Architecture in Asmara
Colonial Origin and Postcolonial Experiences

With the kind support of

Stefano de Martino, the Dean's office of the Faculty of Architecture at the University of Innsbruck

The Office of the Vice-Rector for Research at the University of Innsbruck

The Department of Culture of the Regional Government of Tyrol

FWF (Austrian Science Fund) – Project Funding: Asmara: The Sleeping Beauty. Biopolitics and Architecture (P 25242)

Architecture in Asmara
Colonial Origin and Postcolonial Experiences

Edited by Peter Volgger and Stefan Graf

DOM
publishers

Contents

PART II: POSTCOLONIAL EXPERIENCES

First Chapter: Tracing Postcolonialism

Second Chapter: A Geography of Memories

Third Chapter: City and Migration

Fourth Chapter: Asmara's New Images

CONVERSATIONS

Abbreviations

AHP	Asmara Heritage Project
AHPMD	Asmara Heritage Project Management Database
AI	Asmarino Independent (website)
AOI	Africa Orientale Italiana (Italian East Africa)
AUF	Asmara Urban Forum
BMA	British Military Administration
CARP	Cultural Assets Rehabilitaion Project
CIS	*Congresso Internationale della Strada* (International Road Congress)
CIAAO	*Compagnia Immobiliare alberghi Africa Orientale* (East African Hotel Construction Company)
CITAO	*Compagnia Italiana Trasporti Africa Orientale* (Italian Transport Company of East Africa)
CMP	Conservation Master Plan
DAZ	*Deutsches Architekturzentrum* (German Architecture Centre)
DCD	Department of Construction Development
EUR	*Esposizione Universale del 1942 di Roma* (International Exhibition of Rome)
EPLF	Eritrean People's Liberation Front
GAA	Greater Asmara Area

HUL	Historic Urban Landscape
IAO	*Istituto Agronomico per l'Oltremare* (Agronomic Institute for Overseas)
IMP	Integrated Management Plan
IsIAO	*Istituto Italiano per l'Africa e l'Oriente* (Italian Institute for Africa)
LUCE	*Istituto Luce / L' Unione Cinematografica Educativa* (The Educational Film Union)
MAI	*Ministero dell'Africa Italiana* (Ministry of Italian Africa)
NGO	Non-Governmental Organisation
OND	*Opera Nazionale Dopolavoro* (National Leisure Hours Organization)
PFDJ	People's Front for Democracy and Justice
RACI	*Reale Automobile Club Italiano* (Royal Italian Automobile Club)
SAI	*Società Africana d'Italia* (Italian African Society)
SGI	*Società Geografica Italiana* (Italian Geographical Society)
SECA	*Società di Esplorazioni commerciale in Africa* (Society for Commercial Exploration in Africa)
TCI	*Touring Club Italiano* (Italian Tourism Company)
UoA	University of Asmara
WHL	UNESCO World Heritage List

Acknowledgements

The origins of the present book date back to a research project entitled *The Sleeping Beauty*, carried out at the Institute for Architectural Theory (Innsbruck University), where preliminary drafts of the book were discussed. Research work dealing with colonial architecture does not receive a great deal of funding as a matter of course. We therefore wish to express our deepest gratitude to the Austrian Science Fund (FWF) for grant P 25242; the FWF's generous support made it possible to conduct our field research in Asmara.

I wish to thank the following individuals for their role in the production of this book. My thanks go first and foremost to all the contributors to this volume – both authors and photographers – for their great patience during the completion of the volume. Furthermore, I am deeply indebted to them not only because their articles contain such a vast amount of carefully conducted research, but also because they were willing to share their knowledge and contribute to the ongoing international debate about Italian colonial architecture in Africa, including the problem of how to deal with the colonial and fascist heritage. Scientific meetings dealing with these issues were held in the course of the production of this book; these meetings and discussions will continue. None of the contributors, I hasten to add, can be blamed for any shortcomings this book may have – these are entirely my own.

Much has been written about Asmara in recent years, and the city's rediscovery in the fields of architecture and urbanism is certainly due to Edward Denison's book *Asmara – Africa's Secret Modernist City* which was always a landmark. Edward has kindly shared with us his knowledge and materials many times. In addition, he always eagerly encouraged us to go our own way and he still is doing a great deal of work in Asmara. My graduate students at the University of Innsbruck have also been a constant source of ideas for the book, namely: Stefan Graf, Katharina Paulweber and Arno Hofer. Stefan has been a cheerful and thoughtful analyst of this project right from the beginning. I thank him for his help.

As regards our research trips, we are indebted to the Austrian Science Fund, which enabled us to visit Asmara several times. I have presented some parts of the book during a number of lecture series, at conferences and workshops, including talks at the Archtheo '12 – Theory of Architecture Conference at the Mimar Sinan Fine Arts University in Istanbul (2012), the UdK Berlin (2012), the Pasinger Fabrik Cultural Centre in Munich (2012), the Images of the City Conference at the Austrian Cultural Forum in Istanbul (2013), the African Workshop in Linz (2016), the Young Bauhaus Research Colloquium in Weimar (2016) and the Migrating Objects – Material Culture and Italian Identities Conference at the John D. Calandra Italian American Institute in New York (2016). My sincere thanks go to all who have commented and critiqued these presentations over the last years.

In Eritrea we received great support from several government departments, in particular the Asmara Heritage Office. We wish to thank Medhanie Teklemariam (from the Asmara Heritage Office), who hosted and supported our research undertakings so actively more than once, and is so tirelessly dedicated to Asmara's archive and to promoting the nomination of Asmara to the UNESCO World Heritage List. Anyone who reads this book will see my debts to Medhanie in numerous places; I greatly valued his warm friendship and ideas. We wish to thank Thomas Tedros (from the travel office in Asmara) who kept communication between Asmara and Innsbruck running and helped us immensely with gaining a feel of Asmara. Thomas also helped us to bring the unwieldy Bookeye Scanner from Innsbruck University to Asmara.

Christoph and Konrad Melchers, from the 4Asmara Arbate Asmera group, provided special assistance, and tireless energy and encouragement; they have made Asmara's legacy available to a much larger audience through their exhibition. The origins of the present book also dates back to an exhibition and a conference on Asmara in Munich on July 3–4 2012. We share the same aim as this exhibition, i.e. to support the Eritrean people and its diaspora all over the world in their endeavours to preserve Asmara's architecture as a unique world heritage.

Many other individuals and institutions have made it possible to publish this book, and we would like to express our gratitude to them: Vice-Rector for Research and the Faculty of Architecture. Furthermore, we are also greatly indebted to the Department of Culture of the Tyrolean Regional Government for its financial support for the publication. Special thanks go to Clarice Knowles for the proofreading and Roxanne Powell for the revision of our parts of the manuscript, assisting us with the English translation, and her constructive comments. We also thank Nicole Wolf for all her help and thoughtful advice in preparing this book for publication. Finally we would like to thank Philipp Meuser, from DOM publishers, for publishing this book.

FIAT
TAGLIERO

Introduction

Peter Volgger

The ancient city of Asmara (known locally as Asmera), the subject of this book, is the capital of Eritrea and its largest settlement, with around 649,000 inhabitants. It is situated at 2,325 m above sea level. Its beautiful architecture was rediscovered by outsiders in the early 1990s. Inspiration for writing this book about Asmara came from de Boeck's and Plissart's personal excavation of Kinshasa. The authors offer an original analysis of the colonial city, that provides a history not only of the physical and visible urban reality of Kinshasa, but also of a second, invisible city as it exists in the imagination in the form of a mirroring reality lurking underneath the surface of the visible world.[1] De Boeck and Plissart play off of Italo Calvino's *Invisible Cities*, a book that has often been used to visualise how cities can be, their secret folds, when human imagination is not necessarily limited by the laws of physics.[2] The colonial city becomes a fantastical Venice, a set of cities where each one reflects the others as if in a kaleidoscope, for it contains many cities in one as well. The image of a multiplex is where this ambitious book breaks new ground, and moves us a little further along in the attempt to read Asmara into contemporary theory.

I am grateful for the project funding provided by the Austrian Science Fund (2012-2015, P 25242), which enabled me undertake the research presented in this book; based on what I had seen in research on Italian postcolonialism elsewhere, I felt it was important to broaden the initial scope of the grant, namely colonial architecture. Indeed the last years have seen a resurgence of interest in the Italian colonial style, resulting in impressive, empirically rich and theoretically engaged studies. Several important surveys have been

The famous Fiat Tagliero petrol station seen in a mirror
Source: Courtesy of J.Robert

initiated, along with studies of individual cities that are often multidisciplinary in nature. At the same time, the scope of inquiry into Italy's colonial past has experienced a dramatic transformation. Influenced by new theoretical approaches to colonialism, nationalism and globalisation, these new studies are re-evaluating and redefining the parameters within which we understand Italian colonialism. Because Italian colonial history had been relegated to the ambiguous, unstable sphere of instrumentalised and nostalgic reminiscing, the book takes into account the Italian colonial period as a closed chapter of historical activity and connects the colonial archive to different aspects of the postcolonial present and its discourse. This will enable us to gain a more interdisciplinary understanding of the city of Asmara; it will also allow a more contextual and comparative reading of Asmara.

This book offers a two-part reflection, focusing on contemporary Asmara as it is caught in the contradictory logics of a colonial past and the postcolonial struggle for identity. The first part – entitled *Colonial Origin* – focuses on the concepts of modernity and colonialism which can each be read as embodying the characteristic of the other. Rather than building on the notion of modernism as having developed and moved as a universal modern project from the West to the rest of the world – and which has been left back by the colonisers as a frozen city – the emphasis in this book is on the exchanges and interrelations among international and local actors and concepts, a perspective in which modernity is not passively received, but subject to constant renegotiation and reinterpretation, a modernity in circulation, moving in several different directions at once.

In the second part – entitled *Postcolonial Experiences* – we would like to clean up a few myths that have arisen, deconstructing the romantic and nostalgic *bella Asmara* – image. What has not been examined in depth, however, is the connection between Asmara and the global postcolonial setting. It was our aim to explore the cultural role of colonial architecture and urbanism in the production of meaning, the embodiment of colonial power, as well as the dynamic construction of identities in the present. On the other hand, despite the spatial imagery employed by many postcolonial narratives, the debate around postcolonialism mostly does not focus on architecture and urbanism issues.

Our work encourages African studies and scholars from different fields to engage with the complexity and richness of Asmara with fresh eyes. The book brings together scholars from a multiplicity of disciplines who have shown the ways in which colonial and postcolonial criticism has served as a platform for new, diversified readings of Asmara. These bring together cultural and social history, critical and political theory, anthropological fieldwork, visual culture studies, literary and cinematic analysis, gender studies, diaspora and urban studies. Our analysis, however, goes beyond the historical review of materials and scientific knowledge; it examines the current realities of Asmara in order to address the continuing effects of the legacy of colonialism upon the people living in the city.

State of the Art

Up until the late 1970s, scholarly accounts of Italian colonialism have been rare. This happened for different, complex, and partly unclear historical and social reasons, including the peculiar way in which the period ended, the difficulty of digesting the fascist past and the lack of a decolonisation process in Italy. For a long time, both African and colonial studies were underdeveloped. Starting in the 1970s, the historiography has slowly begun to develop, mostly thanks to Angelo **del Boca's** pioneering research.[3]

Although Asmara boasts the most extensive manifestation of modern architecture in Africa, until the independence of the country in 1993 this attracted little attention or systematic enquiry. But in the last few years, a number of scholars have debated the relative absence of Asmara within the framework of Italy's colonial and postcolonial history. An important point needs to be stressed: these new studies on Asmara stem from different disciplines and are not limited to the historical scholarly tradition. In many respects they constitute new themes and areas of research. They also deal with social studies, anthropology, sociology, the humanities in general and postcolonial studies. Hence I would now like to discuss the importance of this new wave of studies and to mention the names of key scholars and titles from different study fields.

Architectural and Urban History

The tradition of architectural and urban history is both well-established and very well known. In Italy architectural criticism was centred on style for a long time. Thus, most buildings were labelled as works of *futurismo*, *rationalismo* or *architettura metafisica*, and architectural critics created conceptual labels that allowed the loosening of form from context. But before turning to the architecture itself, it is important to examine the ideological setting in which the debate regarding the colonies took place.

What is so often referred to as an Italian amnesia concerning the colonial past is partly the result of active disinformation and the construction of the *italiani brava gente* myth (Italians as good people?). Giuliano **Greslieri** and his assistants Pier Giorgio **Massaretti** and Stefano **Zagnoni** were the first to classify colonial architecture as part of the Italian architectural history.[4] Recently, the

Istituto Italiano per l'Africa e l'Oriente (IsIAO) has been making parts of its archives accessible with the assistance of local experts, such as Giulia **Barrera**, Alessandro **Triulzi** and Gabriel **Tzeggai** in 2008.[5]

The discovery of Asmara by outsiders began in the early 1990s with publications based on archival material held in Italy. The ending of Eritrea's struggle for independence made it possible to visit the city after a long period of war. Peacetime also enabled local efforts to preserve the built colonial heritage, culminating in 2003 with the publication of *Asmara: Africa's Secret Modernist City* (Edward **Denison**, Guang Yu **Ren**, and Naigzy **Gebremedhin**).[6] This book, with its many beautiful photographs drawing on local archives, not only unveiled new material, but also attracted international attention – the aim being to open up the city to tourism. A set of tropes were generated, such as *The Forgotten City* (Mike **Street** 1997), *The City of Dreams* (Ruby **Ofori**, Edward **Scott** and Naigzy **Gebremedhin** 2005), *The Frozen City* (Stefan **Boness** and Jochen **Visscher** 2006), or **Asmara Dream** (Marco **Barbon** 2009),[7] portrayals of Asmara that suggested that the city could be re-discovered. In most cases all these images are a combination of a romantic spirit of discovery, an exploration of the exotic, and an aestheticising of timelessness, combined with political disillusionment with the present and the mechanisms of colonial nostalgia. Mia **Fuller** examined the ideological setting in which the debate regarding the colonies took place, as well as the different ideology that coloured the colonisation project. She described "Italy's colonial inertia, or how Italy's once-vigorously implanted colonial signature has sustained momentum and shows every promise of continuing to do so."[8]

Initiated by 4Asmara Arbate Asmera (*Deutsch-Eritreische Projektgruppe Asmara*), a German-Eritrean project group was at the forefront of the re-discovery of Asmara. It made the city popular for a broader public through an exhibition at the DAZ (Deutsches Architekturzentrum) in Berlin, curated by Naigzy Gebremedhin (former Director of Eritrea's Cultural Assets Rehabilitation Project, CARP) and Prof. Dr. Omar **Akbar** (Director of the Bauhaus Foundation Dessau), and coordinated by Christoph and Konrad **Melchers**. For the first time, the rich architectural heritage of the Eritrean capital was presented in the exhibition, which then went on tour. It was based on Denison's abovementioned book, Asmara: *Africa's Secret Modernist City*, which focuses on iconic buildings and created the *bella Asmara* image (see *Conversation* with Christoph and Konrad Melchers).[9]

Since 2014 the Asmara Heritage Project has been trying to obtain Asmara's inscription on the UNESCO World Heritage list. This is the latest in a series of initiatives spanning two decades, starting with the Cultural Assets Rehabilitation

Project (CARP, 2001–2007) and including the EU-funded Heritage Project (2008–2010). The CARP initiative, financed with a loan from the World Bank and headed by Gebremedhin,[10] included cultural assets beyond Asmara's buildings — intangible as well as tangible heritage, and rural as well as urban – but it excluded the very same areas that Italian colonisers had excluded as *quartiere indigeno* (indigenous quarters). For this reason, the Asmara Heritage Project's new proposal includes both the historic city and its surroundings, and classifies Asmara into three different zones: the historic urban layout (Historic Perimeter) related to the colonial foundation with some additions; the integrated expansion zone (Buffer Zone) with the city that developed following Eritrean tradition; and the surroundings (Historic Urban Landscape).

Results of the earlier preservation initiative have been recorded in works on Asmara's architectural heritage, for example an investigation into the work of Italian architects in the colonies (Filippo **Amara** 2008), or the development of new urban-historical approaches to an increasingly rich range of accessible materials, including local archives and oral histories (Anna **Godio** 2008 and Simone **Bader** 2011).[11] Caterina **Borelli's** film, *Asmara, Eritrea, Asmarini* portrays Asmara as the embodiment of the Eritrean nation; likewise CARP director Gebremedhin had justified his emphasis on preserving the colonial heritage by pointing out its essential place in the formation of Eritrean identity.[12] Christoph **Rausch** demonstrates that in the past governmental and international mechanisms have enabled or supported the preservation of Asmara, while manipulating and capitalising on the value of this colonial heritage to gratify national feelings and foster colonial nostalgia.[13]

Social and Other Studies

A second area of research about the city of Asmara stems from Social Sciences, including social history, anthropology, ethnography, and postcolonial studies. Social studies of the colonial milieu have given rise to lively discussions. Giulia **Barrera**, Francesca **Locatelli** and Sandra **Ponzanesi** discuss racial relations in Italian colonies and examine critically the dynamics of colonial power and the politics of segregation. Giulia Barrera is an authority on racism and on the *madamato* (or native concubinage system) in Italian colonies, while Sandra Ponzanesi adopts a postcolonial critical perspective on literature and visual culture.[14] Urban anthropologist Magnus **Treiber** explored how symbolic pollution can occur in the discourse and actions of both people in power and people lacking in influence. Treiber's key argument is that the Eritrean government uses the colonisers' rhetoric in order to enforce differentiation.[15] Brian **McLaren** addressed the lack of attention to the issue of tourism in the Italian colonies in his book on architecture, tourism and Italian colonial politics in Libya.[16] Studies on domestic culture in former Italian colonies are scant, maybe because domestic matters occupy a space that is neither heroic, nor particularly eventful. Sean **Anderson** has dedicated his work to the colonial interior which, in his vision, is much more complex than a simple domestic space. In that interior space of the colonial conscience, the colonial woman lived; here the colonial architect expressed his ideas regarding society, technology and modernity.[17] Cristina **Lombardi-Diop** has examined the representations of the private and public space of the colonies in diaries and works by Italian women who travelled there since the founding of Asmara as a colonial capital.[18] The study of economics was pursued by Gian Luca **Podestà** and Nicola **Labanca** (2002), who published two interesting books arguing that the economic history of the Italian dominions in Eastern Africa ran through all the major stages of Italian policies until 1941.[19]

Italy and Postcolonialism

Until very recently, Italy did not perceive itself as a postcolonial nation. Indeed it did not receive a significant number of immigrants from its former colonies during the era of decolonisation. Only in the last two decades have Italian scholars started to produce original work on Italian postcolonialism. Historically speaking, *postcolonialism* defines a critical approach and a type of consciousness arising after colonisation from the countries that were once colonised and are now independent. Postcolonialism focuses on the impact that the legacy of colonial history and culture bear on the present. It implies a reversal of roles in the relationship between the ex-colonisers and the ex-colonised. It implies the reversion of the role of the postcolonial from an object that is scrutinized and spoken for into a subjective role in which the postcolonial represents her/himself and speaks back. For the purpose of our book we will use the term in its broadest meaning, which is not confined solely to the period immediately following the end of the Italian empire in Africa; as it is, it is still ongoing in our globalised world.

In the last two decades there has been an increasing interest in the history of Italian colonialism from a postcolonial perspective. However, many of its aspects remain unexplored, particularly those related to the history of culture. New research on Asmara includes another field of studies, namely photography, film and documentaries. To sum up, research on the Italian colonial era now seems to be very well established and more multifaceted than before. Within the framework of postcolonial studies, scholars have been dealing with many subjects and multiple perspectives, focusing on diverse aspects of contemporary Italian literature and culture such as migration, postcoloniality, orality, diaspora, ethnicity, multiculturalism, nationhood and subalternity.

Patrizia **Palumbo**, Cristina **Lombardi-Diop** and Caterina **Romeo** have assembled over a dozen essays on Italian colonialism, its history and its characteristics. Finally, they have defined the key elements of postcolonialism in the peninsula, such as Italy's long history of emigration, its contemporary immigration, and the racial legacy of colonial history.[20] The history of colonial photography has been examined by scholars following some previous work by authors such as Alessandro **Triulzi**, Luigi **Goglia** and Silvana **Palma**.[21] Ruth **Ben-Ghiat** analysed Italian cinema and photography and contented that reconstructing the circumstances of the production and consumption of colonial images can yield insights into the daily interactions of Italians and Africans and the psychological climates and social fabrics of Italian colonial society.[22] Sabrina **Marchetti**, Domenica **Ghidei Biidu** are mainly specialised in issues of gender, welfare, labour and migration, with a specific emphasis on the question of migrant domestic work.[23] Anna **Arnone** explores the narratives of Eritreans in Milan going to Eritrea on holiday and returning from their vacation, and explores the impact on their perception of Eritrea/Asmara as a place for leisure and tourism.[24] Automotive mechanical engineers in Eritrea are at the centre of Stefano **Bellucci** and Massimo **Zaccaria's** work, which shows how automobility – as a socio-technological system of innovation introduced by Italian colonisers – came to be appropriated and transformed by Eritreans.[25]

Beside the work of scholars, filmmakers and writers have devoted themselves to postcolonial issues. Recently, Alan **Maglio** and Medhin **Paolos** presented their documentary *Asmarina*, filmed within the *habesha* community of Milan; it showed collective memories based on photographic documents.[26] Igiaba **Scego** and Rino **Bianchi**, in *Roma negata. Percorsi postcoloniali nella città* filled the gaps in the individual and collective memories of Italian colonialism in Africa, through stories, documents, texts, and autobiographical and literary references. In this fascinating journey between past and present, monuments and places more or less well-known were described through an estranged perspective, thus recovering meanings that were generally had been ignored or excluded.[27] *Aulò! Roma postcoloniale* is a pair of documentaries on Italian colonialism and on migration from former Italian colonies to Italy, directed by Simone **Brioni**, Graziano **Chiscuzzu** and Ermanno **Guida**. *Aulò* assigned new symbolic meanings to some monuments and places in Rome that refer to the colonial past.[28]

As this overview has shown, the ever-expanding studies bookshelf has much to offer to both colonial and postcolonial research on Asmara. In our book we tried to engage with the diversity and range of Asmara's history, including the imaginary dimension, literary and everyday practices. Our task was to combine the new writing about Asmara into a manageable set of themes, mixing wider scholarly reading with our own specific research. Without being blind to socio-economic or political problems in Eritrea, we set out to resist an overarching crisis narrative.

Reflections in the Mirror

Let us begin with a brief reflection on the structure of the book while at the same time highlighting some of its main ideas. Some of the key categories we used in our research were rapidly expanded to include photographic essays, conversations and an increasing number of contributors from different disciplines. In addition, photographs from various sources, working sketches and analyses, and seemingly casual views and vistas of Asmara infiltrated the increasingly heterogeneous array of essays. Once the volume grew, we began to orchestrate it in terms of an overall composition, establishing an overall rhythm, alignments and references among the parts. What initially had a contingent, improvisational, cumulative character has taken on a certain internal logic and dynamic peculiar to itself. This book does not promise any definiteness of the kind vouchsafed in an archive and makes no attempt to offer an overriding interpretation or a kind of fixed master narrative of Asmara. Instead, it proposes a new reading of Asmara. We argue that the catoptricity of Asmara is not simply a post-Modernist hall-of-mirrors play. Like Lewis Carroll's *Alice*, we frequently cross and thus subvert a number of looking-glass boundaries; these, in turn, get the self and its double, light and shadow, and the city and its narrator, to reflect each other in new ways. The book concisely assesses the diverse, mirror-like gazes and representations through which Asmara is captured. More importantly, we try to move beyond a perspective authored solely by external viewpoints to start understanding Asmara's internal struggle to create its own identity. This is also where the metaphor of the mirror is pushed to its limits. Asmara is not merely represented in the mirrors held up to it by colonial modernities or national myths. Asmara does not merely reflect, it often moves beyond this representation in an unexpected, surprising way.

The mirrors we will use to introduce each chapter of the book do not reflect each other symmetrically; they do not pretend to reflect the true Asmara. It was the leitmotif of the colonial speculum that we wanted to expand into a larger project, in order to manage the size and dynamics by means of which the metaphor of the mirror becomes alive in the context of Asmara today. Mirrors (like a metaphor) introduced into colonised societies have interacted with local forms of mirroring in ways that have not been investigated yet. The reflection in the mirror is what Lacan called the mirror stage. This is central to our readings, as we believe that it encapsulates what happens in the stereotyping productions of the colonial discourse. According to Lacan, the mirror stage is a stage of development in which a child recognises himself or herself in the mirror and becomes conscious of selfhood. This is at least a good model for the colonial situation. In the end, we hope that Asmara will have resisted objectification, summarising and colonisation. It may be that if a writer from outside Asmara wishes to portray a specific world, (s)he has to deal with broken mirrors, some of whose fragments may have irretrievably been lost. These fragments are not only linked through their common axis – historical narration – but also through various reflexive and textual mechanisms, the most important of which are intertextuality and self-criticism. However there is a paradox here: a broken mirror may actually be as valuable as one that is supposedly unflawed. For example, in Marc-Antoine Mathieu's innovative graphic novel *3 Seconds*[29] the reader can follow the path of a particle of light as it arrives on the scene of a murder (what happens at the centre of this book is constantly out of focus); Mathieu zooms into each image frame by frame before letting the particle of light bounce off a reflective surface to allow a new perspective. The single trail of light shows the reader one scene from several angles, zooming in on a series of surprising reflective surfaces: earrings, retinas, a spoon, a mobile phone screen or even the distant camera of a satellite, on and on, this way and that, up into the heavens, out into the universe and all the way back again, each frame representing a fraction of a moment. We have translated this pictorial approach into a trajectory towards understanding Asmara.

An undertaking of this type also involves working out decomposition. We have chosen a fragmented structure for the book to insist on the importance of discontinuity; this refers not so much to the rejection of previous insights, but rather to the unfolding of a series of reconfigurations that come out of the colonial past. This structure allows for an open-ended understanding of the continual composition of a multiple Asmara that is caught up in a historical and cultural play of mirrors, like a net that stretches over time. Implicitly it suggests that the final meaning of Asmara never was, or will be, nor could be, coherent. Texts and photographs are only fragments of a wider structure that cannot successfully reproduce the coherence of the city. The photo essays that we have included offer a perfect medium to reflect on the themes upon which this book touches. Our reading of the multiple meanings of Asmara is an invitation to pay attention to the city as a system that reflects the contradictions of production and is open to a range of interpretations. The photographs, along with the other voices in the book, provide an opening through which we may peer into other dimensions of Asmara – beyond the screen of its well-established imaging. The photo essays are situated between the individual sections that constitute the body of this book. The voices of the authors and the eyes of the photographers alternate and together produce a polylogue on the city of Asmara.

Notes

1 Filip de Boeck and Marie- Françoise Plissart, *Kinshasa: Tales of the Invisible City*, Tervuren: Royal Museum for Central Africa, 2004.

2 Italo Calvino, *Invisible Cities* (*Le città invisibili*), transl. William Weaver. London: Vintage, 1974.

3 For the discussion about Italian colonialism and memory see Angelo Del Boca, *Italiani, brava gente? Un mito duro a morire*, Vicenza: Neri Pozza, 2005; Angelo Del Boca, *Gli Italini in Africa Coloniale*, vol 1-4, Bari: Laterza, 1975–1986; Angelo del Boca, *Africa nella memoria degli Italiani: miti, memorie, errori, sconfitte*, Milan: Mondadori, 1992; Nicola Labanca, *Oltremare. Storia dell'espansione coloniale italiana*. Bologna: Il Mulino, 2002; Irma Taddia, "Italian memories/African memories of colonialism", in Ruth Ben-Ghiat and Mia Fuller (eds.), *Italian Colonialism*. New York: Palgrave McMillan. Mia Fuller, "Italy's Colonial Futures: Colonial Inertia and Postcolonial Capital in Asmara", *California Italian Studies*, 2 (1) 2011, pp. 3-5.

4 Giuliano Gresleri, Pier Giorgio Massaretti, and Stefano Zagnoni (eds.), *Architettura italiana d'oltremare: 1870–1940*. Venice: Marsilio, 1993, pp. 178–201; Giuliano Greslieri, *Architettura d'oltremare. Atlante iconografico* (Italian Architecture Overseas. An Iconographic Atlas). Bologna: Bononia University Press, 2008; Giuliano Gresleri, "Architecture for the Towns of the Empire", *Rassegna* 14 (Sept. 1992), pp. 36–51.

5 Giulia Barrera, Alessandro Triulzi, and Gabriel Tzeggai (eds.), *Asmara. Architettura e pianificazione urbana nei fondi dell'IsIAO, Istituto Italiano per l'Africa e l'Oriente*. Rome: Istituto italiano per l'Africa e l'Oriente, 2008. Greslieri and Massaretti (op. cit. note 4) also based on Italian archives, but in combination with local expertise, the IsIAO has been making parts of its archive accessible.

6 Edward Denison, Yu Ren Guang, and Naigzy Gebremedhin (eds.), *Asmara: Africa's Secret Modernist City*. London: Merrell Publishers Ltd, 2003 & 2006. See also: Edward Denison and Yu Ren Guang (eds.), *Asmara Architecture Archives: Final Report CARP*. Asmara, 2002; Edward Denison, Yu Ren Guang, *Asmara City Map & Historic Perimeter 2003*; Naigzy Gebremedhin, Edward Denison, Abraham Mebrahtu and Guang Yu Ren, *Asmara: A Guide to the Built Environment*. Asmara: (Cultural Assets Rehabilitation Project) Francescana Printing Press, 2003.

7 Mike Street, "The Forgotten City", *Perspectives on Architecture 31*, 1997, pp. 50-55, 1997; Ruby Ofori, Edward Scott (directors), and Naigzy Gebremedhin, *City of Dreams*, Washington, D.C.: Eye Level 2005; Stefan Boness and Jochen Visscher, *Asmara. The Frozen City*. Berlin: Jovis, 2006; Marco Barbon, *Asmara Dream*. Trèzèlan: Filigranes Èditions, 2009.

8 Mia Fuller, "Italy's Colonial Futures: Colonial Inertia and Postcolonial Capital in Asmara", *California Italian Studies*, 2 (1), 2011; Mia Fuller, *Building Power: Italy's Colonial Architecture and Urbanism, 1923–1940*, Cultural Anthropology, vol. 3 (4), 1988, pp. 455-487; Mia Fuller, "Wherever You Go, There You Are: Fascist Plans for the Colonial City of Addis Ababa and the Colon Suburb of EUR '42", *Journal of Contemporary History*, vol. 31(2), 1996, pp. 397-418. Mia Fuller, "La colonia: Italiani in Eritrea", *Quaderni Storici* (special issue), vol. 109, 2002, pp. 294-297; Mia Fuller, *Moderns Abroad: Architecture, Cities, and Italian Imperialism*. London: Routledge, 2007, pp. 449-450.

9 See: Mekonnen Mesghena, Christoph Melchers, and Konrad Melchers, *Asmara – Africa's Secret Capital of Modern Architecture*, Dossier Editorial Asmara Architecture Exhibition Project Group, in: http://www.asmara-architecture.com/Dossier_engl.pdf [9-6-2015]

10 Naigzy Gebremedhin, Edward Denison, Abraham Mebrahtu, and Guang Yu Ren, 2003 (op. cit. note 6). See also: Naigzy Gebremedhin, *Asmara, Africa's Secret Modernist City*. Paper prepared for the African Perspectives: Dialogue on Urbanism and Architecture, The Faculty of Architecture, TU Delft 2007, in: http://www.bk.tudelft.nl/fileadmin/Faculteit/BK/Actueel/Symposia [5-5-2015]

11 Some works focus on preservation along with Asmara's architectural history: Filippo Amara, *Un progetto urbano per Asmara. Guido Ferrazza e i nuovi mercati della capitale eritrea, 1935–1938. Un caso di restauro del moderno tra interpretazione e progetto*. Rome: Aracne, 2007; Anna Godio, *Architettura italiania in Eritrea/ Italian Architecture in Eritrea*. Turin: La Rosa Editrice, 2008. Others have been developing new architectural and urban-historical approaches to an increasingly rich range of accessible materials: Simone Bader, *Moderne in Afrika. Asmara – Die Konstruktion einer italianischen Kolonialstadt*. Berlin: Gebrüder Mann Verlag, 2016. See also: Sean Anderson (op. cit. note 17).

12 Caterina Borelli and Anonymous Productions, Asmara, Eritrea, MA: Documentary Educational Resources 2008. In this film *Asmarinos* from different walks of life guide us through the streets of their city and bring us to places of their choice. In doing so, and by talking about their own Asmara, each person locates personal memories in public spaces, investing the urban environment with individual meanings.

13 Christoph Rausch, *Modern Nostalgia: Asserting Politics of Sovereignty and Security in Asmara*. Washington and Brussels, 2011; Christoph Rausch, *Rescuing Modernity? Global Actors in the Heritage Valorization of Modern Architecture in Africa*, Ph.D diss., University of Maastricht/Delft, 2013.

14 Francesca Locatelli, "Colonial Justice, Crime, and Social Stratification in the 'Native Quarters' of Asmara, 1890–1941: Preliminary Insights from the Court Records oft the Indigenous Tribunal of Hamasien", *Northeast African Studies* 10 (3) 2003, pp. 101-115; Francesca Locatelli, "Oziosi, vagabondi e pregiudicati: labour, law and crime in Colonial Asmara, 1890–1941", *International International Journal of African Historical Studies* vol.40 (2) 2007, pp. 134-186; Francesca Locatelli, "La comunitá italiana di Asmara negli anni Trenta tra propaganda: The Italian community of Asmara in the 1930s between propaganda, racial laws and social reality", in: Riccardo Bottoni (ed.), *L'impero fascista. Italia ed Etiopia (1935–1941)*. Milan: Il Mulino, 2008, pp. 369-391; Francesca Locatelli, "Beyond the Campo Cintato: Prostitutes, Migrants and 'Criminals' in Colonial Asmara (Eritrea), 1890–1941", *Africa-Europe Group for Interdisciplinary Studies*, vol. 3, 2009, pp. 219-240; Giulia Barrera, "The Construction of Racial Hierarchies in Colonial Eritrea: The Liberal and Early Fascist Period, 1897–1934", in Patrizia Palumbo (ed.), A *Place in the Sun: Africa in Italian Africa in Italian Colonial Culture*, Berkeley – LA: University of California Press, 2003, pp. 81-115; Sandra Ponzanesi, "The Colour of Love: Madamismo and Interracial Relationships in the Italian Colonies", *Research in African Literatures* 43 (2) 2012, pp. 155-172; Sandra Ponzanesi, "Beyond the Black Venus. Colonial Sexual Politics and Contemporary Visual Practices", in Jacqueline Andall, Jacqueline and Derek Duncan (eds.), *Italian Colonialism. Legacies and Memories*, Bern: Peter Lang, 2005, pp. 165-189.

15 Magnus Treiber, "The Choice between Clean and Dirty. Discourses of Aesthetics, Morality and Progress in Post-revolutionary Asmara, Eritrea",

in Eveline Dürr and Rivke Jaffe (eds.), *Urban Pollution. Cultural Meanings, Social Practices*. Oxford: Berghahn Books, 2010, pp. 123-143; Magnus Treiber, *Der Traum vom guten Leben. Die eritreische warsay-Generation im Asmara der zweiten Nachkriegszeit*. Münster: LIT-Verlag, 2005.

16 Brain McLaren, *Architecture and Tourism in Italian Colonial Libya. An Ambivalent Modernism, Studies in Modernity and National Identity*. Washington: University Press, 2006.

17 Sean Anderson, "Modernità e Interiorità in Colonial Asmara", *Italian Studies* 61 (2) 2006 (a), pp. 233-250; Sean Anderson, *In-Visible Colonies: Modern Architecture and its Representation in Colonial Eritrea, 1890–1941*, Ph.D diss. UCLA 2006 (b); Sean Anderson, *Modern Architecture and its Representation in Colonial Eritrea. An In-visible Colony, 1890–1941*, London and New York: Routledge, 2016 [First published 2015 by Ashgate Publishing].

18 Cristina Lombardi-Diop, "Mothering the Nation: An Italian Woman in Colonial Africa", in Sante Matteo (ed.), *ItaliAfrica: Bridging Continents and Cultures*. New York: Stony Book (Forum Italicum), 2001, pp. 173-191; Cristina Lombardi-Diop, "Pioneering Female Modernity: Fascist Women in Colonial Africa", in Ruth Ben-Ghiat and Mia Fuller (eds.), *Italian Colonialism*. New York: Palgrave MacMillan, 2005, pp. 145-154; Cristina Lombardi-Diop and Caterina Romeo (eds.), *Postcolonial Italy: Challenging National Homogeneity*. New York: Palgrave MacMillan, 2012; Cristina Lombardi-Diop, Residence Rome: "The Making and Unmaking of a Migrant Vertical Village in Rome", in Isabella Clough Marinaro and Bjorn Thomassen (eds.), *Global Rome*, Bloomington: Indiana University Press, forthcoming 2013.

19 Nicola Labanca, *Oltremare,* 2002, pp. 570. (op. cit. note 17); Gian Luca Podestà, *Sviluppo industriale e colonialismo. Gli investimenti italiani in Africa orientale 1869–1897*, Milan: Giuffrè 1996; Gian Luca Podestà, *Il mito dell'impero. Economia, politica e lavoro nelle colonie italiane dell'Africa orientale 1898–1941*, Torino: Giappichelli, 2004.

20 Patrizia Palumbo (ed.), *A Place in the Sun: Africa in Italian Colonial Culture from Post-Unification to the Present*, Berkeley and Los Angeles: University of California Press, 2003. Cristina Lombardi-Diop and Caterina Romeo (eds.) 2012, (op. cit. note 18).

21 Silvana Palma, "Fotografia di una colonia: L'Eritrea di Luigi Naretti (1885–1900)", *Quaderni storici* 109, a.XXXVII, (1) 2002, pp. 83-147; Silvana Palma, *L'Italia coloniale*. Rome: Editori Riuniti, 1999.

22 Ruth Ben-Ghiat, *Fascist Modernities: Italy 1922–1945*. University of California Press, 2001; Ruth Ben-Ghiat and Mia Fuller (eds.), *Italian colonialism*. New York: Palgrave Macmillan, 2005; Ruth Ben-Ghiat and Stephanie Malia Hom, *Italian Mobilities*, London and New York: Routledge, 2015; Ruth Ben-Ghiat, *Italian Fascism's Empire Cinema*, Bloomington: Indiana University Press, 2015.

23 Sabrina Marchetti and Domenica Ghidei Biidu, *Abbecedario coloniale: Memorie di donne eritree alle scuole italiane di Asmara*. Zapruder: Storie in movimento, n. 19/ 2009; Domenica Ghidei Biidu and Sabrina Marchetti, "Eritreans's Memories of Postcolonial Time: Ambivalence and Mimicry at the Italian Schools in Asmara", in Jacqueline Andall and Derek Duncan, (eds.), *National Belongings: Hybridity in Italian Colonial and Postcolonisl Cultures*. Bern: Peter Lang, 2010, pp. 107-126; Sabrina Marchetti, *Le ragazze di Asmara. Lavoro domestico e migrazione postcoloniale*. Rome: Ediesse; Sabrina Marchetti, *Black Girls. Migrant Domestic Work and Colonial Legacies* Boston: Brill, 2014.

24 Anna Arnone, "Talking about identity: Milanese-Eritreans describe themselves", *Journal of Modern Italian Studies*, 16 (4) 2011, pp. 516-527. Anna Arnone, "Tourism and the Eritrean Diaspora", *Contemporary African Studies*, 29 /4), pp. 441-454.

25 Stefano Bellucci and Massimo Zaccaria, "Wage Labour and Mobility in Colonial Eritrea, 1880s to 1920s", *International Labour and Working-Class History*, 86, 2014, pp. 89-106; Stefano Bellucci and Massimo Zaccaria, "Engine of Change. A social history of the car-mechanics sector in the Horn of Africa", in: Jan-Bart Gewald, Andrè Leliveld and Iva Pesa (eds.), *Transforming Innovations in Africa. Exploratie Studies on Appropriation in African Societies*. Leiden and Boston: Brill, 2012, pp. 237-257.

26 Alan Maglio and Medhin Paolos (directors), in collaboration with Docucity – Documenting the City, *Asmarina*, 2015.

27 Igiaba Scego and Rino Bianchi, *Roma negata. Percorsi postcoloniali nella città* (Rome denied. Postcolonial routes in the city), Rome: Ediesse, 2014.

28 Simone Brioni, Graziano Chiscuzzu and Ermanno Guida (drs.), *Aulò. Roma postcoloniale* (written by Sinome Brioni and Ribka Sibhatu). Rome: Kimerafilm, 2014.

29 Marc-Antoine Mathieu, *3" (3 Secondes)*, Paris: Éditions Delcourt, 2011.

FIAT
TAGLIERO

COLONIAL MIRRORS
Photo Essay

Jean Robert

The mirror is, after all, a utopia, since it is a placeless place. In the mirror I see myself there where I am not, in an unreal, virtual space that opens up behind the surface ... such is the utopia of the mirror. But it is also a heterotopia in so far as the mirror does exist in reality, where it exerts a sort of counteraction on the position I occupy. From the standpoint of the mirror I discover my absence from the place where I am since I see myself over there ... The mirror function as a heterotopia in this respect: it makes this place that I occupy at the moment when I look at myself in the glass at once absolutely real, connected with all the space that surrounds it, and absolutely unreal, since in order to be perceived it has to pass through this virtual point which is over there.

Our book invites an exploration of the unseen, the testing of authenticity and of the accepted, and, finally, the cultivation of the creative metaphor of the mirror. The approach to Asmara produces images that were meant to be both looked at and then in turn reflected. This led to readers experiencing the city through constant self-observation. Throughout our book we look at mirrors for assurance. The mirror is in fact not a blank space, but one that conceals the dominant gaze and makes it invisible in order to provide a new insight. In another variation of this idea, the street becomes a mirror, providing a mobile vantage point that destroys distinction between the private and the public, self and other. This mirror reaches into our consciousness even as it moves outwards to the interiors of bars, hotels and houses to that of the shop windows and streets.

ritrean Airlines
MANUTD

NEW

PART I

COLONIAL ORIGIN

Colonial cities are the key to an understanding of colonialism as a historical process, for housing and urban planning projects acquired a symbolic meaning during the creation of a new society and a modern way of life. At the same time these cities are often thought to be the products of the singular visions and needs of the colonial regimes that founded them. Mussolini saw Asmara, in East Africa, as the nexus of his new Roman Empire; clearly the city was envisioned, then built jointly by colonial rulers, mercantile and industrial elites, to serve their various interests, but we still do not know much about how colonial cities came into being and functioned beyond the history of their architectural styles. In any case, the Modernist ideal, i.e. projecting into an empty territory, as well as the concept and technologies used to plan, order and develop, is not specific to colonialism, but is connected to the very emergence of modern urbanism and capitalist societies. Italian modern architecture is thus a very good example of the political implications of modernity, because it stood for a society that actually invented the historical form of fascism.

Essentially, the colonial city was the location for a range of new social spaces, from an acknowledgement of the pre-modern through its translation into modern forms to the recognition of everyday practices. How can we reconstruct colonial architecture in an entirely unromantic fashion and without aestheticising it? How does this architecture function in the political and economic circumstances of the present? How can we reconcile renewed efforts to preserve this valuable architecture with its nefarious colonial associations?

First Chapter

COLONIALISM AND MODERNITY

Asmara has frequently been portrayed as the most modern of all African cities, although it can hardly be described as the most vital one in modern day Africa. This is because of Asmara's Modernist design, which results from the region's unique history of contact with Italian colonialism. After Mussolini took power, Little Rome became the African capital of what the Fascists hoped would become a new Roman Empire. On many levels, the *Oltremare* (overseas territories) was one of the driving myths – with a great symbolic relevance for Italy's attempts at modernisation – and brings to the fore the linkage between colonial systems and ideologies of modernity.

Over the last three decades, numerous books and articles have examined the affiliations between the formal audacities of avant-gardism and the historical atrocities of colonialism. Modernism and colonialism doubtlessly share a certain frame of mind, and it is this frame of mind that we wish to discuss at the beginning. The languages of colonialism and modernism can each be read as mirroring halves. Indeed today the idea of combining the terms modernity and colonialism within a title provokes neither alarm nor surprise. The rediscovery of modernism in Africa offers not only the opportunity to observe the urban and architectonic potentials of the modern European city in an exotic context, but also to reflect on the Modernist project itself critically. The first section will examine the history of Modernism and colonial Modernity in Asmara and suggest that the boundaries of modernism are constantly shifting, indicating that the definition of a Modernist project is a question of reading strategies as much as identifying formal features.

The book opens with the following question: Is modern architecture good? Leaving the European continent and departing from a homogenising, universal view, **Kathleen James-Chakraborty** argues that modernity may be considered as a distinct practice of representation, resulting from multiple figurations that are negotiated through various spaces in fragmented and potentially conflicting ways by a range of different modernising actors. There are multiple modernities and modernism was not an exclusively Western phenomenon. In her essay Kathleen James-Chakraborty claims that modern architecture has often been associated by its opponents, as much as by its supporters, with progressive social positions. And yet this is mostly a myth. Much modern architecture was built under circumstances that were certainly modern, but not necessarily in any way socially progressive. The architecture of Asmara, the Italian colonial capital, is emblematic of this. Two things need to be considered about this architecture today. The first is to reconstruct the circumstances of its creation in an entirely unromantic fashion. What did the builders intend to communicate and why? The second is to understand how this architecture can be made to function effectively in the very different political and economic circumstances of the present. Partly this involves mapping out appropriate preservation strategies, but it is equally important to find uses that keep these buildings alive for the people who live amidst them. Architectural historians, when dealing with heritage, should engage less in producing a discourse of action aiming to preserve a building and more in explaining architecture or the built environment in the light of its historical production context.

Asmara, which Italian colonisers had started to develop through intense construction activity, turned into a model of modern urbanism that embodied the vision of the city of tomorrow. But it never became a canvas on which the dreams of a large modern metropolis could be projected. **Stefano Zagnoni's** contribution focuses on some features that make Asmara's historical centre unique, thereby endowing it with an overall value. Asmara was a peculiar manifestation of the mental outlook of European colonialism in Africa, but later became a symbol of Eritrean national identity. It was conceived in the first two decades of the twentieth century when Eritrea was the forgotten colony; hence the plans and the well-defined framework of rules that set up an interesting experiment were at the time almost completely unknown in Italy itself. It was only in the second half of the 1930s that Italian architectural culture started to reflect about the colonial town and colonial house. Nevertheless, and as in previous periods, in Asmara the urban environment and the houses of the colonisers were mainly a transfer of models and concepts that had just been established and applied in Italy.

Nigisti
House
Hold
Nigisti House Hold

IS MODERN ARCHITECTURE GOOD?

Kathleen James-Chakraborty

Beginning with its origins in the Arts and Crafts movement, modern architecture has been associated throughout it history with progressive social positions. Much of its appeal results from this supposed confluence between abstract industrial form and the political and social interests of the working classes. Yet this is largely myth. Most members of the working class never preferred the architecture that supposedly represented their empowerment. From the beginning modern architecture there were many other reasons to turn to modern architecture. These included the clear break it made with the past, its relatively low cost, and its apparent informality.

The architecture of the Italian colonial capital of Asmara offers a paradigmatic example of modern architecture allied to political repression.[1] Two things matter about Asmara's Modernist heritage today. The first is reconstructing in an entirely unromantic fashion the circumstances of its creation. What were the clients and their designers intending to communicate and why? This architecture has survived intact, after all, in part because the local economy and political situation has never completely recovered from Italy's catastrophic effort to build an empire in the region. At the same time, however, we need to understand how this architecture can function effectively in very different political and economic contemporary circumstances, in which it has apparently become the subject of considerable local pride, probably in part nostalgia for the short-lived prosperity of the period in which many of these structures were erected, as well as foreign curiosity. This entails mapping

One of the many modernist buildings in Asmara
Source: K.Paulweber 2013

out appropriate preservation strategies, but equally important are uses that keep these buildings alive for the people who live amidst them. Ideally this architecture will finally fulfil the utopian aspirations that its modern style appears to promise, but which was so often at cross purposes with the intentions of its original builders, who were part of an inherently racist and exploitive enterprise. Simply making them part of a tourist itinerary of exotic modernism will not in itself suffice.

The architecture of colonial Asmara, and most especially that erected between 1935 and 1941, was by no means unique, except to the degree to which it was specifically Italian. It shares important characteristics with other colonial showcases of the new. These included Casablanca, Cairo (technically the capital of an independent Egypt, but still carefully watched over by Britain), Tel Aviv, Bombay, and Shanghai.[2] Buildings in all of these cities were in the 1930s much more likely to be in overtly modern styles than were structures of the same urban prominence and serving the same functions in the imperial capitals and the smaller cities of the ruling powers. Such innovation in supposedly marginal settings was not unprecedented, as the sophistication of Mexican colonial architecture in the sixteenth century and Brazilian building two centuries later makes clear.[3] Indeed, the popularity of modernism across Latin America as well as in newly independent nations in Africa and Asia after 1945 makes this but one chapter in a longer story of the degree to which modern architecture was, if anything, more popular outside Europe and the English-speaking world than within it. The most modern architecture erected in these cities only very seldom displayed the influence of abstract painting or the industrial aesthetic that were two of the main sources of the International Style architecture of the period.[4] Instead, an understated classicism or even respect for a stripped down version of the local vernacular co-existed with the impact of Art Déco and of streamlining, often with more than one of these currents present in the same design.

Although much colonial architecture, for instance that erected in what is now the United States and Canada across the seventeenth and eighteenth centuries, appears provincial in relation to its metropolitan sources, Spanish and Portuguese colonists had already demonstrated in the sixteenth and seventeenth centuries that far-flung colonial outposts could prompt architectural experiments that would be radical at home. Paul Rabinow and Gwendolyn Wright have shown the degree to which this was also the case for the French colonies in North Africa in the early decades of the twentieth century.[5] Nonetheless, even when there were continuities of style between an imperial power and its colonies, differences arose immediately in the colonies in how buildings were inhabited and thus also in how they were planned.[6]

Multiple factors encourage the use of colonies as showcases of the new. First, state control was typically much stronger, and the power ceded to architects and city planners much greater than in truly capitalist economies, much less democracies, which neither Italy nor Eritrea were at the point when most of Asmara's most memorable architecture was erected. Even in fascist Italy, displacing established landowners to build new showcases was far from easy; in France and Britain it was all but impossible for the state to do this without paying close to market value for what it appropriated. Second, the lack of an indigenous context appreciated by the colonisers encouraged a stronger break with established architectural ways of building than would have been permissible at home, where the same men (and they were almost always men) had a far greater appreciation of their own architectural heritage than of what they found in the Horn of Africa.[7] In much of North Africa, where much larger urban settlements had existed for millennia, the French erected their new cities next to existing Arab ones, which they appreciated as markers of the past they hoped to supersede. Italy followed suit in Libya.[8] In Casablanca and Tripoli during the 1920s colonial architecture often referenced the local but, just as had been the case with nineteenth-century historicism in Europe, new functions, building materials and spaces all ensured that the transposition of sacred and palace precedents into civic and commercial structures nonetheless produced buildings that were easily distinguishable from their indigenous sources. Asmara, however, was little more than an overgrown village when the Italians arrived and did not provide them with anything that they recognised as a significant, although they adapted the *tukul* as uniquely appropriate for housing Eritreans. Finally, modern architecture was usually less inexpensive than the alternatives. Concrete (or stucco covered brick, which often ends up looking like much the same thing) was and remains cheap, especially when labour costs are low, especially in comparison with carefully dressed stone.

Beyond such pragmatism, however, was the issue of how people who understood themselves, as colonial subjects and administrators, to be on the margins of the world as they themselves defined it took pride in the environment they inhabited. In Bombay (now Mumbai) in the 1930s, architects and developers from the minority Parsi community were largely responsible for the creation of Marine Drive. Lining the Indian Ocean just north of the city centre, this string of apartment buildings and hotels provided well-off Indians as well as British officials and business people with modern conveniences, including an Art Déco style whose obvious break with both European and Indian precedent appeared on the cusp of Independence to offer everyone a fresh start. Cairo boasted a number of enormous Art Déco cinemas, one of which was designed by Thomas Lamb, an American architect employed by the Hollywood-based studio Metro Goldwyn Meyer.[9] Here the city's middle class could watch the latest imported movies in much the same fashionable settings as their counterparts in California. In Tel Aviv, recent Jewish arrivals from Europe used abstract modern architecture, typically derived more from the example of Erich Mendelsohn than the Bauhaus, to distinguish themselves from the other claimants for control of this space, including the British authorities and western Christians as well as Arabs.[10] That these forms had vernacular Mediterranean precedent, especially in Greek and Arab villages, as both their supporters and detractors already realised, only appeared to make them more appropriate for such settings.[11] By the European standards of the day, the forward-looking architecture of these North African and Asian cities was optimistic, if not strictly utopian.

Undoubtedly those inhabitants of Asmara who were responsible during the 1930s for its fashionable new buildings shared this optimism. Here it emerged, however, out of fundamentally different aspirations than the hopes, for instance, that many, but by no means all, of those who moved into apartments on Marine Drive had for an independent India, that Cairene's elite had of being *au courant*, or that those who had recently made *aliyah* had of escaping Europe's deadly anti-Semitism. Like many of the European inhabitants of Casablanca, a city whose new buildings during the 1930s increasingly shaded from the simplification of classical or Islamic precedent into actual abstraction, they probably also appreciated the boost in their social status that came from living in a colony. The liberation implied by Asmara's buildings was from the immediate Italian past; the political empowerment that accompanied it was achieved in relation to colonial subjects rather than as part of the creation of a more participatory democratic, much less socialist, society. Particularly in the context of territory that had never been part of the Roman empire, new architectural forms symbolised the new start Fascism promised Italians, as well as the national pride that was to accompany it. It is no accident that Asmara's most celebrated buildings from this period are a cinema and a petrol station, building types that serve as emblems of a consumer-oriented prosperity, most of which – with the movies being an important exception – would become available to working and lower middle class Italians only after World War II.[12] The short-lived building boom during which much of the city's best buildings were constructed was prompted not by any locally generated prosperity, however, but by the Asmara's role as a staging ground for the Italian conquest of Ethiopia, one of the last and most sordid chapters in the unsavory history of European empire building in Africa.

The pride of being up to date transcended politics, however, as did the freedom that distance from the metropole provided from European standards of decorum, although this was also often accompanied as well by increased anxiety about being provincial, something modern architecture also helped assuage. Modern architecture was also considered particularly appropriate for tropical climates, not least because European formalities could often be dispensed with as middle-class entertaining as well as domesticity spilled out easily on to verandahs and balconies. Nor were colonial cities expected to maintain the standards of grandeur set by imperial capitals or even major financial and industrial centres like Milan and Turin. Indeed avant-garde design went out of fashion in both Germany and the Soviet Union as nationalism waxed, and the construction of major civic structures resumed. Style, often coupled to scale, made the point that remoteness did not equal backwardness, and on Europe's fringes as well as its colonies. Bucharest, the environs of Helsinki, and Ankara, were also places where modern architecture flourished, although only the work of Alvar Aalto became widely known outside the country in which it was built.[13]

How exactly, however, did the rest of this architecture convey that it was new? The leading lights of the modern movement were almost never involved in the design of anything erected outside Europe and the United States; Le Corbusier's role as a consultant for the Ministry of Education in Rio de Janeiro marks the major exception and Erich Mendelsohn's work in Mandate Palestine are major exceptions.[14] Many modern buildings probably did not have architects at all, although the rapid expansion of Asmara certainly attracted well-trained Italian professionals, whose Casablanca counterparts had often studied at the École des Beaux Arts in Paris.

The modernism that fills survey books may have comprised the most highly theorised and aesthetically sophisticated architectural representation of the new during the 1920s and 1930s, but it was never the only or even the most popular means of signifying modernity. In Sao Paulo and Shanghai towers that would have been at home in Chicago or New York employed the latest technology and fashionable new forms and ornament without engaging the avant-garde styles inspired by the same steel frames; in Calcutta as in Cairo, new cinemas testified to the global popularity of new forms of mass-produced entertainment. And concrete frame construction brought versions of Le Corbusier's *Maison Domino*, almost always erected without any awareness of the Swiss architect's understanding of the potential it created for elaborate new conceptions of space, to cities around the world. Breaking with the past never required even a passing acquaintanceship with the International Style. What was instead crucial was the sense that dressing up in historical styles was as old-fashioned as horse and carriages, or skirts that swept the ground; indeed in India one might retain the rickshaw and the sari and still be enthusiastic about a suburban apartment whose plan completely broke with inherited social conventions.[15]

Studies of Asmara have done much to define the precise styles employed there shading from Novecento through Art Déco to streamlining and at least a hint of Rationalism. These nuances are often ignored by those who tie the modern architecture in Africa, Asia, and Latin America back to the International Style, even as they appreciate the lack of the asceticism that characterised the work of Europe's most celebrated modern architects (indeed one of the obvious appeals of Asmara's modern heritage today is the obvious care with which these buildings were originally constructed, including a level of detail that can be found in only some of the best International Style buildings). The situation is little different in Europe and the English-speaking world, where architectural historians have not yet developed the tools to explain the wide range of architectures that were built by architects of various levels of distinction during these years, not to mention those erected, often with considerable sophistication, without the assistance of architects at all. Lumping all of this together eliminates the fine gradations of expression of individual and group identity and taste as well as aesthetic achievement that, along with politics and economics did so much to shape cities and suburbs alike.

The builders of Asmara were not concerned about model housing for the working class or workers' clubs that could serve as alternatives to churches and pubs, nor were they much interested in marketing the latest style in dress or providing showcases for a new scale of capitalist or civic bureaucracy, all briefs for the creation in the 1920s and 1930s of structures that looked radically different from anything that had been seen before. But like their ambitious urban middle-class counterparts across Latin America, Africa, and Asia, neither were they satisfied with anything that appeared as if it could have been built in either Europe or at home more than a few years earlier. This required no interest in communism, socialism, or even democracy. Instead what we find in Asmara, in Casablanca, in Cairo, in Tel Aviv, in Bombay, and in Shanghai, to name only the most architecturally dynamic cities of this kind during these years, is a client base as well as an architectural profession committed to change. The form this change took would soon itself seem passé. To establish itself as more than simply modish, modern architectural culture would in the post-war period pay more attention to the ideas and designs of a relatively small group of stars whose appeal was often greater to the profession than the general public. Asmara was not alone in being forgotten. To appreciate its importance requires a new kind of history, one is not driven by the need to defend modern architecture but by the importance of understanding it.

Notes

1 Edward Denison, Guang Yu and Naigzy Gebremedhin, *Asmara: Africa's Secret Modernist City*. London: Merrell, 2003; Mia Fuller, *Moderns Abroad: Architecture, Cities and Italian Imperialism*. London: Routledge, 2007.

2 Jean-Louis Cohen and Monique Eelb, *Casablanca: Colonial Myths and Architectural Ventures*. New York: Monicelli, 2002; Mercedes Volait (ed.), *Architectes et architectures de l'Egypte modern: Genèse et essor d'une expertise locale*. Paris: Maisonneuve & Larose, 2005; Mark Levine, *Overthrowing Geography: Jaffa, Tel Aviv, and the Struggle for Palestine, 1880–1945*. Berkeley: University of California Press, 2005; Nahoum COHEN, Bauhaus Tel Aviv. London: Batsford, 2003; Norma Evenson, *The Indian Metropolis: A View Towards the West*. New Haven: Yale University Press, 1989; Edward Denison and Guang Yu Ren, *Shanghai: The Story of China's Gateway*. New York: Wiley, 2002.

3 Kathleen James-Chakraborty, *Architecture since 1400*. Minneapolis: University of Minnesota Press, 2014.

4 This term, which was just coming into use at the time, was not invented by Henry-Russell Hitchcock and Philip Johnson, but can already be found in Frederick Kiesler, *Contemporary Art Applied to the Store and Its Display*. New York: Brentano, 1930.

5 Paul Rabinow, *French Modern: Norms and Forms of the Social Environment*. Cambridge: MIT Press 1989; Gwendolyn Wright, *Politics of Design in French Colonial Urbanism*. Chicago: University of Chicago Press, 1991.

6 Dell Upton, "White and Black Landscapes in Eighteenth-century Virginia", *Places* , vol. 2.2, 1984, pp. 59-72; Swati Chattopadhyay, *Representing Calcutta: Modernity, Nationalism and the Colonial Uncanny*. London: Routledge, 2006.

7 For an earlier example of this see William Cronon, *Changes in the Land: Indians, Colonists and the Ecology of New England*. New York: Hill and Wang, 1983.

8 Brian McLaren, *Architecture and Tourism in Italian Colonial Libya: An Ambivalent Modernism*. Seattle: University of Washington Press, 2006.

9 http://cinematreasures.org/theaters/12765, consulted 26 October 2015.

10 Cada Karmi-Melamede and Dan Price, Architecture in Palestine during the British Mandate, 1917–1948. Jerusalem: The Israel Museum, 2014.BegleitProgramm2007/DAZ_Presseinfo.pdf [27.06.2015].

11 The impact upon Le Corbusier of his voyage to the Orient is well known, as is the castigation of the Weisssenhof Siedlung in Stuttgart as an Arab village.

12 Victoria de Grazia, *Irresistable Empire: America's Advance through Twentieth-century Europe*. Cambridge: Belknap Press, 2006.

13 Luminita Machedon and Ernie Scoffham, *Romanian Modernism: The Architecture of Bucharest, 1920–1940*. Cambridge: MIT Press, 1999; Eeva Liisa Pelkonen, *Alvar Aalto: Architecture, Modernity, and Geopolitics*. New Haven: Yale University Press, 2009; Sibel Bozdogan, *Modernism and Nation Building: Turkish Architectural Culture in the Early Republic*. Seattle: University of Washington, 2001.

14 Zilah Quezado Deckker, *Brazil Built: The Architecture of the Modern Movement in Brazil*. London: Taylor & Francis, 2001; Ita Heinze-Greenberg, *Erich Mendelsohn, Bauten und Projekte in Palästina*. Munich: Scaneg, 1986.

15 Nikhil Rao, *House but No Garden: Apartment Living in Bombay's Suburbs, 1898–1964*. Minneapolis: University of Minnesota Press, 2013.

ASMARA
A Modern Historic City

Stefano Zagnoni

"Wherever they [ed.: the Italians] go, the thought they take with them is not to invent a new world, different from the familiar world they have just left, but to rebuild a small patch of Italy".

Curzio Malaparte[1]

Varied Unity

The urban centre that developed during the years of Italian occupation in the undulating plain between Fort Baldissera and the pre-existing native village of Arbate Asmera tends to defy all attempts at definition. We will simply call it Asmara, despite being well aware that we are referring only to a part of it, which at the time was largely out of bounds for the majority of the population, those of Eritrean descent. Initially scattered around the plain, they became increasingly concentrated in the north-east of the colonial city, relegated to settlements not at all dissimilar to shanty towns, which maps of the era in general tended to omit.

As generic as it is, the term Modernist city, used repeatedly in the research carried out over the last quarter of century,[2] encapsulates a characteristic feature of that which appeared in the second half of the 1930s: a striking expression of the myth of modernity, which goes beyond the extremely short-lived myth of the fascist empire from which it also descends. On the other hand, it fails to grasp Asmara's distinctive features, leaving out the different traits that co-exist there and that make it unique.

The Mai Jah Jah Fountain
Source: K.Paulweber 2013

The research and initiatives carried out locally immediately following Eritrea's independence have the merit of defining the border of what is now the historic centre of the city, considering it a unique case that is worthy of safeguarding, and surveying its heritage.[3] Nonetheless, studies of urban morphology and building typology that go beyond the identification of stylistic references, some more relevant than others, are still largely incomplete. Likewise, research into the main figures, architects and entrepreneurs who worked there, and who are almost entirely unknown in Italy, is also still at a very early stage.[4]

All phases of the urban formation undoubtedly bear the hallmarks of an Italian city, but it also stems from something derived from Italian culture, with its own distinctive features. Whilst this relative autonomy has its origins in the fact that for its first few decades Eritrea was a forgotten colony, the same attitude remained when faced with the centralising intentions of fascism, and survived beyond the end of colonial rule thanks to the establishment, at a local level, of an entity that embraced administrative management, the entrepreneurial system and technical professionalism. More so than in Italy's other colonies, even in the 1930s the work of well-known Italian architects in Eritrea was extremely sporadic. This certainly affected the results, but rather than diminishing them, it serves to highlight that there were trained specialists in situ, and it matters little if in many cases these were only surveyors. The city's features mimic an Italian city, but there is no city in Italy like Asmara.

It was, to all extents and purposes, a New Town. Nevertheless, despite a fervour that exceeded anything in Italy for regulating and controlling its growth with a succession of urban plans and building codes,[5] it did not take shape following a predefined design. In this sense, it lends itself more to being considered as a stratified city, analysing the process of urban development. While only a few traces remain of the 1890s buildings, constructed in a proto-urban context, there is much more left of the first centre of aggregation from the years immediately following its declaration as capital of the colony. The *Map of the City of Asmara with the New Urban Plan*, published in 1910, and the accompanying article[6] give us a rather detailed depiction both of the state of things at the time and the planned developments, which anticipate the dimensions of the urban centre up to the mid-1930s. Even the overall structure had already been defined, along with the criterion of racial segregation which was an integral part of the city's design from its origins.

As well as showing the division between the European zone and the native zone, the map also shows and defines the borders of the native settlements which were still present within the planned urban scheme, but from which the inhabitants "will soon have to move out", as the author makes clear

Former Piazza Roma with the northern façade of the Post Office
Source: K.Paulweber 2013

without any qualms at all in relation to one of them. At opposite sides of the Mai Bela River the European zone and the mixed zone (not shown on the map, but outlined in the 1908 urban plan) had been developing within a rather dense network of blocks, based around the thoroughfare of Corso del Re (now Nakfa Avenue). The guiding principles of the city's design, based around roads and squares, did not depart from those traditionally found in the historic European city. Due to the low number of Italian residents and meagre resources, the small size of the main public spaces in the European zone is striking: Piazza Roma, which Ferdinando Martini even described as a "vast square",[7] and the even smaller Piazza della Posta, to the south on the opposite side of the block. Alongside the public buildings, the urban fabric that took shape along the streets comprised buildings with at most two storeys. Only in some cases did these contain intentional stylistic features; they often had commercial premises on the ground floor and were built using rather elementary building techniques. As has been observed several times, it had the appearance of a small Italian provincial town, rather than a capital city.

The views of the mixed zone from the early 1910s give us a rather different picture: around the open space used for the market, the only large public area in the city, the geometric precision of the grid pattern framed very basic one

The former mixed zone of Asmara is still today the market zone and a vital hotspot in the city
Source: K. Paulweber 2013

storey buildings with corrugated metal roofs. Anyhow, the situation evolved more quickly than elsewhere, which is testament to the vitality of the area. Odoardo Cavagnari's urban plan, which, along with subsequent modifications, remained the key urban planning tool until 1939, from 1914 onwards imposed the same building rules set for the European zone in part of the mixed zone. As a result, by the second half of the decade, the mixed zone also had a small Italian piazza overlooking Corso del Re (Piazza Italia, later Piazza Michele Bianchi).

Anyway, if one considers it as a whole, Asmara, unlike the historic city, is not a formally unified structure. Instead it is a fragmentary city, which since its foundation has accepted the changes thrown at Western cities in the modern era. Of all the aspects that have led to this state, that which most clearly highlights the intention behind it is the district of *villini* on the southern slopes, where the individualism of the architectural typology methodically rejects any aggregational logic. However, this is not a typical residential suburb separated from the city, but rather an integral part of it, which incorporates public functions both on a city and regional scale. In general, adaptation to the environment did not go beyond adapting to the topography of the land. The most significant exceptions to this are the two later reconstructions of the Nda Mariam Orthodox Cathedral and the Degghi Selam building that stands immediately opposite: a pre-existing place of worship for the Eritrean population has become a monumental compound where the architecture enters into dialogue with the native tradition, and reinterprets it. But it must be noted that the operation was also instrumental in the dismantling of the native village that surrounded it.

The Deggi Selam building in front of Nda Mariam Orthodox Cathedral evokes precolonial architectures of Eritrea (left). The Modernist villa (right) is a contrasting example of the 1930s.
Source: S. Graf 2013

The Very Modern City

Italy's conquest of the empire radically altered the organisation of the land of colonial Eritrea. The huge resources set aside for it meant a change from planning without any systematic development to unbalanced, unplanned development that, along with exponential growth in the Italian population, affected only part of the colony, and mainly the capital.[8] Pre-imperial Asmara thus became, almost out of the blue, the city centre of an expanse of outskirts, settlements that grew up chaotically as a result of the military operations. A city council official used the expression "the city of Asmara and its outlying area" when describing the work that "with true fascist speed" gave "the city the appearance of a very modern urban centre".[9] The efforts of the municipal administration to tackle the emergency did not manage to provide a complete solution to the problem, nor could they possibly have hoped to do so, but they revealed significant operational skill: the planning and urbanisation of the new southern districts, the infill of the urban fabric to the west, the construction of workers villages intended as satellite settlements, as well as a major reinforcement of the city's infrastructure.

The urban layout of the pre-existing consolidated city in general withstood the impact of the jump in scale well. While the public spaces (squares and streets) were affected by considerable urban renewal work, the incisive transformation of the morphology and image of the city predominantly took place through increasing urban density and replacing existing buildings. The new constructions were mostly concentrated on Viale Mussolini (now Harnet Avenue), which is now the central thoroughfare of the settlement, and on the main roads into the city. The urban plan issued in 1939 and devised by Vittorio Cafiero foresaw the complete demolition and reconstruction of the compact central section of the European zone, thus wiping out the memory of an era seen in a negative light, but only a few buildings were actually replaced. The mixed zone, on the contrary, was subjected to more incisive transformations that radically remoulded it, although without completely reshaping it. All buildings aim for individual architectural features, but they continue, in general, to remain aligned with the streets and around the edge of the block. To this end, the vast range of corner solutions employed was primarily a response to the need to make the buildings fit the urban form, rather than a stylistic exercise. The very modern city therefore had very little to do with theories regarding the Functional City. Based on a method that had cemented itself over the centuries, the shape of the compact city centre had much more in common with the concepts of Camillo Sitte than those of the Athens Charter.

Guido Ferrazza's design for the market area is an excellent example of architectural definition of the urban space,[10] linking the European zone with the native zone, and, although it did not represent a step away from the dominant racism of the time, it expressed a total aversion to the "concept of a clear separation or outright gap between the two centres".[11] The Maj Jah Jah stepped fountain is another urban project that recalls Sitte's Art of Building Cities, even though the rapid pace of events changed the role for which it was originally conceived: from a monumental backdrop standing in front of the new railway station (planned here at the time of its construction in 1938) at the end to the (never completed) diagonal axis, it became an access gate to the Gheza Banda district that was under construction to the south.

The nineteenth-century penchant for zoning is ingrained in the urban layout, but it is separated both in terms of time and concept from the theoretical work on functional zoning carried out in the 1920s and 1930s. Even the regime's press complained about Asmara's mixed-up zoning, revealing a certain acquaintance with these theories, since in various parts of the city "it is difficult to identify their respective definition and function and the logic of where the various arteries begin and end".[12]

On the contrary, and despite the intended rationalisation, the mixture of different functions remains one of the elements that bring the urban fabric to life, and that, like in the historic city, gives rise to a unity that spurns homogeneity. According to Curzio Malaparte, Asmara, at the peak of its boom, went beyond the concept of colonial city itself. "Asmara immediately appears, in its form and its spirit, similar to certain cities in the central United States (...). The wide, straight streets, the layout and style of the buildings, the heavy traffic, the incredible number of luxury cars that drive quickly and silently along its large avenues flanked by pure white houses with plain, modern lines, and buildings made of glass and concrete, (...) all reveals the intimate spirit of this city which sprang up in just four years."[13] Falling prey to the regime's rhetoric, Malaparte maintained that fascism has abandoned the model of nineteenth-century colonialism, which aimed merely to exploit the subjugated countries, and that instead it was decisively accelerating the history of these places. In Asmara and Dekemhare he therefore thought he recognised the early signs of a developing White Empire.

Leaving aside his imperial dreams, Malaparte's impressions are not as unfounded as they may appear, just as the hyperbole with which he compared the city to American metropolises offers a further example of the strength of the myth of modernity. Unlike the radical avant-garde movements, which searched for renewal that would free humanity from oppression and dominion, this was a modernity that can be associated with the multifaceted phenomenon retrospectively named Art Déco. Rather than stylistic, the focus is once more on substance: the brand new celebrates the state of things as they are and has a strong impact on the collective imagination of the oppressed, who, moreover, are not allowed to do anything other than admire them. In cinemas the captivating power of the architecture was then multiplied by the images projected on the screen and, whether or not it was done intentionally, the cinemas of Asmara are amongst its most surprising pieces of architecture, much more so than the regime buildings. Given that the discrimination did not end even once colonial rule had come to an end,[14] it begs the question of whether the myth of modernity had a positive role in the no less surprising process of the reappropriation by the Eritrean population, both of the physical places and of the customs that took place within them.

If cinemas were the monuments, mixed real estate (shops and/or offices combined with dwellings) was the building type that made up the majority of the part of the urban fabric where the skyline of the city centre increased in height by two or three storeys. The types of dwelling were not dissimilar from those currently in use in Italy and, like the methods of construction, differed from the first drafts of colonial norms that Italian architectural culture was only just creating in those years.[15] On the one hand, the city's climate meant that the solutions adopted were not completely incongruous: "The mild, spring-like climate that features neither bitter cold nor scorching temperatures dispenses with all those devices that are necessary elsewhere", Guido Ferrazza wrote about the upland area.[16] On the other hand, and most importantly, it must be borne in mind that both Ferrazza and the other authors that tackled knowledgeably the topic of the colonial house in Eastern Africa based their writing on the problems that had occurred in recently conquered regions. It was above all the exorbitant cost of imported building materials that made, albeit temporarily, "the daring and very modern cantilevers of reinforced concrete" unthinkable and forced the recommendation of a return to the past, using local materials as much as possible and even adopting solutions adapted from the native tradition.[17] The prices of cement and steel remained significantly higher in Asmara than in Italy, but not to the same extent as in Ethiopian cities. A reinforced concrete frame structure (usually combined with a load-bearing wall following a practice which was common at the time) thus became widespread. The pitched roof, protruding from the perimeter wall to offer protection from the sun, is another recurring recommendation for colonial houses, whilst in Asmara, in general, flat roofs were adopted. And there is no shortage of other examples.

In summary, a rationalism of forms that favoured the use of languages, techniques and materials that denoted what was considered modern at the time tended to dominate, even, to a certain extent, where it made little financial or functional sense. The widespread quality of the architecture is symbolically intended to reflect a clear break from the past and to prove that the city had reached a position where it could keep up with a developed metropolitan area. Similar Italian and modern features also characterised the new districts on the peripheral residential zones, where a certain portion of the tens of thousands of Italian workers that flooded the city could leave behind the poor and promiscuous conditions in which they often lived, and which led the regime to worry seriously about contamination of the purity of the race. In terms of the types of dwelling, diversification seems to have prevailed decisively over repetition of house types, even in coordinated projects, whilst the unity of the whole was entrusted to the urban layout and the community hubs which, at a local level, acted as meeting places. Here, more than elsewhere, however, much still needs to be ascertained before we have a sufficiently clear picture of the types of settlement and the specific nature of the context, both physical and social, in which many of Asmara's Italians recreated an environment familiar to them, and achieved a standard of living beyond that which they had experienced in Italy.

Notes

1 Curzio Malaparte, "L'Africa non è nera", Il Corriere della sera, May 4, 1939; now in Enzo R. Laforgia (ed.), *Viaggio in Etiopia e altri scritti africani. Curzio Malaparte*. Florence: Vallecchi, 2006, p. 46.

2 Cf. in particular Edward Denison, Guang Yu Ren and Naizy Gebremedhin, *Asmara. Africa's secret modernist city*. London-New York: Merrell, 2003.

3 Cf. in particular Naizy Gebremedhin (ed.), *Asmara. A Guide to the Built Environment*, Asmara: Francescana Printing, 2006 (1st ed., 2003).

4 Cf. in particular Anna Godio, "The men who built the Italian architecture in the colony: pioneers, architects, engineers, property developers and builders" in ID., Anna Godio, *Italian architecture in Eritrea*. Turin: La Rosa, 2008, pp. 227-264.

5 cf. in particular Belula Tecle-Misghina, *Asmara – An Urban History*. Rome: Nuova Cultura, 2014 (e-book).

6 Michele Checchi, "Asmara", *Rivista Coloniale*, Sept. 25– Oct. 10, 1910, pp. 346-355. This map has been published multiple times in contemporary publications, but is dated 1913, the year of one of its printed versions.

7 Ferdinando Martini, "Relazione sulla colonia Eritrea – 1900/1901", Atti parlamentari, Camera dei Deputati, Legislatura XXI – 2a sess. 1902, Rome: Tip. Della Camera dei Deputati 1902, p. 33.

8 Cf. Stefano Zagnoni, "L'Eritrea delle piccole città", in Giuliano Gresleri, Pier Giorgio Massaretti and Stefano Zagnoni (eds.), *Architettura italiana d'Oltremare 1870–1940*. Exhibition Catalogue (Bologna, Municipal Modern Art Gallery, Sept. 26,1993/Jan. 7, 1994), Venice: Marsilio, 1993, pp. 145-163.

9 Pietro Galli, "Cenni sulla città di Asmara", in *Guida della città di Asmara*. Bologna: il Resto del Carlino, 1938, passim.

10 Cf. in particular Filippo Amara, *Un progetto urbano per Asmara. Guido Ferrazza e i nuovi mercati della capitale eritrea, 1935–38. Un caso di restauro del moderno tra interpretazione e progetto*. Rome: Aracne, 2007.

11 Guido Ferrazza, "Relazione al Progetto di Piano regolatore della Città di Harar", Nov. 24, 1936, Private Archive Ferrazza Milan.

12 "I piani regolatori", *Annali dell'Africa italiana*, vol. IV, 1939, p. 386.

13 Curzio Malaparte, "Città d'Impero bianco", *Il Corriere della sera*, May 13, 1939; now in Enzo R.Laforgia (ed.), *Viaggio in Etiopia e altri scritti africani. Curzio Malaparte*, op. cit., p. 56.

14 Giulia Barrera, "Asmara la città degli italiani e la città degli eritrei", in Giulia Barrera, Alessandro Triulzi and Gabriel Tzeggai (eds.), *Asmara. Architettura e pianificazione urbana nei fondi dell'IsIAO*. Rome: Istituto Italiano per l'Africa e l'Oriente, 2008, pp. 12-27.

15 Cf. in particular Giorgio Rigotti, *Edilizia e urbanistica nell'Africa Orientale. La zona di Addis Abeba*. Turin: Editrice libraria italiana, 1939; Cesare Valle, *Corso di edilizia coloniale con particolare riferimento all'A.O.I.* Rome: R.Pioda 1938.

16 Guido Ferrazza, "Il problema del costruire nell'impero", *Rassegna di architettura*, n. 1 – 1937, pp. 19-22.

17 Ibid., passim.

Second Chapter

CONSTRUCTION OF THE COLONIAL SPHERE

Although our collection of essays primarily intends to cast light on the specificity of Italian colonialism in Asmara and its economic, cultural and discursive articulations, its aim is also to dismantle resilient notions of a single colonial project tied to fantasies of an impenetrable Italian national identity. This chapter contrasts a theorised colonial architecture and urban planning with untheorised approaches to the colonial sphere (of course, they constitute theoretical approaches unto themselves), such as those concerned with car racing, colonial archives, business organisations or private housing. Architects in those days conceived architecture and urban planning as symbolic signs of Italian modernity and as the means to spiritual domination. It is difficult to investigate the colonial project and to formulate any judgement on it without referring to this symbolic order, because the fascists' objectives were mainly of an ideological-spiritual nature. From the very beginning, the colony was a myth employed to mobilise the nation.

This chapter focuses on the construction of the colonial sphere and describes how Italian colonial settings were managed away from architecture. In other words, Italians defined the colonial built environment independently from what they erected there. This perspective opens the way to examining the discursive construction of the colonial sphere as a foundational landscape – both material and immaterial – that could be accessed, consumed and dominated. The settlers coming to Eritrea did not seem to conform to the myth of the new Italian and little is known about how urban dwellers, especially Africans, experienced European notions of modernity, becoming agents of urban transformation.

Pier Giorgio Massaretti investigates the foundation of colonial Asmara through historical-geographic patterns and the socio-political context. Based on this genealogical and historical interpretation, Massaretti probes the real foundational value that the story of the capital of the Italian colony in the Horn of Africa, both immaterial (political and social) and material (physical-constructional), has had on the entire national colonial design. He makes an exemplary survey of the experimental diagnostic governance implemented by the National Liberal Right for a modernising civic and urban development of the native Asmara; this investigation recovers, refines and integrates Massaretti's precedent text: *Prolegomeni coloniali. La genesi dell'imperialismo nazionale nell'innovatività del modello urbanistico asmarino*, originally partially edited by the Italian Institute for Africa and the East (2008).

Gian Luca Podestà shows that the planning and building of the new Italian areas in Asmara and Addis Ababa, in which even Le Corbusier tried in vain to take part, was going to be important both at the economic and symbolic levels. The situation in Asmara was quite exceptional. By 1939 the population, which in 1935 had amounted to 4,000 Italians and 12,000 Africans, had grown to 48,000 and 36,000, respectively. It was a phenomenon without any precedent in history, determined by the town's economic importance as a logistics base for the war. By 1938, over 12,000 civilian vehicles were already circulating in Eritrea (one for every six inhabitants). Private housing therefore played a very relevant role in Asmara. Public expenditure for the war and various building projects promoted economic growth in Eritrea, the region most endowed with infrastructures and productive factors. It was also the region where most workers had received some basic education, thanks to a network of newly-created primary schools.

The aim of **Francesca Locatelli's** piece is to question the process whereby spatial relations were constituted along gender, race and class lines within the colonial context. Scholarly literature on the growth of Asmara during the Italian colonial period has primarily been interested in the study of the spatial development and architecture of the city, perceived as symbols of a form of modernity imported from abroad. Colonisation represented a turning point in the life of thousands of settlers. Yet little is known about how urban dwellers, especially Africans, experienced European notions of modernity. Francesca Locatelli shows how the rapid, turbulent processes that occurred between the end of the nineteenth and middle of the twentieth centuries were destined to have a strong impact on the ways in which urban dwellers asserted their presence and forged their lives in Asmara, and on the subsequent development of the city: in other words, on the making of the modern Asmarini and on the transformation of Asmara into a microcosm of fundamental national changes.

Silvana Palma's essay focuses on pictures of Asmara in the two Italian colonial archives (especially IsIAO and that of the *Società Africana d'Italia*), on how and when they were collected and, above all, how the documentary material has been organised. In search of the colonial discourse, she proposes to read Asmara through archives assembled in Italy, investigating the place that Asmara and its architecture occupy within these spaces. The story and fate of the two archives – especially of the Roman one – is also emblematic of the country's controversial relationship with its colonial past and of the refusal that, at the institutional and social levels, still characterises it. This, in turn, has a significant and often tragic impact on the reception of Eritrean refugees in Italy.

Federico Caprotti investigates the representation, in 1930s newsreels and documentaries, of Asmara as both the quintessential, fascist, modern colonial city, and as a hub connecting Italian East Africa with the imperial centre. He analyses how strategies of visuality were deployed, through the moving image, to hold together the representation of Asmara as either a self-sustaining colonial city, or as a city whose importance lay less in its architectural solidity than in its constructed interdependence with Italy and other colonial cities. Notions of interdependence within the context of colonial city networks are explored by excavating the depiction of Asmara as a veritable hub of Empire; the moving image clearly focused on the city as a node in modern technological networks, from air transport to rail, roads and trade.

Massimo Zaccaria deals with car travel and motor racing in Asmara and Eritrea. His sources comprise a rare collection of sport articles published in Eritrean newspapers. His history of motor sports in Asmara/Eritrea deals with their symbolism and the appearance of the first Eritrean drivers. Asmara offers a good example of the Fascist regime's desire to infuse the infrastructural programme with a symbolic meaning: the road as a symbol of life and civilisation. In many cases elite motor racing attracted people influenced by the Futurist mythology surrounding engines and engineering. The motor car thus became incorporated in local popular culture as a symbol of modernity. In addition to the services that were strictly related to the car industry, automobiles acquired a central place in Eritrean society. In order to understand this, Massimo Zaccaria discusses the unique significance of the recreational, social and even symbolic roles of the car. From 1938 onwards, motor car and motorbike races were organised in Asmara and immediately enjoyed widespread popularity among the Italian and Eritrean public.

View of one of the oldest governmental buildings in Asmara, today's Regional Government Offices
Source: S. Graf 2015

COLONIAL PRELIMINARIES
The Genesis of Italian Imperialism in the Experience of the Governance of Asmara

Pier Giorgio Massaretti

The Colony of Eritrea and the Governorship of Ferdinando Martini

In his two long articles devoted to the activity of Ferdinando Martini as governor of Eritrea, Alberto Aquarone[1] addresses the history of the firstborn colony through a careful examination of the relationship between the mother country and the colony, especially in the delicate moment of transition from a military administration – the direct consequence of the physical occupation of those African territories, for the sake of preserving the geo-political boundaries acquired – to that of a special civil commissioner, namely Martini. On the other hand, the issue of the difficult relationship between military and civilian actors in administering the Italian colonies at its inception was a central element of Aquarone's historiography and of his commitment as teacher and researcher.

On this historiographic core, the reflection I intend to develop here – with the irreplaceable contribution of Aquarone himself and the timely document references in the work of Carlo Rossetti on the Asmara Congress of 1905[2] – is to unravel that chaotic tangle of political and strategic relationships and vocations that connects Martini's management to the weak governance of the Nation in matters of colonies and colonialism; that unresolved conflict between opposing grandstanding (public vs private) inherited from the post-Risorgimento national government, which would be ineffectively metabolised by the hegemonic leadership (Fascism vs totalitarian state) of the Fascist regime.

Former Piazza Italia in Asmara
Source: K.Paulweber 2013

The military but above all political cataclysm that followed the defeat at Adua (1 March 1896) first of all testified to the weakness and inefficiency of Crispi's imperialism. It was, politically, the product of a precise choice of sides for the national government, which never officially gave up the idea of a possible policy of colonial expansion, which between public opinion and some organised political forces (the Socialists, among others) was beginning to make headway. In this divergent perspective there was even an attempt to establish, between the two vectors of expansion – that of a peaceful economic penetration and of the organised protection of mass emigration and territorial occupation, regardless of a military conquest – a special department of the Colonies which would extend its work beyond the ordinary administration of the colonial possessions, to rule instead over all affairs and events regarding emigration and Italians abroad, but also the systematic promotion of domestic exports on foreign markets.

The appointment of Ferdinando Martini Real as Special Commissioner of the Colony of Eritrea (21 November 1897), cannot but be interpreted as a decisive government action for resolving the catastrophic political short-circuit after Adua. Early in his political and parliamentary career Martini had taken positions that were avowedly different from the colonial enterprises under way in Africa;[3] however – lashing out angrily against the alleged civilising mission Italy had cut out for itself in Africa – he decisively supported the international policy that the great European colonial powers had agreed on in Berlin in 1885, at the close of the Congo Congress (1882).

The transition decreed by the tortuous appointment of Ferdinando Martini as Commissioner of the Governorship of Eritrea should have ushered in a profound internal reorganisation of the territory, which was still colonised militarily, with a view to activating a targeted process of economic exploitation, which would be "prudent and maybe modest but secure and steady, now based definitively more on the exploitation of local resources than on ambitious plans for encouraging settlement by migration from the motherland".[4]

Martini's was a mandate with a wide margin of discretion, to be exercised "after careful consideration of the situation and an equally thorough study of the appropriate measures." It was a programme of reflection, cautious and modest, primarily concerned with "preserving at all costs the internal and external peace by eradicating any cause of friction with the Emperor of Abyssinia and turmoil and rebelliousness among the local population," and with avoiding any further exacerbation of anti-African public opinion, which in Martini's wait-and-see solution could not fail to see the declared bankruptcy of his political aspirations.

The Italian Colonial Congress in Asmara (1905)

After the trauma of Adua the appeals and exhortations to get to work, first of all to learn about the colony's resources and potentials, and then to direct and elucidate a coherent and effective colonial policy, multiplied, and gradually took the pragmatic shape of a colonial consciousness. What followed was the start of a campaign of consolidation for a dedicated colonial culture, which Martini had already laid as a cornerstone of his term as governor: the need to heal both the political and collective inattention concerning colonies which had produced the scarcely exhilarating results of the military experience up to then in Eritrea. It was a revival promoted by the progressive convergence around a new strategic alliance between a government policy that by now had taken an ineluctable direction – although with an equally fatal delay – and a deficient international economic expansionism, and the public and journalistic work of the scientific-cultural elite of Italy during the reign of Umberto I of Savoy.

A promotional, informative commitment accredited by both the multiplication of conference activities and targeted public programmes that the interest groups of geographical interest then produced periodically, and specific commercial agencies then committed to supporting an advanced international-colonial target of national economic policy. It was in this context of socio-cultural promotion that the 1905 Colonial Congress of Asmara was placed.

Already called for in the conclusions of the fourth Italian Geographic Conference of Naples in 1901, the African Congress was, however, characterised since its inception by a problematic connotation of ambiguous semi-officiality. A true *deus ex machina* of the whole operation was Lieutenant Colonel Carlo Rosselli: already a speaker at the Naples conference – then curator of the proceedings of the Asmara conference – as an officer of the Colonial Office of the Ministry of Foreign Affairs "he worked for over a year, faithfully and tenaciously overcoming burdensome difficulties of men and things, thus the only true keeper of order of this Congress".[5] But despite the important adhesions (ministerial, business, associative and intellectual) it received, the event was bound to trigger some justified concern in ministerial circles, precisely because of the still considerable government impreparedness and indecision concerning the colonial policy of Eritrea.

Although Aquarone made an unflinching assessment of the Congress results – "Of course there were, on the whole, no particularly original and revolutionary positions and solicitations. Mostly, the agendas presented and the discussions that accompanied their approval did nothing but retrace concepts and proposals that have long become traditional in 'Africanist' circles"[6] – starting precisely with these, the task I now undertake is to review the results of that "desired and conscious action of state" in implementing the structural and cultural paradigms that had inspired the city planner of Asmara or suggested to him the main lines of action for optimising the growth and affirmation of the Eritrean capital.

The Urban Experiment of Re-founding the Colonial City

The effective and timely reporting that the Official Bulletin of Eritrea Colony produced about the works undertaken by Ferdinando Martini in Eritrea allows me to illustrate the valuable efforts implemented by his governorship (1897–1907) for local public works.

— In 1898 there is the first government decree "to provide the centre of Asmara [what would later become the colony's capital] with a decent urban plan."

— In 1899 Martini moves the capital from Massawa to Asmara; in the new capital he then inaugurates a plethora of projects: architectural (the construction of two large high-reception hotels); urban and infrastructural (the facilities of a still primitive aqueduct system, the activation of competitions for the arrangement of streets and central squares, the work of transforming the caravan trails from Asmara to Keren, Adi Ugri and Seghenetei); and public regulation (for collecting and storing rainwater; plastering and whitewashing for the decorum of the buildings of the European quarter; for refuse disposal).

— In 1900 he concludes the Treaty of Addis Ababa, which defines new boundaries between Eritrea and Ethiopia, and consequently transforms and develops the road network linking the two countries.

— In 1901 he strengthens the inner road network; inaugurates the Asmara-Addis Ababa telegraph line; lays out (Government Decree 10 of 1901) the first sewer system [improved in 1917 and enlarged in 1936 and 1939].

— In September 1902 (Government Decree 137) there is "the approval of the first part of a master plan for the central area of the European quarter" – a project never brought to fruition.

— In 1903 the governorship approves some urgent public services: the founding of the *Istituto Siero-vaccinogeno* [Serum Vaccine Institute]; the inauguration of the first Italian secular elementary school; the endowment of the great market area – near the central mosque – with a caravanserai, a slaughter-house, a vehicle scale, small wells and a large cistern for water collection.

— In 1904: the railway from Massawa reaches Ghinda. In the same period there is the inauguration of "the first electrical plant powered by vegetable fuel [...] to replace kerosene lighting."

— In 1905 [coinciding with the staging of the colonial Congress?] three major public works have been completed: in the water treatment and distribution network for domestic use; the construction of the Governor's Palace; the planting of trees along the banks of the Mai Belà, some streets and central squares.

Asmara, 1910: *Raduno per un picnic a piazza Roma*
Source: A. Comini, source: IAO (Istituto Agronomico per l'Oltremare)

— In the closing years of Martini's special mandate, his activity is limited to: February 1906, "The construction of the Asmara synagogue is concluded." The most important urban planning and transformation projects were implemented later on.

— In 1908 (the information-documental reference is still the aforementioned *Bulletino*), the repeal of the unrealised 1902 plan and the approval of a new plan, zoned along racial lines (the European zone; a mixed zone for Europeans and assimilated natives, an exclusively indigenous zone; a belt of suburban housing – meant for what specific racial or social class?).

September 1912 sees the opening of "the 118 km steep railway line joining Massawa to Asmara." In 1913 the urban plan, in 1914 its approval and the relevant building regulations, set up by the Civil Engineering Unit of Eritrea Colony – signed by Odoardo Cavagnari – and that designs Asmara as represented in the 1929 Italian Touring Club Guide.

The exhaustive survey produced by Zagnoni in his: *L'Eritrea delle piccolo città*[7] starts precisely from this point. And to emphasise the novelty of the Eritrean experiment, it recalls two exemplary events: the successful demilitarisation (in 1898, during Martini's governorship) of the local administrative bodies, and their endowment of an autonomous capacity for legislative enactment; the simultaneous activation of a Technical Office of the colony trained by the Civil Engineering staff, a technical-administrative adjunct, the latter indispensable for guiding with the help of its experienced and advanced professional skills the long series of interventions listed above, and even able to prepare innovative urban planning measures, governance and planning guidelines earlier than in Italy itself and even internationally.[8]

But in the shareable intention of emphasising a healthy distance from the accredited innovation of the disciplinary experience of Eritrea with respect to the backward conditions of the planning discipline of the motherland, the author identifies a solution that, in my opinion, is ineffectual. He says: "The incident is all the more notable because it takes place virtually unbeknownst to the national culture, of which it is yet a product" – it turns out, despite the absence of direct evidence – to be rather unlikely; an improbable "informational masking," which does not take into account how the actual difference between the two diverse disciplinary events (in the motherland vs in the colony) is supported by far more enlightening strategic reasons. The exemplary capacity of Martini's Special Commissariat to experiment his effective, innovative gubernatorial leadership in the territorial programming and in urban planning was permitted and facilitated by the endemic tabula rasa which the archaic and unregulated conditions of colonial territories inherently presented. Regulatory and legislative capacity, mature technical expertise, advanced models of planned development of the territory and its urban centres – which even in the young national unitary state were being experimented and consolidated – for a complex range of socio-economic, political and cultural reasons (which could be summarised in the attestation of an endemic "incapacity of state governance" of post-Risorgimento Italy), in Italy at the turn of the century, had little and localised chances of application. In Eritrea Martini's idea of an Asmara as metropolitan capital – so strongly in keeping with the genealogical Haussmann model of modern European urban planning – in order to take root, certainly paid for the lack of necessary economic investments coming from Italy, but – just as clearly – was the strategic reason for confirming the innovative partnership of interdisciplinary technical expertise that had animated the 1905 Colonial Congress of Asmara.

But what drove the educated intellectual and professional elite to take up in such a disadvantaged form the cultural challenge and the material risk of a colonial adventure? The main imprinting is what I would summarise in the encompassing paradigm of the frontier and/or boundary myth: the physical and intellectual challenge that the knowledge and/or conquest of new worlds inherently triggers in the modern man. This epiphenomenon – the blinding challenge of the unknown, the heady appeal of boundlessness – which excites the popular imagination (and the explosion of the exotic literature and iconography of the period well attests to it), but which also triggers an overwhelming scientific and technological creativity: the omnipotence of the Engineer, who redraws the Earth and its physical features – to adapt them to Mankind's "magnificent progressive destiny" – and at the same time (with the strictly positivist invention of "sanitary engineering"[9]) rescues Man from suffering and from physical and moral degradation. From this metaphorical exploration of the limes there re-emerges the constructive pragmatism that distinguishes the *Romanus ordo* – integrally revived by the two great modern revolutions: the French one, but especially the American one; and relaunched rhetorically by the illusory Fascist revolution – whose models and corporate rules were being developed simultaneously with the conquest of the new territories, and with the civilisation of the "*barbari moribus incondite*".[10] But I think it was above all the icon of the sacred and ritualistic "founding regeneration"[11] of the *moris ordo et traditio* that had forcefully motivated and sustained – in tune with the Catholic missionary theology of plantatio ecclesiae[12] – the Italian colonial explorations and conquests.

Why then, in spite of this more doctrinal than pragmatic adhesion of Italian Africanist culture to the founding axiom, was there no mature development of a national colonialism (that re-foundation which in Roosevelt's New Deal was the very backbone of the social programme of the Farm Security Administration)? It would take a much longer and demanding critical reflection to probe into how it was the different religious matrix of the two different models of capitalism in question (the Central European-American one against the national-Mediterranean one) that produced such a gap, and therefore decreed the delay and inaction of entrepreneurial and national political elites in the overwhelming international competitiveness unleashed by the scramble for colonies. In the joint efforts of the two doctrines in the process of community foundation, while for Protestantism its moral vocation of solidarity was expressed in a singular professional cosmopolitanism[13] of the role of a Christian in the community, for Catholicism the permanence in its doctrinal system of an ecclesiological hierarchical matrix retarded the development and maturation of responsible professional figures, keeping alive instead the "solidarity in sin"[14] typical of an archaic rural culture. In this general socio-cultural scenario Pope Leo XIII's *Rerum Novarum* (1891) – the first of the social encyclicals of the Roman papacy – was definitely a valuable ideological device, meant mainly to moralise the growing discontent of the working classes, and whose enunciation of the christianum mandatum for Italy's dominant middle-class elite was part and parcel of the training of the professionals who in Eritrea worked with Ferdinando Martini for the albeit failed modernisation of the Italian colony.

An entrepreneurial elite that was unable (or insufficiently equipped?) to compete with the momentous socio-economic transformation of full-fledged Western industrialism; and, significantly, the largest financial investments of the embryonic Italian capitalism were concentrated – with great technological and managerial delay with respect to other European countries – in slow and inadequate processes of modernisation in the agricultural sector: the mechanisation of its production and marketing, while most were economic commitments in the mammoth work of reclamation redemption that for nearly a century intensively involved the entire national territory.

Inevitably, the blatant ineffectiveness of the Italian colonial policies during Martini's tenure was motivated (as evidenced in Aquarone's opening insightful critique) by a strategic-structural inadequacy of the national economic apparatus, compounded by political and governmental choices – prejudicially anchored to the non-competitive "ruralist ideology of 'bread and work'"[15] – which, however, were able to mobilise conveniently that dragging effect which the critical mass of a thriving class of Italian labourers was able to bring about through a willing nationalistic fervour of public works. Why, then, to conclude – in the case of Italian colonialism in particular – did the re-founding challenge I outlined above not develop? Was it perhaps a delay motivated by that endemic but pathological attachment to the rural communitas and its reassuring religious constellation? Can the at times downright mock-heroic history of the founding of the demographic colonisation villages by Fascism in Italy and in the former African colonies perhaps supply a suitable answer?

Notes

1 In his 1989 text: Alberto Aquarone, *Dopo Adua: politica e amministrazione coloniale* (ed. or., Ist. Poligrafico e Zecca di Stato, Rome), Ludovica De Courten gathers Aquarone's lessons from his History of the Risorgimento courses at Rome's Sapienza University, and two well-annotated texts on the figure of F. Martini during his governorship of Eritrea (1897–1907): i) Ibid., La politica coloniale italiana dopo Adua: Ferdinando Martini governatore in *Eritrea, Rassegna storica del Risorgimento*, LXII, 1975; ii) Ibid., "Politica estera e organizzazione del consenso nell'età giolittiana: il Congresso dell'Asmara e la fondazione dell'Istituto coloniale italiano", *Storia contemporanea*, VIII, 1977 (respectively, at pp. 75-160 and pp. 161-254 of the 1989 volume cited).

2 See Carlo Rossetti (eds.), "Proceedings of the Italian colonial congress", in *Asmara* (September–October 1905): vol. I: *Relazioni, Comunicazioni e Conferenze*; vol. II: *Verbali delle discussioni*; Rome: Tip. dell'Unione Cooperativa Ed., 1906.

3 Again in 1891, in Parliament Martini declared that he "did not know how to resign himself to believing that there are two justices, one white and one black, two rights, one white and one black", see Ferdinando Martini, *Cose Affricane. Da Saati ad Abba Carima. Discorsi e scritti*. Milan: Treves, 1896, p. 215.

4 See Alberto Aquarone, *La politica coloniale italiana dopo Adua* [...], cit., p. 142.

5 For the preparatory work of the Congress, the documents drafted by a special authorising committee of the initiative (Naples, November 24, 1904), see ACS-Asmai, pos. 34/2, folder 52. In this case too reference is made in Aquarone's 1975 text to the careful reconstruction of the Congress being analysed (pp. 301-304).

6 See Alberto Aquarone, *Politica estera e organizzazione del consenso nell'età giolittiana* [...], cited on p. 313; significantly, the author himself delegates to Martini's *Diario eritreo* the task of listing – though not exhaustively – the relations-discussions that took place here.

7 See Stefano Zagnoni, "L'Eritrea delle piccole città", in Giuliano Gresleri, Pier Giorgio Massaretti, Stefano Zagnoni (eds.), *Architettura italiana d'oltremare 1870–1940*. Venice: Marsilio, 1993, pp. 150-153.

8 "Over more than a decade a comprehensive regional planning was carried out, on the basis of the now clearly established interventionist strategies when, in 1913, Regent General Lyautey called Henri Prost to Morocco to entrust him with [...] the first example of applying the new urban planning discipline to an entire country (BB Taylor); or when, in the same years, the urban development plans of Tripoli and Bengasi are prepared, in which the national sector handbook identifies the beginnings of Italian colonial urban planning," Stefano Zagnoni, *L'Eritrea delle piccole città*, cit., p. 146.

9 For a more general assessment, see Jaffry Herf, *Il modernismo reazionario. Tecnologia, cultura e politica nella Germania di Weimar e del Terzo Reich*. Bologna: Il Mulino, 1988. Concerning health systems and disciplinary devices, and their effect on processes of urban hegemonisation: see Jeremy Bentham, *Panopticon, ovvero La casa d'ispezione*, Michel Foucault and Michelle Perrot (eds.). Venice: Marsilio, 1983.

10 The most updated essay reflections on the geo-history of Italy and its generative matrices of ancient Roman layout are all indebted to the famous text by Carlo Cattaneo, "La città considerata come principio delle istorie italiane", in Idem, *Scritti storici e geografici*, G. Salvemini and E. Sestan (eds.), vol. II, Florence: Le Monnier, 1957, pp. 364-385.

11 In reference to the sense used here, I do not much agree with the hegemonising interpretation of the foundational event that Zagnoni, in his oft cited text, states as: "an authoritarian gesture that, in opposition to the 'disorder' of the native village, imposes with its rigidity an unmistakable form on the first nucleus of 'urban condensation' (the native area in *tukul*, arranged orthogonally)," p. 151.

12 Pier Giorgio Massaretti, "Il tragico 'òikos' dei villaggi di fondazione della Libia", in Pasquale Culotta, Giuliano Gresleri, Glauco Gresleri (eds.), *Città di fondazione e "plantatio ecclesiae"*, Bologna: Compositori, 2007; see especially the chapter: Plantatio ecclesiae e vocazione fondativa. Il kerygma missionario ed i modelli egemonici del regime, pp. 220-222.

13 See Max Weber, *The Protestant Ethic and the Spirit of Capitalism*. Milan: Rizzoli, 2013, pp. 101-102.

14 Adriano Prosperi, *Tribunali della coscienza. Inquisitori, confessori, missionari*. Turin: Einaudi, 1996, p. 12.

15 Pier Giorgio Massaretti, "Le esperienze degli enti di colonizzazione demografica in Libia e in AOI", *Terre d'Africa*, special issue., 2002, Milan: *Unicopli*; see especially paragraph 3.1. "L'esportazione dell'ideologia ruralista e l'esperimento coloniale", pp. 171-172.

ASMARA
The Real Capital of the Italian Empire in East Africa

Gian Luca Podestà

Autarchy, War and Economic Planning: Public Expenditure and Private Investments in Italian East Africa

After the great 1933 crisis, the most important Italian industries were united into the *Istituto di Ricostruzione Industriale* (IRI – Institute for Industrial Reconstruction), the public body managing state shareholdings. The Great Depression and the birth of the IRI stimulated a new debate on the future of the Italian economy. In 1932 the Central Corporate Committee had decreed that the state had the power to regulate the construction and extension of factories manufacturing products subject to compulsory trusts. On the eve of World War II, state industries contributed 77 per cent of the national cast iron production, 45 per cent of steel, 75 per cent of pipes, 67 per cent of iron mineral, 80 per cent of shipbuilding, 22 per cent of aeronautic construction, 39 per cent of engines and tractors, 50 per cent of armaments and munitions, and an average of 23 per cent of mechanical production; they also controlled 90 per cent of subsidised maritime lines.[1]

The turning point, however, only came after the Society of Nations had decreed sanctions against Italy for its aggression on Ethiopia. On 23 March 1936 Mussolini had launched a "planning scheme for the New Italian Economy", in which he had delineated the main points of a new autarchic policy, as well as the necessity to assess all available resources in the country and in the colonies, in order to prepare for war.[2] Between 1936 and 1940 the conquest of Ethiopia and the proclamation of the Italian Empire set in motion a radical transformation of economic structures in Italian Africa. Though the war put

Former apartments for Alfa Romeo in Asmara
Source: K. Paulweber 2013

a sudden end to the most ambitious projects, the programmes of economic valorisation undoubtedly incremented capitalistic economy and at the same time notably reduced the importance of traditional economy both in Libya and in Italian East Africa (IEA). The most remarkable innovations were a huge increase in public expenditure, destined to build the towns and all the infrastructures necessary to promote economic development, and the start of regular immigration from Italy.

Between 1935 and 1940 Italy spent 53,000 million current lire for the war and civilian building projects in East Africa. This remarkable sum (no other power had spent so much money on the colonies, and in such a short time) reached over 10 per cent of GNP in 1936, the year of greatest expenditure. According to a document elaborated by the Ministry for Italian Africa (MAI), total state expenditure for civilian works in IEA between 1937 and 1941 increased to about 10,000 million current lire, of which over 8,000 were spent on roads and about 2,000 for other building work.[3] The total sum equalled 56 per cent of the expenditure forecast by the government as necessary to provide the colonies with the indispensable civilian infrastructures (17,800 million lire). The year of greatest financial investment was 1937. Total expenditure forecast in the Italian East Africa government budget was 5,843 million lire, of which 3,100 million was allocated to civilian projects, ordinary and extraordinary, whilst 2,743 million were destined for ordinary and extraordinary military expenses.[4] Financing expenditure in IEA was covered by the issue of Government Bonds. Ordinary expenses were covered by an ordinary contribution by the Italian State, to balance the budget of the IEA government amounting to 1,000 million lire; by a special extraordinary allocation for the Road Company of 1,100 million and by another special extraordinary allowance of 1,000 million provided for in a special twelve-year plan for public works in IEA.[5]

It is impossible to evaluate precisely the money invested by private citizens. Some Ministry of Italian Africa's estimates only stated that total Italian investments were equivalent to about 4,000 million current lire.[6] Lacking more reliable data, I believe it would be only fair not to underestimate the effects that valorisation of the empire had on the Italian economy, in terms of both increase in production and sales for military and civilian orders, as well as absorption of manpower and movement of capitals from Africa to Italy.

The Corporative Colonialism

In IEA il Duce intended to create a new organic social system conjugating demographic colonisation with other forms of valorisation, transferring from Italy "the whole machinery of its own civilisation".[7] Fascist colonisation should be understood, in space and time, as "the settlement and empowerment of a people", that is the transposition to the colonies of all the productive elements of the mother country, such as farmers, workers, artisans, clerks, traders, small entrepreneurs and intellectuals, thus shunning the loathsome model of capitalistic colonisation exclusively aimed at benefiting a restricted class of privileged individuals. This conception met with three crucial objectives: preserving and increasing the country's numerical power, cementing Italians' racial cohesion in the empire and in Italy itself and, finally, promoting the social elevation of large popular masses.

That the conquest of Ethiopia had little to do with traditional colonialism is shown by the unusual and unorthodox economic policy devised, though characterised by numerous contradictions and changes of mind: "Implement as far as you can all practical measures to create living conditions in the area, and only ask the mother country for the strictly indispensable" Mussolini telegraphed Marshal Graziani, the newly appointed General Governor, in May 1936.[8]

The economic policy differed from other colonial models: Mussolini had ordered to take all necessary measures to limit imports from Italy. The empire should gradually progress not only towards food self-sufficiency, but also towards the creation of its own industrial facilities to produce the most common consumer items, such as construction materials, textiles and drinks. Naturally IEA should also contribute to economic autarchy in the mother country, by developing the production of cotton, wool, leather, meat, oil seeds, coffee and minerals. Autarchy in the empire would meet with three objectives:

1) decreasing food supply and financial difficulties back in Italy (the cost of shipping and duties for the Suez Canal, for example);

2) allowing provision of resources for at least one year in case of war, given the foreseeable interruption of communications;

3) restarting exports of IEA's produce (like coffee and salt, for example) in order to increase currency reserves and help improve Italy's balance of payments.[9]

The former soap factory in the south of Asmara's city centre
Source: K.Paulweber 2013

There is no precise data on the European and African populations in IEA. An estimate carried out in the spring of 1939 indicated 165,267 Italian civilians,[10] against about twelve million Africans. The greatest number of settlers, amounting to 72,408, lived in Eritrea (43.8 per cent). The percentage of women was very small and only in Eritrea did it exceed 20 per cent: in 1939 there allegedly were 26,628 women, of whom 14,827 in Eritrea (55.7 per cent).[11]

The first Italians to come to Eritrea in the summer of 1935 were the workers charged with building infrastructures to house the army as well as roads to transport troops to the front line. After the war they were employed to build the most important IEA roads and other infrastructures. The workers amounted to over 200,000 individuals. Salaries were higher than in Italy. Between 1935 and 1938 workers' remittances sent back to Italy reached over 5.2 billion of current lire (Italian Lira = £), a sum corresponding to over 1 per cent of the national GDP in 1936 and 1938, and about 2 per cent in 1937.[12] From 1937 onwards Italian workers were gradually removed and replaced by African workers. Repatriation was decided by Mussolini because in his opinion the workers did not uphold the prestige of the Italian race vis-à-vis its African subjects.[13] Many Italians worked for the public sector (about 25,000). Civil servants' salaries were notably higher than back in Italy, also because of the numerous perks, though of course they varied according to the function. Workers employed in the private sector were estimated at about 20,000, but probably their number was much higher, if we also take into account temporary residents. Self-employed professionals who practised their activities in IEA amounted to 871 in 1939. Doctors made up the largest professional group, followed by engineers, land surveyors, lawyers, pharmacists and vets, but there were also architects, notaries, midwives, journalists and artists.

Besides workers, the military and all those who depended on the public administration, and private companies' employees, a large number of Italians, not quantifiable but certainly amounting to some tens of thousands, had set up their own business. These were hard-working people who had shown great adaptability, initiative and inventiveness. A multitude of small entrepreneurs, traders, managers of small, often itinerant, catering businesses, drivers and owners of means of transport, skilled workers who doubled as artisans, owners of small building firms, trade representatives and intermediaries.

In April 1939 the MAI carried out a survey of Italian industrial and commercial enterprises registered in IEA and their invested capitals.[14] There were 4,007 industries with a total capital of over 2.7 billion of current lire. The highest concentration of businesses and capitals was in Eritrea with 2,198 companies (54.8 per cent) worth about 2.2 billion current lire (80.4 per cent), followed by Shewa with 561 (14 per cent) with 305 million (11.1 per cent). The most relevant sector was road transport with 1,262 private businesses (31.5 per cent) worth about 1.7 billion lire (62.2 per cent) followed by building with 823 companies (20.5 per cent) with invested capitals amounting to about 745 million lire (27 per cent). Commercial enterprises were 4,785 with invested capitals of over £1.1 billion. Economically, the most important regions were Eritrea with 2,690 businesses (56.2 per cent) worth about 486 million lire (43.7 per cent) and Shewa with 634 businesses (13.2 per cent) valued at about £500 million (45 per cent).

State intervention in IEA had two aims: on one hand, to replace private capital in the riskiest sectors, such as mining, or in some monopolies, like bananas or tourism, which had evident political implications; on the other hand, it aimed at creating some large mixed-capital companies, with private and public capitals, to rationalise the imperial economy and reduce costs. The most important mixed-capital company was the *Compagnia Italiana Trasporti Africa Orientale* (CITAO – Italian Transport Company of East Africa), created to manage the delicate and strategic transport sector.[15] During the war and immediately after, besides the largest Italian companies, hundreds of small transport businesses operated in IEA. The fragmentation of the sector and the army's impelling necessities had produced a remarkable increase in costs. CITAO was supposed to rationalise the sector and reduce costs, by subdividing orders among all the transport firms regularly recorded in the register set up by the MAI. Moreover, the company was in charge of recovering and dealing with scrap metal. Between 1935 and 1938, for example, about 30,000 vehicles had been brought into IEA, a third of which, because of wear, could only be used as spare parts. CITAO was given the task of dismantling unusable vehicles and selecting parts, estimated at about 20,000 tons, and then sending some back to Italy. The most renowned private car industries such as FIAT, Lancia, Alfa Romeo, OM, Isotta Fraschini, Breda and Pirelli took part in these activities. To alleviate at least partially the housing problem and create the premises for future tourist development, the state created the *Compagnia Immobiliare alberghi Africa Orientale* (CIAAO – East African Hotel Construction Company, established to build hotels in the largest cities.[16]

In IEA the relationship between the number of businesses and the resident population was therefore rather high. This phenomenon was more evident in Eritrea, the most important region in terms of Italian settlers, number of companies, amount of capitals invested and weight of the private sector compared to the public sector. In summer 1939 the MAI published new data concerning Eritrea that also included smaller enterprises and retail dealers.[17] Commercial enterprises were 5,174, whilst 653 were registered as activities auxiliary to trade (banks, insurance companies, brokers and shipping companies). Industries had risen to 2,769, while there were 1,737 registered artisans. In total 10,333 Italian business enterprises had been recorded. Paradoxically, although Mussolini had declared that the empire's true wealth consisted of Italian people's work, the new economic situation managed to involve a consistent part of the African population too. Both the state and private businesses needed labour. In 1940 estimates recorded 750,000 African workers employed in constructions, road-building and agriculture. If we add those recruited by the armed forces and those working for private businesses, their number surpasses one million, about 10 per cent of the estimated African population.

In the agricultural sector too, the planned emigration of Italian farmers had been suspended for financial reasons, deeming more opportune to involve African farmers and their families in co-partnership agreements. In the road-building sector, despite Mussolini's orders to avoid intermingling between the races, at the end of 1938 thousands of Africans were still working side by side with Italian workers. Many were employed directly by the Italian government as temporary workers: 800 in Somalia, 1,000 in Shewa, 3,200 in Oromo-Galla and Sidama and 1,800 in Eritrea. Their salaries were on average 25 per cent of those earned by Italian workers, although they varied according to the different regions and functions. In Eritrea wages were higher.

Albergo Italia was the first hotel in Asmara built in 1899. After Eritrea's Independence it was called Keren Hotel and only in recent years was it given its former name again.
Source: K.Paulweber 2013

The scarcity of manpower and competition by the army contributed to raise salaries, although the government tried to limit them by law. In Eritrea some industrial enterprises like the cement works in Massawa and later, during the war, the match manufacture of Asmara employed thousands of Eritrean workers. Because of the improved level of education, a minority of Eritreans could have access to more qualified professions and thus become interpreters, drivers, shop assistants, etc. The Italian East Africa Hotel Company (CIAAO) employed 250 Italian and 450 African workers.

A large number of Africans were involved in trade and handicraft. Without African trade the European population of the towns could not survive. A total of 2,698 African traders were registered in Eritrea. To avoid the mixing of the races Mussolini had forbidden Italians access to the African market, but the government had to revoke the order after a few days to avoid penury.[18] The council built a new market and organised new shops to improve sanitary conditions. The participation of a rising number of Africans to market economy clearly contributed to the growth of capitalist economy, to the diffusion of the use of money (both Marie Therese's talers and Italian lire) and to stimulate the increase of consumption along Western lines, at least for those classes of workers at closer contact with Italians. It is undoubtedly true that Italian colonisation had a remarkable influence on the life of a consistent part of the African population.

Asmara was the real capital of the Italian Empire in East Africa. The town had the headquarters of the most important Italian firms. Addis Abeba was the artificial capital: the remote seat of government in the heart of Ethiopia. The situation was slightly different in Eritrea. Asmara's development had been chaotic. Each firm (especially transport and building companies) had built their own factories and storehouses in the suburbs, also providing them with accommodation for their employees. Of course dozens of unauthorised edifices had sprung up. To remedy this situation at least in part, the local government granted some lots of land free of charge to war veterans authorised to remain in East Africa, who managed to build their own homes with government help and the workers' club's contribution. Besides public initiative however, some large private companies in Asmara were allowed to build new residential areas for Italians and Eritreans. These new homes somewhat helped to keep rent prices under control, though they were still very high practically everywhere. In all cities, but especially in Addis Ababa, Asmara and Massawa, a thriving black market of rented houses and rooms developed at the hands of both Italians and Africans. In Eritrea, near the strategic hubs where companies had dislocated their logistic quarters during military operations, there materialised almost out of nothing some new urban agglomerates, such as Dek'emhare and Nefasit. The most fascinating case was that of Mai Edaga, also called Capronia because it had developed around the Caproni factory in the Gura plains. Not only had the industrial buildings been added to the few pre-existing *tukuls*, but also houses and villas for the Italian employees, technicians and workers, as well as new huts for the indigenous workforce, a school, a nursery, a post office, the workers' club, a church, some shops and great water storage tanks: Capronia had become a small town in its own right, built along the most modern criteria according to a rational town planning scheme, and capable of a truly autonomous life.

Conclusions

The economy of the empire was artificially supported by the State. Mussolini after the Great Depression had acquired heterodox views: he was convinced that the capitalist system, just like liberal democracy, was doomed. However, not even Mussolini could do without monetary policies. Italy had suffered from a constant haemorrhage of the Bank of Italy's reserves and had been forced to redefine its own plans for AOI and Libya. The reduction in programmes was influenced by the winds of war in Europe, but by then it was already clear that the empire could only exist thanks to the State's financial support. But in a totalitarian system such as Fascism, in which ideology was elevated to the role of a political religion, and where form was therefore equivalent to substance, autarchy and the empire played a mainly political role.

Notes

1 IRI's Historical Archive, Rome (from now on ASIRI), *Serie Nera* (from now on N), b. 24, *L'IRI ente di carattere permanente (1937–1943)*.

2 Edoardo and Duilio Susmel, *Opera Omnia di Benito Mussolini*, XXVII, *Dall'inaugurazione della provincia di Littoria alla proclamazione dell'Impero* (19 December 1934–9 May 1936), Florence: La Fenice, 1959, p. 244.

3 *Archivio Storico Diplomatico del Ministero degli Affari Esteri*, Rome (from now on ASDMAE), *Archivio del Ministero dell'Africa Italiana* (from now on ASMAI), Africa III, b. 73, *Direzione Generale Affari Economici e Finanziari. Riassunto delle spese per opere pubbliche o di pubblica utilità raggruppate secondo la loro natura*, 1945.

4 ASDMAE, ASMAI, *Archivio Segreto di Gabinetto* (from now on ASG), MAI to Governo Generale AOI, 07.02.1938.

5 Gian Luca Podestà, *Il mito dell'impero. Economia, politica e lavoro nelle colonie italiane dell'Africa orientale 1898–1941*. Turin: G.Giappichelli editore, 2004, p. 245.

6 ASDMAE, ASMAI, ASG, *Situazione delle aziende industriali e commerciali*, June 1939.

7 Renzo Meregazzi, "Lineamenti della legislazione per l'Impero", *Gli annali dell'Africa Italiana*, 3, 1939, p. 12.

8 ASDMAE, ASMAI, ASG, b. 160, telex, Mussolini to Graziani, 26.05.1936.

9 *Archivio Centrale dello Stato*, Rome (from now on ACS), *Fondo Graziani*, b. 46, telex, Lessona to Graziani, 10.11.1937.

10 Raffaele Ciferri, "I cereali dell'Africa Italiana", *Rassegna economica dell'Africa Italiana*, 1, 1942, p. 12.

11 ACS, *Ministero dell'Africa Italiana* (from now on MAI), b. 2123, Italian female population resident in AOI and enrolled in women's fascist organisations on 31 December 1939.

12 Gian Luca Podestà, "L'Emigration Italienne en Afrique Orientale", *Annales de Démographie Historique*, 1, 2007, p. 74.

13 ASDMAE, ASMAI, ASG, b. 67, Teruzzi a Governo Generale Africa Orientale Italiana, 20.12.1937.

14 ASDMAE, ASMAI, ASG, b. 151, *Situazione delle aziende industriali e commerciali*, June 1939.

15 "Le industrie e il commercio", *Gli annali dell'Africa Italiana*, 3, 1940, p. 1122.

16 Gian Luca Podestà, *Il mito dell'impero. Economia, politica e lavoro nelle colonie italiane dell'Africa orientale 1898–1941*, op. cit., p. 308.

17 "Attività economiche esercitate nell'Eritrea al 30 aprile 1939", *Rassegna economica dell'Africa Italiana*, 8, pp. 763-765.

18 Gian Luca Podestà, "Colonists and 'Demographic' Colonists. Family and Society in Italian Africa", *Annales de Démographie Historique*, 2, 2011, p. 219.

መደበር

SHAPING THE CITY FROM BELOW
Asmarini's Struggle for the City between the End of the Nineteenth and Mid-twentieth Centuries[1]

Francesca Locatelli

In an article published in 2006, *The Observer* described Asmara as "the Art Déco gem baking in the African sun".[2] The Eritrean capital's Modernist architecture, the Italian colonial buildings, its bars and Mediterranean lifestyle have always attracted both tourists and travellers alike, and scholars have expressed interest in its architectural and spatial features. But among elderly citizens of Asmara, the same buildings, streets and modernism invoke the memory of a painful past and of long-lasting struggles for citizenship in a city which was primarily conceived as a colonial city for European settlers, and whose exclusionary and segregationist roots are still imprinted in its structure to this very day. This paper sheds light on some understudied and hidden aspects of African urban dwellers' struggles in Asmara, on the way they asserted their presence, and forged their own life, becoming the main agents of urban transformations. Basically, it is on how they came to be from colonial subject to *Asmarini.*

The Development of the City

Asmara was primarily built during the period of Italian colonialism, which lasted in Eritrea from 1890, when Asmara was occupied by the Italian troops, to 1941, the year of the Italian defeat in the Horn of Africa by the Allies, and the replacement of the Italian administration with the British Military Administration (BMA). Throughout the fifty years of Italian domination, the city underwent major transformations and a rapid growth in terms of

Former caravanserai in Asmara, today a large recycling market
Source: K.Paulweber 2013

population, space, architecture, and economic and social development. Its population increased from approximately 5,000 at the end of the nineteenth century to more than 100,000 by the early 1940s, with more than 60,000 of its urban dwellers being Italian.[3] Its service sector expanded dramatically, alongside commercial and industrial activities, and the city also became a laboratory for major Modernist experiments in architecture and engineering, and in urban planning. Nonetheless, the survival of Asmara primarily relied on private and public investment from Italy, which created a dependency that often rendered its economic development unstable and unpredictable, with a consequential exacerbation of competition for resources, and an increase in ethnic and social tensions among urban dwellers.

The outbreak of World War II and the process of decolonisation, enhanced by the BMA from 1941, worsened the economic situation of the city, deepening the ethnic and social divisions of the urban communities. Riots and incidents spread throughout Asmara, transforming the city into a hotbed of violence against the administration and, from the late 1940s, among urban dwellers, who were divided over both social issues and community values. In the 1940s, the city also became a contested space among the different international and local political actors involved in the intricate and contradictory decision-making process regarding the future of the country.

Asmara and its Communities

Since its foundation, Asmara was both conceived and developed as a highly divided city: socially, racially and ethnically. Divisive policies were implemented by colonial authorities and city officials in order to impose order on the urban space and on the urban dwellers, with predictable consequences. The scarcity of resources triggered competition among communities; racial policies increased tension; and social hierarchisation created forms of exclusion which inevitably degenerated into conflict. By the end of the Italian colonial experience, the city was inhabited by Italian settlers – the first wave settled between the end of the nineteenth and the beginning of the twentieth centuries (the pioneers) and the second wave reaching Africa in the mid-1930s when the fascist regime enhanced the policy of massive settler colonialism – a small community of Indians, Jews and generically defined Arabs (mostly Yemeni) and a consistent native population segregated in specific quarters of the city.

Similarly to other African colonial contexts, throughout the colonial period the city continued to attract people. Why people move to overcrowded and unwelcoming cities is a question still widely debated within African scholarship, which tries to understand the rapid urbanisation that the Continent experienced in the twentieth century.[4] In the past – as in the present – the most consistent explanation for urbanisation was that people found different and varied ways of shaping their own lives in the city, even in the most divisive, exclusionist, and alien environments, such as that of colonial Asmara. This because colonialism produced structures between which African urban dwellers managed to find some opportunities or to create new ones.

In the case of Asmara, the city primarily attracted men from all Eritrean regions and from neighbouring Ethiopia, hoping to start a military career in the Italian colonial army, especially in the 1930s at the outbreak of the war against Ethiopia. However, being the most remunerative, prestigious, and therefore competitive career, only a few of them achieved this aim. The majority lived in the city working as casual labourers, in urban businesses, bars, restaurants, shops, workshops and small industries, or managed to survive by improvising activities such as temporary vendors and cultural mediators. These urban dwellers complemented the first nucleus of the indigenous urban community formed by the *askaris* (local soldiers employed in the colonial army) who contributed to colonise Eritrea at the end of the nineteenth century, the local authorities, the merchants and white-collar workers.[5] The city also attracted women who were endeavouring to escape from the traditional patterns of life, such as forced marriage, and were looking for alternative lifestyles or simply trying to improve their economic conditions by selling home-made beers or by practising prostitution.

All of them formed the bulk of the population of the overcrowded native quarters, the areas in which they were forced to live according to the segregationist urban-planning policies which were imposed by the colonial governments throughout the Italian period, and institutionalised during the fascist regime, in order to create different areas and spheres of life between the natives and the massive population of Italian settlers. It was in Abashewel, Haddi Addi, Ghezza Berhanu, Acria, and Ghezza Atal that African urban dwellers found their own ways of organising their existence, of forging their own experience and of structuring their community life. Indeed, while it is true that the life of African urban dwellers was shaped by urban infrastructures, structural policies and colonial power relations, it is also true that the same African urban dwellers changed and transformed the urban spaces in which they lived through their daily interaction and/or struggle with the municipal authorities. It was in the streets of Asmara, in its native quarters, that Africans established their own social networks and individual relationships, created their leisure areas, and set up their informal economy through which they managed to survive the restraints of the formal economic structures.[6]

View of the native quarter
Source: IsIAO (Istituto per l'Africa e l'Oriente), Rome

Struggle for the City

Archival sources highlight fascinating aspects of African dwellers dynamics and life in the city during both the Italian and British administrations.[7] Indeed, even within a restrictive context like Asmara, Africans (mainly Eritreans and Ethiopians) managed to find their own space of sociability. The development of Asmara as a commercial city, and later as an industrial city, in conjunction with the military presence, led to the sudden growth of services such as restaurants and bars, with *sewa* houses[8] run by women becoming the main feature of African urban life.

Sewa houses were overcrowded during the colonial (and postcolonial) period, and increasingly became hotbeds of social and political tension. They constituted a fundamental aspect of African social life and played a crucial role in the creation of indigenous urban networks. They attracted a variety of customers drinking *sewa*: urban migrants, casual labourers, civil servants and soldiers. A study by Christine Matzke on female performers in postcolonial Eritrean *sewa* houses aptly documents the role of music, theatre, and performances by women in *sewa* houses, in politicising the urban dwellers of Asmara in the 1940s and the 1950s, when anti-colonial feelings and later anti-Ethiopian and Eritrean nationalist sentiments began to spread.[9] We can assume that similar social dynamics had already existed during the Italian period, although police controls in the *sewa* houses were frequent and very strict. The Italian colonial administration used to delegate to the local military police, the *zaptié*, the task of controlling the indigenous locations. A sarcastic song testifies the method used by the *zaptié* in exercising their power over the "uncontrollable" customers who attended the *sewa* houses: "Asmara is a pretty town, there are many places where you can drink, there is some meat to eat, there is almost everything....but beware of the *zaptié*!".[10]

The *sewa* houses represented indispensable, if not the only, places for urban social and political networking. Here people socialised, shared their own experiences, drunk together, expressed their own feelings and opinions which often escalated into fights against the police or against other urban dwellers. Drunkenness and violence were testimony to the growing social tension in the city. By the beginning of the 1940s, social tension acquired a more politicised form. It was from the *sewa* houses that anti-colonial tumults arose in the early 1940s, both against Italian settlers still numerous in the city, and against the new British administration and its policy of continuity with the past regime. The ongoing economic and social unrest in the native areas of Asmara and the uncertainties which surrounded the future geo-political set-up of Eritrea, contested by different international and local actors, ignited the atmosphere of tension in the city.[11] A wave of violence, generically defined as incidents or sometimes disturbances by the British administration, spread throughout Asmara, involving urban dwellers of different communities, whose actions were clearly aimed at dismantling the colonial structures of the city.

In July 1946 a group of approximately 300 Pan-Ethiopians (claiming the reunion of Eritrea to Ethiopia) participated in a demonstration on the streets of Asmara without authorisation. Political leaders were arrested, triggering violent reactions (n.b. even from urban dwellers who did not participate in the demonstration), which were expressed through stone throwing and attacks on police stations. As a result, some people were injured and two Eritreans killed.[12] A furious crowd followed the police and began to damage the police station by throwing stones and destroying police vehicles. Violence escalated the day after, when a crowd of approximately 400 Eritreans gathered in front of the court and demanded the release of the arrested leaders. The intervention of the police and the arrest of other Eritreans triggered further violence. A "very hostile *mob in an ugly mood*" composed now of more than 2000 people from the native quarters of the city assembled in front of the Central prison and engaged in stone throwing and further violence. Piles of stones were later found in the "native quarters".[13]

Just one month after the first disturbance, another riot occurred in the native areas, following a clash between drunken Sudanese police forces of the BMA and local urban dwellers in a *sewa* house for "not clear reasons". A Sudanese soldier was killed and as retaliation Sudanese soldiers began shooting all over the native areas randomly. Thirty-nine Eritreans, three Sudanese soldiers and one Italian were killed, and several other people injured.[14]

The nature of these incidents has been the subject of different interpretations, particularly contemporary interpretations, which attempt to explain the violence of the 1940s primarily as a reaction to the uncertainties concerning the future of Eritrea after the demise of the Italian empire and mainly caused by exogenous factors, or as isolated criminal events. However, a more attentive and all-embracing analysis of some of the social dynamics involved in the events of the 1940s can help to shed light upon both the nature and the causes of this wave of urban violence. The incidents displayed several similarities in their development, although they originated in different situations. They all stemmed from general quarrels, which subsequently led to disproportionate acts of violence. Moreover, they quickly shifted from small- to large-scale actions: i.e., groups of people immediately gathered around the locations of the quarrels; the number of people engaged in violent actions – the "mobs in ugly mood" as defined by British accounts – easily increased (i.e., 2,000 as reported in some accounts). Finally, despite their spontaneous appearance, they showed a high degree of organisation and co-ordination: stones were accumulated in the streets of the native quarters, rumours spread quickly in specific areas of the city, and *sewa* houses were often the centre of political awareness and of the co-ordination of political action.

The incidents of the 1940s can therefore be interpreted as evidence of a wider atmosphere of violence, underlying which there was the need, on the part of the urban dwellers of the native quarters, to re-claim the city. The crowds involved in these incidents were composed of men and women, mainly (but not only) young unemployed, casual laborers and migrants, whose social distress was channeled into common political action against foreign administrations, their symbols and their institutions. They engaged in violent actions because of the visibility which these actions could guarantee to their primary expectation, namely, to re-claim the city. Despite their ethnic, religious and cultural differences (which became particularly evident and confrontational in the 1950s), African urban dwellers in the 1940s expressed their right to citizenship in a city which they had physically built with their work, forged through their struggles, and shaped with their daily experiences. Their fight was a fight to assert their right to become *Asmarini*, in a space that they recognised as their own space of political activism and sociability, and in which their sense of belonging lay, because, as James Greham has noted in the context of street violence in late-Mamluk and Ottoman Damascus, the streets of a city and the "itinerary of a demonstration […] could be as eloquent in setting forth aims and expectations as any public manifesto".[15]

Notes

1 The expression "struggle for the city" is borrowed by Frederick Cooper and his inspiring book, *Struggle for the City: Migrant Labour, Capital and the State in Urban Africa*. Beverly Hills CA: Sage, 1983.

2 Paddy Magrane, "The Art Déco gem baking in the African sun", *The Observer*, 26 February 2006.

3 For comprehensive analyses on the spatial and demographic development of Asmara, including examination of policies of urban segregation see Edward Denison, Guang Yu Ren & Naigzy Gebremedhin (eds.), *Asmara: Africa's Secret Modernist City*. London-New York: Merrell, 2003; Giulia Barrera, Alessandro Triulzi & Gabriel Tseggai (eds.), *Asmara: architettura e pianificazione urbana nei fondi dell'IsIAO*. Rome: Istituto per l'Africa e l'Oriente, 2008; Mia Fuller, *Moderns Abroad: Architecture, Cities and Italian Imperialism*. London; New York: Routledge, 2006; Giuliano Gresleri, Pier Giorgio Massaretti & Stefano Zagnoni (eds.), *Architettura italiana d'oltremare, 1870–1940*. Venice: Marsilio, 1993; and Eugenio lo Sardo (ed.), *Divina geometria: modelli urbani degli anni Trenta: Asmara, Addis Abeba, Harar, Oletta, Littoria, Sabaudia, Pontina, Borghi*. Rome: Maschietto & Musolino, 1995.

4 See for instance Bill Freund, *The African City: A History*. Cambridge: Cambridge University Press, 2007; Andrew Burton, "African Underclass: Urbanisation, Crime and Colonial Order", in *Dar es Salaam*. Oxford, Dar es Salaam, Athens OH: James Currey, 2005; Catherine Coquery-Videovitch, *The History of African Cities South of the Sahara: from the Origin to Colonization*. Princeton NJ: Markus Wiener Publisher, 2005.

5 See Francesca Locatelli, "Beyond the Campo Cintato: Prostitutes, Migrants and 'Criminals' in Colonial Asmara (Eritrea), 1890–1941", in Francesca LocatelliI and Paul Nugent (eds.), *African Cities: Competing Claims on Urban Spaces*. Leiden: Brill, 2009, pp. 219-240.

6 Ibid.

7 My research on Asmara is based on sources collected at the archives of the Municipality and the High Court of Asmara in 2001, 2002 and 2006, in Italian colonial archives of the Ministry of Foreign Affairs in Italy, and the National Archives in London. These consisted of court records of different colonial tribunals, demographic records, municipal reports, military records on riots in the city. In this paper I am only using the records found in the National Archives in London.

8 The *sewa* houses were drinking places. They were houses in which women used to produce and sell *sewa* (local beer).

9 Christine Matzke, "Of Suwa Houses and Singing Contexts in Eritrea: Early Urban Women Performers in Asmara, Eritrea", in Martin Banham, James Gibbs and Femi Osofin (eds.), *African Theatre: Women*. Oxford: James Currey, 2002, pp. 29-46.

10 Interview with Mr. Gebremedhin Tessema, April 22, 2002, Asmara.

11 Its future set-up also became a disputed issue among the different international forces: Ethiopia, whose aim was the annexation of Eritrea; Great Britain, which aimed at the partition of the country between the Sudan and Ethiopia; and Italy, which claimed the right to obtain a mandate over Eritrea. On top of this, the dynamics of the Cold War transformed the ex-Italian colony – and the whole Horn of Africa – into a contested area between the USA and the USSR, both of whom were seeking to replace the British Empire. Ruth Iyob, *The Eritrean Struggle for Independence. Domination, Resistance, Nationalism 1941–1993*. Cambridge: Cambridge University Press, 1995, pp. 61-64.

12 National Archives (NA), Kew Gardens, London, Foreign Office (FO) 371/53511 Cipher telegram from C. in C. Middle East Land Forces to the War Office, SECRET 35957/OE7, Recd. 1 August 1946.

13 NA, FO 371/53511, "Report on the political disturbances in Asmara". SECRET. HQ Eritrea District. 3 Aug. 46. (Sgd) Jackson Maj. for Brig. Comd.

14 NA, War Office (WO) 32/11757 "Asmara Incidents", "Final Report on Disorders in Asmara".

15 James Grehan, "Street Violence and Social Imagination in Late-Mamluk and Ottoman Damascus (c.1500–1800)", in Stephanie Cronin (ed.), *Subalterns and Social Protest. History from Below in the Middle East and North Africa*. London-New York: Routledge, 2008, p. 40.

T.Z
FURNITURE

SLEEPING MEMORY IN ITALIAN ARCHIVES

Historical Photographs of Asmara and Italy's Controversial Relationship with its Colonial Past

Silvana Palma

The essay focuses on the images collected in two Italian colonial archives (especially the IsIAO's and that of the *Società Africana d'Italia*); on how and when they were collected, and how the documentary material has been organised. It will describe what place Asmara and its architecture occupy within these spaces. The story and the fate of the two archives, especially the Roman one, are particularly emblematic of the Italian controversial relationship with its colonial past, marked by long-standing denial at the institutional and social levels – whose significant and often devastating effects are apparent in the reception of African refugees, for the most part Eritrean, in Italy.

1. Referred to as an "Italian city" in *Guida dell'Africa Orientale Italiana* (A Guide to Italian East Africa), Asmara was "the fastest booming outpost of the Empire", having grown exponentially in preparation for the war on Ethiopia: in 1938, Italians were 53,000 – up from a pre-war estimate of about 3,000 – out of a total population of 98,000.[1] Understandably, the photographic and cartographic records of the Italian city eventually came to be part of the documentary heritage of various public institutions and private military and religious archives scattered throughout the Italian national territory. Unfortunately, though, their dispersal has hindered all meaningful attempts at appraising and therefore studying them. Most of the fonds have never been catalogued and neither their size nor their subjects are known with certainty. In spite of the great archival recovery efforts undertaken by Italian Africanist scholars over the years (which is one of their merits), significant gaps remain in our knowledge of the documentary collections on the former colonies available in the country.

A shop and apartment building near the train station in Asmara
Source: K.Paulweber 2013

Hosted in Naples by the Università L'Orientale and in Rome by the Italian African Institute, the first international conference on colonial photography took place in 1992.[2] Its aims were to draw historians' attention to an until then neglected documentary source and break the isolation experienced, at times even within the scientific community itself. In the same period, recovery of the Africanist photographic fonds held by the two institutions, and lying abandoned since war's end, was being carried out by the Author. These were the fonds of the *Società Africana d'Italia* (Italian African Society, hereinafter SAI) of Naples and of the ex-Colonial Museum of Rome; the latter was managed by the *Istituto Italo Africano* (later renamed Italian Institute for Africa and the Orient – IsIAO).[3] Indeed, giving Africanist and colonial photography a central role in research was the stated goal, besides recovering a documentary source that had been until then disregarded by historians.[4] Quite tellingly, those same years saw the emergence of a new generation of Italian scholars who, unencumbered by nostalgia and ties to the colonial and fascist past, finally put the country's African past at the centre of historiography,[5] according to renewed methodological approaches and investigative tools.[6]

2. The Neapolitan collection was created and developed as an essential documentary corpus for the scientific-commercial and markedly colonialist activity of the *Società africana d'Italia*. Established in 1880,[7] the organisation rapidly turned into the southern pole of Italian colonialism alongside two other major associations of the time: Rome's *Società Geografica Italiana* (Italian Geographical Society) and Milan's *Società di Esplorazioni commerciali in Africa* (Society for Commercial Exploration in Africa). In the late 1880s, Italy experienced a transition from individual pioneer expeditions to the action of organised groups that combined the original geographical mission with more overtly economic-commercial and colonial purposes.

SAI was the youngest and poorest of the three organisations but from the outset it became the fiercest supporter of the Italian colonial expansion, even when heavy political and military failures, such as the Adwa defeat, brought the other associations' expansionist thrusts to an abrupt halt.[8] Backed by turn-of-the-century Neapolitan intelligentsia and entrepreneurs, who looked to Africa as a promising area for an increased Italian presence, SAI promoted a series of scientific, commercial and educational endeavours. Indeed, it supported geographical exploration and trade reconnaissance missions, some of which were worthwhile, organised conferences and promoted language courses, collaborating in particular with the *Istituto Orientale* (now Università L'Orientale) of Naples. In support of its activities, SAI urged its correspondents to send written and photographic documentation that would be used to promote a better understanding of the African continent and its economic-trade potential. Thus, it accumulated a significant photographic heritage of the entire African continent, carefully stored in thick metal binders that preserved its integrity throughout the troubled history of the association.

Today, SAI's photographic heritage consists of about 7,000 images,[9] preserved for the most part in eighty-nine albums divided by region and holding photographs from much of the African continent, although the bulk (forty-two volumes) is, quite understandably, devoted to the Italian-occupied areas. Sixteen volumes are related to Eritrea and about sixty images were taken in Asmara. Dating approximately between 1890 and 1918, when the association was indeed particularly active in building consensus towards the colonial option, the photographs show city views as well as official and religious ceremonies, groups of natives, and construction work on the railroad connecting the city with Massawa. While SAI's industrious efforts persisted throughout World War I, they were eventually dampened by fascism – which downsized the association and gradually reduced its autonomy until none was left. In 1928, SAI became the Campania regional branch of the Colonial Fascist Institute in Rome, which was directly controlled by the National Fascist Party, and, in the same year, designated as being "in charge of colonial propaganda in Italy".[10]

Given its history as the "heart of Italy's colonial life",[11] in 1953, the Institute – in the meantime renamed *Istituto Italiano per l'Africa* (Italian Institute for Africa) – was chosen as the natural recipient of the collections, as well as the activities, of the ex-*Ministero dell'Africa Italiana* (Ministry of Italian Africa, hereinafter MAI) and of the Colonial Museum (formerly under the jurisdiction of the MAI). Additionally, it later took over the building previously occupied by the Colonial Museum, which currently houses the IsIAO. Rather than being motivated by clear documenting purposes, the photographic collections at the IsIAO had a fortuitous beginning at the time of the Italian landing in Africa, during the Liberal period, when recurring donations to the Ministry turned into involuntary (often begrudging[12]) accessions – further proof of the peculiar traits, delays and sloppiness affecting the initial stage of the Italian scramble, even photographically.

It was only in the 1930s, especially with the proclamation of the Empire, that the photo library in Rome found itself the object of intense attention by virtue of which it grew exponentially, proving indispensable to the consensus-building machine that the regime was striving to create, whose strength lied indeed in spreading ideals and myths through images. However, as pointed out earlier, the story of the photo library is yet to be written: no trace was found of its history, its managers and curators, its accession policy, its accession register or the original size of its collections. This is appalling, to say the least, considering that its extraordinarily relevant documentary collection is estimated to contain over 100,000 images, covering Italy's entire colonial period up until the Italian-British war of 1940–1943,[13] and over 20,000 between plates, slides and negatives. These figures confirm both the essential role of photography and the ever greater depth and breadth of the discourse on Africa over time.

The absence of documentation on the collection is largely ascribable to the vicissitudes that marked the Italian colonial experience and the state of neglect of the material and documents – crammed into inadequate storage spaces during Republican Italy's long-lasting denial of the overseas experience. The neglect certainly led to the loss or destruction of the documents that, over a period of fifty years, were often relocated or rearranged, leading to increasingly difficult and precarious conditions. Misuse and misappropriation of the documentary material, especially after the war, caused remarkable losses, too. "Thousands and thousands of photographs – states a report by M.A. Vitale, Director of the Colonial Museum – were temporarily loaned for propaganda purposes such as illustrating newspaper articles, miscellaneous publications, reading books, textbooks, encyclopaedias, etc."[14] In those years, in fact, the documentation of the photographic library was used extensively, both in Italy and abroad, to support Italian ambitions towards the pre-fascist colonies as it proved, better than any other evidence, the substantial improvements accomplished in Africa.[15]

Sorting more than 100,000 photographs, randomly stacked in piles after decades of neglect and carelessness, was a necessary preliminary to cataloguing the images from Eritrea and Ethiopia. Identifying and classifying the records – first by region and then by subject – and finding duplicates required a considerable amount of time, despite being just the preliminary steps in cataloguing. The photographic material on Eritrea and Ethiopia was then separated from the rest of the inventory: today nearly 35,000 images are individually catalogued.[16] Asmara holds a prominent place in the collection: about 3,300 photographs show the area where the capital of the colony was going to be founded at the time of the first Italian forays in the late nineteenth century, and the earliest buildings during the Liberal period. From the first group of huts and Ras Alula's *tukul* to the first masonry buildings, the photographs document the expansion of the city, gradually showing military buildings, schools, hospitals, railways and the political, social, religious and economic life of the city. Above all, the images show Asmara's development in the 1930s, with the preparations for the Italo-Ethiopian war, the reconstruction and urban effervescence in the second half of the 1930s, and the new 1938 master plan.

A portion of the images is collected in albums: fifty-six albums are devoted to Eritrea. In these volumes Asmara's images are conspicuous and dating from the end of the nineteenth century. Many albums are devoted to the accomplishments of the colonial Government (roads building, the Massawa-Asmara railroad, the radio-telegraphic service, etc); other albums donated by the Catholic Mission document its activities (as well as Asmara's political, religious and social life); still others document special events, such as the 1905 Colonial Congress or the visit of King Vittorio Emanuele III in 1932.

A larger portion of the images is represented by loose photos, mostly dating from the 1930s. These images are now grouped by subject. Pictures of Asmara can be found in several sections (economic and commercial activities/events/colonisation/communications/buildings/justice/panoramas and views/healthcare/schools/public services). Obviously the bulk of images of the city is present in the section *views* and especially in the section more specifically dedicated to *buildings*, where hundreds of photos, divided into subsections, prove the breadth of the documentation on Asmara gathered by the archive. Additionally, the documentation of the map library, which was also accessioned from the former *Istituto italo africano* and provided by the Cartographic Unit at the MAI, offers City and Public Works master plans, blueprints and revisions. It consists of about seventy maps, not available elsewhere, that the library accessioned from the Eritrean Colonial Offices.[17]

Identification and classification of the photographic records, even when they were still in progress, had allowed a large number of research projects, including some relevant works on the city of Asmara.[18] Paradoxically, Asmara was the subject of the last project completed before years of work aimed at recovering the colonial historical memory were wiped out: on November 11, 2011, the IsIAO was compulsorily wound up due to severe financial losses, owing at least partly to government's delinquency. The IsIAO's documentary heritage was once again unavailable for consultation and research, and rather than being donated to scholars, university libraries or any interested library, the institution's publications were destroyed. That was how a unique source for colonial studies, Africanist studies in general, and the historical reconstruction of many African countries faded back into the limbo from which it had been painstakingly recovered. Italian and foreign scholars pleaded for the protection and preservation of the IsIAO's heritage and scientific activity, to no avail. More recently, yet another plea went unanswered. In September 2015, Federico Cresti, President of the Association for African Studies in Italy (Asai), called on the Ministry of Foreign Affairs and the Ministry of Cultural Heritage to preserve the IsIAO's historical and archival heritage and prevent the likely dispersion that would heavily penalise research.[19] To date, the government is yet to show interest in the conservation of this part of the country's scientific and cultural heritage, let alone its promotion or the preservation of its integrity.

3. The Ministry's is indeed a time-honoured indifference, only partly caused by the economic downturn of recent years or policies that have increasingly favoured, for example, military spending over a cultural policy that is in the least worthy of the name. The denial of the country's colonial past and the ever greater distance between politics and historical research also play a role. The colonial and postcolonial questions have very little space and weight in the Italian public debate and so does Academia, for that matter.

In Italy, while today the transition between colonial historians and historians of colonialism, however arduous and belated, is seemingly complete, the divide between historiographical research findings and part of society and its institutions, which continue to relate to the colonial past with a never fully decolonised and defascistised approach, essentially remains unbridged. Italy's complex relationship with Africa feeds on denial, myths and self-acquittal whose influence on the national policy towards the former colonies is of no little significance: according to Angelo Del Boca, the policy is "not providing reparations, not forward-looking, misallocating aid, wasting money and failing to honour debts".[20] Mostly, this relationship feeds on ignorance. Although the building of the nation and of a national image derived many of its themes from the colonial experience, the country still seems to ignore that story and especially its most violent and ruthless aspects.[21]

Several reasons have prevented Italy from confronting its African past and facing the inevitable throes that elsewhere in Europe accompanied this dialogue/confrontation with the peoples struggling for self-determination and independence. First of all, major Italian war criminals were never tried. Moreover, having lost its colonies as a result of an international decision, following defeat in World War II, Italy never had to deal with any kind of confrontation (or negotiation) with the ruled countries in the years of decolonisation. Thus, the myth of the uniqueness of the good-natured and benevolent Italian colonialism became firmly established in the popular consciousness. For its part, the state built, preserved and protected a public memory of the colonial past which very closely resembles the anti-fascist narrative that, since right after the war, has led to separating the responsibilities of the Italian people from those of fascism and, above all, has endeavoured to disavow the fascist crimes.[22] This effort certainly had the characteristics of a therapeutic denial and was motivated by the political need to allow a new republican and democratic course in the country following the end of the war and the fall of fascism. However, it now prevents the construction of a firmly democratic identity and allows the widespread belief, in the country and among its institutions, that fascism was, after all, a good-natured regime. Likewise, the state became the custodian and promoter of a public memory of the colonial past based on denial, censorship and amnesia and, above all, on denying the validity of others' memories. This explains restrictions on access and use of the archives, especially the Historical Archives at the MAI – not a minor matter in the thirty-year-long controversy over the use of poison gas;[23] or the censorship of *Lion of the Desert* (1981), a film by Moustapha Akkad. Based on the story of Omar al-Mukthar, hero of the Libyan resistance to the Italian occupation, the film was never shown in Italian movie theatres and, like any attempt, Italian or foreign, to shed light on the Italian colonial past was depicted as damaging to the honour of the Italian Armed Forces.[24]

The vague promises made by the Italian government when meeting with representatives from the ex-colonies or its propensity to purely symbolic concessions, as long as Italian crimes or responsibilities are not rehashed, follow the same logic. To mention but one recent example, it took Italy fifty-eight years to fulfil the pledge to return the Axum Obelisk to Ethiopia, an obligation assumed under the 1947 Peace Treaty. At the insistent behest of Addis Ababa, the obelisk was returned, amid a storm of controversy, only in 2005.

These are just a few examples but they reveal how the persistence of the politics of memory at different times and in different circumstances prevented the opportunity to shed light on a colonial past that is crucial to understanding the country's history. It is because of these knowledge gaps that recent events and colonial recollections came to be, not accompanied by a critical review of the past but, on the contrary, supported by a resurgence of revanchist and self-celebrating tendencies. Among them were the 2004 exhibition on the Eritrean Askaris[25] – one of the most celebrated symbols of fascist colonialism – and the shrine built in 2012 by the municipality of Affile (a municipality in the Metropolitan City of Rome) and dedicated to general Rodolfo Graziani, guilty of crimes against humanity and still remembered as "the butcher" in Ethiopia and in the Arab world. International outrage and protests were not met with equal reactions in Italy.[26] "Returns of the colony" violently resurfaced in the country with the increasingly frequent arrival of African migrants. The crisis of the post-colony and the influx of migrants have reopened the question of relations with the African otherness, bringing back xenophobic and racist currents in the country and triggering aggressive identity-affirming impulses. Today the legacy of the colonial experience, with its hierarchy of the world and citizenship rights, and the role of racism in the organisation of social and productive relations, govern relations with the other, increasingly perceived as an invader and a threat.

Consistent with this reality, the Italian government adopted a summary deportation policy – an action condemned by the Council of Europe[27] – and engaged in refoulement practices following the 2008 agreement between Berlusconi and Qaddafi which, among other things, provided funding for migrant detention centres in Libya where human rights violations were systematic, according to reports by Amnesty International and Human Rights Watch.[28] Paradoxically and tragically, the Italian-Libyan Treaty used the colonial past (the provisions on migrants were part of a broader agreement designed to settle the long-standing colonial-era litigation) to push back African women and men in search of a better future, many of whom came from the ex-Italian colonies in the Horn of Africa.[29]

The implosion of Libya marked a new turn in the Italian containment policies aimed at regulating migration flows: a new agreement was signed with transit countries in the Horn of Africa migration route such as Tunisia, Egypt and Sudan. Known as the Khartoum Process, the agreement signed on November 28, 2014 in Rome provides for an additional control of migration flows through partnerships with the same countries from which migrants are fleeing at the cost of their lives.[30] These countries, in particular Eritrea, are expected to readmit the runaways in exchange for financial incentives and funding to unspecified development projects. In 2012–2015, Eritreans were reported to be the largest refugee group arriving in Italy: in 2014, they accounted for 27 per cent of total arrivals.[31] The number of children is also increasing: 16,362 minors arrived to Italy by sea in 2015 alone – 12,272 of whom were unaccompanied – mainly from Eritrea (3,089).[32] And for those migrants who succeed in reaching Italy, the government has not only stepped up security measures and surveillance systems, but also streamlined detention and custody procedures in specially established camps, reactivating old racial separation practices. In a system of this sort, the Eritrean descendants of that *colonia primigenia* (first-born colony) towards which Italy has historical obligations have a sad privilege: humanitarian protection status (not refugee) and a residence permit valid for one year.[33] They don't get anything else. Neither accommodation, nor a job, nor support, nor certainties.

Notes

1 *Guida dell'Africa Orientale Italiana*. Milan: Consociazione Turistica Italiana, 1938, p.199.

2 A. Triulzi (ed.), *Fotografia e storia dell'Africa*, Proceedings of the symposium (Naples, Istituto Universitario Orientale-Roma, Istituto italo africano, September 9-11, 1992). Naples: Istituto Universitario Orientale, 1995.

3 IsIAO was formed by the 1995 merger of the *Istituto italiano per il Medio ed Estremo Oriente* (*Ismeo*), established in 1933, and the *Istituto italo africano* (*Iia*), established in 1906 as *Istituto coloniale*. The latter was frequently renamed over time, so as to reflect adaptation and repositioning within new socio-political scenarios: *Istituto coloniale fascista* (1928), *Istituto fascista per l'Africa Italiana* (1937), *Istituto italiano per l'Africa* (1947), *Istituto italo africano* (1971).

4 For more information on the reasons for this disregard, partly related to the not easily decodable nature of the medium itself and partly owing to the very limited knowledge of the existing colonial photographic heritage, cf. S.Palma, *L'Africa nella collezione fotografica dell'Isiao. Il fondo Eritrea-Etiopia*. Rome-Naples: IsIAO-Università di Napoli L'Orientale, 2005, pp. 9-16.

5 M. Lenci, "Dalla storia coloniale alla storia dell'Africa", *Africa*, II, 2000, p.207-218; S. PALMA, "Half–devil and half-child. Africanist historical studies and studies on colonialism in Italian University", in P. Bertella Farnetti and C. Novelli (eds.), *Colonialism and national identity*. Newcastle upon Tyne: Cambridge Scholars Publishing, 2015.

6 One of the most influential voices in Italian Africanist Studies recently stated that "the discovery of photography as a source for colonial history [...] is one of the most significant innovations in the last few years". Cf. G.Calchi Novati, "La controversia sull'Eritrea: popolo, nazione, stato", in A.Giovagnoli and G. Del Zanna (eds.), *Il mondo visto dall'Italia*. Milan: Guerini e Associati, 2004, p.138.

7 Established as *Club Africano*, a private membership association, after two years it was renamed *Società africana d'Italia*, with bylaws stating its new scope and ambitions.

8 S. Palma, "La Società africana d'Italia. 'Sodalizio di agitazione' napoletano di fine Ottocento", *Archivio Fotografico Toscano*, vol. 21, 1995, pp. 12-16.

9 S.Palma, *Archivio Storico della Società africana d'Italia – vol. II: Raccolte fotografiche e Cartografiche*. Naples: Istituto Universitario Orientale, 1996.

10 "L'Istituto Fascista dell'Africa Italiana – Ieri oggi domani", *Africa Italiana*, VI, 1941, p. 4.

11 According to words and programmatic lines of Ernesto Artom, founder and president of *Istituto coloniale* from 1914 to 1925. See "Il programma dell'Istituto Coloniale esposto dall'on. Ernesto Artom", *Rivista Coloniale*, vol. I, IX, 1914, pp. 331-334.

12 S. Palma, "Ricerca africanistica e fonti fotografiche. Il recupero di due collezioni italiane", in T. Serena (ed.), *Fotografia e raccolte fotografiche, Centro di Ricerche informatiche per i beni culturali*, VIII, Pisa: Scuola Normale Superiore, 1998, pp. 185-196.

13 Actually, photographs were sent from the former colonies at least until 1946, and from Italian and foreign trade shows well into the 1950s.

14 Cf. the report of M.A. Vitale, in: Archivio Storico del MAI (ASMAI), *Africa*, IV, pp.11-12.

15 For more information on the MAI's awareness campaigns and propaganda and colonialist lobbies supporting Italian rights before the 1949 UN General Assembly, cf. G. Rossi, *L'Africa italiana verso l'indipendenza (1941–1949)*. Milan: Giuffrè, 1980; A.Del Boca, *Gli Italiani in Africa Orientale. Nostalgia delle colonie*. Rome-Bari: Laterza, 1984.

16 S. Palma, *L'Africa nella collezione fotografica dell'Isiao. Il fondo Eritrea-Etiopia*, op. cit.

17 C. Cerreti, *La raccolta cartografica dell'Istituto Italo Africano*, Rome: Istituto Italo Africano, 1987.

18 G. Gresleri, P.G. Massaretti and S. Zagnoni (eds.), *Architettura italiana d'oltremare 1870–1940*. Venice: Marsilio, 1993; E.Denison, G.Yu Ren and N.Gebrebedhin, *Asmara, Africa's Secret Modernist City*. London: Merrel, 2003; G.Barrera, A.Triulzi and G.Tzeggai, *Asmara. Architettura e pianificazione urbana nei fondi dell'Isiao*. Rome: Isiao, 2008.

19 http://www.asaiafrica.org/wp-content/uploads/2015/09/APPELLO-INT-ASAI-1.pdf (10/15).

20 A. Del Boca, *L'africa nella coscienza degli italiani*. Milan: Mondadori, 2002, p. 127.

21 For more on the concise and belated accounts of Colonial history offered in history textbooks, Cf. G.de Michele, "La storia dell'Africa e del colonialismo italiano nei manuali di storia in uso nelle scuole superiori", *I sentieri della ricerca*, vol. 3, 2006, pp. 131-168.

22 F. Focardi, *La guerra della memoria. La Resistenza nel dibattito politico italiano dal 1945 a oggi*. Rome-Bari: Laterza, 2005, p. 11. Più in generale see A. Del Boca (ed.), *La storia negata. Il revisionismo e il suo uso politico*. Vicenza: Neri Pozza, 2009.

23 A. Del Boca, *I gas di Mussolini. Il fascismo e la guerra d'Etiopia*, Rome: Editori riuniti, 1996.

24 The same motives were behind the prohibition to air the BBC documentary *Fascist Legacy* (1989), on Italian war crimes in Africa and the Balkans. The documentary, purchased by the Italian public television station RAI and never broadcast, was the subject of a parliamentary interpellation.

25 S. PALMA, "Il ritorno di miti e memorie coloniali. L'epopea degli ascari eritrei nell'Italia postcoloniale", *Afriche & Orienti*, vol. 1, 2007, p. 57-79.

26 "Quel mausoleo alla crudeltà che non fa indignare l'Italia", *Corriere della Sera*, 30 September 2012.

27 See Thomas Hammarberg's report: http://www.meltingpot.org/IMG/pdf/Hammarberg_Rapporto_16-2-09_.pdf (09/16).

28 https://www.hrw.org/node/254236 09/15).

29 See the documentary directed by A.Serge, Dagmawi Yimer and R.Biadene, *Come un uomo sulla terra*, 2008.

30 http://www.nigrizia.it/notizia/roma-khartoum-accordi-sui-migranti (08/15).

31 http://www.UNHCR.CR/ARRIVALS/italy – (08/15). However, ours is not among the destination countries in their migration project: data confirm that countries in Central and Northern Europe, e.g., Germany and Sweden, receive a higher number of asylum applications (UNHCR global trend).

32 http://www.savethechildren.it/IT/Tool/Press/All/IT/Tool/Press/Single?id_press=1013&year=2016 (30/16).

33 Storia di Abrham. O della condizione dei migranti eritrei a Bologna: http://www.bologninabasement.it/4063-2/ (03/16).

ASMARA
Making (Colonial) Modernity Work through Transport Networks and Infrastructure

Federico Caprotti

Urban planning and the design and installation of infrastructural and architectural elements was a complex endeavour in the context of Asmara, and indeed in the Eritrean context as a whole. Urban planning can be seen as a technology of the regime, in the sense that Mussolini's planners and architects used the new discipline as a way of promoting fascism's totalitarian vision and unstable ideology, solidifying it in urban public spaces.[1] This is the case, most visibly, in Rome and Italy's other major urban centres, as well as in the Pontine Marshes land reclamation and urbanisation drive. The latter, in particular, was conceived as a way not only of experimenting with new cities, but with changing a pre-fascist, negative nature and landscape, into a rationalised, productive fascist nature, subordinate to the New Towns – Littoria, Sabaudia, Aprilia, Pontinia, and the various smaller new *borghi* – that were to be the organisational nodes around which the new Pontine Marshes rotated.[2] While these elements are clearly in evidence in the architectural and infrastructural interventions in Asmara's urban form in the 1930s, it has to be acknowledged that the urban context in Asmara was also highly complex prior to fascism, including, as it did, pre-colonial and pre-fascist colonial urban roots. As a result, fascist urban interventions were not as focused on urban cleansing as those found in other fascist colonial city plans, but had to integrate within them elements of the Eritrean, and pre-fascist city.[3]

Asmara was known as Little Rome by the late 1930s. This was for several reasons, including its central role in Italian East Africa; its urban redevelopment along Modernist and Rationalist lines; and its technological, cultural, and symbolic connection with Rome as the capital of Italy's empire.[4]

A garage for automobiles
Source: K.Paulweber 2013

These connections included elements of static infrastructure, such as: the rail station (opened in 1911), on the highly advanced (for the time) Massawa-Asmara rail line; Asmara airport (opened in 1922), a key node on the *Linea dell'Impero* air route to Rome; the paved main road to Addis Ababa known as the *Via della Vittoria* (built in 1935–1938); paved roads throughout Asmara itself; and the cableway between Asmara and Massawa, opened in 1937 and, at 75 km in length, the longest cableway in the world at the time. Ceretti & Tanfani, the corporation responsible for the construction of the cableway, described the construction of the cableway not just as a technological feat, but as a way of enabling Asmara to reach its potential as a colonial urban centre. Indeed, the first pages of a book commissioned by Ceretti & Tanfani on the cableway focus on the key role of Asmara in networks of empire, in "becoming one of the principal hubs for trade and commercial traffic arriving by sea and headed for the heart of empire".[5]

Nonetheless, Asmara was not simply a static container of architectural designs and static elements of urban and transport infrastructure. The airport, paved roads, rail lines and the rail station, among others, can be seen as solid nodes within fluid networks of empire facilitated by the modern technologies of transport and mobility. By briefly focusing on just three aspects of Asmara's centrality within networks of colonial transport – the airport, rail station, and roads – the chapter highlights the way in which Asmara was constructed as a central node of within Italy's fascist visions of Empire. In so doing, the chapter consciously draws on newsreels from the *LUCE* Institute, which was the regime's chief moving image propaganda institution in terms of intensity and frequency of production of newsreels during the fascist ventennio. In addition, analysing newsreels as visual cultural artefacts enables an investigation of the production of particular, specific visions of Empire in fascist Italy.

There are some caveats to this brief chapter. Firstly, the chapter focuses on flows and networks rather than on the more obvious architectural and planning components of Asmara. Secondly, the chapter focuses mostly on the fascist period, which is a significant part of a larger whole in terms of Italian presence in Asmara. By focusing on Asmara during the 1920s and 1930s, this chapter also omits to consider the pre-fascist colonial experience of the early wave of Italian colonists who settled in and around Asmara, and for whom the fascist ventennio was, initially, a parenthesis or evolution in their experience of Eritrea, and finally, a painful conclusion. Some of these families of colonists lived in Asmara for several decades, and their connection with Italy became ever more exiguous. A case in point is the memoir of Asmara written by Erminia dell'Oro, who lived in Asmara from her birth to age twenty, and whose family lived in Asmara from 1886 until the end of the fascist era.

The *teleferica*: the cable car connecting Asmara with Massawa on the Red Sea
Source: Biblioteca-Archivio "Africa"

According to dell'Oro, the advent of the fascist period meant little for these long-standing colonial families, for whom the only connection with Italy were the free holidays back in Italy granted by the regime to colonial families, and a notion that Italy was, by the 1930s at least, a country "on the road towards Great Power status".[6]

Asmara Airport – Airmindedness and Connections to Empire

Asmara airport was built in 1922. Initially an airfield with little in the way of buildings, the field was located several kilometres to the southwest of the city centre, and is still the site on which the current Asmara International Airport is situated. It quickly became integrated within the *Linea dell'Impero*, the key route that linked Rome with its colonies. Although the *Linea dell'Impero* did not have as its terminus Asmara (the end of the line was in Addis Ababa), Asmara was nonetheless one of the most established air stations on the route. The entire *Linea dell'Impero*, at its height in the late 1930s, was 6,400 km in length and could be flown in two and a half days, an enormous improvement on just a decade earlier, when the only travel option was likely to be ship-based, through the Suez Canal. By 1940, the *Linea dell'Impero* could be flown in two days from Rome. The building of the airport, the use of air transport and aviation technologies, and the linking of Asmara with Rome as well as with other cities in Italian East Africa, was also part and parcel of a process of promotion of airmindedness throughout Italy and her colonies.[7] The airport became the central piece of infrastructure through which highly technological flows – of officials, goods, visitors, mail, communications, and violence and military hardware – flowed and were perceived as co-constituting Empire in Italian East Africa.

The link between aviation technology and imperial symbolism can be seen in a 1937 newsreel which narrated the delivery, by air, of military banners to Asmara for the Eritrean components of the Italian air force.[8] The banners, sent by "His Majesty the Emperor King" according to the newsreels narrator, were shown being paraded through Asmara airfield. The banners were reminiscent of Roman military banners in their design, and significantly, the newsreel also shows the banners being hung from the propellers of aircraft stationed on the airfield. This symbolically linked Asmara and Rome, via aviation technology and a recourse to historical symbolism in the design of the banners.

Asmara's role as the capital of Italy's colonies in Italian East Africa can also be seen in a 1935 newsreel celebrating the start of the airmail link between Eritrea and Ethiopia.[9] The reel devoted a significant amount of time to overviews of the engines of the airmail aircraft and to its loading operations (the narrator proudly announcing that the aircraft was able to carry 87 kg of mail as well as several passengers), in so doing underlining the focus on modern technology in fusing together networks of empire. In addition, the newsreel presented aviation technology, and the links made possible by connecting airports such as Asmara with other colonial cities, as a sign of state power and of the self-sufficiency of empire. Indeed, the reel concluded with the image of the airmail aircraft taking off and flying into the distance, while a slogan becomes visible. The writing on the slogan – "Italians, boycott those who are placing sanctions on Italy" – point to a riposte to international sanctions on Italy as a result of its invasion of Ethiopia. Infrastructure such as Asmaras airfield was clearly seen as (symbolically, if not in actual practice) enabling autarchy through a solidification of imperial networks of self-sufficiency.[10]

In addition to the civil air duties to which Asmara airport was assigned, from 1932 the airport was also the headquarters of a flight of eight military aircraft. In light of Italy's invasion of Ethiopia in 1935, Asmara airport became the centre for the orchestration of technologies of war and murder from the air.[11] The central role of Asmara airport in Italy's aerial warfare against Ethiopia during this time can be seen in a *LUCE* newsreel from December 1935, which celebrated a medals ceremony at Asmara airport.[12] The newsreel showcases the airport as a centre for Italy's colonial military aviation by showing general De Bono surveying serried ranks of military personnel, including Vittorio Mussolini, in front of parked military aircraft. On this occasion, medals were awarded to aviators including Galeazzo Ciano, who was awarded a silver medal to military valour for his leadership of the Disperata air squadron. While the visual representation of the military aspects of Italian colonialism in East Africa cannot be explored here, it is nonetheless key to highlight the fact that the filmic representation of infrastructural and transport prowess went hand-in-hand with a darker celebration of violent oppression and a will to erase or at least dominate a colonised Other.[13]

Asmara Train Station

While air travel and the *Linea dell'Impero* arrived in Asmara during the fascist period, and were directly linked to the regime's colonising focus, the epoch of rail transport and rail travel had been a feature of Asmaras urban landscape, and of its connections. Indeed, the line from Massawa to Asmara was built from 1887 to 1911, although the line was upgraded in the 1930s. Therefore Asmara rail station stands as a signifier of Italian presence in Asmara for over half a century. Indeed, its architecture – a standard station building which could originate from any small town on the peninsula – is a far cry from the bold modernism found in many railway stations built by Mussolini's architects

Asmara train station
Source: K.Paulweber 2013

in the 1920s and 1930s. Nonetheless, what connects Asmara station to the regime is the wider, fascist focus on Asmara, and rail, as parts of a colonial system of transport and exchange. While in earlier decades the railway had been a means to an end, and a celebrated technological feat in and of itself, by the 1930s it had taken on a different, ideologically-infused meaning in the context of aspirations to Italian imperial expansion.

An example of this is the way in which the train station was the central feature in a 1936 newsreel featuring governor Guzzoni welcoming the new bishop for Eritrea to Asmara.[14] The reel posits a close link between Empire and the city through transport networks by showing a series of three static images before the narrated footage of the bishops arrival at the station. The first static image is of a statue of Julius Caesar. This fades into the second image: a map of Italian East Africa, with the word *Impero Italiano* superimposed upon it. The third image is a Modernist, stylised representation of a worker, with the word Asmara next to the worker. In the background are visible some fasces rising out of the ground. The reel thus links Roman imperial history, Mussolini's colonial ambitions, and Asmara as a colonial centre and work-in-progress. The first moving image in the reel shows the new bishop arriving in a littorina carriage, festooned with Italian flags: military and administrative officials greet the bishop on the station platform. Thus, the station – modest as it was in terms of size and design – can still be seen in the context of its importance as an interface between imperial ambitions and networks of rapid travel and transport which the fascist regime, as a modern political-ideological phenomenon, relied upon for the realisation of their projections of power.

Roads of Empire

In addition to rail, air, and cableway links to the rest of Empire, Asmara was also envisioned as a road-based transport node for Eritrea. Road-building has been described as a technology of Empire.[15] In fascist Italy, road-building enterprises lent themselves to symbolic justifications linking 1930s road construction to the layering of road networks in the Roman Empire. In this light, then, the construction of road links in the colonies became not just an infrastructural project to enable transport, trade and control of territory, but a project to weave together disparate parts of Empire, and ultimately to link colonial capitals to Rome.

The road between Asmara and Gondar, for example, was described in contemporary accounts as an imperial road: opened in 1937, the 580 km connection between the two cities was celebrated in a newsreel which showed Minister of Public Works Giuseppe Cobolli Gigli inaugurating the last stretch of the road to be built.[16] The road was seen as an imperial artery, and as the result of a modern, fascist struggle against the colonial Other in this case represented by the East African natural environment. An example of this celebration of fascist technological prowess to bring order to East Africa was the erection of a large stone slab on a cliff face near Uolchefit. The slab was inscribed with the road's opening date, and with the following inscription:

> "Italian labour has, in this land conquered by the heroism of the Motherland's sons, mastered this land's harsh mountains. The Duce ordered the battle that was won by the 3rd Company of Workers' Groups of Asmara's Military Engineers".[17]

The inscription clearly pointed to the importance of transport links between Asmara and other cities in Italian East Africa, to Asmara's importance as an imperial transport node, and to the construction of these transport links as a key example of the fascist regime's battle with Nature: the battle ordered by the Duce in the inscription was not a military battle, but a struggle with the elements. In this struggle, Nature was almost personified and turned into an unruly, primal Other that could then be mastered, controlled and disciplined by fascist technology and labour.

Conclusion: Asmara as a Technology of Empire

The brief discussion above has used Asmara's airport, train station, and road network as gateways into the weaving together of webs of Empire, linking Asmara to other cities in Italian East Africa, and ultimately to Rome. Although links to Rome were in all actuality very limited – after all, airplanes could only carry a very limited number of passengers, mail and goods in to and out of the colonies, when compared to the thousands who could arrive via ship transport – what is important about these networks is the fact that they were ideologically envisioned, and constructed to be something that they were not, at least in reality: backbones of Empire. The visual and textual representation of air, road, cableway, and rail links to and from Asmara, and the construction of the static components of transport infrastructure in and around the city, could be put to use by the regime's cinematographers and journalists so as to construct an image of colonial coherence, of close connection to Rome, of dominance and control. Although this image was, in reality, thin and wavering – and ultimately dispelled by the start of World War II and the attendant severing of the fragile spider's web of air and other links in Italian East Africa – it nonetheless served the ideological purpose of framing a colonial reality that the regime wanted displayed at home. In this context, the representation of transport networks was part and parcel of showcasing (mostly to the national public) an image of coherent modernity.

Notes

1 David Atkinson, "Totalitarianism and the street in fascist Rome", in Nicholas Fyfe (ed.), *Images of the Street: Planning, Identity and Control in Public Space*. London: Routledge, 1998, pp. 13-30.

2 Federico Caprotti, "Destructive creation: fascist urban planning, architecture, and New Towns in the Pontine Marshes", *Journal of Historical Geography*, vol. 33, 2007, p. 651-679. For contemporary projects in a wider European context, see Hans Renes and Stefano Piastra, "Polders and politics: new agricultural landscapes in Italian and Dutch wetlands, 1920s to 1950s", *Landscapes*, vol. 12, 2011, p. 24-41; see also Marco Armero and Wilko Graf von Hardenberg, "Green rhetoric in blackshirts: Italian fascism and the environment", *Environment and History*, vol. 19, 2013, pp. 283-311.

3 Uoldelul Chelati Dirar, "From warriors to urban dwellers: Ascari and the military factor in the urban development of colonial Eritrea", *Cahiers d'Études Africaines*, N.175, 2004, pp. 533-574.

4 Maristella Casciato, "Da campo militare a capitale: Asmara colonia italiana e oltre", *Incontri: Rivista Europea di Studi Italiani*, vol. 28, 2013, p.44-57.

5 Ceretti & Tanfani, *La teleferica Massaua-Asmara*, no date (1930s). Milan: Ceretti & Tanfani, p. 3.

6 Erminia Dell'Oro, *Asmara Addio*. Pordenone: Edizioni Studio Tesi, 1988, p. 49.

7 Gordon Pirie, "British air shows in South Africa, 1932/33: 'airmindedness', ambition and anxiety", *Kronos*, vol. 35, 2009, p. 48-70; Gordon Pirie, *Cultures and Caricatures of British Imperial Aviation: Passengers, Pilots, Publicity*. Manchester: Manchester University Press, 2012.

8 Cinegiornale LUCE B1117, "Il rito della consegna dei labari", 23 June 1937.

9 Cinegiornale LUCE B0789, "Il servizio aereo di collegamento tra l'Eritrea e la Somalia si è inaugurato con la partenza del trimotore 'Ala Littoria' carico di 87 chili di posta", 27 November 1935.

10 Federico Caprotti, "Profitability, practicality, and ideology: fascist civil aviation and the short life of Ala Littoria, 1934–1943", *Journal of Transport History*, vol. 32, 2011, p. 17-38.

11 Roberto Gentilli, "L'aeronautica in Libia e in Etiopia", in Paolo Ferrari, *L'Aeronautica Italiana: Una Storia del Novecento*. Milan: FrancoAngeli, 2004, p. 301-337.

12 Cinegiornale LUCE B0803, "Consegna di medaglie al valor militare per la squadriglia aerea Disperata", 24 December 1935.

13 Federico Caprotti, "The invisible war on nature: the Abyssinian war (1935–1936) in newsreels and documentaries in fascist Italy", *Modern Italy*, vol. 19, 2014, pp. 305-321. See also Federico Caprotti, "Visuality, hybridity, and colonialism: imagining Ethiopia through colonial aviation, 1935–1940", *Annals of the Association of American Geographers*, vol. 101, 2011, pp. 380-403.

14 Cinegiornale LUCE B1016, "Impero italiano. Asmara. L'arrivo del nuovo vescovo dell'Eritrea ricevuto dal governatore Guzzoni", 30 December 1936.

15 Libbie Freed, "Networks of (colonial) power: roads in French Central Africa after World War I", *History and Technology: An International Journal*, vol. 26, 2010, pp. 203-223. See also Suzanne Moon, "Place, voice, interdisciplinarity: understanding technology in the colony and postcolony", *History and Technology: An International Journal*, vol. 26, 2010, pp. 189-201.

16 Cinegiornale LUCE B1119, "L'inaugurazione della strada che conduce da Uolchefit a Debivar", 30 June 1937.

17 Giuseppe Cobolli Gigli, "Dall'Asmara a Gondar", *La Stampa*, vol. 71, 10 June 1937, p. 1. See also Giuseppe Cobolli Gigli, *Strade Imperiali*. Milan: Mondadori, 1938.

RACING ACROSS ASMARA
Engines, Speed and the Colour-line in Eritrea (1938–1954)

Massimo Zaccaria

For the history of transportation in Italian East Africa, the year 1938 had a special meaning. The fascist regime had sponsored the creation of an ambitious road network in its African domains, for clear military and economic purposes.[1] The road network also had propaganda value. The roads were conceived as the clearest expression of the superiority of the system brought in by fascism and embodied its desire for modernity. In 1938, over the thousands of kilometres that made up this road network, about 16,000 vehicles circulated, of which two-thirds were registered with the Government of Eritrea.[2] If we take into account the relationship between residents and vehicles, the motorisation rate of Eritrea was, at the end of the 1930s, higher than the Italian one. From the conjunction of road symbolism with car symbolism there sprang, precisely in 1938, the idea of organising the first Grand Prix of that Country.

Auto races in the Italian colonies had made their debut in 1925, when Libya had begun to host the Grand Prix of Tripoli and in August of 1938 motor racing had reached Somalia with the Mogadishu circuit. But the arrival of motor racing in Eritrea had a special meaning in its priority intent to celebrate the new fascist road system. Before 1938, motorcycle racing had monopolised the Eritrean scene, and over that decade a crowded competition calendar had built up. On July 31, 1938, for example, there took place the Asmara-Keren-Asmara circuit of the motorcycle regularity rally for young fascists.[3] Two months later, forty-five motorcycles belonging to the Eritrean motorcycle association took part in another sortie, this time on Agordat.[4] In the same period the Hamasien Cup had seen the participation of forty-two contenders.

View on Harnet Avenue
Source: S. Graf 2015

Cover of the special issue of the *Corriere Eritreo* dedicated to the *Coppa di Natale* and *Coppa di S. E. il Governatore*. Asmara: Percotto, 1938.
Source: M.Zaccaria

Auto racing made its debut in the country in 1937, with the Nefasit-Asmara hill climb, destined to become a classic of the Eritrean motorsport calendar. A year later, the first Eritrea Motor Speedway was organised and immediately became the main event of the country's motorsport calendar. The initiative was undertaken by the Eritrean headquarters of the Royal Italian Automobile Club (*Reale Automobile Club Italiano*) and the Federation of Fascist Combatants of Eritrea (*Federazione dei Fasci di Combattimento dell'Eritrea*). The competition took place along a twenty-lap city circuit (75,540 km), along the main road axis of Asmara (Viale De Bono, Viale Mussolini and Corso del Re). To further stress the importance of the event, eight trophies and the Asmara Lottery were added to the first Motor Speedway of Eritrea (*1° Circuito Automobilistico dell'Eritrea*), while the event was commemorated in a special issue edited by sports journalist Mario Melani and printed by the *Corriere Eritreo*[5] [Photo 1]. The competition categories were two, the first with cars of up to 1,500 cc. (10 participants) and the second with cars of above 1,500 cc. (thirteen participants).

Racing was only one aspect of the first Motor Speedway of Eritrea. The fascist regime wanted to infuse the competition with a symbolic meaning, which ultimately constituted the true motivation for the initiative. In the first place, there was a clear intention to celebrate the road as a symbol of life and civilisation. Mussolini was especially fond of this metaphor and had revived it on several occasions. On September 13, 1926, during the International Road Congress (*Congresso internazionale della strada*), Mussolini had said: "I am personally a road fan. Roads are the nervous system of the organism of a people, useful for economic purposes, strategic purposes and especially moral purposes".[6] The other symbolism evoked was linked to movement, rhythm and speed, attributes considered typical of the fascist spirit, namely a system that presented itself as frenetic and pervaded by an eagerness to act and get things done. The idea for the first city circuit of Eritrea was the fruit of this combination of road symbolism and speed symbolism, as demonstrated by the official publicity of the initiative: "Dauntless racing cars speed by, sliding away swiftly on these smooth, perfect roads. Booming civilisation on the backs of imperial signs of Rome. They dart on the steel strip that flashes the dark gleams of the rulers' sword, a dizzying carousel, arrows of audacity. And the incomparable thrill of the Italian people, who have found their Man and their soul, march to the beat of a giddy excitement and an indomitable will, to encounter their grandiose destinies".[7]

Even the date chosen for the rally had a symbolic intent, since by overlapping with Christmas Day it emphasised the will to counter the traditional religious celebration with a more up-to-date, secular, fascist celebration of modernity.[8]

Already back in the Liberal era a clearly segregationist principle had been imposed on the major sports events of the colony. The fear of seeing their racial superiority threatened by the often unfavourable competitive results of Italian athletes had urged avoiding any sports contact between the two sides. The Italian athletes competed in their own categories, separated from the indigenous element, for which special tournaments and rounds were created. The distinction had become still more marked since 1937–1938 by the enforcement of the racial laws. Among the sports events, auto racing, displaying the most advanced technological component, was conceived as the highest demonstration of the technical and cultural superiority of the Italian colonisers[9]: "The hovels disappear as grandiose buildings surge up. Lavish department stores and vast theatres are built. Both sides of the splendid new streets are lined with dazzling rendezvous places, emporiums of every kind. A massive industrial complex is launched. Banks, aqueducts, covered markets, neighbourhoods rise up. The Eritreans gape before the teeming grandeur of Rome. In their oriental fatalism they believe it a miracle not of this world".[10]

In the case of motor sports, the expensiveness of the events long hindered the emergence of Eritrean racers and teams, and so made the sport an entirely Italian domain. However, it must not be forgotten that the Gran Prix also had a controversial internal aim specifically linked to the dynamics of the Italian community. It marked the arrival of a new kind of coloniser, representative of a new Italy that was opposed to the old liberal-oriented colonial system. When the Christmas Cup was being presented, this element forcibly emerged: "The Asmara of the old colonials, going around on the backs of mules prancing lazily on clay dirt, with their placid bourgeois airs, their typical tarot games with the parish priest, the mayor, the pharmacist and the chief of police, is now a bygone memory, an idea for a likely writer of *A Little World of the Colonial Past*".[11] A concept reinforced by sports journalist Mario Melani: "From two streets to a hundred streets, from a hundred homes to a thousand palaces, from a thousand men of goodwill to 50,000 new Italians. Those of the Mussolini's era".[12]

The King's Cup (*La Coppa del Re*) enjoyed a resounding success. Thirty thousand spectators from all over the country crowded the sidelines of the circuit track. The highest officials of the colony, starting with the Governor, attended the event. Five days later the streets of Asmara hosted the First Motorcycle Circuit of Asmara, with a great public attendance. But the future of motor sports was destined to be far from rosy. The events of the war and the economic crisis of the 1940s completely halted the competitions. In 1946, for example, the British authorities prevented the organisation of motorcycling rallies, given the scarcity of tires and fuel.[13] A partial recovery of the competitions took place

Mario Manzini and (second to his left) Solomon Ma'ashio, Asmara, June 1947. The picture is dedicated to Solomon ("to Solomon [my] chief mechanic"). Asmara.
Source: M. Zaccaria, courtesy of Solomon Ma'shio's family

only in 1947, when a motorcycle race was run in Asmara, and in the following year, when in Massawa, on February 15th, the first automotorcycle-racing circuit of Taulud took place.[14] There followed, at the end of September 1948, a Gymkhana organised in the Ferrovieri-Melotti field of Asmara by the Eritrean Moto Club[15] and a motoring festival in Campo Polo a month later. However, the great event of 1948 was, exactly ten years after its first edition, the return of the Auto-motorcycle Circuit (*Circuito Automotociclistico*) of Asmara organised by the Eritrean Automobile Club, among which two motorcycle categories (250 and 500 cc.) and two categories (under 1,500 cc and over 1,500 cc.).[16] In the same year, the Eritrean Motorcycle Club organised the social regularity rally on a track, which, in addition to Asmara, included Addi Keyh, Sageneiti and Dekamhare. Although the vehicles and drivers were all Italian, the same cannot be said of the public, which usually included a broad Eritrean attendance. Thus automobiles became a standard feature of the popular culture, which embraced vehicles and drivers as clear symbols of modernity. Asmara loved to present itself as a city on wheels, proud to have its streets cluttered with cars even during hard economic times, such as the early 1950s.[17] The disappearance of the Italian administration had led to the gradual removal of the racial laws. In the 1950s the presence of an Eritrean urban middle class became increasingly visible. The two phenomena provided the conditions for the appearance of the first Eritrean racing car pilots.

Picture celebrating Solomon Ma'ashio's winning at the Campo Polo's circuit (Asmara) on 8th February 1953. Solomon Ma'shio is driving a Moto Guzzi 250 cc. Asmara. Campo Polo, 2nd Feb.
Source: M. Zaccaria, courtesy of Solomon Ma'shio's family

In motorcycle racing, the 1950s were dominated by Solomon Ma'ashio, the first Eritrean motorcycle racer. Solomon's career started at the garage of Mario Manzini, one of the most famous 1940s pilots in Eritrea. Possessing uncommon qualities for tending to and setting up the Moto Guzzi, Solomon had become Manzini's top mechanic [Photo 2]. In the early 1950s he opened his own motorcycle workshop, which became a mecca for all the Guzzi freaks of Asmara. At the same time he devoted himself to racing, to become one of the most popular pilots in the country up to 1958, when he retired.[18]

Solomon Ma'ashio took part in competitions where the vast majority of participants were Italians. His, however, was no token participation, since Solomon ran to win and had the means and skills to do so. His arrival on the scene introduced an unexpected variable in an environment unaccustomed to seeing Eritrean pilots win. Solomon Ma'ashio's victory lead took place on February 8, 1953, when he won, after an epic race, the finale of the 250 cc category on the Campo Polo circuit, ahead of Leo Cicolari. The *Giornale Eritreo* wrote that Cicolari had given "an indisputable world-class performance" and that the young driver was "ready at the commands, steady at gripping the curves, and when it came to outmaneuvering, his style showed no hesitation whatsoever".[19] Yet it was Solomon Ma'ashio who made it first to the finish line [Photo 3]. Nor was Solomon Ma'ashio an isolated case, since already back in January of 1950 the pilot Uoldai had arrived eighth in the 250 motocross category of Bet-Gherghis. In the 1952 Mountain championship races at least four Eritrean motorcyclists participated with excellent placings.[20]

As for auto racing, 1952 was without doubt the year in which the first Eritrean pilots began to get on track. The sports newspapers of the period tell us that, at the Asmara-Adi Quala-Asmara regularity rally, Mansur M. Ramadan, aboard a Fiat 1100, finished second joint place.[21] Two years later, during the fifth Massawa circuit, in the presence of Emperor Haile Sellasie and his wife, two Eritrean pilots, Tewolde Baraki (Alfa Romeo 1750) and Goitom Tesfazien (Alfa Romeo 1750) also ran.[22] It was especially G. Gheresghier who excelled, finishing third in the June 20, 1954 Nefasit-Asmara (Alfa Romeo 1750).[23] In the following years the newspapers reported the participations of Zeggai Berhe, Ghebru Yemane, Uodal Tekleghier, Tesfai Abtesghi and Berane Geber. The Italian community, after totally losing its political clout and suffering a dramatic drop in attendance, (between 1938 and 1950 Italians in Eritrea had gone from 48,000 to 21,000), had also lost much of its economic influence. The spaces that opened up were filled by Italian-Eritreans and by an increasingly self-confident Eritrean middle class. Motor sports, perhaps a footnote in the history of the country, offer yet another way of getting a better understanding of the dramatic social changes that took place in Eritrea from the 1940s to the 1960s.

Notes

1 On the Africa Orientale Italiana's road network see: "Le opere stradali", *Gli Annali dell'Africa Italiana*, 2, 4, 1939. See also Marco Antonsich, "Addis Abeba 'Caput Viarium' le strade del Duce in Abissinia", *Limes*, 3, 2006, pp. 133-144.

2 Davide Fossa, *Lavoro italiano nell'impero*. Milan: A. Mondadori, 1938, p. 433.

3 "L'Asmara – Cheren – Asmara", *Corriere Eritreo Sportivo*, 25 Jul. 1938, p. 8.

4 "Quarantacinque centauri in gita ad Agordat", *Corriere Eritreo*, 21 Sep. 1938.

5 *I° circuito automobilistico dell'Eritrea Coppa di Natale*. Asmara: Tipografia del Corriere Eritreo, 1938.

6 Antonio Cederna, *Mussolini urbanista. Lo sventramento di Roma negli anni del consenso*. Rome-Bari: Laterza, 1979, p. 27.

7 Mario Melani, "Natale 1938", in *I° circuito automobilistico dell'Eritrea Coppa di Natale*. Asmara: Tipografia del Corriere Eritreo, 1938, p. 9.

8 *Mario Melani, "Nostro Natale", Corriere Eritreo*, 26 Dec. 1938, p. 1: "We wrote that a familiar sedentary Christmas was not for us [...]. The cars rumbled by on the broad smooth roads of the first-born capital of the Colony, between two orderly, compact, impressive lines of crowds that felt no desire to linger before the Christmas feast".

9 Gianluca Gabrielli, "L'attività sportiva nelle colonie italiane durante il fascismo. Tra organizzazione del consenso, disciplinamento del tempo libero e "prestigio della razza", *I sentieri della ricerca*, 2, Dec. 2005, pp. 109-136.

10 Guido Ghezzi, "E' nata una metropoli...", in *I° circuito automobilistico dell'Eritrea Coppa di Natale*. Asmara: Tipografia del Corriere Eritreo, 1938, pp. 11-12.

11 Sandro Sorbaro Sindaci, "A ritmo fascista", in *I° circuito automobilistico dell'Eritrea Coppa di Natale*. Asmara: Tipografia del Corriere Eritreo, 1938, p. 10.

12 Mario Melani, "Natale 1938", in *I° circuito automobilistico dell'Eritrea Coppa di Natale*. Asmara: Tipografia del Corriere Eritreo, 1938, p. 9.

13 Alfeo Maramotti, "Dateci un gallone di benzina", *Orizzonte eritreo*, 1, 3, Mar. 1946, p. 59.

14 R. Tani, "A Taulud è nato lo sport motoristico eritreo", *Orizzonti Africani*, 2, 11, Mar. 1948, pp. 20-21.

15 "La Gymkhana del Moto Club Eritreo", *Luci sportive*, 1, 6, Oct. 1948, pp. 14-15.

16 Pippo Rolio, "Il raduno auto-motociclistico", *Orizzonti Africani*, 2, 19, Nov. 1948, p. 21.

17 Alce, "Asmara città su quattro ruote", *Giornale dell'Eritrea*, 10-11 Nov. 1954. On the role of cars in Eritrean society see: Stefano Bellucci, Massimo Zaccaria, "Engine of Change. A Social History of the Car-Mechanics Sector in the Horn of Africa", in Jan-Bart Gewald, André Leliveld, Iva Peša (eds.), *Transforming Innovations in Africa. Explorative Studies on Appropriation in African Societies*. Leiden-Boston: Brill, 2012, pp. 237-256.

18 Interview with Isaa Ma'ashio, Asmara, 22 July 2011. In his career Solomon Ma'ashio won numerous individual trophies and awards: 1951: 3rd place, Nefasit-Asmara hill climb, cat. 250 cc., (4 Nov. 1951).1952: 4th place, Eritrean Motorcycle Regularity Championship, cat. 250 cc. 1953: 1st place Campo Polo's circuit speedway, cat. 250 cc. (8 Feb. 1953).

19 Piero Zannoni, "Solomon, Ronzoni e Pace vincitori assoluti di categoria", *Giornale dell'Eritrea*, 10-11 Feb. 1953.

20 "2.a Corsa in salita. Piana d'Ala – Decameré Km. 5.500", *Giornale dell'Eritrea*, 21 Nov. 1952.

21 "Quattro ex aequo (Dal Re, Monteguti, Colabello e Salvatori tutti su Lancia", *Giornale dell'Eritrea*, 29 Jul. 1952.

22 "Circuito di Massaua", *Giornale dell'Eritrea*, 30-31 Jan. 1954, p. 2.

23 "A Bigi e a Barattolo i trofei "Cornara" and "Cicolari", *Giornale dell'Eritrea*, 21-22 Jun., 1954, p. 4.

Third Chapter

ASMARA'S COLONIAL ARCHITECTURE AND URBANISM

Asmara was built as the cornerstone of Mussolini's short-lived dream of an Italian empire and a springboard for the conquest of Ethiopia. In a very short period – between 1935 and 1941 – the city experienced a boom during which striking examples of Futurist and Rationalist architecture were commissioned. A Modernist core was added to the former village which, after the re-discovery of Asmara in the 1990s, was celebrated as an architectural treasure and a unique manifestation of Modernism in Africa. The city centre hosts an exceptional range of late nineteenth- to early twentieth-century architectural styles, including a number of iconic buildings from the 1930s that have remained largely untouched. The reasons for this are manifold: there was economic stagnation and interstate conflict in the past century, violent events have luckily by-passed the city and it has never been engulfed by the kind of construction boom that raced ahead elsewhere in Africa.

Here, our book offers a shift in perspective: it will not focus on the unique Modernist city, a frozen ensemble of monuments, but rather on the historical conjuncture of modernity and its internal critique. The term *laboratory of modernity* should therefore not be imported too hastily. Asmara's urban planning makes a series of suggestions about the function of colonial space, which accommodated experimentation, and was controlled and controllable. The merging of imperial projects with Modernist aesthetics and fascist motives yielded a complex built environment. On the other hand, no famous architect was involved and in this regard Asmara is unique in that it developed less according to a rigid, holistic modern plan than as an ensemble of parts.

In order to break down the conception of Asmara as a *città metafisica* or a frozen city – which has been considered a dubious aestheticisation of fascist architecture – we have developed an interpretive approach to an extra-artistic reality. Asmara is renowned for the quality of its architectural and urban landscape, made before World War II, and mostly for its historical centre (Historic Perimeter), which is often considered as a lingering memory of a formerly Italian place. This, however, leads one to consider architecture as a pure design object belonging to its designer and not to the land in which it stands – in this case the history/identity of the Eritreans who live there. Asmara also consists of elements of an urban organism linked to the history of its inhabitants and geographic context.

In recent years, a sense of national belonging as a fundamental public value has been revived in Italy, and not only by the political right. **Harald Bodenschatz** outlines the reception of Italy's colonial past from this point of view. The new nationalism provides the essential context for a critical assessment of the shifting patterns in which Asmara's architecture has been received recently. His essay traces some of the most significant elements that have conditioned the response to, and development of the colonial heritage in Italy. It explains how Italy once implanted its colonial signature, which sustained the city and therefore became a benchmark for its future development. This indicates that these remains are valuable even today. The fascination with Asmara's architecture and urban planning must be weighed against our knowledge of the background of their inception; thus we must examine the contradictory era when fascism, race divisions and avant-garde claims to modernism all appeared simultaneously.

The deep engagement of Italian architects in the vernacular buildings of their country for over sixty years, from the 1910s to the 1970s, ran parallel to years of wrenching transformation from a rural Italy to an industrial urban society, both throughout fascism and the boom of the 1950s. Colonialising impulses under the fascist government prompted Italian architects to work beyond their national borders, where they discovered and appropriated the vernacular traditions of foreign countries. **Michelangelo Sabatino** shows how, through the multiple meanings that could be assigned to it (Italian, authentic, peasant, local, etc.), the vernacular helped Italian Modernist architects to do battle with academicism, both engage in and resist fascism, negotiate the transition to post-war democracy, and more generally address the very specific conditions in Italy at that time.

In their contribution **Peter Volgger** and **Stefan Graf** investigate the spatial and morphological logic of colonial Asmara's urban planning, using the concept of the palimpsest to bring to light the multiple layers of colonial history and investigate the layered construct of this urban morphology. The authors take up a number of concepts briefly touched upon in Filip de Boeck's *Tales of the Tangible City of Kinshasa*, focusing on several structuring urban elements that can be discerned in the palimpsestuous urban fabric of the city and unravelling the way they have structured the city's development and fabric over time. Yet, looking more closely, one can easily find different signs of their permanence in contemporary Asmara since most of its urban structure and built environment are uncannily close to the image the Italians left behind.

The contribution includes the analysis of a large series of figure ground plans representing urban planning decisions in different periods. The excavation of these layers reveals a military city, an ethnic city and a hedonistic city. Colonial cities are often thought to be the products of the singular visions and needs of the colonial regimes that founded them. Asmara was envisioned, then built jointly by colonial rulers, and mercantile and industrial elites, to serve their various interests; it was divided up according to these interests. At the same time, we still do not really know how colonial cities came into being and operated beyond a pure history of their buildings.

Belula Tecle Misghina's essay is based on her doctoral thesis. Her investigation is important in that it puts in order various documents, both known and unpublished, in order to sketch a chronology of Asmara. The essay ends with Mezzèdimi's master plan for the city. Urban structures and architecture can positively influence the sustainability of cities despite the colonial and political circumstances in which they were conceived, and Asmara is proof of this. It is a successful example of a liveable city that did not decline at the end of Italian colonialism. Indeed it has continued to play an important part in shaping local history (home to socio-political debates, as well as demonstrations for the rights of its citizens and the fate of Eritrea as a unified nation). This essay briefly outlines the growth of the city and its development from 1941 until the early years of the twenty-first century. In some cases this urban growth was shaped by major planning studies (Arturo Mezzèdimi's master plan in the 1970s and the study *Asmara Infrastructure Development Study* in early 2005).

Eritrea, and so its capital Asmara, did not gain independence immediately after the end of Italian colonialism. A period of several consecutive governments and administrations (British trusteeship administration, government federated with Ethiopia, the imperial regime of Ethiopia and the Derg regime) ensued – until independence in 1991. During this period Asmara and Eritrea pursued their own political, social and economic agendas. It is therefore difficult to easily access architectural and city planning information; however, an outline of the city's development could be sketched by using indirect sources.

Between 1940 and 1974 Arturo Mezzèdimi designed and built more than 1,600 buildings in Ethiopia. His work, which covers an incredible variety of styles and types of buildings, has been totally forgotten in the official history of architecture, although it was deeply appreciated by Hailé Selassié, quickly embodying the pan-African dream of the Ethiopian Emperor; the site work of the new Africa Hall was completed within eighteen months, between 1959 and 1961. **Benno Albrecht, Filippo de Dominicis** and **Jacopo Galli** present this architect's work. Until 1974, when the Marxist revolution tried to wipe away the whole legacy of a millenary Empire, Mezzèdimi shaped the appearance of the Ethiopian capital, Addis Ababa, making it the most prestigious hub of Africa. His overall Modernist ambition, well represented by the countless works spread throughout the Empire, was also mentioned by Alberto Sartoris in his masterpiece about Functionalist Architecture.

Sean Anderson's essay attempts to read Asmara from its edges. Immediately prior to and following the creation of the Italian Empire, the substantial increase in the number of colonists throughout the overseas territories dramatically affected the organisation of urban and domestic spaces. Commencing in 1936 within the bounded areas that had been reserved specifically for the Eritrean or regional populace, the extra-territorial zones of Via Tevere in the northeast quadrant of Asmara are also spaces in which the telling of a modern history seemingly slows down, where photographic images are not as plentiful, and the boundaries that demarcate the binaries of colonial power are understood but not relayed. But this is not to say that the blurring of such limits within Asmara did not previously exist. Rather, these transactional sites allow for the interrogation of a homologous interior that enfolded citizenry while also reflecting the sanctioned violence for imperialised metropolitan spatial codes.

Günter Wett's series of photographs explores Asmara's theatres and cinemas. Modernisation and urbanisation of the country were associated with the construction of cinema and theatre houses in centres such as Asmara. The first theatre — Teatro Asmara — was constructed by the Italians immediately after World War I in 1918. Throughout the 1920s and 1930s the construction of a number of other cinemas in Asmara continued and by the 1930s major towns (Keren, Dekemhare and Akordat) in the whole country had cinemas or film houses. Owing to the segregation policy introduced by the fascist state, most of the urban zones that contained movie theatres were reserved for Europeans.

MINISTRY OF

ASMARA AND ROME
Architecture and Urbanism of the Fascist Italian Empire and their Reception[1]

Harald Bodenschatz

Not many visitors to Rome accidentally stray to the northern part of the city. The Foro Italico, a peculiar urban quarter, which most German travel guides do not even mention, is located in this part of the city. Those who stumble upon it discover a wonderful urban complex, which has, in some places, been significantly damaged by recent developments. The Foro Italico, a masterpiece by Italian architect Enrico Del Debbio, fits perfectly between the Tiber River and Monte Mario. Never heard of it? At best, a visitor might read in his travel guide that the Foro Italico was the site of the Olympic Games 1960 or that it was once called Foro Mussolini and was built as a sports city for the Fascist Italian youth. Looking around more closely, he will become irritated or even unsettled when he sees an obelisk with an engraving *Mussolini Dux* and a number of large marble blocks that commemorate historical events – but which events and how they are commemorated! On the central square, he will see mosaics similar to those of Ancient Rome – but what messages they display! These mosaics have obviously been restored in post-war years. The name of the central square sounds harmless today. However, on an old plan, the square is labelled Piazzale dell'Impero. What does all this mean? What might be the connection of all this to Asmara?

Eighty Years Ago: Proclaiming the Fascist Empire

May 9, 1936 was a memorable day, not only in Italian history, but also in European and African history. On this day, Italian dictator Benito Mussolini proclaimed a new Fascist empire in a speech from the balcony of his office in the Palazzo Venezia on Piazza Venezia, located in the centre of Rome.

The former Casa del Fascio and today's Ministry of Education in Asmara
Source: K. Paulweber 2013

Foro Italico, previously called Foro Mussolini, the former Piazzale dell'Impero with mosaics in the Ancient Roman style – original (left) and restored (right)
Source: H. Bodenschatz 2009

The reason and condition for this proclamation was the victorious end of the war in Ethiopia. Mussolini had announced the victory a few days prior, also from the balcony of Palazzo Venezia. Just before the dictator's speech on May 9, 1936, the Grand Council of Fascism, the dictatorship's main institution, named Mussolini the Founder of the Empire. May 9th became a Fascist holiday.

At this time, hardly anyone knew or was interested in the circumstances that had facilitated a victory in Ethiopia. Marshal Badoglio had used poison gases, illegal according to international law, against the Ethiopian opposition. Mussolini ordered the use of poison gases on March 29, 1936 in a telegram to Pietro Badoglio, after the Ethiopian resistance turned out to be stronger than expected. Up until then, the Second Italo-Ethiopian War was the bloodiest of Italy's already very brutal colonial wars. It is estimated that the war of seven months claimed 150,000 Ethiopian lives. Between 80,000 and 230,000 people died in the guerrilla warfare that followed. The war also claimed the lives of approximately 25,000 Italian soldiers.[2]

May 9, 1936 not only changed Italy. It changed the political map of the world. After the League of Nations' condemnation of Italy, this date prompted closer ties between Fascist Italy and National Socialist Germany and strengthened Mussolini's ambitions in the Mediterranean. This resulted in Italy's increased support of Franco during the Spanish Civil War. After the proclamation of the empire, no architect – regardless whether Modernist or traditional – could design as before. Italy's new imperial power now had to be presented to the nation and internationally. In the competition among Europe's three main dictatorships, the demonstration of superiority – with spectacular architecture, especially comprehensive, nearly neo-baroque urban restructuring plans – became increasingly important. The aim was to rebuild the recently conquered and established Fascist empire according to master plans – especially the newly constituted Italian East Africa (*Africa Orientale Italiana* – AOI), which included Eritrea, Italian Somalia and Ethiopia.

Asmara: The Logistic Base of the New Empire

Ever since the turn of the century, before Mussolini gained power, Asmara expanded step-by-step as the central foothold of Italian power in East Africa.[3] Asmara first gained significant importance, however, as a bridgehead in preparation for the invasion of Ethiopia. Later, it was crucial for the appropriation of conquered land. Most of the Italian buildings were constructed between 1934 and 1940. It is no secret that the most impressive architecture of Asmara belongs to the logistic base, which orchestrated the conquest and seizure of Ethiopia by Italian aggressors. An Italian travel guide from 1938 describes Asmara as a supplies centre during the Italo-Ethiopian War 1935/36 and emphasises the racist double nature of the city: the "Italian city, rich with remarkable buildings" on one hand and the "city of the local people" on the other.[4] A master plan was to be developed for Asmara in order to control the immense growth of the city. Vittorio Cafiero completed the plan in 1937. It features a traditional urban order with regular streets and squares, similar to those of the existing city. Asmara featured a combination of Modernist architecture and traditional urbanism, which was not uncommon at the time.[5] This apparent contradiction effectively increased the attractiveness of the city. However, the planned expansion of Asmara was never finished, since the Italian rulers had to retreat from Asmara by 1941.

Rome: The Centre of the New Empire

Following the proclamation of the Fascist empire, architecture and urbanism in the capital had to be redefined in a new, "magnificent" way.[6] Two sites played a key role: Foro Mussolini, the sports city in the north and *Esposizione Universale di Roma*, the grounds of the World Fair in the south. The two sites were to be connected by an enormous North-South axis: the Via Imperiale. The already existing Via dell'Impero, today's Via dei Fori Imperiali, was to become the core of the Via Imperiale. The Foro dell'Impero Fascista, the location of Mussolini's government offices – today's Piazza Venezia with the Palazzo Venezia – was the central node of this axis. Empire everywhere!

Casa
24

The Foro Mussolini in northern Rome had already been constructed as a sports city in 1928, on commission of the *Opera Nazionale Balilla*, the youth organisation of the Fascist Party. Enrico Del Debbio, one of the most influential architects of Fascist Italy, was responsible for planning the complex. After the proclamation of the new empire, the sports city was propagandistically laden according to plans by Luigi Moretti, who is still highly celebrated today. The new imperial orientation concerned mainly the central square, the Piazzale dell'Impero – the Empire Square. Moretti created the square, which is 280 m in length, in 1937. Since 1932, an obelisk honouring Mussolini has stood in the southern part of the city, near the Tiber River. Additional marble blocks were erected and mosaics added. The mosaics depicted the Fascist promise and portrayed the actions and development stages of Fascist Italy, including the invasion of Addis Ababa and the establishment of the Empire on May 9, 1936. The parole *Duce a noi* is featured in endless repetition, alternating with lictor axes. The dictator's name appears a total of 264 times on the square. The trapezoid-shaped square constituted the most elaborate place of cult of the now imperial Fascist regime in Rome.

The last major urbanism project of Italian Fascism was realised on the grounds of the World Fair in southern Rome. It was called Project E 42 and is known today as EUR. On June 25, 1936, forty-five days after the proclamation of the new empire, Italy was selected by the *Bureau International des Expositions* (International Exhibitions Bureau) to host the World Fair in 1941. The application had been submitted in November of 1935. The unanimous decision to award the exhibition to Italy, made by the international exhibition office, occurred before the League of Nations lifted sanctions imposed in response to the invasion of Ethiopia.

The exhibition – which was soon postponed to 1942 – aimed to celebrate the twentieth anniversary of the Fascist Revolution and the fifth anniversary of the proclamation of the empire. Furthermore, the power of Fascist Italy was to be presented to the world. On December 13, 1937, Marcello Piacentini took over the overall urbanism direction of the project. In March of 1938, his new plan was complete. The main building of the exhibition grounds was the Palazzo della Civiltà Italiana, the Palace of Italian Culture. The reinforced concrete building's resemblance to the ancient Coliseum resulted in its popular name *colosseo quadrato*. The large building dominating the exhibition grounds features an inscription that pays homage to the Italian people: "A people of poets and artists, heroes and holy men, thinkers and scientists, seafarers and emigrants." Most of the words of the inscription, which is entirely in capital letters, were first spoken by Mussolini in a speech on October 2, 1935.[7] At that time, the dictator reacted to the sanctions of the League of Nations after the invasion of Ethiopia. The construction of the 68 m tall palace began in

The Casa degli Italiani in Asmara – today a restaurant and cultural centre – still shows fascist symbols
Source: K.Paulweber 2013

Central Square (Piazza Imperiale) of the district of the (planned) 1942 World Fair (*Esposizione Universale di Roma* – EUR) with museum buildings and an obelisk honouring Guglielmo Marconi, Rome
Source: H. Bodenschatz 2009

1928 and ended in 1940. The building encompassed six floors with nine arches each – corresponding to the number of letters of Benito (6) Mussolini (9). Construction plans for the World Fair had to be downsized because of the war. They ceased entirely in early 1943. Although only a few buildings had been completed by then, thirty-eight of forty were already in progress.

War, Silence and Enthusiasm

On June 10, 1940, after lengthy hesitation, Italy declared war on France and England. In September of 1940, Mussolini ordered the invasion of Egypt. The extremely brutal war in the Balkans, which began on October 28, 1940, resulted in catastrophe and revealed the military limitations of Fascist Italy. On May 20, 1941, Italy was forced to retreat from Ethiopia. The empire collapsed five years later. Even Asmara had to be abandoned. The regime's crisis intensified after the invasion of the Soviet Union on June 22, 1941, which Italy participated in, and the defeats on the African continent. The situation became increasingly critical after Allied Forces landed in Sicily on July 10, 1943. On July 19, 1943, Rome was bombed. On July 25, 1943, Mussolini was arrested on order of the King and the regime collapsed.

There was no real debate about the urbanism of Fascist Italy after the end of World War II. Post-war research, publications and exhibitions ignored the issue. It would take several decades, especially until a major exhibition on the 1930s, in Milan, in 1982, until the dam would break. A new wave of research, but also new enthusiasm about the architectural and urbanism products of the Mussolini era emerged. Since then, countless exhibitions and books have celebrated the products of the Mussolini era using pleasant terminology, such as *Metafisica, Futurismo, Razionalismo, Mediterraneità*.

Today, enthusiasm regarding the EUR exhibition grounds, the sports city Foro Mussolini and Asmara, the Eritrean capital, is almost boundless. Whether or not these sites feature architecture or are works of art is not called into question, not only in Italy. The world exhibition grounds are presented as an artwork, the Foro Mussolini as a model of landscape-oriented urbanism, Asmara as the wonderful capital of African modernism. However, memories of the socio-political context of this art, such as of the invasion of Ethiopia and support of General Franco during the Spanish civil war, are often vague.

Asmara: Ideal Modernist City?

"Asmara – Africa's secret capital of modern architecture" – in 2006, the Deutsches Architekturzentrum (German Architecture Centre) coined this message for an exhibition featuring photography by Edward Denison.[8] The exhibition was co-curated by the Bauhaus Dessau Foundation. *Baunetz* swarmed: "Piccola Roma in the desert: An ideal Modernist city is rediscovered". "We see a breathtaking city with a Modernist layout [the city's layout is by no means Modernist], designed by talented young Italian architects, whose style shimmers between typical Italian *Razionalismo*, Art Déco, somewhat neo-baroque and even classical modernism. That which fascinates so gruesomely in the motherland is a sensation of global proportions here."[9] Asmara, according to the Deutsches Architekturzentrum,[10] boasts the most historic Modernist architecture worldwide – more so even than Miami Beach, Napier and Tel Aviv!

The joy opposite this "mysterious, slightly crumbling ideal city of modernism" receded after a few sentences. Asmara was, without a doubt, a colonial city of the Fascist Italian empire. The city played a significant part in the invasion of Ethiopia. A contradictory time, as some call it? The book accompanying the exhibition clearly refers to Asmara as the "*città più progressista del continente*", Africa's most progressive city![11] Who, however, was able to stay in the hotels pictured and who could watch films in the Cinema Impero (one notices the name)? Who was able to fill his car at the winged service station and who could live in the many houses?

If this wasn't enough: In the exhibition, Asmara appeared as an echo of the functional city of the International Congresses of Modern Architecture (CIAM)[12]

Poster for the exhibition *Asmara. Afrikas heimliche Hauptstadt der Moderne* (Asmara. Africa's Secret Capital of Modernist Architecture) in the Pasinger Fabrik (Munich) from July 5 to August 19, 2012. The poster depicts the Cinema Impero.
Source: H. Bodenschatz 2012

and Athens Charter. But can we even speak of Modernist urbanism in Asmara? Not in the least! It could easily be recognised that Eritrea's capital is by no means a functional city such as defined by Le Corbusier. Asmara's often Modernist architecture was built on the foundations of a traditional urban layout.

When the exhibition was shown in Munich six years later, those responsible had the chance to respond to the few critical comments.[13] However, their enthusiasm had obviously not been tarnished. The following description appeared on the website of the exhibition space, the Pasinger Fabrik: "A unique Modernist architecture ensemble developed as a result of Italian colonisation, mainly in the 1920s and 1930s. A downright building boom caused Asmara to develop from a provincial city into one of the most vibrant cities on the African continent within a short period of time. [...] In the metropolitan area, all style directions of classic modernism can be found in unique cohesion, which is a global phenomenon."[14]

The wide range of myths and associations implied by the exhibition demonstrated the lack of reflection regarding Fascist Italian architecture and urbanism, not only within Germany. The goal of the exhibition, officially, was to support the 2005 application for Asmara to be recognised as a UNESCO World Heritage site. The purpose of this application is not to be questioned here. However, it is important to pose the questions of which cultural arguments should be used to support such an application and how people should be informed about this time period. It is also important to ask what such a submission means for the conflict in Eastern Africa. Wouldn't a joint submission of Asmara and Addis Ababa[15] be more appropriate? The fact that this question seems totally strange demonstrates the necessity for further reflection of the relationship between culture and politics.

EUR World Fair Grounds: Twentieth-century Artwork?

Current appreciation for the EUR World Fair grounds is at least equal to the appreciation for Asmara. Today, EUR is a popular, privileged district in the Rome metropolitan area. It is a greened administrative and cultural district featuring expensive residential neighbourhoods. The development agency EUR AG (federal share: 90 per cent, municipal share: 10 per cent) aims to renovate EUR and market it as a unique twentieth-century artwork. It is to be developed further with spectacular new buildings, such as the new convention centre La Nuvola by architect Massimiliano Fuksas.

At the end of the war, most of the buildings in the EUR district remained unfinished. The Olympic Games 1960, awarded to Rome in 1955, were a deciding factor in the completion of the district. Marcello Piacentini was called upon to be the project's leading architect. The large artificial lake was also constructed at this time. The metro line Stazione Termini – EUR was completed in 1955. In that same year, the church SS. Pietro e Paolo was inaugurated. Between 1958-1960, the Palazzo dello Sport was built according to plans by Pier Luigi Nervi and Marcello Piacentini.

Rome's booth at the *Internationale Tourismus Börse* (ITB) Berlin (International Travel Trade Show Berlin) 2012. Not an ancient ruin, but the Palazzo della Civiltà Italiana, the main building of the planned 1942 World Fair (*Esposizione Universale di Roma* – EUR), built between 1938–1943 and restored since 2006, was used to market the booth. A quote by Mussolini can be seen above the prominent archways.
Source: H. Bodenschatz 2012

Glorification of the complex, however, began only in recent years. In 2007, the Rome travel guide of the *Touring Club Italiano* called the EUR district a "grand project, which unites urbanism, architecture and art." Now, the Palazzo della Civiltà Italiana serves as a highly attractive advertising medium. Examples include the title page of *The New Art of Building in Italy*, a real-estate brochure, in 2008, in Miami, and a tourism poster at the *Internationale Tourismus-Börse Berlin* (International Travel Trade Show Berlin), in early 2012, which advertised Rome's booth. The restoration of the Palazzo della Civiltà Italiana was the most important project in the EUR district since 2006. In 1999, the announcement was made that the building was to be used as Museo Nazionale dell'Audiovisivo and complemented by the exhibition *Made in Italy*. Between 2006–2011, the Ministry of Cultural Heritage and EUR AG laboriously restored the building as a "monument of particular cultural value". As a result, the inscription featuring the words of Mussolini has been shining again for a number of years.

Drastic spending cuts to Italy's state budget in 2002 led to the disappearance of financing for the planned exhibition and museum. It became known, in the summer 2013, that the building was to be leased to a private company, the French group LVMH Louis Vuitton, Moët Hennessy. Since 1999, LVMH had gradually taken over the formerly Italian Fendi label. Beginning in 2015, LVMH would market the label from the Palazzo della Civiltà Italiana. Outrageous? Yes, for parts of the Italian public. The reasoning behind the outrage is interesting. On July 18, 2013, the newspaper *Il Giornale* wrote: "The French take over the Palazzo della Civiltà Italiana in Rome, a centrepiece of Italy's cultural heritage." The newspaper also wrote that Italy was giving away one of its "jewels" and "today, the doors close to the Italians."[16] Meanwhile, the building, "one of the world's most beautiful palaces",[17] has been sold to the French group.

Mussolini Dux: Cultural Heritage?

What about the sports city Foro Mussolini? It was renamed Foro Italico in the 1950s and expanded for the Olympic Games. The regime's marble blocks on the Piazzale dell'Impero, which was renamed Piazzale and Viale del Foro Italico, were not removed. Rather, additional marble blocks now inform of the regime's collapse in 1943, the referendum to abolish the monarchy and the establishment of the Italian Republic in 1946. The continuing existence of such a place of cult is surely unparalleled, even in comparison with central places of cult of other dictatorships. In 2006/2007, a major exhibition about Enrico del Debbio,[18] one of the most important architects behind the Foro Mussolini, acknowledged the urban complex. However, in April 2015, a debate about the Fascist features of the sports city developed. The president of the Italian parliament, Laura Boldrini, dared to demand the removal of the inscription *Mussolini Dux* from the obelisk that stands on the central square. The right wing of media and politics immediately drew a comparison to the Taliban and ISIS – cultural desecration! There was opposition even from within Boldrini's own *Partito Democratico*. According to the opposition, the obelisk and its inscriptions were a historical testimony and represent no dangerous agenda.[19]

Remembrance in Italian?

One thing is obvious: Italy handles remembrance much different than Germany. In Germany, almost every urbanism project of the National Socialist era is coded per se as negative. It is inseparably linked to its violent creators. In Italy, Mussolini-era urbanism and architecture are isolated as works of art – with almost fundamentalist consistency – from the conditions under which they were built. This goes so far that even the content communicated by these products – including Fascist propaganda – can be perceived as an artwork. In Italy, there are no state-run documentation centres, such as in Munich or Nuremburg.[20] Not only the case of Asmara, therefore, raises a fundamental question: Should a dictatorship's architecture and urbanism ever be isolated from its political context? Another question that must be posed: Must architecture and urbanism – regardless of their form – be negatively valued because of their political context? I would say no to both questions. It is sensible, even necessary, to differentiate analytically between the built products and production conditions of urbanism, but to neither isolate nor link them. However, they must always both be examined – through a pair of glasses with both art history and social science lenses. Only then can we comprehend why the built products could be realised, why they were designed a certain way and why they might still be useful and attractive today.

Notes

1 The article is based on research, publications and lectures realised by the author since 2007. Cf. Harald Bodenschatz, "Metafisica, Futurismo, Razionalismo, Mediterraneità ... Die Architektur des italienischen Faschismus und ihre unkritische Rezeption", *Bauwelt* 06/2007, pp. 8-10; Harald Bodenschatz (ed.), *Städtebau für Mussolini. Auf der Suche nach der neuen Stadt im faschistischen Italien*. Berlin: DOM publishers, 2011; Harald Bodenschatz, *Städtebau für Mussolini. Auf dem Weg zu einem neuen Rom*. Berlin: DOM publishers, 2013; Harald Bodenschatz, "Schwieriges Erbe – in Nürnberg und Rom", *Merkur. Deutsche Zeitschrift für europäisches Denken*, April 2015, pp. 69-78.

2 For information on the invasion of Ethiopia cf. Aram Mattioli, *Experimentierfeld der Gewalt. Der Abessinienkrieg und seine internationale Bedeutung 1935–1941*. Zürich: Orell Füssli Verlag, 2005.

3 Cf. on Italian urbanism in Eritrea Uwe Altrock in Harald Bodenschatz, (ed.): *Städtebau für Mussolini. Auf der Suche nach der neuen Stadt im faschistischen Italien*. Berlin: DOM publishers, 2013, pp. 371-377.

4 *Consociazione Turistica Italiana: Guida dell'Africa Orientale Italiana*. Milan, 1938, p. 199.

5 One famous example of this combination of style is the city of Sabaudia, located southeast of Rome, which was inaugurated in 1934.

6 On urbanism in Rome since the mid-1930s cf. Harald Bodenschatz, *Städtebau für Mussolini. Auf dem Weg zu einem neuen Rom*. Berlin: DOM publishers, 2013, pp. 141-197.

7 Benito Mussolini, Opera Omnia. Ed. Edoardo e Duilio Susmel. Band XXVII. Florence: La Fenice, 1959, pp. 158-160.

8 The exhibition was later shown in the German Museum of Architecture in Frankfurt, in Kassel, Stuttgart and Munich. It was presented again at the World Architects Congress 2008 in Turin as well as in Tel Aviv, London, Bologna and Graz, in Egypt, Nigeria and Togo. An exhibition book was published: Jochen Visscher, (ed.)/Stefan Boness, (Photography): *Asmara. The Frozen City*. Berlin: Jovis, 2006.

9 www.baunetz.de/baunetzwoche/baunetzwoche_ausgabe_90424.html [27.06.2015].

10 Cf. http://www.asmara-architecture.com/BegleitProgramm2007/DAZ_Presseinfo.pdf [27.06.2015].

11 Cf. Jochen Visscher, (ed.)/Stefan Boness, (Photography): *Asmara. The Frozen City*. Berlin: Jovis, 2006, pp. 10-11.

12 The functional city was the topic of the fourth CIAM congress.

13 Cf. for example Harald Bodenschatz, "Metafisica, Futurismo, Razionalismo, Mediterraneità ... Die Architektur des italienischen Faschismus und ihre unkritische Rezeption", *Bauwelt* 06/2007, pp. 8-10.

14 http://pasinger-fabrik.com/en/ausstellungen/archiv/detailansicht-archiv-programm-pasinger-fabrik/cal/event/detail/2012/07/05/asmara_afrikas_heimliche_hauptstadt_der_moderne/view-list|page_id-67|offset-1.html [27.06.2015].

15 For more on Italian building heritage in Addis Ababa, cf. Fasil Giorghis/Denis Gérard, Addis Ababa 1886–1941. *The City & Its Architectural Heritage. La Ville & son Patrimoine architectural*. Addis Ababa: Shama Books, 2007.

16 http://blog.ilgiornale.it/franza/2013/07/18/i-francesi-si-prendono-il-per centE2per cent80per cent9Cpalazzo-della-civilta-italianaper centE2per cent80per cent9D-a-roma-cuore-dei-beni-culturali-italiani/ [27.06.2015]. In fact, the ground floor will probably be open to the public.

17 According to a Fendi representative, cited from *La Repubblica*, 18.07.2013.

18 Maria Luisa Neri, Enrico Del Debbio. Exhibition catalogue. Milan: Idea Books, 2006.

19 Cf. among others: *La Repubblica* and *Corriere della Sera*. 17.04.2015

20 Since July 21, 2014, there is a small documentation centre in South Tyrol under the Bolzano Victory Monument, which itself remains controversial. Cf. *Autonome Provinz Bozen Südtirol* (21.07.2014): *Dokuzentrum unter Siegesdenkmal eröffnet: Historisierung und Normalisierung* [03.07.2015]; *Südtirol News* (19.03.2015): *FAI empfiehlt Siegesdenkmal als Ausflugsziel* [03.07.2015].

TWENTIETH-CENTURY ARCHITECTURE AND THE VERNACULAR TRADITION IN ITALY

Michelangelo Sabatino

The deep engagement of Italian architects with the vernacular buildings of their country for over sixty years, from the 1910s to the 1970s, parallels years of radical transformation in Italy, from a rural to an industrial urban society, through both fascism and the boom of the 1950s.[1] Colonial ambitions under fascism prompted Italian architects to work beyond national borders and to adapt approaches to respond to the conditions of the African context. By assigning multiple meanings (Italian, authentic, peasant, local, etc.), the vernacular helped Italian Modernist architects working in Italy and in some instances working in the colonies to battle academicism, to both engage and resist fascism, to negotiate the transition to post-war democracy, and more in general to address the very specific conditions of Italy at that time. Thus the vernacular tradition is key source of mediation between architecture and society, for Italy in those years.

Italian Modernist architecture emerged in a cultural context characterised by distinct and competing regional traditions unified primarily by a deep-seated agricultural heritage that had since antiquity coexisted with the urbane aspirations of city dwellers. Although the key events and issues that shaped Italy's modernity are by now well known, little attention has been given to looking at how the rediscovery and appropriation of ordinary things – anonymous preindustrial vernacular buildings and objects – informed and transformed the practice and discourse of architecture from the 1910s well into the 1970s. The robust volumes, basic plans, unadorned façades, and modest local materials of extant vernacular buildings located in hamlets, villages, and hill towns throughout the Italian peninsula provided formal, practical, and poetic inspiration for Modernist architects during a period of sixty years and spanning two major world wars.

Despite shifting social, political, and economic contexts and differing points of view, the influence that vernacular buildings exerted on Modernist architects cannot be submitted to such neat time frames. Over the *longue durée*, from the 1910s through the two world wars and the post-war period

A rustic villa in the villa quarter in Asmara
Source: S.Graf 2015

of reconstruction, and even into the 1970s, it seems only logical to look at this phenomenon as one that gained momentum in Italy but also as an international phenomenon. In Italy, the vernacular tradition informed Modernist design practice, inspired critical debates and the production of exhibitions and publications, and also spurred legislation pertaining to the preservation of traditional buildings and sites.

For the historian writing in English about a phenomenon of appropriation of the vernacular tradition that unfolded in specific political and aesthetic contexts of Italy, and whose manifestations were expressed equally specifically in Italian, use of a blanket term like vernacular in another language threatens to blur or even obliterate vital nuances that distinguish highly diverse practices and intentions.[2] Cultural historian Lucien Febvre's dictum "it is never a waste of time to study the history of a word" has relevance for historians exploring the impact of vernacular buildings on Modernist architecture and theory in Italy and beyond.[3] Perhaps nowhere so much as in the Italian language is the definition of what in English is called vernacular architecture so elusive. Some of the expressions employed over a sixty-year span are: *fabbricati etnografici* (ethnographic buildings), *architettura minore* (minor architecture), *architettura naturale* (natural architecture), *architettura rurale* (rural architecture), *architettura rustica* (rustic architecture), *architettura spontanea* (spontaneous architecture), *arte paesana* (peasant art), *arte popolare* (popular or folk art), and *arte rustica* (rustic art). Depending on the perspective of the writer or speaker, the same category could be assigned different value. For example, negative attributes were ascribed by Rationalist architects during the 1930s to the Italianised term folklore, but not to *architettura rurale*. These differences are especially interesting within the context of the Anglophone world, where folklore, folk art, and folk architecture are generally considered to be synonymous with the vernacular tradition. In the Italian context expressions like *architettura rurale* referred to architecture, *arte paesana* to arts and crafts, and *tradizioni popolari* referred to folklore in the English sense. One is hard-pressed to invoke debates of this period in Italy which generated a variety of charged terms reflecting political and cultural stances when using the English term vernacular, borrowed from linguistics where it refers to dialect has specific associations with the uninflected notion of common, familiar, or ordinary.

More importantly, in almost all cases, the appropriation of the vernacular tradition by professionally trained architects helped negotiate class division that surfaced in architectural history up until then between style-driven historicist or classical and vernacular buildings. The etymology of the word vernacular is rooted in class distinctions: the Latin *verna* refers to the status of slave. In the romance languages, various words for peasant allude to the pastoral context, stemming from the Latin root *pagus*, meaning *village*. The plurality of expressions coined by practising architects, critics, and historians to describe the phenomenon of *vernacular architecture* implies the multifarious readings it received as well as the disparate approaches of designers. If the architect Giuseppe Pagano referred to vernacular buildings as "*architettura rurale*," (1936) he spoke of his own architecture as Rationalist. If Giancarlo De Carlo employed the term *architettura spontanea* (1951) to refer to vernacular buildings and demonstrated in the role that participation by the end-user could transform his work, he spoke of it in terms of architecture.

Under fascism, the vernacular tradition was appropriated by second-generation Futurists and Rationalists who were reacting against historicism and sterile Classicism imposed by party officials known as *gerarchi* and epitomised by state-sponsored projects in Rome like the *Esposizione Universale Rome* (EUR, 1935–1943). Yet with less then progressive intentions, the regime employed mimetic, neo-vernacular to promote anti-urban values through the design and realisation of the fascist New Towns. It was only thanks to a cluster of Rationalist architects who were critical with the fascist regime's interference with the arts and architecture and deployed the vernacular tradition to help undermine anti-urban and anti-Modernist attitudes. Whereas second-generation Futurists infused mechanisation with the primitive expressivity of vernacular buildings and landscapes, Rationalists appropriated extant vernacular buildings as a source of *Mediterraneità* or *Mediterranean-ness* to broaden the parameters of what constituted *Italianità* or *Italian-ness* according to the fascist regime. During the 1950s, neo-realist architects adopted elements of extant vernacular buildings to counteract the alienation and displacement they imagined to be experienced by peasant farmers moving en masse from rural and village dwellings into new urban housing projects, and likewise patterned the design of public spaces on the experience of Italian hill towns. In both cases, memory was engaged, but nostalgia was avoided. Rationalist architects who aspired to *Mediterraneità* in the 1930s admired the whitewashed surfaces and serially repeated forms of vernacular buildings typical of the seaside towns along the Mediterranean coast of Italy, Spain, and Greece, their counterparts of the 1950s were inspired by the hill towns of central Italy, where exposed brick and pitched roofs clad with terracotta tiles evoked the rugged vitality of rural environments from whence the new working-class proletariat came. In the 1960s and 1970s, Italy's vernacular heritage provided neo-Rationalists with a tool to sidestep naïve functionalism.

Writing in the late 1960s, architect and theorist Vittorio Gregotti (1927–) was one of the first to acknowledge continuity in the interest for the vernacular tradition between the 1930s and the post-war era:

Interest in spontaneous architecture had long existed in Italy. Since Giuseppe Pagano's and Guarniero Daniel's book Architettura Rurale Italiana (1936), this architecture had been considered as naturally connected with Rationalist architecture, inasmuch as it related the natural and functional styles of building. The ninth Triennale (1951) devoted substantial research to spontaneous architecture and dedicated a remarkable exhibition to it. Its extraordinary formal repertory had for many years a direct influence on the attempt of Italian architecture to make contact with the working class.[4]

Italian architects who worked under fascist patronage but took issue with the regime, and instead of working in the idiom of bombastic Classicism sought to appropriate vernacular sources as a form of resistance were regarded with respect by the Left-leaning architects who identified with the social reform agenda of the regime and served as examples for those who felt they could persuade the regime to adopt a progressive Italian modernism. A case in point is Giuseppe Pagano (1846–1945), who pleaded with fascist officials to embrace the pride in modesty exemplified by those vernacular buildings he and Werner Daniel showcased in the 1936 exhibition *Architettura Rurale Italiana* (Italian Rural Architecture) installed at the Milan *Triennale*. In reaction to the visual and spatial hysteria of the *Mostra della Rivoluzione Fascista* (Exhibition of the Fascist Revolution) mounted in 1932 in the nineteenth-century *Palazzo delle Esposizioni* at Rome, Pagano and Daniel abandoned the museum in motion approach of Giuseppe Terragni's Sala O, along with the monumentality of Mario Sironi's Sala Q, in order to draw attention to the social and architectural problems of their time. Their straightforward exhibition eschewed visual drama in favour of simplicity and convincingly demonstrated the extent to which vernacular buildings and urban forms suggested vital, functionalist design solutions in contrast to the stale, historicising tendency of official fascist architecture like Marcello Piacentini's scheme for the EUR complex. Although Pagano died as a political prisoner of the regime he once supported, his endorsement of Italy's rural vernacular architecture as a means of tempering the elitism of Classicism was inspirational for architects like Franco Albini (1907–1977) and Giancarlo De Carlo (1919–2005), who perpetuated his passion with their *Architettura spontanea* (Spontaneous Architecture) exhibition in 1951 at the Milan *Triennale*. During the late 1930s, as the novelist Curzio Malaparte built his Casa Malaparte on Capri in collaboration with Rationalist architect Adalberto Libera and stonemason Adolfo Amitrano, Finnish Modernist Alvar Aalto designed and built the Villa Mairea in Noormarkku. Whereas Malaparte embraced the ultra-nationalist ideology of the reactionary milieu of *Il Selvaggio*, his architectural proclivities for bold volumes and sweeping views of the surroundings were essentially Modernist in opposition to the prescriptive attitudes that prevailed under fascism. National Romanticism in Finland, on the other hand, was an invented tradition, experienced as a Democratic phenomenon. While the villas of Aalto and Libera were produced in vastly different political contexts, there was in both cases a dynamic engagement with materiality and forms based on vernacular architecture.

Although the impact of Classicism on Italian Modernism has been studied in depth, the vernacular tradition has not received the same intense scrutiny as a force in the Modernist movement. Just as Classically inspired Modernist buildings had "many souls," to use a felicitous expression of historian Giorgio Ciucci, ranging from the metaphysical Novecento to Rationalism and the stripped monumentality of *Stile Littorio*, the appropriation of vernacular forms generated a number of different expressions.[5] For example, in the act of reassessing Rationalism and *Mediterraneità*, with all of its attendant regional, national, and transnational implications, architects and scholars drew attention to the role played by both Classical and vernacular traditions in shaping Italian modernism during fascism.[6] In their influential overview of Modernist architecture published in 1976, Manfredo Tafuri and Francesco Dal Co claimed:

In the Rationalist position, the concern with preserving a bond with tradition while still achieving a renewal of forms became the occasion for re-proposing Mediterranean myths or the anti-rhetoric of purportedly spontaneous or peasant-style architecture.[7]

To be sure, the use of spontaneous or peasant-style architecture was not limited to the interwar years or to Italy, for that matter. An indication of shifting attitudes toward modern architecture in Europe and North America, coupled with a growing awareness of the role played by the vernacular tradition, surfaced after the war in 1957 with British architect James Stirling's seminal essay *Regionalism and Modern Architecture*.[8] Stirling wrote that "The most visually stimulating chapters of Kidder Smith's recent book Italy builds were not those on Italian Modernism and Italian Renaissance but that on the anonymous architecture of Italy."[9] Stirling drew attention to American critic, George Everard Kidder-Smith's juxtaposition of traditional buildings and urban spaces with examples of Italian Modernist architecture realised between the 1920s to the 1950s. Stirling also wrote an article on Le Corbusier's recently completed chapel of Notre Dame du Haut in Ronchamp.[10] Acknowledging its debt to Mediterranean vernacular architecture, he remarked:

... If folk architecture is to re-vitalise the movement, it will first be necessary to determine what it is that is modern in modern architecture. The scattered openings on the chapel walls may recall de Stijl, but a similar expression

is also commonplace in the farm buildings of Provence. The influence of popular art is also apparent in the priest's house and the hostel buildings.

The discovery of Le Corbusier's Mediterranean-inspired work – from Villa Mandrot to Maisons Jaoul and Ronchamp – led to a gradual loosening of tensions that had arisen between the modernism of the industrialised North and that of the agrarian South.[11] Le Corbusier and Italian Rationalists were part of a strain of Mediterranean Modernists who integrated functionalist agendas with culture through a process of dialogue and hybrid practices. Although the vernacular tradition was associated with the primitive by virtue of its preindustrial building techniques and materials, it also comprised a regional heritage shared by other countries bordering the Mediterranean region, a geographical area that touches three continents – Europe, Asia, and Africa. While the pioneering narratives of the modern movement by figures such as Nikolaus Pevsner acknowledged the role of the northern preindustrial vernacular tradition in the emergence of modernity, most ignored the impact of vernacular and anonymous architecture of the Mediterranean region on Modernists such as Josef Hoffmann in Austria, Le Corbusier in France and José Luis Sert in Spain.[12] Paul Schultze-Naumburg's comparison of a Mediterranean village with the Weissenhof and Schönblick housing estates in *Das Gesicht des deutschen Hauses* (1929), and the racist collage he published in 1941 in the *Bund für Heimatschutz's Schwäbisches Heimatbuch*, in which the Weissenhof housing estate was compared with an *Araberdorf* (Arab village), reveal the resistance to Mediterranean modernism among Northern architects.[13] They also reveal how the vernacular tradition – not unlike Classicism, was appropriated by Modernists and historicist architects. The conflation of modernity and the vernacular tradition raises issues of anonymity and authorship for theorists and practising architects. The notions of *timelessness* and *anonymity* that have adhered to the vernacular tradition conveyed one meaning in the nineteenth century, when provenance and authorship established the value of a work of art or architecture, and another for avant-garde practitioners of the twentieth century, for whom anonymity came to be revered as an antidote to historicism and academicism. Writing in the same year that he abandoned the fascist party, Giuseppe Pagano explained that the design of what was to be his last completed work, a weekend home in Viggiù, near Milan (1942), was motivated by his desire to make something that did "not offend the landscape" and that was truly "*una cosa qualunque* (just an ordinary thing)."[14] Indeed, ordinary things offered Italian architects the possibility to combine modernism with tradition while avoiding banal nostalgia. Some sixty years later, within a context of globalisation and heightened concern over the environment, the tension between the past and present, between approaches that are constructive but do not offend the landscape, is still the most compelling ingredient of the "made it Italy" brand.

Notes

1 This essay draws on the introduction of my book: Michelangelo Sabatino, *Pride in Modesty: Modernist Architecture and the Vernacular Tradition in Italy* (Toronto – Buffalo: The University of Toronto Press, 2010); Italian translation: *Orgoglio della modestia: Architettura moderna italiana e tradizione vernacolare*. Milan: Edizioni Franco Angeli, 2013.

2 Difficulties associated with translation complicate and enrich the story; whereas Benedetto quipped that a translator is a traitor, Walter Benjamin on the other hand declared that: "It stands to reason that kinship does not necessarily involve likeness." Walter Benjamin, "The Task of the Translator", in Hannah Arendt (ed.), *Walter Benjamin: Illuminations*. New York: Schocken Books, 1968, pp. 69-82.

3 Lucien Febvre, "Civilisation: Evolution of a Word and a Group of Ideas", in Peter Burke (ed.), *A New Kind of History and Other Essays*, trans. K. Folca. New York: Harper and Row, 1973, pp. 220-257.

4 Vittorio Gregotti, *New Directions in Italian Architecture*, trans. Giuseppina Salvadori. New York: George Braziller, 1968, pp. 54-56.

5 See Giorgio Ciucci, "Italian Architecture during the Fascist Period: Classicism between Neoclassicism and Rationalism: The Many Souls of the Classical", *The Harvard Architectural Review*, 6 (1987), pp. 76-87.

6 On the topic of *Mediterraneità* in architecture, see Silvia Danesi, "Aporie dell'architettura italiana in periodo fascista – mediterraneità e purismo", *Il razionalismo e l'architettura in Italia durante il fascismo*, 21-28; Benedetto Gravagnuolo, *Il mito mediterraneo nell'architettura contemporanea*. Naples: Electa, 1994; see also Vojtech Jirat-Wasiutynski (ed.), *Modern Art and the Idea of the Mediterranean*. Toronto and Buffalo: University of Toronto Press, 2007, and Jean-François Lejeune and Michelangelo Sabatino (eds.), *Modern Architecture and the Mediterranean: Vernacular Dialogues and Contested Identities*. London: Routledge, 2009.

7 Manfredo Tafuri and Francesco Dal Co, *Modern Architecture*. New York: Rizzoli, 1976, pp. 259-261.

8 James Stirling, "Regionalism and Modern Architecture", *Architects' Year Book 8* (1957), pp. 62-68, republished Joan Ockman and Edward Eigen (eds.), *Architecture Culture 1943–1968: A Documentary Anthology*. New York: Rizzoli, 1993, pp. 243-248.

9 George Everard Kidder-Smith, *Italy Builds: Its Modern Architecture and Native Inheritance*. New York: Reinhold Corporation, 1955; London: Architectural Press, 1955; and Milan: Edizioni di Comunità, 1955.

10 James Stirling, "Ronchamp: Le Corbusier's Chapel and the Crisis of Rationalism", *The Architectural Review* 119:711 (March 1956), pp. 155-161.

11 Caroline Maniaque Benton, *Le Corbusier and the Maisons Jaoul*. New York: Princeton Architectural Press, 2009.

12 See Julius Posener, "Häring, Mies, and Le Corbusier", *From Schinkel to the Bauhaus: Five Lectures on the Growth of Modern German Architecture*. New York: George Wittenborn, 1972, pp. 33-41.

13 See Richard Pommer, "The Flat Roof: A Modernist Controversy in Germany," *Art Journal* 43:2 (Summer 1983): 158-169; Christian F. Otto and Richard Pommer, *Weissenhof 1927 and the Modern Movement*. Chicago: University of Chicago Press, 1991; and Karin Kirsch, *The Weissenhofsiedlung: Experimental Housing Built for the Deutscher Werkbund*; Stuttgart, 1927 and New York: Rizzoli, 1989.

14 Giuseppe Pagano, "Una casetta in legno", *Domus* 77 (Sept 1942), pp. 375-379.

FIAT

COLONIAL SPECULA
Re-mapping Asmara

Peter Volgger and Stefan Graf

This paper outlines our research about the city of Asmara carried out to clarify the properties of the historically generated structural layers. The concept of the palimpsest has recurrently been used by architects to explain the layered construct of urban morphologies. The text presented here reflects the analyses of a large series of figure ground plans representing essential urban configurations from different periods of urban development of the city of Asmara. The focus is put on the urban layers which have been the outcome of planned developements. Unlike social historians, architectural historians place their emphasis on the physical frame of things and the spatial characteristics of the city.[1] The concealed aspects of the urban palimpsest can easily be investigated in Asmara, as most of the architectural and urban interventions have been preserved quite faithfully. Andreas Huyssen goes one step further, when he claims: "If the city is a palimpsest, its legibility relies as much on visible markers of built space as on images and memories repressed and ruptured by traumatic events".[2] Therefore, we also point to the power relations at play in the production of the urban plans. The creation of, and interaction between, urban layers reflect the characteristics and potentials of different planning strategies of the colonial administration.

The Military City

The aim of the first part of our analysis is to discuss the role played by the military component in the process of Asmara's urbanisation, f.i. the role played by military investments in determining lines of development in the colonial urban planning. Military infrastructures reveal how the criteria of

Fiat Tagliero petrol station
Source: K. Paulweber 2013

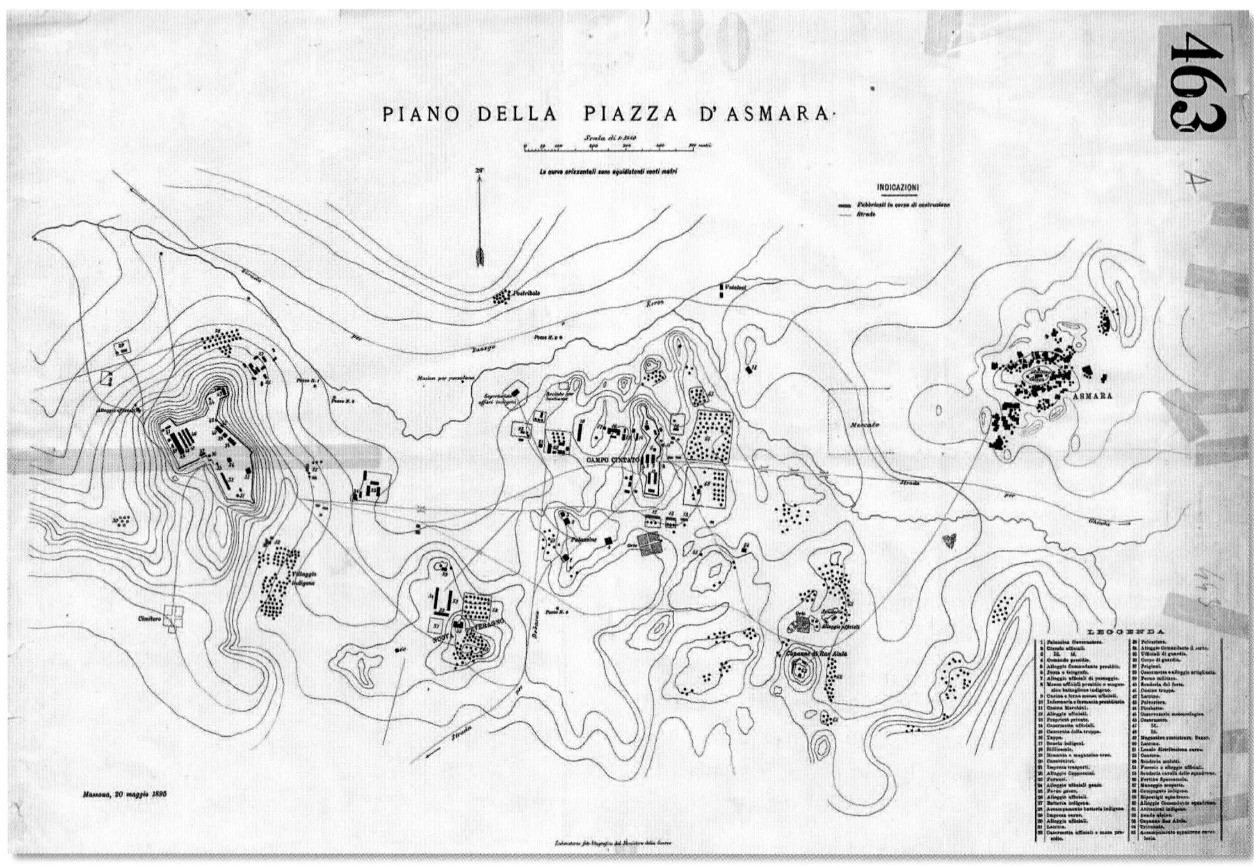

Plan dated 1893/1895, 1:5,540

The Italian colonisation of the high plateau of Asmara began with the fortification by General Baldissera on a simple elevation he called Campo Cintato (1). When he realised the strategically not so advantageous position of the complex, he decided to construct a new fortification to the west on a higher hill. The area could be well monitored from the new Forte Baldissera (2). In the south of Campo Cintato the first villas (*palazzine*, 3) appeared. Shortly after 1890 the new settlement *Nuova Peveragno* (4) was founded between Campo Cintato and Forte Baldissera. Also the hospital is visible in the plan. A red dotted line shows the market; the caravan route is also outlined in red. The round huts of the indigenous are well visible which are naturally agglomerated but already subordinated to a European grid. *Ascari*, Eritrean soldiers fighting in the Italian army, were housed in settlements like these. These camps are to the east of Campo Cintato (5). Around 1900 Asmara seems to be totally occupied by the military. Around Forte Baldissera are located the camps of the local soldiers, around Campo Cintato the Carabinieri and the cavalry. The Alpini are located near the hill of Ras Alula (6), an Eritrean tribal leader, in the south.

Source: ISIAO (*Istituto Italiano per l'Africa e l'Oriente*), figure ground plan by Stefan Graf and Arno Hofer

Military facilities

1893

1 Campo Cintato
2 Forte Baldissera
3 Governor's Palace
4 Nova Peveragno
5 Military camps
6 Ras Alula's hill

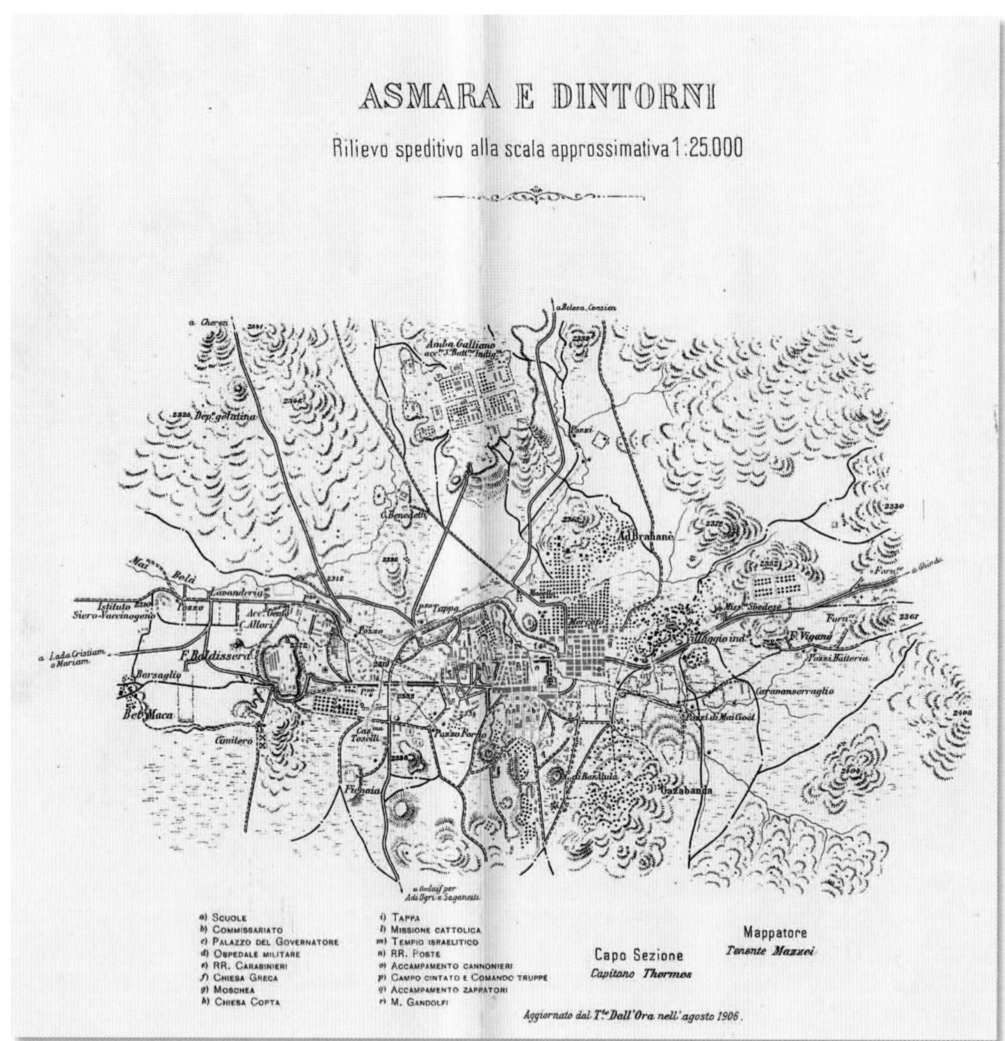

Plan dated 1906, 1:25,000

This plan should improve the level of hygiene in the city, and is restricted to the area of the Italians and the Campo Cintato (1). The city of Asmara came into existence around the Corso del Re (the old caravan route): administrative buildings, schools (4), banks, the post office (5), shops and hotels. The hospital (6) in the east of the city undergoes expansion. One of the reasons for this was that several outbreaks of diseases occurred amongst the Italians as well as the natives, leading to the belief that the natives were the cause for the diseases. The plan shows the grid with the European zone and the market, as well as the already rasterised huts for the natives to the north of the market. The first years in Asmara were marked with the construction of essential infrastructure: wells, aqueducts, a telegraph network, markets (7), caravanserai, post and telegraph buildings, health centres, schools and churches. This plan took the form of four distinct urban quarters and reveals the zoning of the colonial city. The first and most extensive quarter accommodated Europeans only. The second was a mixed quarter centreed on the market for Europeans, other foreigners and Eritreans. The third was the quarter for the indigenous population to the north of the city. The fourth was an outlying area reserved primarily for industry.

Source: ISIAO, figure ground plan by S. Graf and A. Hofer

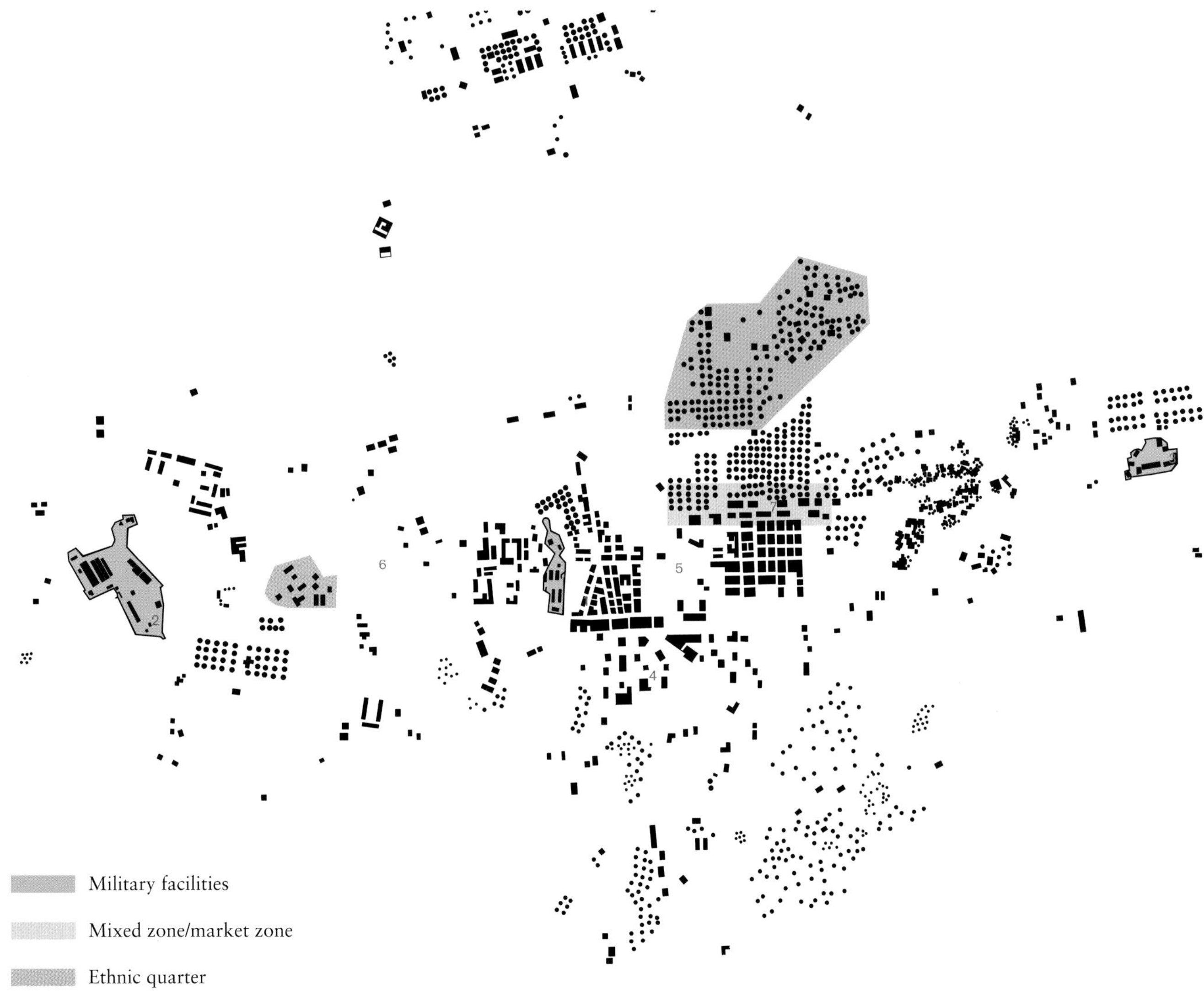

1906

1 Campo Cintato
2 Forte Baldissera
3 Fortino Viganó
4 School
5 Post office
6 Hospital
7 Market

defensibility, rather than economic priorities, had a significant influence on the main patterns of Asmara's early settlements on the Hamasien Plateau.[3] What General Baldisera witnessed when he marched to the highlands were the *agdos* and *hedmos* (traditionally built homes) of the village of Asmara. This place was of military importance. Two fortified areas – the original Forte Baldissera and that of the Biet Mekae – were built immediately after 1890 and small settlements began to appear in the area between.[4] The fortifications were established as a safeguard to the main supply route from the east (Massawa). The Campo Cintato was the seat of the earliest colonial administration. Around the hills, round dwellings for the *Ascari*, Eritrean soldiers, were built, which were intended to evoke traditional Eritrean shepards dwellings.[5] The colonial government considered the first implementation of an urban plan for Asmara because the small town became an important crossroads. Around 1900 Ferdinando Martini, the first civilian Governor, arrived, marking the end of the military administration. Under his guidance a formal town plan was prepared in 1902, mainly focusing on improving public hygiene in the Italian sector, Campo Cintato. After Martini left in 1907 three formal plans were prepared in 1908, 1913 and 1916[6]).

The military was primarly responsible for the planning of infrastructure and thus for the whole colonial landscape. Until the 1930s, Italian policy essentially imposed over the existing Eritrean structures a colonial superstructre in which Eritreans participated primarily as soldiers. Organisation of military space and logistics become key elements for the origination of political and economic life in general. Streets and railways were built which are fundamental for the future urban development.[7] The railway was finished in 1911 and was to retain the mobility of the military forces. Soon it couldn't supply the city anymore and a ropeway was built and connected Asmara across 75 km directly with the port. In comparison with other colonial powers, Italy focused more on streets than on the railway, not least for financial issues.[8] After the conquest of Ethiopia Mussolini pumped enormous amounts of money into the construction of roads in East Africa. No other colonial power had spent more on infrastructure. The infrastructure was considered Roman since ancient Rome had gained its importance through it. Before the campaign against Ethiopia began 50,000 Italian soldiers were garrisoned in Asmara. These were placed in the villa quarters in the south but also in the city centre and in areas which were reserved for the Eritrean population. As a reaction to this development architect Vittorio Cafiero designed his master plan.

In 1938 Vittorio Cafiero came to Asmara to finalise his master plan. He kept the four ethnic zones but destroyed Aba Shaul, the indigenous quarter to the north of the market, and planned a new indigenous quarter far away from the

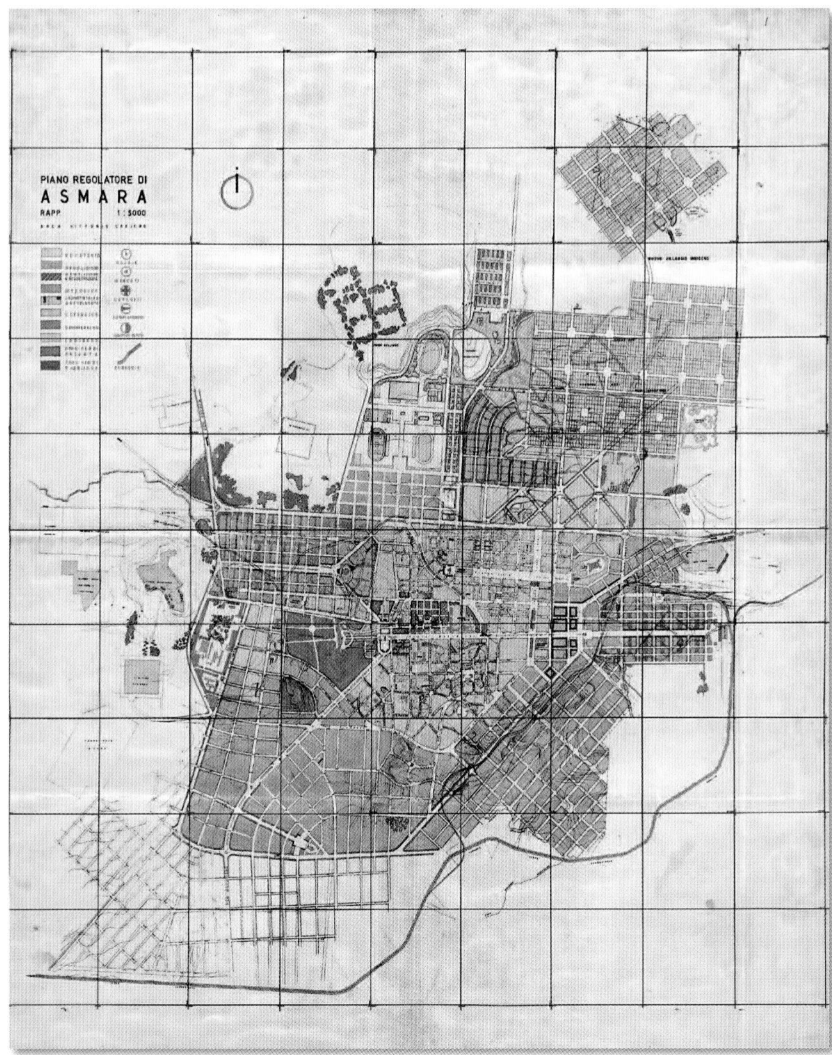

Cafiero's plan from 1938
Source: IsIAO, Rome

centre in the northeast. The Governor refused to evict the natives from their quarters, underlining the loyality Eritreans had always shown toward Italy. Thus Asmara maintained at its core an indigenous zone that contradicted the regime's racial policy and that determined the peculiar social structure that Asmara maintained for a long time after the war.[9] A bigger trade and industrial zone was to act as a buffer zone between Italians and Eritreans. Cafiero's plan provided many broad boulevards which end at important buildings or places. He planned the extension of the Viale Mussolini, which connected the Governor's Palace with the new railway station.[10]

The Ethnic City

In this section we will discuss the nature and extent of the interaction between colonial urban planning and the urban social landscape. During the 1920s and 1930s urbanism was a central technology for implementing the reform of society on the principles of modified production and living circumstances. Referring to Foucault, Paul Rabinow explored how the formation of the colonies had involved a series of new technologies of governance, education, scientific research, forms of industrial production, planning methods and legal experiments which where then actually often brought back to the West.[11] That structure is colonialism in general, but specifically it is the spatial organisation of bodies and built forms during the colonial period. The Italian colonisers organised Asmara in accordance with racial and cultural stereotypes. As a symbolic universe the colonial city was a triumph of hegemony as well as symbolic edifices, as a symbolic order it legitimates the world order it creates. This symbolic order represented in the colonial city was the product of a union between Darwanian theories about racial development and utopian dreams about Italy's national progress. Lefebvre continued the same long Modernist traditions which underpinned the creation of difference in the colonial period, and which is characterised by its conceptualisation of the world within a polarised framework opposing, for example, modernity and tradtion, city and countryside, centre and periphery, culture and nature.[12]

The binary structure of the colonial city was typically organised on a scale from barbaric to civilised, so that everybody could easily see the distinction between European culture and Africa. It is also the same colonial mirror that gives birth to Asmara's two reflecting halves: the Italian *quartiere dei villini* and the *villaggio per gli indigeni*. The native quarter emphasised the inferiority of exotic and primitive races, while the European quarter showed the evident superiority of the industrialised white culture. These impressions were reinforced if the people in the native quarter were housed in structures associated with a barbarian status. For instance, native Eritreans might be thought to live in round *tukuls* (a type which was used by shephards) in order to produce a differing and primitive lifestyle. Separation plays an important part in defining otherness and allows for a critical distance needed for surveillance. Behind the clear message conveyed by the image of dual cities at first sight, however, hide more complicated implications. This reflected not only the colonial endeavour to control the city's growth rate, but also the simple fact that the indigenous quarters mainly functioned as depots of cheap African labour.[13]

In 1914 a new building code was issued to serve as the base for the zoning of successive planning actions. It was based on racial separation and the consequent organisation of the area into four distinct urban quarters. The purpose of the urban planning was to provide a functional urban environment reminiscent of home for the Italians, and also to control the native population, which consistently far outnumbered the Europeans and was forced to live in unplanned settlements. In many colonial cities indigenous areas were consistently separated from the central areas by stretches of no man's land, by the main railroad, as well as by a number of other buffer zones. Unlike the layout of many other colonial cities, which reflect the implementation of urban plans with little regard for pre-existing structures, the division of Asmara was determined by the location of pre-existing elements, such as Campo Cintato or the native market and the village of Arbate Asmera. This leads to the fact that the native quarter came very close to the city centre and that "Asmara's development was founded on a curious amalgamation of pre-existing social and physical realities".[14]

As argued by Homi Bhabha and others, the colonial relationship is not symmetrically antagonistic due to the ambivalence in the positioning of the colonised and the coloniser. Ambivalence is connected to hybridity, in which the other's originality is rewritten but also transformed through misreadings and incongruities, resulting in something different.[15] Bhabha's hybridity is a useful concept to question the methods that have been used to historicise cities whose morphological development has been determined by colonialism. Colonial cities have often been described on the basis of a binary system of antagonism between the pre-colonial and the European part of the city. The dismantling of binary systems and the foregrounding of cultural difference that Bhabha advocates brings about an opportunity to overcome such antagonism and to argue along with Bhabha that binary methods of analysis are insufficient to fully address the complex urban conditions whose development was determined by colonialism.[16]

Between 1935 and 1941, when Mussolini began to plan the invasion of Ethiopia using Eritrea as a primary base, Fascist race laws were imposed and public facilities strictly segregated between natives and Italians. The massive influx of Italian urban settlers and the development of an urbanised industrial economy had a profound social and cultural impact on Eritrean society that has lasted to the present. Under Fascist rule, the urban palimpsest of Asmara was subjected to a relentless reordering that went far beyond anything envisaged in the decades before, masterminded by a succession of regulatory ad hoc plans. During this period Asmara's visible layer changed dramatically. Spatial reconfigurations and new additions were all strategies geared towards forcing the urban palimpsest as a whole to conform to an overriding Fascist legibility. The visible layer of Piccola Roma was subsumed to a Fascist hemegonic discourse.

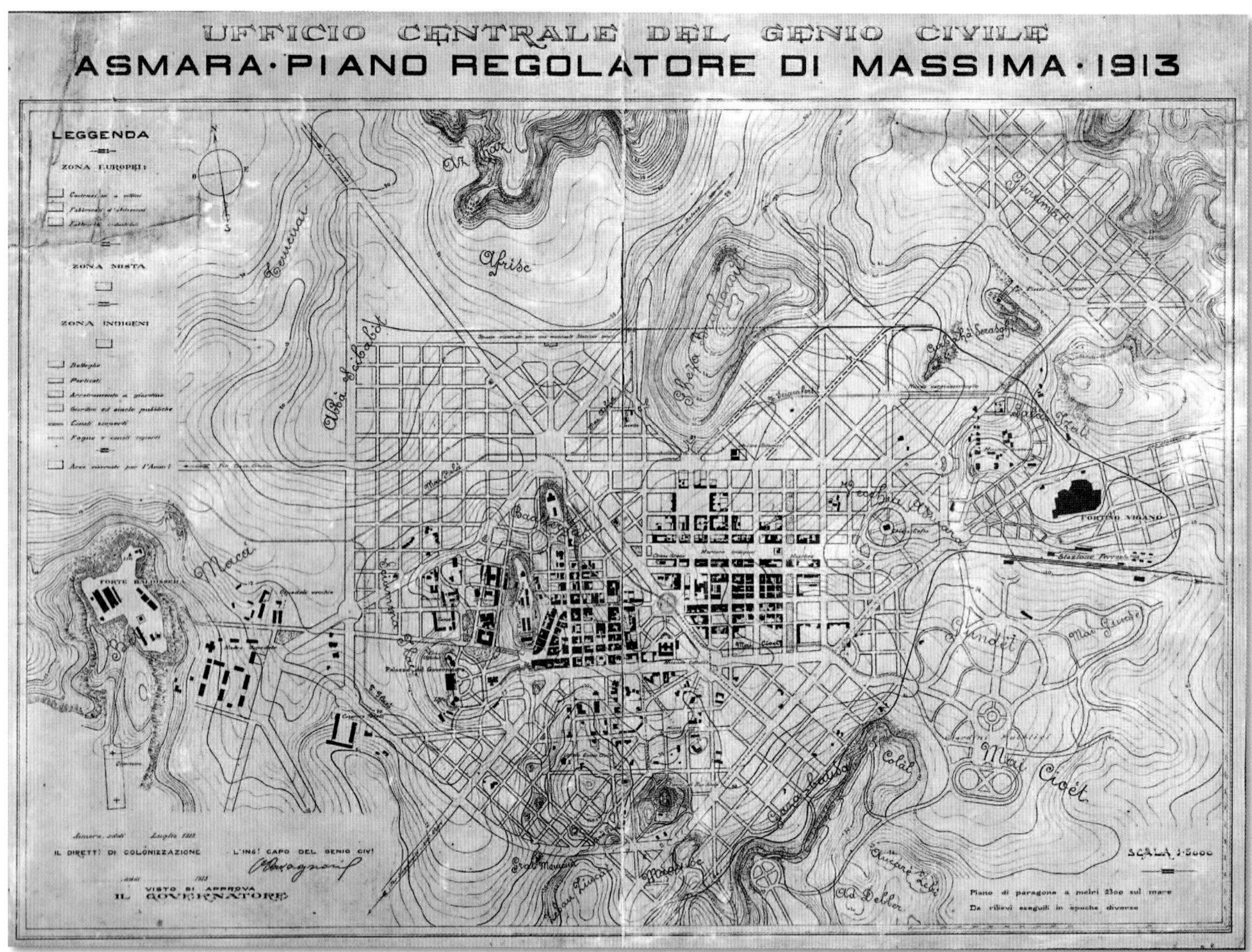

Plan dated 1913, E. Cavagnari, 1:5,000

Eduardo Cavagnari changed the plan of 1902 and 1908, but the attempts of racial separation with the four zones stayed the same. The plan aims to erect a functional city that reminds Italians of their home country and at the same time considers and controls the natives, who outnumbered the Italians. The settlements of the natives are not important anymore – in fact they don't appear on the plan. The Eritrean inhabitants shall settle in the north of the industrial zone. The ones that own land in the European zones are forced to sell it and move out. The objective of the plan is to prepare for the spatial expansion of the city, especially in the European zones. The lots are rasterised, the network of roads is laid out, leading far beyond the existing city. There is a new emphasis in the layout of the streets: until now Corso del Re (1) was the main east-west connection of the city, but now what would become Viale Mussolini (2) is the main thoroughfare. In the north of the city another bypass (3) is planned so that the old city centre – Corso del Re and the market (4) – is enclosed by these two boulevards. A broad road (5) connects these two boulevards and replaces the river Mai Bela (which was overbuilt in 1937) from the planned suburb Gheza Banda (6) in the south-east to the street that leads to Keren in the north-west.

Source: ISIAO, figure ground plan by S. Graf and A. Hofer

1913

1 Corso del Re
2 New main road
3 Northern bypass
4 Market
5 Newly planned road
6 Gheza Banda
7 Train station and railway

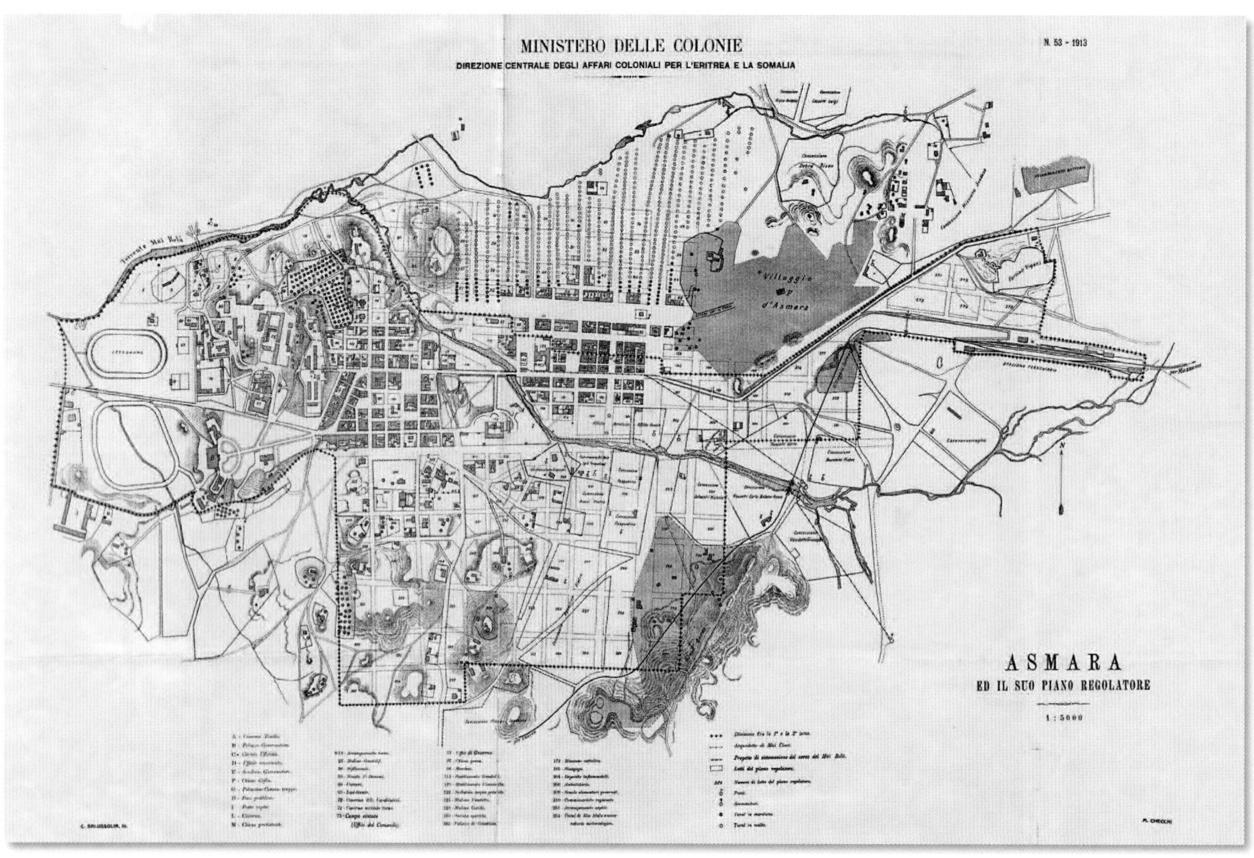

Plan dated 1913, M.Checchi (Pico), 1:5,000

The plan from 1913 shows the existing centre of Asmara, the area in the south is rasterised and the lots are delineated. The remarkable detail is the indigenous quarter to the north of the market. The round huts built by the Italians for the Eritrean population form straight lines (1). In this way the indigenous huts become part of European modernity: although they are not supplied with running water and sanitary facilities the linear orientation of the huts should provide fresh air and prevent the spread and transmission of disease.
Racial segregation also plays a role in this plan. There is a distinct line separating the European zone from the Eritrean one (2), marking the perimeter around the European area. The hippodrome (3) to the north-west of the Governor's Palace is also depicted.

Source: ISIAO, figure ground plan by S. Graf and A. Hofer

Border of the European zone

1913

1 Indigenous huts
2 Separating line
3 Hippodrome

The fight against disease and the new consciousness for hygiene manifest in terms like pure and impure resorts to metaphors from the physiology of the human body. Diseases – according to urban planners – came from the African chaos. The fight against tuberculosis for instance lent itself to a variety of symbolic manipulations – a central one was the link between illness and blackness, racial purity and sanity. One of the centrepieces of colonial propaganda was the lack of *civiltà* of the natives, considered backward and underdeveloped on the basis of lack of hygiene of their dwellings. The need for isolation was regarded as an efficient protection from diseases found in indigenous life.[17]

Plan Dated 1913 by M. Checchi

A new general plan for the city of Asmara, signed by Odoardo Cavagnari, was entitled: "Drafting of a new town plan, with provision for a significant extension of the city centre and a more defined racial segregation than in the following scheme of 1908". The plan gives more importance to civil rather than military settlements. To the north of the market square is a settlement for natives, the Villagio indigeno di Asmara (with a differentiation between two types of *agdò* in masonry and in mortar) already with a regular organisation overlapped by a lot division plan that, located beyond the dividing line between the two zones (Italian and Eritrean), allows for the supposition of a complete substitution of the native settlement with a new buildable area for Italians. Many critics assert that the arrangement of these settlements exhibited racial and ethnic biases and were consciously designed to proclaim the superiority of white culture.[18]

The Hedonistic City

This article is a detailed look at Asmara as the site of colonial policies, based on an understanding that architecture and urban forms are key players in definitions of culture and identity. The imagery and the rhetoric of the conquest of the colonies were conceptualised in gendered terms empowering the coloniser to take possession of the "virgin lands of virgins".[19] Asmara as a place where these phantasies were fulfilled first in imagery and then physically. Postcards with naked African women and the song *facetta nera* – which talks of the arrival of the Italians in Ethiopia and the black women who expect their arrival – were topics responsible for a erotication of the colony and therefore form part of the Porno-tropic tradition.[20] Naked women adorned travel posters and postcards while the Italian photographer in the colonies exposed the bodies of subjugated women. In addition, the colonial state, as a rationalising project and a panoptical Foucautian milieu, developed new "geographies of perversion".[21] These *othered* the beggar, the black, the criminal, the prostitute and the homosexual. Paradoxically, the colonial government, as a homogening project, continuously produced differences as well. It is indeed interesting to see how these differences become visible in the urban plans. The management of the male bourgeois self brings about conflicts of race, class and gender take the form of racialisation of domestic space as well as that of the domestication of the colonial space.

Tourism also played an important role. The construction of an infrastructure of roads and public services undertaken during colonialism provided the necessary preconditions for the development of a well-organised and efficient tourist system. Albergo Italia, Asmara's first hotel, was built in 1899. In 1919 the Albergo Hamasien followed. Under fascism, early consumer culture was managed within mass organisations, projects in the colonies were closely tied to Fascist concepts of mass society and social hierarchy. Thus, Fascism not only introduced aesthetics into politics, as Benjamin described, but also invested them with leisure. And this collective domestic space of leisure was delineated, and also domesticated, by the actions of touristic praxis. Tourism was positioned as a colonising strategy.

Stephanie Malia Hom intends to tease out the connective tissue between tourism, colonialism, and imperial formations – one filament being that Italian colonial tourists, conditioned to the pleasures of Empire, were more open to new forms of cultural imperialism predicated on consumerism, mobility, and leisure – the very stuff of tourism – that emerged in the post-war era.[22] Italian propaganda considered it important to extol the colonies as tourist sites. To alleviate at least partially the housing problem in Asmara and create the premises for future tourist development, the state created the *Campania Immobiliare alberghi Africa Orientale* (CIAAO – East African Hotel Construction Company, established to build hotels in the largest cities. Under the regime more than half a dozen tourism organisations (*Opera Nationale Dopolavoro, Touring Club Italiano*, Italian Tourism Company) were formed and colonial tourists grew exponentially during this time. The tourist architecture of the colony was a product of a regime whose reactionary views of the local culture were aligned with the integration of the region into metropolitan society. The experience of tourism and travel was a liminal state where such contested identities were negotiated.[23]

Colonisation represented a turning point in the life of many settlers. The regime conceived a new social plan for the colonies, consisting of a society made up of hard-working people with a remedy for the evils of bourgeois hedonism. The situation was slightly different in Asmara. The colonial towns were important tools for spreading hedonistic lifestyles. In the culture of advertisement of the

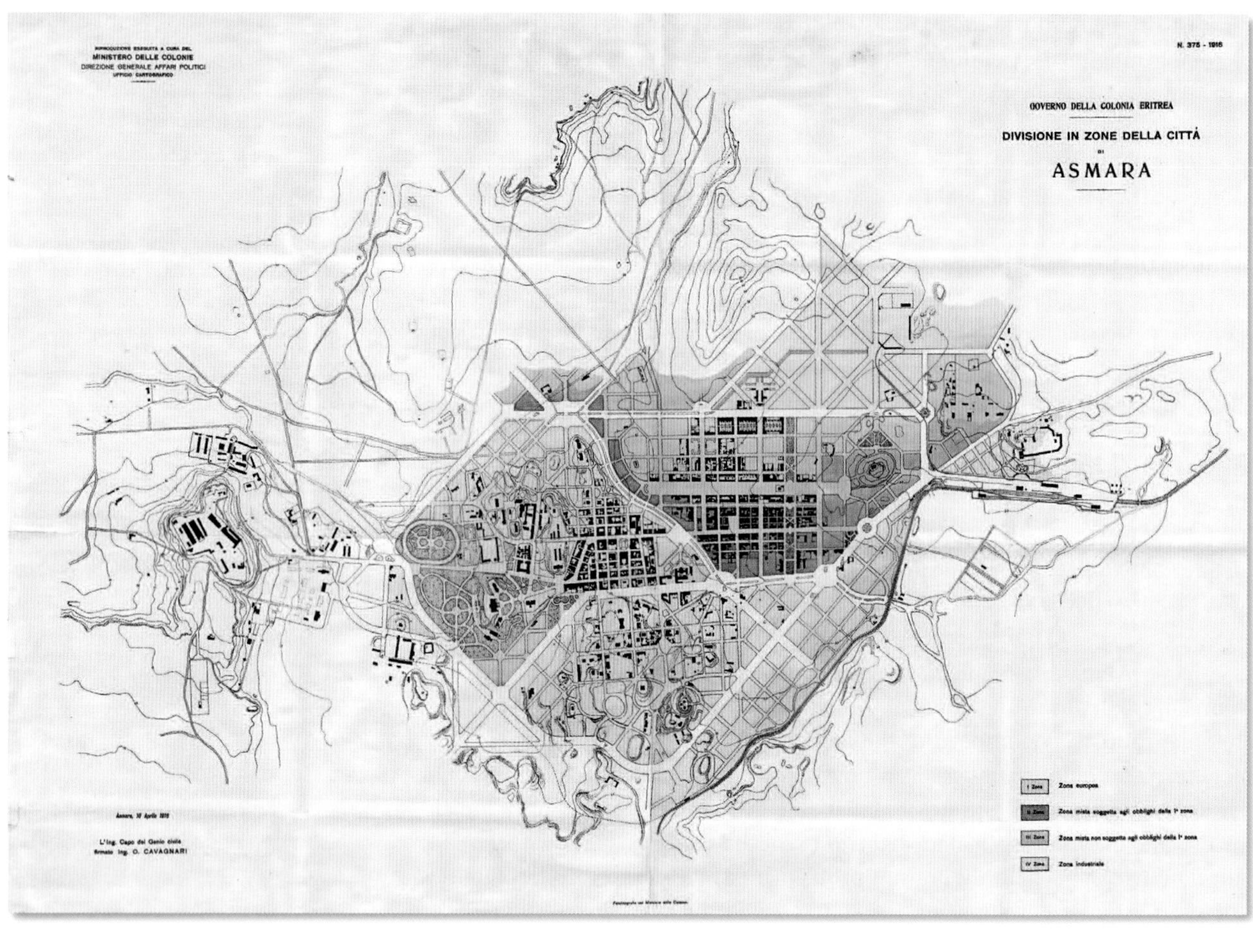

Plan dated 1916, E.Cavagnari

This plan is a revised version of the plan of 1913 and shows racial segregation with a colour scheme. The grid in the north of the Governor's Palace is replaced by the hippodrome. The street leading to the north-west copies the winding course of the river Mai Bela. This street and the eastern part of the later Viale Mussiolini constitute the ethnical line of demarcation. This line is no longer arbitrary, like in the Checchi plan, but follows the river which gives the racial segregation the impression of naturalness. Racial segregation is defined in four zones throughout the city plan. The first area is for the Europeans and is located to the west of the Catholic mission (city centre) and the south (living zone). The second zone is the mixed zone, an area around the market for Europeans, other foreigners (Jews, Greeks, Arabic merchants) and Eritreans. The third zone is for the natives around the coptic church and in the north of the city. The fourth zone is situated outside the city and contains industry. Despite this plan the city grew in an unregulated fashion and prices in the centre rose enormously.

Source: ISIAO, figure ground plan by S. Graf and A. Hofer

European zone
Indigenous and mixed zone
Industrial

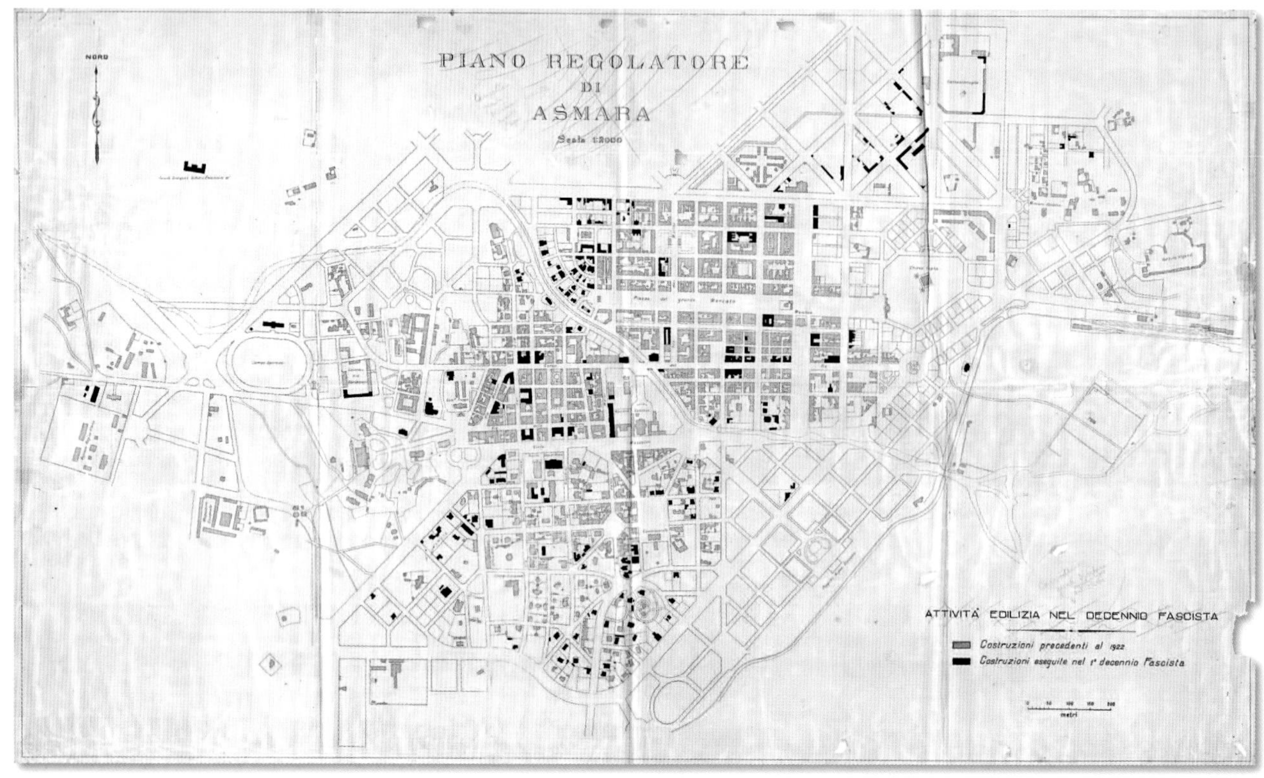

Plan dated mid-1930s, 1:2,000

This plan dates from the mid-1930s and shows the existing city. Buildings that were erected before 1922 are depicted in grey; those from the first ten years of fascist rule are in black. The plan corresponds more or less to the Cavagnari plan from 1916. The city centre has been redensified and in the *quartiere dei villini* to the south many new villas were built. The indigenous quarters are not shown.

Source: ISIAO, figure ground plan by S. Graf and A. Hofer

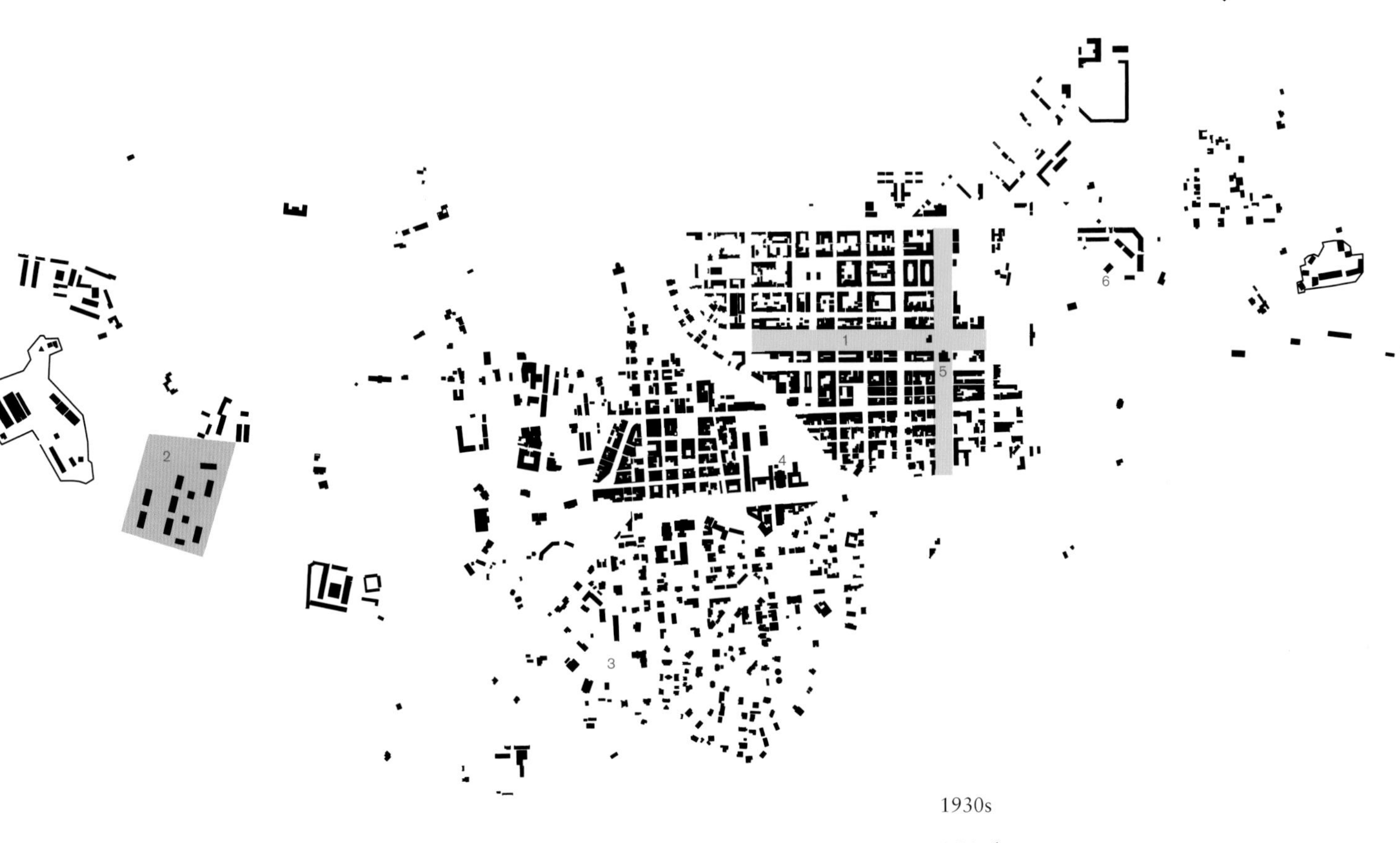

1930s

1 Market
2 New hospital
3 Italian villas quarter
4 Catholic Church
5 Mosque
6 Coptic Church

Aerial view of Asmara (1930s)
Source: Photographic archive of the IsIAO (E 15/A I/2))

Fascist *ventennio*, the hygienic benefits of water and swimming were soon aligned with the practice of sunbathing and the realm of travel and pleasure. Lower-class Italians acquired typically bourgeois habits and practised sports which in their mother country were reserved for the higher classes.

Life in the colony explored the crucial nexus of whiteness, racial superiority, and femininity. "At night, social life moved to the ever expanding number of entertainment and leisure facilities. New dancehalls, restaurants and bars were being opened everywhere. The working men's clubs and numerous sports and recreational societies, supported by local government and by the PNF, organised the colonists' free time."[24] Dozens of shops and even department stores were opened in both cities. Leisure activities also boomed: in Asmara eight cinemas had been built for Europeans and one for Africans. Cinemas, theatres, the press and above all the radio were considered the most important instruments for the persuasion and involvement of both settlers and indigenous people in the regime's policies.[25] The fascist regime gave importance to sport activities in the colonies and one of the most followed were those related to car races. A more visible trace of the hedonistic life in Asmara was the Asmara circuit, where the Italians started running competitions. Asmara had a higher density of cars during the colonial time than cities in Italy (Y8) and was a real car city. One report submits that there were approximately 50,000 cars in Asmara mid-1939.[26]

Notes

1 Spiro Kostof, *The City Shaped: Urban Patterns and Meanings Through History*. London: Bulfinch, 1993 (4th), p. 25.

2 Andreas Huyssen, *Present Pasts: Urban Palimpsests and the Politics of Memory.* Stanford: Stanford University Press, 2003, pp. 51-52.

3 Belula Tecle-Misghina, "Asmara, an urban history", *L'Architettura delle città, UNESCO-Chair Series – The Journal of Scientific Society Ludovico Quaroni*. Rome: Edizioni Nuova Cultura, 2014, pp. 23-29.

4 Uoldelul Chelati Dirar, *From Warriors to Urban Dwellers. Ascari and the Military Factor in the Urban Development of Colonial Eritrea*, 2004, in: http://www.ssoar.info/ssoar/bitstream/handle/document/28476/ ssoar-ceafri-2004- (12.04. 2013), p.6.

5 Maristella Casciato, *Da campo militare a capitale: Asmara colonia italiana e oltre*, Igitur publishing (website: www.rivista-incontri-nl), 2013.

6 Naigzy Gebremedhin, *Asmara, Africa's Secret Modernist City*. Paper prepared for the African Perspectives: Dialogue on Urbanism and Architecture, The Faculty of Architecture, TU Delft, 2007, pp. 4-5.

7 Uoldelul Chelati Dirar 2004, p. 11.

8 Marco Antonsich, Addis Abeba: *Caput Viarium. Le strade del Duce in Abessinia*, 2006, in: www.academia.edu/2286490/Addis_Abeba_caput_viarium. (August 2013), p. 143.

9 Giuliano Gresleri, "1936-40: programma e strategia delle città imperiali", in Giuliano Gresleri, Pier Giorgio Massaretti, Stefano Zagnoni (eds.), *Architettura italiana d'oltremare 1870–1940*. Venice: Marsilio, 1993, p. 198.

10 Naigzy Gebremedhin 2007, pp. 8-9.

11 Paul Rabinow: *French Modern: Norms and Forms of the Social Environment*. University of Chicago Press, 1995.

12 Kanishka Goonewardena, Stefan Kipfer, Richard Milgrom and Christina Schmid (eds.), *Space, Difference, Everyday Life. Reading Henri Lefebvre*. New York and London: Routledge, 2008.

13 See also: Francesca Locatelli, "Colonial Justice, Crime, and Social Stratification in the (Native Quarters of Colonial Asmara, 1890–1941: Preliminary Insights from the Court Records of the Indigenous Tribunal of Hamasien", *Northeast African Studies*, vol. 10, no. 2, 2003 (New Series), pp. 101-115.

14 Edward Denison, G.Yu Ren and Naigzy Gebremedhin, *Asmara. Africa's Secret Modernist City*. London-New York: Merrel Publisher, 2003, p. 36.

15 BHABHA

16 Mia Fuller, *Moderns Abroad: Architecture, Cities, and Italian Imperialism*. London: Routledge (*Architext* series, series editors Anthony D.King and Thomas Markus), 2007, p. 264.

17 Homi K.Bhabha, "The Other Question: Difference, Discrimination and the Discourse of Colonialism", in Russell Ferguson, Martha Gever, Trinh T.Minh-ha, Cornel West (eds.), *Out There: Marginalization and Contemporary Culture* (Cambridge, Mass., 1990), p. 72, pp. 85-86.

18 IbId. Belula Tecle-Misghina, "Asmara, an urban history", *L'Architettura delle città, UNESCO-Chair Series*, pp. 43-46.

19 Giulia Barrera, *Dangerous Liaisons: Colonial Concubinage in Eritrea 1890–1941*. African Studies Program in Working Paper 1, 1996, p. 26.

20 Anne McClintock, *Imperial Leather: Race, Gender and Sexuality in the Colonial Context*. London: Routledge, 1991.

21 Rudi C.Bleys and Charles Darwin, "The Geography of Perversion: Male-To-Male Sexual Behavior Outside the West and the Ethnographic Imagination, 1750–1918", *Journal of the History of Behavioral Sciences*, vol. 34 (4) 1998, pp. 388-389.

22 Stephanie Malia Hom, *The Beautiful Country. Tourism and the Impossible State of Destination Italy*. Toronto: University of Toronto Press, 2015, pp. 105-127.

23 Brian McLaren, *Architecture and Tourism in Italian Colonial Libya: An Ambivalent Modernism*. Seattle, Wash.: University of Washington Press, 2006.

24 Gian Luca Podestà, "The Eighth Vibration. Asmara and Dek'emhare, Cities of Work, Cities of Leisure, Diacronie", *Studi di Storia Contemporanea*, (21) 2015, p.3.

25 Gian Luca Podestá, "I luoghi della cultura nell'Impero fascista", in Scarpa, Domenico (ed.), *Atlante della letteratura italiana*, vol. 3, *Dal Romanticismo ad oggi*. Turin: Einaudi, 2012, pp. 655-670.

26 Rita di Meglio, *Gli Italiani in Eritrea. Italian Embassy in Eritrea*. Asmara, 2004.

ASMARA AND THE DEVELOPMENT OF ITS MODERN URBAN ENVIRONMENT POST 1941

Belula Tecle Misghina

The historic built environment of Asmara, modern while partly eclectic, is the result of a canvass in which architects could practise and realise products of Modernism, with influences of local and Arab building systems[1] – modern in itself although influenced by the Italian Modern[2] from which it originated. Asmara architectural and urban heritage must therefore be preserved and enhanced by recognising this inherent richness and not only as a former Italian place. Definitions such as living museum, the frozen city or the forgotten city, used to describe Asmara architectural heritage, consider architecture as pure design objects belonging to their designers and not as part of Eritreans' Asmara identity. This implicitly placed Asmara as witness to a process that would seem not to have been part of its Eritrean heritage and culture but rather a symbol of oppression, which could easily threaten its preservation. Asmara however consists of elements of an urban organism linked to the history of its inhabitants and geographic context. What would the area of the city's historic market, for example, referred to as public space, be without its pre-colonial history,[3] its character as a place of social and cultural exchange throughout the history of the city also during colonialism? Preservation of Asmara therefore means preserving a successful example of a liveable city on integrated urban planning and architecture from the late nineteenth century to the early twentieth century, a contingency of components such as architecture, heritage and culture, which have favoured the flourishing of an Eritrean society founded on the idea of the modern city concept (World Heritage Convention 2004), human-scaled and multicultural. Multiculturalism was largely due to the flows of migrants[4] (Indian, Greek, Israeli, Arab, Yemenite, etc.) mainly engaged in trade, until the early 1970s. Furthermore, Asmara must be protected as it is one of the few examples where the construction of

A contemporary building in Asmara
Source: S. Graf 2013

a capital has strengthened the sense of unity of an entire region. This is evident in the period that followed the end of Italian colonialism and the period of the federation with Ethiopia which were the years when Asmara, while maintaining its original political, economical and cultural functions, was also home to the socio-political debates and demonstrations on the rights of its citizens and the fate of Eritrea as a united nation. Asmara hence became the nucleus shared by a growing number of Eritreans.

Asmara is well known for its architectural and urban landscape quality before World War II; below is an outline of the fate of the city and its development from 1941 – the end of Italian rule – until the early years of 2000. During this period Asmara grew from a number of around 98,000 inhabitants[5] in the late 1930s to more than 400,000 by 2005. This rapid increase in population led to tensions between social needs and urban planning that resulted in attempts to control urban growth which in some cases took the form of major planning studies, such as the Master Plan of Arturo Mezzèdimi (1972–1973) and the study *Asmara Infrastructure Development Study* (2005). Asmara did not decline at the end of Italian colonialism; conversely it strengthened its economic (commercial) power and extended its influence beyond Eritrea, mainly in Ethiopia, until the regime of the Derg.[6] It is noted that at the end of Italian colonialism Eritrea did not gain its independence until 1991. The demise of the Italian colonial government took place during a period of several consecutive governments and administrations: the British trusteeship administration (1941–1952), the government federated to Ethiopia (1952–1962), the imperial regime of Ethiopia (1962–1974) and finally the Derg regime (1974–1991). Subsequent to the Italian era, Asmara and Eritrea focused on political, social and economic agendas. It is therefore difficult to easily access architectural and city planning information; however, an outline of the evolution of the city can be drawn by using indirect sources.

a) British Trusteeship Administration (1941–1952)

During the 1940s Eritrea was under British trusteeship while awaiting a United Nations decision on its future. The British maintained the status quo, i.e. an Italian administrative structure with its public officials and its laws, including the racial ones, only later abolished. As a result the city perpetuated a regulated coexistence between Europeans and natives and only later started the slow appropriation of the city by Eritreans. The British appreciated the modernity of the Eritrean cities and the infrastructure in the country but simultaneously progressively dismantled significant infrastructural assets of the Eritrean territory (port facilities, cableway, etc.), even to the detriment of Asmara.

b) Period of the Federation with Ethiopia (1952–1962)

This period was characterised by the transfer of control mechanisms and direction of society from the Italians to the Eritreans. Asmara became the seat of the federal parliament, a change that increased its power nationwide. This consequently enhanced the factors of attraction to the city, which impacted on Eritrea as well as Ethiopia. During the federation, the Municipality of Asmara was headed by Eritrean mayors, and it was then that part of Aba-Shawl[7] area was demolished and replaced by modern buildings, organised on parcelled plots ordered along aligned roads.[8]

c) Period of Union with Ethiopia: The Ethiopian Imperial Regime and the Derg Regime (1962–1991)

After its forced annexation to Ethiopia, Eritrea became a province of Ethiopia and Asmara was reduced from the capital city of a federal state to the capital city of a province. This caused deep frustration among the Eritrean people, who saw their rights and autonomy shattered. It is important to note here that Asmara, since its modern foundation (1899), had acted as the capital city of a country for most of sixty three years, only interrupted in 1936–1941 when the capital of the Italian colony moved to Addis Ababa. The city still continued to maintain a leading role as a commercial and industrial centre with the best infrastructure of the new *Africa Orientale Italiana* – Empire of Italian East Africa. During the early years of union with Ethiopia, Asmara maintained its original role as the node of administration, commerce and major infrastructure, re-establishing itself on the wider territory of Eritrea as a link between the sea and the whole of Ethiopia. During the subsequent Derg period stagnation and the slow decline of the city occurred as the dismantling and transfer of its industries to Ethiopian territories took place. Asmara, however, continued to be subjected to immigration and growth, mostly from rural areas, as a consequence of the war of independence. This urbanisation was largely characterised by spontaneous settlements in the form of barracks accumulated around the nucleus of the existing city, thereby lowering the quality of many urban districts which were in economic decline.

It is therefore evident that during those decades, the city of Asmara functioned either as capital of country, or of province, depending on the political situation. This helped entrench its role as the urban node and the future capital of the State of Eritrea. It should be noted that the Eritrean population had never rebelled against the city as a symbol of colonial oppression due to the fact that Asmara was considered an outcome of a collective good which had already been experienced by the Eritrean population which also participated in its

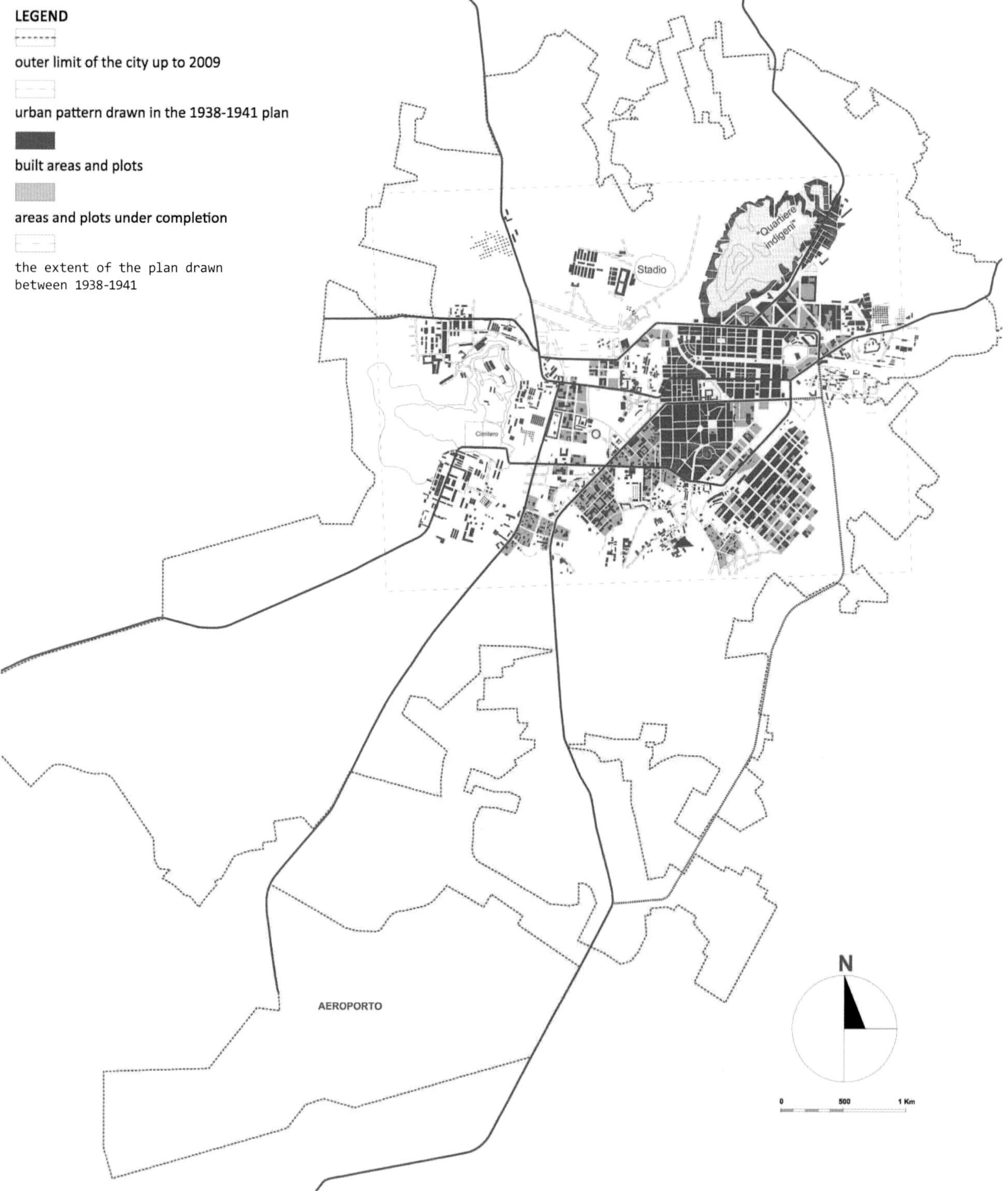
LEGEND
outer limit of the city up to 2009
urban pattern drawn in the 1938-1941 plan
built areas and plots
areas and plots under completion
the extent of the plan drawn between 1938-1941
"Quartiere indigeni"
Stadio
AEROPORTO
N
0
500
1 Km

construction. The sequence of Italian urban planning ended around 1939 with the development of the town plan drawn by Vittorio Cafiero,[9] which could not be completely realised due to the fall of the Italian colonial government in 1941. During the following decades Asmara continued to grow; the reality of this urban progress is mainly documented as a list which includes: a tourist map entitled *Asmara* (around 1938–1941), a multilingual plan undated, and by the complete file of studies for the Master Plan of Asmara prepared by Arturo Mezzèdimi[10] (1972–1973).

Image of Asmara around 1941 (fig.1)

The development of the city around 1941 is illustrated in a plan drafted by an unknown author.[11] It is a technical plan which is assumed as developed for information/orientation (it indicates the primary services and facilities) for the use of English speaking people. This plan illustrates the completed new costructions along the axes of the Piazza del Mercato, the historic market place. When comparing the abovementioned unknown author's plan with the plan of Cafiero, it is evident that the city grew along two different approaches: the west, north and east area continued to grow, ignoring Cafiero's town plan and its guidelines, while in the south area the concept was adopted and adapted in the extension of the city. The north-east areas of the town in the Cafiero plan corresponded with the zone that the Italians intended to provide for the natives. For this reason they were not considered worthy of attention. It is thus reasonable to assume that, after the end of the Italian rule, no plans were developed for this part of the town. The term *Quartiere Indigeno* (Indigenuous Quarter) is still used in the plan to indicate the area of Aba Shawl.

Image of Asmara between the Years 1950–1970 (fig.2)

The growth of the city between 1950–1970 is represented by a multilingual plan,[12] elaborate although undated, with handwritten inscriptions and signs. This was most probably elaborated between the years 1953–1969, an assumption based on the new buildings in it. However, this plan was used well before the period of the Derg. As such the city was divided into subzones corresponding to that of *kebeliye*[13] as had been evident during the period of the Derg. The plan illustrates that the city had grown by absorbing surrounding villages whose autonomous identities remained, as evident in the names of the urban neighbourhoods that replaced them – Acria, Gajeret, Godaif, Never Temenay, etc. It is not clear in the plan where the proposed new extensions overlap the existing ones. In order to determine which are the newly planned subdivisions and which existed, a comparison with the current layout of the city was necessary. By analysing the plan (fig. 2) it is understood that, for areas

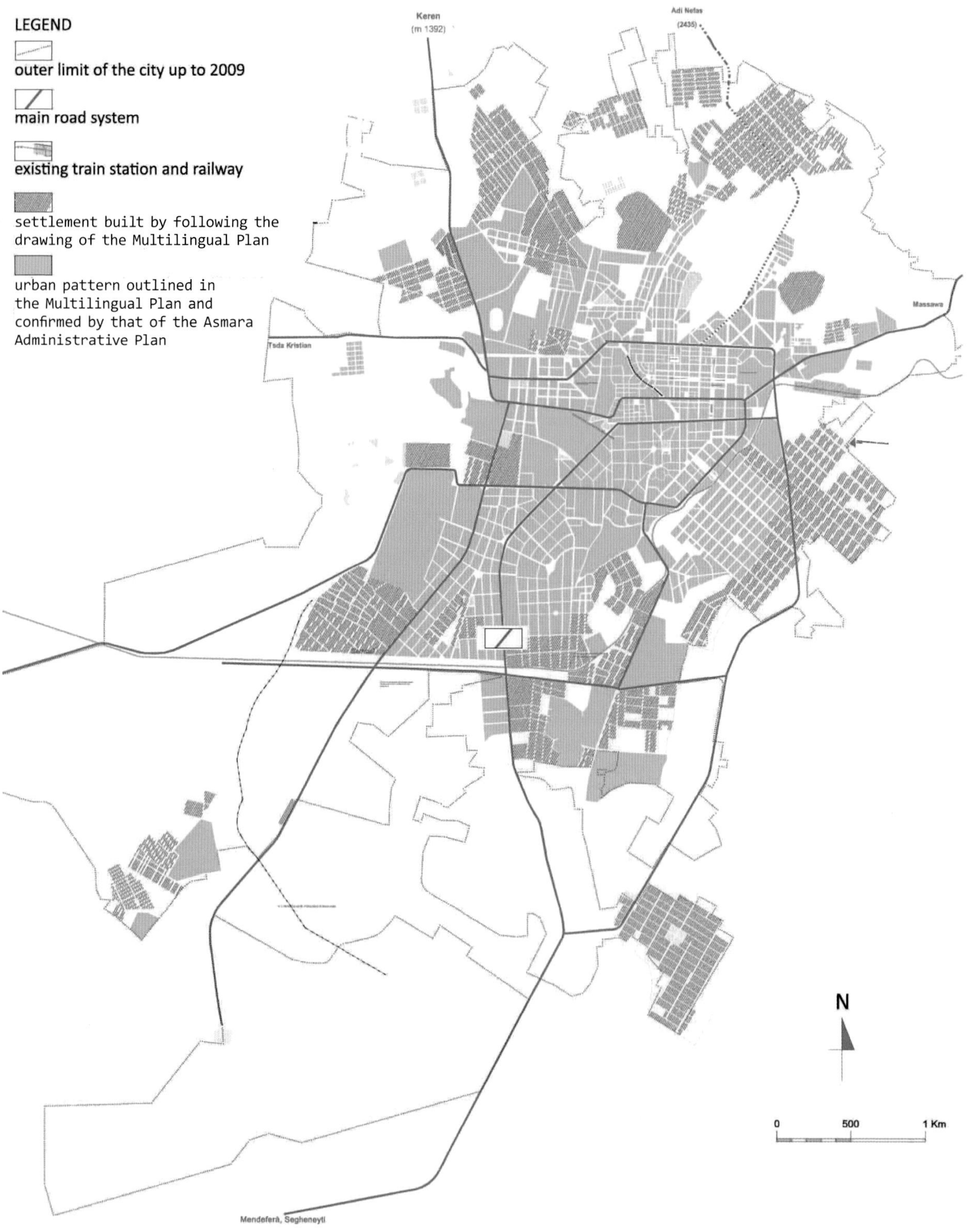
LEGEND
outer limit of the city up to 2009
main road system
existing train station and railway
settlement built by following the drawing of the Multilingual Plan
urban pattern outlined in the Multilingual Plan and confirmed by that of the Asmara Administrative Plan
Keren
(m 1392)
Adi Nefas
(2435)
Massawa
Tsda Kristian
Mendeferà, Segheneyti
N
0
500
1 Km

of expansion located in more suburban areas, a parcelled and fragmented system has been used, similar to that adopted by Kitchener in Khartoum. On the other hand, areas in the south and southeast of the old plan were used for low-density settlements. The plan also illustrates the partial urban renewal of the Aba Shawl area, as mentioned above.

Image of Asmara of the Early 1970s: The Mezzèdimi Master Plan

Arturo Mezzèdimi's Master Plan illustrates the detailed image of the postcolonial city. It is a comprehensive study plan based on standard modern town planning principles to govern the expansion of the city that seemed out of control. Here the study of the Mezzèdimi Master Plan is especially important to the analysis of the existing city because it illustrates the state of the city until the early 1970s, tracing urban development, therefore the economic, social and demographic situations. Demographic growth between 1950–1968 led to a population increase of 65 per cent which, in addition to the growth of large informal neighbourhoods, had fuelled land speculation. In his analysis Mezzèdimi highlighted that Asmara, as well as the whole of Eritrea, constituted an important economic hub for the central Ethiopian government, with large capacity for industrial development (Asmara Expo '69, National Expo '72). The activities of the service sector in the city, especially the tourism sector, continued to operate, presenting a growing source of revenue for the city. Asmara was always commercially important because of its proximity to the port of Massawa. The third economic component analysed was the crafts, as well as trade, which were stimulated as a fundamental initiative of the city. According to the architect, this was made possible by the diverse multi-racial and multi-national society which was conducive to exchange and diversified craft and trade. The only critical drawback to such economy was the difficult agricultural sector which also significantly influenced urban migration to Asmara.

The city of Asmara, which Mezzèdimi studied and designed, was much wider than that considered in the plan of Cafiero. It was a development based on the availability of building sites and/or through rudimentary urban regulations. Part of the analysis of the plan also produced data on housing development:

- Over 50 per cent of buildings in total were achieved in the twenty years preceding the plan,
- 42 per cent of buildings were detached and 52 per cent semi-detached,
- 30 per cent of buildings were semi-permanent as a result of immigration,
- 83 per cent of housing (including semi-permanent) were constructed of brick or stone walls,

- 70 per cent of residents rented and only 20 per cent had home ownership,
- Approximately 75 per cent of homes had electricity,
- 90 per cent of households had direct water supply, while a few used ground water.

On conclusion of his analysis, Mezzèdimi drew up a plan (1972–1973) for expansion and reorganisation which became a master plan (fig. 3) comprising a set of strategic objectives and synoptic patterns which requires further detailed action planning to be implemented in line with the reality. Among the various elements of the plan was an interesting system of modular form district (or modular quarter as per Mezzèdimi) expansion (fig. 4) thought of as consisting of high density buildings[14] to the rational use of the site and cost-effective infrastructure. Another important element of the plan is the system of roads designed according to a structuring concept of two concentric ring roads: an internal connection between districts and an external connection between territorial lines. This intended draft master plan by Mezzèdimi was never approved, most likely due to the fall of Hailè Sellassiè I (1974) who had commissioned it. Around 1976, however, the firm Mezzèdimi prepared a town plan (different in many ways from the master plan) which, as the previous draft, does not appear to have been implemented.

Image of Asmara around 1995

Growth data in Asmara until the early 1990s was revealed in a document titled *Asmara Administrative Zone*, produced by the municipality immediately after independence. Although it does not report the exact development of the city at that time (1995 approx), it clearly illustrated the general nature and growth of Asmara since World War II until around 1995 (fig. 2). The growth was based on a replication of the existing adjacent parcels which comprised simple rectangular shapes and proportions. There was no trace of any deviation and no hierarchy of urban spaces. Building typologies, except for those along the main avenues, illustrate growth through expansive, low-scaled built form with very few exceptions.

Planning Asmara would restart in 1998, subsequent to a meeting of the *Planning Committee* which outlined strategies for the urban development of the city. For the first time it took into account an enlarged Asmara, i.e. the existing Asmara Town and its satellite villages[15] which would later be named the Greater Asmara Area (GAA). The Committee had been faced with urban problems generated by simplistic planning and uncontrolled spontaneous building constructions and thus concluded their work with the production of a policy document containing:

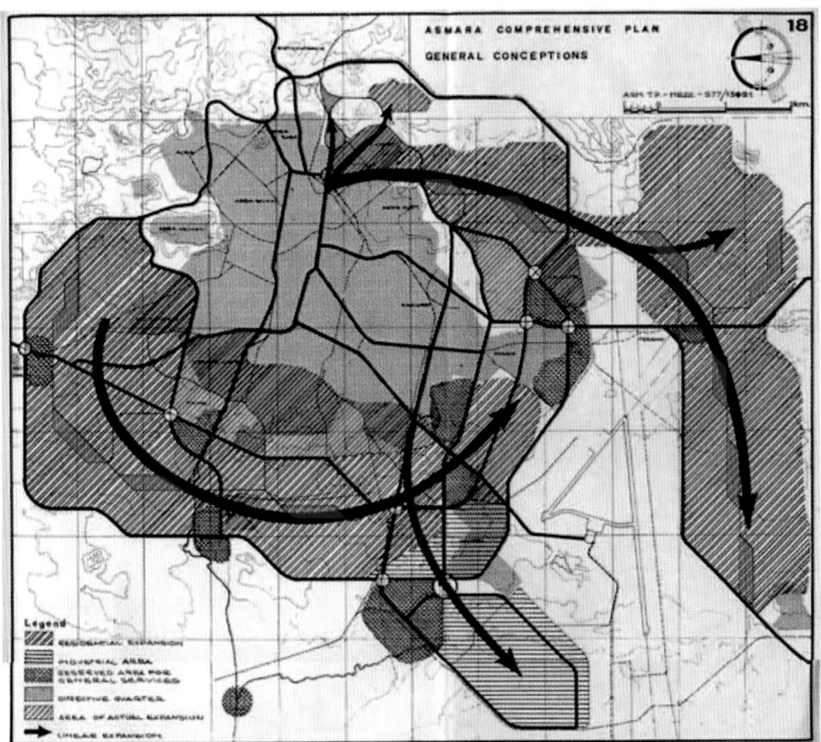

Figure 3. Mezzèdimi Master Plan: Asmara Comprehensive Plan, General Conceptions. The centres of the module quarters are highlighted in red.

Source: Studio Mezzèdimi 1973

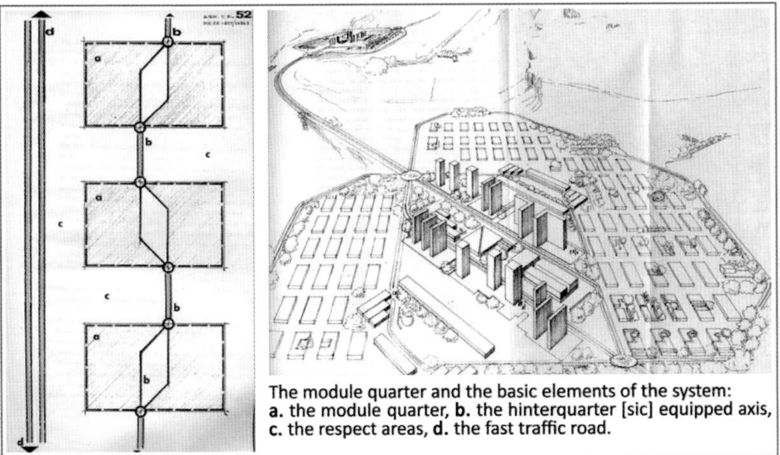

Figure 4. Module quarter and the theoretical scheme.

Source: Studio Mezzèdimi 1973

- Problems, assumptions and projections for the development of GAA (availability of land, water resources, limit population of 600,000 inhabitants);
- Guidelines for the development of Asmara Town (maintenance actions and redevelopment, identification and restoration of buildings of architectural value, etc).

The indications of the Committee initiated studies for the elaboration of a new plan for the GAA. Among these the most complex and significant was the *Asmara Infrastructure Development Study* of which the first phase in 2005 had produced a suite of documents under the title *I fase: Urban profile and projections report*[16] – a very careful study of rich data, proposed developments and maps. Despite this it requires further detail in order to be implemented. The beginning of the study is very significant as a programme aimed to enable the GAA to start a process of redevelopment of its urban fabric and strengthening of its infrastructure. It is interesting that the part of the study on the road system which, although not then completely defined, clearly indicated the need to fully realise the full extent of the ring and to introduce another outer concentric semi-ring to match the new size of the city. These two conceptual principles are aligned with those of the Mezzèdimi Master Plan.

Conclusions

Asmara with its pleasant urban environment, characterised by variable densities of population and the integration of different ethnic and economic groups in commercial and residential areas (World Heritage Convention 2004),[17] has preserved a considerable part of its urban quality. The once Italian city became the centre of a city far larger and more complex; this enabled it to resiliently withstand often terrible difficulties of history, perhaps better than other similar settlements in Africa. This resilience also corresponds to the collective character of the Eritrean people who inhabited the early Asmara city, proudly and tenaciously anchored to its history and to its environment. Asmara today is a city that continues to function despite past political and complex events, even helping to address the political and social transformations. It is proof of the unique ability of urban structures and architecture to influence the sustainability of cities that are independent of the historical colonial and political conditions in which they were conceived. Asmara must be preserved, along with its built heritage, as a great example of what it means to live the culture of the city and not only as a place of nostalgic memories of refined lovers of architecture.

Notes

1 For example, the Nda Mariam Church and Guido Ferrazza's projects in Asmara.

2 Italian modern architecture and urban planning, although rooted in the Mediterranean Rationalism, is different to that of the International Style and has strong identifying characters (e.g. EUR district in Rome).

3 The area was for overnight caravans and trade along the trade routes of the Aksum Kingdom; these routes to and from North Africa and the Red Sea largely occurred in the Eritrean territories, including a route along the old site of the city of Asmara, an area inhabited since the 1st Millennium BC.

4 Except for the number of Italians during colonialism, the number of immigrants from outside Eritrean territories to Asmara has never been massive but still represented a significant amount for the size of the city of that time.

5 The number of inhabitants refers to the town plan of Asmara drawn by Vittorio Cafiero.

6 Military regime inspired by, and allied to, the Soviet Union which ruled Ethiopia from 1974–1991.

7 The area to the northeast of the city and the site of the native quarter during the colonial period.

8 Medhanie Estifanos. 1998. "Asmara, una città unica", in Oriolo L. (ed.), *Asmara Style*. Scuola Italiana: Asmara, p. 67.

9 The town plan of Asmara drawn by Vittorio Cafiero (a Roman architect, 1901–1981) was based on the reorganisation, upgrading and expansion of the city which worsened the racial division. The designated areas for natives seemed to refer to the project study of re-founding the Khartoum city by Lord Kitchener (1899).

10 Arturo Mezzèdimi (Siena 1922–2010) was an important Italian architect active in Eritrea and Ethiopia between the 1940s and early 1970s.

11 Plan available online at http://www.trainweb.org/eritrean/scrapbook/where/maps/0001Asmara.jpg.

12 The name given by the author as the title of the document isn't clear. The definition "multilingual" is due to the various languages employed (Tigrigna, Italian, English and Amhara) and overprints on the same document which seems to have been used and modified several times and by several administrations.

13 The *kebeliye* (districts) were of divisions or groups in which every aspect of daily life was controlled by security organs of the government.

14 Mezzèdimi refers to this as "multi-housing".

15 The satellite villages are suburbs dependent on Asmara for services and more.

16 Work study was directed by the Department of Urban Development Centre in collaboration with BCEOM (*Societe Francaise D'Ingeniere*), the GROUPE HUIT (*Bureau D'Etudes Pluridisciplinaires*), the OPTIMA (Development Services) and the contribution of CARP (Cultural Assets Rehabilitation Project).

17 World Heritage Convention. 2004. The Historic Perimeter of Asmara and its Modernist Architecture. Ministry of Education, p. 2.

ARTURO MEZZÈDIMI
Promises of an African Modernity (Asmara 1940–1959)

Benno Albrecht, Filippo De Dominicis, Jacopo Galli

The days between the 22nd and 25th of May 1963 were the happiest in the life of the Negus Haile Selassie. The Emperor of Ethiopia had managed to unite under one roof thirty-two African heads of state and for three days, "this man with his sharp but serene eyes, always slightly tinged with melancholy, immobile and hieratic"[1] acted as a noble father and mediator: softened differences, weaved strategies and smoothed quarrels. At the end of these efforts, before the opulent banquet that concluded the meeting, the heads of state gathered alone in the assembly hall of the Africa Hall and signed the official document establishing the Organisation of African Unity, finally sanctioning the death of European colonialism. Many protagonists of the struggle for independence were present: Léopold Sedar Senghor, Sékou Touré, Modibo Keïta, Gamal Abdel Nasser, Ahmed Ben Bella, Julius Nyerere e Kwame Nkrumah. Only one European witnessed this historic moment: the architect of the building Arturo Mezzèdimi.[2] Mezzèdimi had just accomplished Haile Selassie's dream and the most important building of his successful career. When, only five years earlier, the Emperor summoned the architect in the Ghebbi to inform him of the decision to build the Africa Hall, Mezzèdimi immediately realised the scope of his task and decided to leave Asmara, where he had been living since 1940, to move permanently to Addis Ababa.

Mezzèdimi perfected the Italian building tradition in the Horn of Africa. Giacomo Naretti, a master builder (*bajerod* for Ethiopians) from Piedmont, who built, years before the battle of Adwa, the Heruy Giorgis church in Debre Tabor, the Dabre Berhan Selassie church in Gondar, the imperial palace in Adwa, the Royal Palace, residence of Ras Mengesha, and the famous throne

View of the Asmara Pool from the inside
Source: S.Graf 2013

of Mekelle, conceived as an imitation of the biblical Throne of Solomon.[3] Sebastiano Castagna, a sergeant of the military engineering corps from Sicily, taken prisoner in Adwa and conducted in Addis Ababa, where he remained at the service of Menelik II and later of Haile Selassie, married a noble Abyssinian and designed many important buildings, such as the famous St. George's Cathedral and the Bank of Abyssinia. He was considered a sort of Public Works Minister.[4]

Mezzèdimi will be the architect of an Emperor and truly uniquely of the Black Messiah: Haile Selassie I. Haile Selassie, literally Power of the Holy Trinity, was the Emperor of Ethiopia, Conquering Lion of the Tribe of Judah, Elect of God, Defender of the Faith and Negus Neghesti, 225th descendant of King Solomon and the Queen of Sheba, born Tafari Makonnen. He was considered the second coming in the majesty, glory and power of Jesus Christ, the Black Messiah for Bob Marley and Rastafarians, as described in the holy book of the Kebra Nagast.[5] This particular position – right-hand of an Emperor and new Messiah – as well as a peculiar attitude to design led Mezzèdimi to the unique opportunity of designing and constructing a shocking number of buildings and plans in a very short time.

The mapped buildings are 281, while the number of the projects catalogued by the firm reaches 1,624. If we consider all of his career, in about thirty years of professional activity, this means an average of fifty-five projects per year. An hyperbolic number that corresponds to about one project per week. In 1958 Mezzèdimi received his most prestigious commission to draft a proposal for the Africa Hall, United Nations' headquarter in Africa, entirely financed by the Ethiopian government and strongly supported by the Emperor, as a tangible symbol of his pan-African policies.

Arturo Mezzèdimi participated to the process of defining an Ethiopian and pan-African architectural identity. Its architectural choices, never dull or repetitive despite the pace of overproduction, were manifest of the imperial will of modernity. Leafing through the enormous list of his works, we can picture Haile Selassie less lonely "in assuming the huge task of starting his millennial empire toward a real evolution of civilisation".[6] Haile Selassie will be engaged for a lifetime in the process of modernisation of a country and a continent to "develop a modern African identity and at the same time a modern Africanity".[7] The Negus will live in constant fascination of Ethiopia in its most traditional and genuine version, but also of Europe, a very different world of which he sensed not the superiority but the essential technical complementarity. The attempt of the Negus, largely failed, was to "harmonise Ethiopian provincialism with European modernism".[8] Architecture in Africa became a tool in the search for identity, and the fact that it was for a long period entrusted to foreign experts stresses not only the technical limitations of the continent, but also the ability to absorb foreign influences, the cosmopolitan vision and the resilience of local traditions. Mezzèdimi lived the unusual condition of belonging to an invader nation and at the same time be a trusted consultant of a prince in his quest for modernity. Architecture, not based on formal research or folk revival but defined by quantitative parameters and respectful of the specific social and cultural conditions, could be a tool towards a renewed African identity.

In these abundance of professional opportunities, the concrete risk is the search for distinction or for arrogant uniformity that could lead to pretentious invention. Mezzèdimi escaped this risk. The cornucopia of innumerable tasks is faced with decorum. It is a measured sobriety, moderation controlled by education, which characterises all his buildings, even in the most challenging, and exposed to criticism, professional opportunities. The investigation of a right middle way is the essential component for the search of decorum, which is an ideal, ethic and aesthetic at the same time, a balance and respect of things, the desire to be fair and comply with the laws of behaviour, to achieve optimum moderation. The birth of this attitude can be found in the conditions that Mezzèdimi lived in the 1940s Asmara, an Italian city de facto even under British occupation. Mezzèdimi will interpret the complex colonial legacy, imagining the future needs of a young bourgeois society. A fertile ground welcomes the young Sienese, not yet graduated: despite the turbulent political events, Amara's dynamic entrepreneurial environment will allow Mezzèdimi to overcome the first economic difficulties and complete his studies as a quantity surveyor and establish himself as an autonomous designer fully careful to all technical and functional implications. Mezzèdimi's work will remain equidistant from the requirements of representativeness and imperialist ideology expressed by the 1963 Cafiero plan and from the Allied propaganda that from 1941 aligned with neo-traditionalist positions.

The extent of equidistance will be clear in his first important work, the Mingardi pool, epilogue of a series of leisure buildings in Asmara and first act of a multitude of private commissions that will allow him to design and build houses, villas, factories, shops, tombs, etc. Few of the 17,000 Italians that remained in Eritrea after the British occupation will identify themselves with the residues of the fascist expression; few reap the provocative British propaganda which, although surprised by Asmara's measured grandeur, deplored the super-fascist spirit of the city and the state of poverty in which the war had left the natives;[9] many, almost all, will continue the controversial but fruitful work of collaboration that led Asmara to be an Italian city with a cosmopolitan vocation.[10]

Arturo Mezzèdimi, Babatin House, Asmara 1946–1947
Source: Mezzèdimi's personal archive, Rome, Italy

Between 1941 and 1949, when the Eritrean case was put under the control of the United Nations, Asmara saw the birth of the Magnotti brothers' nail factory; the Salumificio Torinese; the IVA Asmara Wine Industry, the IFMA Matches Industry Asmara, the PRODEMAR; industry for the production of pearl buttons, and the engineer Carlo Tabacchi's ceramic industry, in addition to the Prodotti Vitale and the Milani Honey Industry which began activities immediately before British occupation. The British mandate, leaving the Italians control over the civil administration, laid the foundations for a transition based on the continuity of relations between former colonisers and ex-colonised: an attitude that will allow, despite some underlying contradictions[11], the growth of a progressive and independent Italian and Eritrean middle class. To understand the different realities that made the postcolonial transition, it's enough to scroll through the names of the clients for whom Mezzèdimi will work in Asmara, Massawa and Assab. Bahobesci, Mingardi, Ceci, Trinci, Babatin, Becchio, Bion, Moledina, Sciausc, Beshir, Kahjee Dossa, Patrignani, Mutahar Said and Shoa Benin were entrepreneurs from Italy, Eritrea, Ethiopia, Israel who invested in the construction of the city and entrusted Mezzèdimi to represent their social status. Measured every time on different demands and needs, the various solutions proposed by the architect combined the satisfaction of private interest with attention to the issues that the controlled expansion of the city posed.

Arturo Mezzèdimi, Piscina Mingardi, Asmara 1944–1945
Source: Mezzèdimi's personal archive, Rome, Italy

The search for economy and for the best possible solution, in functional and technicals terms, imposed to the design a process of continuous refinement, which corresponds to the fluidity of Asmara's urban character and, more generally, with the complex economic and cultural transition of the city during the British mandate. While we can not reconstruct the history of each design, the testing of appropriate solutions from a technical as well as urban point of view encompasses Mezzèdimi's first experiences. The solution prepared for the Mingardi pool, built between 1944 and 1945, is the last in a long series of hypotheses through which the architect perfected the distribution pattern and calibrated technical solutions gradually, depending on available materials and labour. In doing so he built a solid relationship between the building and the city, in spatial and cultural terms, giving architecture the public character that made it an integral part of the urban landscape. From the first solutions, characterised by a long curtain façade, to the complex volumetric configuration that characterises the constructed building, Mezzèdimi proceeded to a progressive simplification. As the technical data were integrated into the architectural discourse, this was becoming more essential and synthetic and the hierarchy of the parts that made up the set became gradually clearer.

The arrangment of the pool, the roof, the distinction between served and servant spaces, the corner solution, the main prospect on Via Bottego and the shed of the terrace are the key steps through which the architect gives form to the design and realises, with the help of the latest technologies, a modern public building. The indoor pool, which was open on the morning of September the 2nd 1945, was constructed on a lot owned by Mrs. Ines Mingardi, between Via Bottego and Via Miani. The building was an unprecedented success for Asmara which had only a modest public bath.[12] The indoor pool was considered, well before its inauguration, as a building of great interest for the entire population of the city. News of its impending opening were already published in July 1945, on the sports pages of *Il Quotidiano Eritreo*, one of the many Italian newspapers published in Eritrea during and after the war. The press gives news of the construction of the building and focuses on the high quality of the implants and of their technical characteristics: the size of the pool of 9 m x 20 m, is considered exceptional, both for the "confined space and the irregularity of the area", as well as for the amount of services that designers have succeeded to build. Great importance was assigned to the mechanisms that allowed the continuous rotation of the water, completely filtered twice a day. In order to build a modern building so well received by the press, Mezzèdimi will work alongside the best Italian companies permanently present in Eritrea: the concrete and steel structures were entrusted to Vincenzo Costa Costruzioni Metalliche, founded in 1936 and still active in Asmara, while the electrical system, "which meets the most modern standards", was assigned to Società Anonima Ingegneri Lucini e Ziliani.

Vincenzo Costa Costruzioni Metalliche was a solid business and was involved in all stages of iron working, from casting to varnishing: already involved in the construction of "many magnificent industrial installations with enormous structures of proven solidity" the company demonstrated its ability to respond to the degree of commitment that the project demanded. During this apprenticeship phase in Eritrea, where private commissions and public competitions alternate, Mezzèdimi worked essentially alone, dealing with the architectural design as well as with structural calculations and cooperating with external technicians only in rare cases, often for the preparation of in-depth implant design. The ongoing professional training that the architect pursued was the indispensable support in the search for the most effective solution, the base for a rational discourse that passes through the various phases of the project, from the initial processing to the final choices, and is never realised in a uniform language: each architecture can be recognised only from its special, domestic and urban conditions for which it was designed and built.

The project for the building in Piazza Toselli, in Massawa, without ever falling into camouflage or easy environmentalism, is a poster of this attitude: the distribution pattern of the building is divided into a triple body and combines the search for climatic comfort with the extreme rationalisation of domestic spaces, while the shed of the terrace, made with a simple concrete system, gives depth to the façade, a reinterpretation of the historical roshan window of the Red Sea, and gives the architect the opportunity to draw an unprecedented façade solution with an important urban value. In the Becchio house extension and in the project for villa Patrignani, both in Asmara, the proposals developed by Mezzèdimi show close attention to the domestic dimension. At the same time, he does not waive to public represent its customers and their social condition, articulating spaces open towards the city, with large windows, terraces and a solarium ready to welcome guests.

In 1948 Mezzèdimi designs a proposal for the redevelopment of Piazza Italia, home of the indigenous market and business centre of the city, already rebuilt by Guido Ferrazza. The design of the new building, located at the centre of the long colonnade, reaffirms the spirit in which Mezzèdimi addressed the issue of post-war reconstruction and postcolonial transition: the architect works on the remains of the existing, recovers its meaning, reinventing it, and lays the foundation for a measured and appropriate urban development. In the design drawings the city around the square grows in height, becomes denser and the market, properly renovated, is again its centre. Having blocked all sorts of imports from the former Italian motherland, in a few years Asmara reconstructs its manufacturing economy. Mezzèdimi is part of this process of reinvention and formalises the creative development that the *Mostra delle Attività Produttrici dell'Eritrea*, held in Asmara in 1943, had already anticipated, reorganising the new production processes despite continuous protests, bombings and strikes.

Only at the end of the 1940s, at the conclusion of a ten-year transition path, with the weakening of the revolutionary spirit and the easing of the class struggle, is Asmara rebuilt as a "city of the white empire".[13] No longer the centre of a futile Italian empire, to which Malaparte had devoted long pages of his diary, but the capital of federal Eritrea, that through the difficult postcolonial transition linked its fate to that of the Negus' empire. Mezzèdimi, who had a leading role in this transition, had acquired the tools to intervene on the city, interpreting each project as an opportunity to rebuild the link between production, urban culture and technical knowledge. A strong relationship that will cause the city to grow in height and densify its fabric: in this atmosphere of renewed growth, Mezzèdimi designs and manufactures alongside the Haile Selassie Avenue, in Asmara's city centre, two dwellings complexes for Ahmed and Omar Bahobesci between 1951 and 1953.

The first one, built for Ahmed Bahobesci, is the revival of issues already tested on a small scale by Giuseppe Cané and Carlo Marchi e Aldo Burzagli

Arturo Mezzèdimi, Piazza Italia, Asmara 1948

Source: Mezzèdimi's personal archive, Rome, Italy

in Palazzo Faletta which they designed between 1937 and 1938. Mezzèdimi overlaps to the building block a large multistory loggia, building on the main front a tripartite façade strongly hierarchical and full of light and shade; the two lower wings, marked by deep loggias and small square windows, complete the open court that is shaped as a urban element. A character accentuated by the coating, made with small yellow and green mosaic tiles.

The second building commissioned by the Bahobesci family is one of the first projects that Mezzèdimi designs and constructs with the engineer Mario Fanano, technical expert and active polemicist. In 1953, upon completion, the building is one of the largest in Asmara. To cope with the change in scale, which is evident from aerial photos immediately after the implementation, designers unhinged the compact character of the first Bahobesci building, just a few hundred metres away, articulating the six floors of the long façade in a multitude of loggias, balconies, terraces and overhangs. Technological appropriateness, wise distribution and urban tradition meet in the search for a new building type: the high density housing block which was unprecedented in Asmara. Also unprecedented is the glass, concrete and steel tower that the study by Fanano-Mezzèdimi will elaborate for the Bahobesci family, a few years later, alongside Haile Selassie Avenue. The proposal, though appropriately assessed in its urban insertion through the use of models, perspectives and photomontages will never be constructed, probably rejected by the building committee or discarded for financial reasons.[14]

Mezzèdimi will have to wait until the 1960s – the transfer to the capital, the major public and private commissions – to see his design ideas fully realised. But it is in Asmara that his thoughts are shaped; in Asmara he gets in contact with the "surreal landscape, controlled by a random and illogical order, that flipped Vignola's four rules",[15] indifferent to human presence. An indifference detected by Malaparte in 1939, while travelling in the ephemeral Ethiopian empire unified by the Italians, to understand what he saw he could only refer to known comparisons: Tarquinia's tombs, Ceri's hunters, the black haired Etruscans. And the Etruscan Mezzèdimi tries to bend this indifference, to meet this illogical landscape, to mediate this upside down order, to find out where it was, "between Mycenae and Manhattan"[16] the Ethiopia that he will build.

Arturo Mezzèdimi, Shoa Benin Building, first solution, Asmara
Source: Mezzèdimi's personal archive, Rome, Italy

Arturo Mezzèdimi, Mario Fanano, Bahobesci Building, Asmara 1953
Source: Mezzèdimi's personal archive, Rome, Italy

Notes

1 Arturo Mezzèdimi, "Hailé Selassié I: una testimonianza per la rivalutazione", *Studi Piacentini*, vol. 12, 1992, p. 179.

2 Angelo Del Boca, *Il Negus. Vita e morte dell'ultimo re dei re*. Rome-Bari: Laterza 2007, p. 280.

3 Alberto Sbacchi, Gino Vernetto (eds.), *Giacomo Naretti alla corte del Negus Johannes IV d'Etiopia (Diari 1856–1881)*. Ivrea: Associazione di Storia e Arte Canavesana, 2004.

4 Beppe Pegolotti, "Un italiano alla corte di Menelik", *Storia Illustrata*, vol. 148, 1970.

5 Lorenzo Mazzoni (ed.), *Kebra Nagast: la Bibbia segreta del rastafari*. Rome: Il Coniglio, 2007.

6 Giuliano Cora, Italian ambassador to Ethiopia, in a letter to Benito Mussolini dated 18th April 1928, see Angelo Del Boca, *Il Negus. Vita e morte dell'ultimo re dei re*, op. cit., 2007.

7 Joseph Ki-Zerbo, *Repères sur l'Afrique*. Dakar: Panafrika/Silex/Nouvelles, 2011, p. 44.

8 Angelo Del Boca, *Il Negus. Vita e morte dell'ultimo re dei re*, op. cit., p. 280.

9 Edward Denison, *Asmara, Africa's Secret Modernist City*. London: Merrell, 2003.

10 For a deepened understanding of the complex history of post-war Asmara see Angelo Del Boca, *Gli Italiani in Africa Orientale – IV. Nostalgia delle colonie*. Milan: Arnoldo Mondadori, 1992, pp. 111-124.

11 Like the strikes and clashes of 1943, which involved workers from Eritrean and Italian companies, see Edward Denison, *Asmara, Africa's Secret Modernist City*, op. cit.

12 *Guida dell'Africa Orientale Italiana*. Milan: Consociazione Turistica Italiana, 1938, pp. 204-205.

13 Curzio Malaparte, *Viaggio in Etiopia e altri scritti africani*, Enzo R.Laforgia (ed.), Florence: Vallecchi, 2006, pp. 51-66.

14 The project was remodelled at the request of new clients, Shoa Benin, who acquired the area in 1957 and constructed in very different forms at the end of 1958. Edward Denison, *Asmara, Africa's Secret Modernist City*, op. cit., pp. 224-225, 227.

15 Curzio Malaparte, *Viaggio in Etiopia e altri scritti africani*, op. cit., p. 59.

16 (note 15), p. 53.

OTHER SCENES – POSSIBLE SELVES
Building the Italian Colonial Interior in Asmara

Sean Anderson

We Italians need the barbarous to renew ourselves, we Italians more than any other population, since our past is the greatest in the world and because of that the most formidable for our life! Our race has always dominated and it is always renewed by barbaric contact.[1]

If one were to replace the word race with architecture in this much-maligned quotation by the Futurist sculptor Umberto Boccioni, we might understand the sphere of Italian modernism as having been strengthened by constructions of the Other, of the autochthonous, as commensurate with imperial ambition. Yet, when examined through the lens of the colonial, however, both conditions – the divisive racial paradigm and that of an imposed architectural culture – are both constructed from without. The overlaps of architecture and race in the establishment of Italian colonies in East and North Africa were performed, in part, by the imaging of its cities, through the displacement of native populations and the consistent reappraisal of their value. A reconstitution of discourses relating to the construction of interiority continues to define Italian and Western European modernism. Adopting a heterotemporal or diachronic rendering of Eritrea and its principal city Asmara affords readings of a colony that was not exhaustively imprinted in the journals, magazines and other media central to the Fascist establishment.[2] In between these gaps of signification, multiple modernities emerged in the localities of Asmara over its near fifty years as an Italian colonial and later imperial city.

A *tukul* still existing in the north of the city
Source: S. Graf 2013

This essay attempts to read Asmara from its edges. Immediately prior to and following the creation of the Italian Empire, the substantial increase of colonists throughout the colonies dramatically affected the organisation of urban and domestic spaces. Commencing in 1936 within the bounded areas that had been reserved specifically for the Eritrean or regional populace, the extra-territorial zones of Via Tevere in the northeast quadrant of Asmara are also spaces in which the telling of a modern history seemingly slows down, where photographic images are not as plentiful, and the boundaries that demarcate the binaries of colonial power are understood but not relayed. But this is not to say that the blurring of such limits within Asmara did not previously exist. Rather, these transactional sites allow for the interrogation of a homologous interior that enfolded citizenry while also reflecting the sanctioned violence for imperialised metropolitan spatial codes.

The introduction of two contrasting visual economies in Asmara illustrate how the colonial interior was conceived within the visual and spatial realms of the modern. The architectonics of a *teleferica* or cableway in 1937 and the perpetuation of Eritrean-only settlements around Asmara will pose architecture as a substitute for power. Rather, by rethinking the motivations for and the material remains of a distinct, yet coeval interior(ity) for Asmara, agency will be construed first inside the unseen domestic spaces given to the Eritreans inhabiting these areas and then transferred to the reflective surfaces of the modern city. An inversion is also possible, in which the fundaments of witnessing the colony's unfolding from above via the *teleferica* signalled a new territorial claim for the unseen and the invisible. Both transits, from the prescribed affinities of locality to a projective unknown, represent a fundamental aspect of Asmara's spatial ordering. It is precisely within this interpolative frame that such fleeting occupations became the emboldened yet dark mirrors of an Italian colonial modernity.

Revising Italy from an erstwhile colonial power to that of an Empire between 1936 until 1943 altered the means by which Mussolini and the Nation operated across its Northeast African protectorates. Located within both a rhetorical spiritualism and an emphatic pragmatism, securing these colonies under the umbrella of an imperial drive was foremost concerned with transcendence. Not content with only territorial ambitions, as these deviations were still being played out in other arenas such as Dalmatia and Albania, the domain of *Africa Orientale Italiana* (AOI) involved a recuperative mission on behalf of Fascist ideologues. While embodying a continuum from ancient to modern employed by Fascism, architecture's aesthetic hierarchies were located within newly-formed urban and domestic spheres. In the colonies of East Africa, this perpetuation was not as clearly defined. Eritrea suffered from a dearth of objectified ancient artifactual evidence such as found in Libya and the Dodecanese. If state-sponsored archaeological pursuits were to confirm the continuities of the Roman Empire, they also opened up the very ground upon which modern Italian architecture and urbanism could be situated. This revelation of historicised stratigraphy was closely aligned with how the past was construed as imaginary while the East African colony and the city were situated within the present perfect: a perpetual state of becoming.

An often-compromised indigeneity was continually promoted throughout the colonies. For Eritrea, and Asmara in particular, within its active urban laboratory of modernity, constructed scenes were established for the encoding of a racialised and gendered present. The misregistration between the fixity of Race and those intersections that fulfilled a more tactical mobilisation of vision were not easily resolved. Rather, over time, architects, engineers and planners in Asmara sought to find methods in which the native Eritrean, while addressed within the dictates of demographic colonisation, might also disappear from the city. Simultaneously, the interior became a dominant, yet unseen, mode for understanding the evolution of the city. To occupy the burgeoning centre of the Italo-African Empire, which would soon be transferred to Addis Ababa, was at once to be emplaced by difference while having one's value consistently in flux.

Demographic colonisation in *Africa Orientale Italiana* transformed Asmara as a setting for the implantation of new visual and spatial systems for which Italy would attempt to transfer "the whole machinery of its own civilisation."[3] Mapping the colonial as modern within Asmara, when defined as interior, is both a bounded yet mobile spatial phenomenon. Leading up to and following the declaration of the Empire, the emplacement of new technologies inflected a counterpart to the modern city. However, among the indigenous zones outside of the Asmara city centre, these narratives fall away and we are left with few images documenting what Okwui Enwezor has termed an *aftermodern*, that is, the countenance of a city, colony, and empire in which uncompromising temporalities were rendered by and through interiors.[4] If, as Silvana Palma has argued, the early photography of Eritrea "sought to construct a reality," that elided conflicts in favour of a domestication of spatial forms, following the declaration of the Empire, such "...recognition of an independent and autonomous power and identity of the colonised" was ultimately diminished in favour of disappearance.[5] The nascence of a modern colonial Asmara allied the simultaneous manufacture of Eritrean-borne realities within a self-conscious Italianità. Prompting a circuit of meanings among the city's inhabitants, the charged interfaces between architecture and interior deployed a spatial language that sought to coalesce visual structures around material referents that suggest passages from embodiment to surface.

Among the earliest instances of colonial Eritrea, the mapping of the physical landscape was coupled with a social ordering of its populations. As Uoldelul Chelati Dirar has described, this twin process was instrumental in determining Italian authority as much as it was to organise imperial knowledge.[6] Later, while political certainties present within the Italian colonial city were made visible through coordinated mass gatherings, syncretic urban planning devices and the co-opting of fascist symbology, the construction of an interior captured but also transgressed these manifestations of external power. The circulation of Eritrean and Italian bodies in Asmara prior to the rise of Empire suggests a hybridisation of urban and interior spaces in which divisions were projective rather than incongruent. Yet, as the establishment of Eritrean settlements outside of the city continued apace, an even more divisive rupture in the figuration of race and identity occurred in Asmara. By 1938, the enactment of Race Laws solidified a shadow city.

For the "anthropological machine" described by Giorgio Agamben, the Italian colonial city established "zones of indeterminacy" in which the state offered forms of inclusion that nonetheless were also exclusive of its subjects.[7] Consequently, the emboldened advent of modern temporalities in Asmara emblematised by new building programmes that privileged cinemas and hotels as well as infrastructures of mobility such as new roads, including the Via della Vittoria to Ethiopia, were easily distinguished but difficult to manage.[8] It was through this institutionalisation of the modern: the simultaneous building of governance and the colonial city that resulted in a disciplining of the spatial. The internal boundaries that formerly defined a singular history of Asmara were now subject to increasing exposure, revelation. For colonial authorities, the desire for an all-encompassing or metropolitan vision accompanied by nationalist sentiments supplanted an autochthonous Eritrean presence and led to fragmentation. Between 1936 and 1938, with an expanding population and a catalytic military-industrial presence, those divisions that reified the dialectics of subject and interior, between Eritrean and Italian, were fortified.[9]

Movements through Asmara also speak to non-static hierarchies in which the city became both stage and backdrop to the course of modern transits of colonial bodies and meanings. These transformations in time fundamentally changed the manner in which urban and domestic spaces were experienced. When observing how the vernacular moved out of the edges of the burgeoning city and into/on to the new buildings that were being proffered by Italian architects (perhaps contrary to the more traditional vein of Catholic neo-Romanesque), what we recognise is an outfitting of buildings as images, their façades eschewing any doubt of who built them, yet their interiors not revealing or slowly fading from language. For the urban and architectural enterprises of late colonial Asmara, the appropriation of filmic controls in which the holistic appearance of apartment blocks and institutional buildings along the dominant streets of Asmara established an almost impenetrable screen through and by which Eritrean identity was assessed. The speed of the visual, akin to spectacle, induced by this resurfacing of the city, culminated in a road race on the principal thoroughfare of Asmara on Viale Mussolini in 1936. For the colonial subject, one's withdrawal into an interior not of their own making may thus be interpreted as a precarious form of safety in which the remediation of living conditions was an attempt to fashion alternative modes of the everyday. Organised, gridded, and rationally dispersed across a lifeless ground, Asmara was first marked by indigeneity and rewritten by colonial and imperial structures.

What then may be the visible traces of a finite colonial interior in Asmara? For the proto-Imperial realm, the overlaps of time and image secured bodies to locations. Akin to W.J.T.Mitchell's concept of a metapicture, Asmara by the late 1930s staged an image of an image in which aspects of the modern colonial city became "...not merely epistemological model(s), but ethical, political, and aesthetic 'assemblages' that allowed..." Italians and Eritreans alike "to observe observers."[10] A constructed hypericonic nature of Eritrean settlements on the peripheries of Asmara forcibly pried apart those bonds that fixed home and ground in which space was not acceded value with the exception of visual occupation. The violence of this partitioning was as perfunctory as it was punitive. Found among the elegiac photographs that accompanied the missions of the Nicotra Brothers and other Italian photographers in Northeast Africa prior to the turn of the twentieth century, the multiple registers of the colonial offer a quantitative but not objective depiction of the Eritrean as a dissolute entity.[11] Furthermore, the documentary imaging of gated areas of Italian-built *tukuls* organised into tight grids on the outskirts of Asmara speaks to a logic of surveillance as much as mistrust. The engineered boundaries between these zones of difference, of primitivity, and those of the Italian colonial city were unmistakable. Terry Smith describes this practice within the dictates of "cultural imperialism" as "a kind of ethnic cleansing carried out by the displacement of unmodern peoples into past, slower or frozen time."[12] Consequently, through the rationing of interiority, Eritreans were fundamentally deprived of their time.

An enforced or coercive mimeticism of the grid implanted within the Eritrean settlements at the peripheries of Asmara challenges the notion of the colonial government's single vanishing point for the city. Homi Bhabha's commentary on the insouciance of colonial mimicry decries "the desire for...the subject of a difference that is almost the same but not quite...also the same but not white."[13]

While the grid of *tukuls* allows for maximal transparency of its inhabitants, the easily reproducible ordering of houses for the Eritrean native also asserts a complex inversion of a modern colonial city's interior. Even if the boundedness of home asserted both in geometric formation (a circular or semi-oval form of the *tukul*) as well as imposed ordering in these areas, the colonised shadow-city is structured within the operative potential of an interior that is both refuge and suspension. Not necessarily a mirror, these dispersed settlements break down the distance between the (white) interior of the city and the marked bodies of Eritreans. These spatial oppositions have not necessarily been countermanded by other diagrammatic instances in the city. Even today many commentators of Asmara suffer from a myopic entrenchment in the descriptive language of the colonial city as frozen, forgotten, and lost. Race, in turn, may thus be presenced within Asmara as an externalised condition of the interior.

For *Africa Orientale Italiana*, this split subjectivity between Asmara as city and Asmara as interior allies an affective positioning through which consciousness is a negotiation of spatial forms. Spatial relationships occured both independently as well as collectively through experiencing the urban and domestic as inherently fragmented. In central Asmara, the delimiting of the so-called Villa Quarter, the covering of the Mai Bela River passage, and separate marketplaces established internal boundaries that enacted spatial and temporal breaks in the city fabric. The modern colonial city, whilst organised in part by one's ability to cross these thresholds, is ultimately disaggregated by an architecture that sought to further demarcate the spatial conditions by which Eritrean and Italian were derived. It is the mark of the colonial subject to reduce these instabilities to a fixity or wholeness, as Walter Benjamin asserts in describing the (modern) city as a panorama. The panorama of evolution proffered by the Italian colonial and later imperial authority in Asmara exists as a form of collection in which the collocation and restructuring of Italian-made Eritrean spaces and Italian-defined Eritrean persons offer a glimpse of a totalising equanimity that only exists within the image. Indeed, within this pan-optic imagining of Asmara, the spaces for Eritrean self-reflexivity were negotiated.

Through an imperialised subjectivity, Eritreans were incapacitated by colonial temporalities that constituted their otherness. With the accompanying shocks of the modern colonial city, an equivalent trauma existed in being removed from it, the framing for a fictive reality. Similarly, for Freud and the psychoanalytic outlining of another scene is distinct from the dreamworld. He deploys the notion of a bounded space that is manifest in its productive capacity.[14] Here, the dream, governed by the colonial city, while existing in an autonomous yet parallel sphere to waking life, is not necessarily drawn from individual desire but from external labour. Encompassing unconscious drives, the other scene and perhaps its formations of interior, becomes a "preconscious repository of the means of signification, images, and associations not repressed but not at the forefront of conscious thought."[15] Subsequent delaminations of the other scene by Jacques Lacan and Maud Mannoni suggest an equivalence between the Other as symbolic currency and the space(s) in which otherness is posited, a psychic locality. In Asmara, the bifurcation of the coloniser and colonised intensifies such borders. One such point in the 1938 *Manifesto della razza* claims, "...the theories that support the African origin of some European peoples...must be considered dangerous, because they establish inadmissible affinities and ideological sympathies."[16] Yet, the mirroring of the colonial subject in Asmara with that of colonial oppressors is highlighted by such urban constructions as those found at the peripheral *tukul* encampments. Meanwhile, indexing traditional components, including thatched roofs and striated stone façades, with the religious buildings of Degghi Selam and Enda Mariam were upended by the visual and economic pleasures afforded by the *teleferica*. For Mannoni, the other scene "constitutes a necessary understanding of the political, for it is composed through the manner in which all people, and not only the deluded, form their realities."[17] Throughout Asmara, this imbalance inscribes the Italian colonial city as binding the signification of imperial dominion to an interior. The visual silencing of Eritreans in Asmara may thus be wrought first through pictorial annexation and second through spatial suppression.

Characterising the (Italian) colony, if not the city, as interior disrupts the monolithic construction of a global modern. Infrastructural and building projects in Asmara throughout its fifty-year involution modified the boundaries between an unseen but occupied interior and an intransigent exterior while introducing new structural orders as thresholds that, until now, had only occupied semi-fictional narratives. A contrapuntal actioning of difference inherent within representations of Italian colonial cities illustrates an oscillation between a regeneration of the colonial modern city as fixed and the bodily/visual movements within it. As much as the peripheral Eritrean settlements embodied division, with the introduction of the *teleferica*, a repositioning of the landscape and bodies (of goods and people) could now literally transect territories of colonial vision, of modern building, that had formerly constituted imperial longing. Akin to the gridded Eritrean settlements existing along the confines of an Italian Asmara, the presence of the *teleferica* from coastal Massawa to Asmara simultaneously systematised landscapes of disavowal and conquest. For both, the disjointed natures of Eritrea and Asmara were harnessed within an interior that underscored the intense workings of a "hierarchy of dominions."[18]

The temporal, visual and spatial vectors of race were redrawn through Asmara and exemplify conflicting associations. At their intersection, the colonial interior was constructed and assumed. The boundedness of (Eritrean) bodily experience and the optical undoing of urban spaces up to and following the declaration of the Italian Empire locates the modern colonial architecture of Asmara both within and without the confines of a present. Both involve congruent designations by which agency is determined externally. In effect, the trap of colonial modernism was to be (re)settled into the very visual and spatial networks that aligned one's body with an exploitative architecture and urbanism. However, without possessing the fleeting images of Asmara's rise that may account for the interiors of modern dwellings, domestic spaces, cinemas, and factories. While this may not seem unusual for the broader reaches of colonialism, with the concomitant over-exposure of Italian colonial cities, this register for an unknown in Asmara is remarkable. It is the modern colonial city's apparitional appearance as the setting of other scenes that challenges narratives of a holistic (Italian) modernity. In Asmara, to escape these engineered boundaries was and continues to be perilous. To become, to not-become: questions for the Eritrean that remain essential testimonies for a city and nation that today are undergoing an unprecedented emptying. The leakage of countless Eritreans escaping into the invisible itineraries of people smuggling routes across the Sahara and into the deadly camps and prisons of Libya are hollowing former Italian colonial cities once again. If the refugees survive, the crossing of the Mediterranean induces a manifold retrenchment of colonial parallels. A return of the oppressed. Without access to an interior, a violent expression of the barest of lives, Eritreans are attempting to escape to the very shores that once signified their own limits as subjects. And being denied entry.

Notes

1 Umberto Boccioni, "Fondamento Plastico della Pittura e Scultura Futuriste", in Zeno Birolli (ed.), *Pittura Scultura Futuriste*. Milan: Abscondita, 2006, p. 81.

2 Dipesh Chakrabarty, *Provinicializing Europe: Postcolonial Thought and Historical Difference*. Princeton: Princeton University Press, 2007, p. xvii.

3 R. Meregazzi, "Lineamenti della legislazione per l'impero," in *Gli annali dell'Africa Italiana*, a.II (1939) no. 3, pp. 5-34; 12. "The regime conceived a new social plan for the empire, consisting of a society made up by brave and hard-working farmers, virtuous and frugal, 'all equal and all poor enough.'" Gian-Luca Podestà, "Colonists and 'Demographic' Colonists: Family and Society in Italian Africa", *Annales de démographie historique*, vol. 122, 2011, pp. 205-231; p. 221.

4 Okwui Enwezor, "Modernity and Postcolonial Ambivalence," *South Atlantic Quarterly*, vol. 109, 3, 2010, pp. 595-620.

5 Silvana Palma, "The Seen, the Unseen, the Invented: Misrepresentations of African 'Otherness' in the Making of a Colony. Eritrea, 1885–1896", *Cahiers d'Études africaines*, XLV (1), 177, 2005, pp 39-69. Palma continues by suggesting that the early photography of Eritrea "...separates the seeable from what must be rejected, according to specificities proper to an instrument which, at the very moment it reproduces reality, is in fact constructing it."

6 Uoldelul Chelati Dirar, "Colonialism and the Construction of National Identities: The Case of Eritrea", *Journal of East African Studies*, vol.1, (2), July 2007, pp. 256-76, p. 260. "However, parallel to the mapping of the Eritrean physical landscape, colonial authorities engaged in an even more complex activity which in the long term had major consequences for both colonial power and Eritrean society. This was the mapping of the social landscape of Eritrea, a multifaceted process which investigated many levels of Eritrean society in the attempt to provide ethnographic and linguistic knowledge to Italian policy-makers and administrators on the ground." Tekeste Negash has described three phases of racial policies enacted in Eritrea with the later Imperial period enforcing "indisputable dominance over the colonised." See Tekeste Negash, *Italian Colonialism in Eritrea, 1882–1941: Policies, Praxis and Impact*. Uppsala: Uppsala University, 1987.

7 For Agamben, the colonial state, in its managerial practice, through states of exception effect "a zone of indeterminacy in which the outside is nothing but the exclusion of an inside and the inside is in turn only the inclusion of an outside." Giorgio Agamben, trans. Kevin Attell, *The Open: Man and Animal*. Stanford: Stanford University Press, 2004, p. 37.

8 This is also suggested by the earlier Futurist appropriation of continental Africa as a timeless present in which visual structures were staged. For the colonial Indian context, "The openendedness of spatial meaning unsettled dearly held ideas of public and private, self and other, by refusing to grant colonisers a sense of interiority within the safe confines of which to construct an imperial self." Swati Chattopadhyay, "Blurring Boundaries: The Limits of 'White Town' in Colonial Calcutta", *Journal of the Society of Architectural Historians*, vol. 59, (2), June 2000, pp. 154-179, p. 177.

9 One census figure places a total of 75,000 Italian persons (mostly men) in Eritrea by 1940 following five years of rapid expansion. This figure was no doubt compounded by the presence of 350,000 Italian soldiers involved with the Italo-Ethiopian War.

10 Metapictures "don't merely serve as illustrations to theory; they picture theory." W.J.T. Mitchell, *Picture Theory: Essays on Verbal and Visual Representation*. Chicago: University of Chicago Press, 1994, p. 49. For Mitchell, the metapicture is "a representation of the relation between discourse and representation, a picture about the gap between words and pictures."(65)

11 See Palma (2005).

12 Terry Smith, "Introduction", in Terry Smith, Okwui Enwezor, and Nancy Condee (eds.), *Antinomies of Art and Culture: Modernity, Postmodernity, Contemporaneity*. Durham, NC: Duke University Press, 2008, pp. 1-19, p. 5.

13 Homi Bhabha, *The Location of Culture*. New York: Routledge, 1994, pp. 85-89.

14 Freud located such transferals within a dream-like "other scene" [*eine andere Schauplatz*] based on previous findings by the psychologist Gustave T. Fechner. In *The Interpretation of Dreams*, Freud writes "the scene of action of dreams is different from that of waking ideational life." SE V (1900), pp. 535-36.

15 Ranjana Khanna, *Dark Continents: Psychoanalysis and Colonialism*. Durham: Duke University Press, 2003, pp. 239-241.

16 The *Manifesto della razza* was first published in the newspaper *Giornale d'Italia* on 14 July 1938 as "*il Fascismo e il problema della razza*."

17 Ibid. 159.

18 See Podestà (2011) 213.

CENTRALE ELETTRICA
PROIBITO L'INGRESSO

LIGHT – GAME – THEATRE
Licht-Spiel-Theater (Play-of-Light Theatre)

Günter Richard Wett

Today, cinemas in Asmara are places where crowds gather in the darkened auditorium for purposes that their architects had never imagined, for instance watching Bollywood films or local films in Tigrinya with English subtitles, American films or football games. After Eritrea's independence in 1991, a number of popular films focused on themes such as Eritrea's liberation war and patriotism. However, newer films deal with themes such as love and sexuality. In the Cinema Roma's foyer café, pictures of Hollywood stars are hung just in front of an image depicting Eritrea's liberation struggle, a vintage projector stands next to vintage movie posters (*Casablanca*, *The Great Dictator* and John Wayne) and Laurel and Hardy statuettes. People sit smoking and drinking coffee in the foyer.

Mussolini had encouraged Italian architects and engineers to transform Asmara into an urban utopia, full of cinemas, cafés, and people enjoying their *passeggiata*. Inside the Asmara Theatre are empty stalls, dress circle, row after row of old wooden seats, grand circle and upper balcony, topped by a domed ceiling fresco in which young women dance surrounded by peacocks displaying their feathers. In colonial times, films contributed to the production and orchestration of a coherent colonial sphere – allowing the spectator to participate in all the stages of colonial conquest – and of new exotic experiences among the many Italians who never set foot in Africa. Cinema and colonialism fortified each other to such a degree that it is impossible to see one without in some way dealing with the other. The majority of Italian Empire films – produced under the auspices of Mussolini's government – were war films and allowed Italy to enter into the international market for the exotic.

Fourth Chapter

ASMARA'S CULTURAL HERITAGE

Eritrea's colonial period lasted until the 1990s, leaving legacies of the various colonial rulers of the twentieth century – Italians, British and Ethiopians. Though Asmara had been designed by Italians and then changed under the following administrations, after Eritrea's independence in 1991 it was undisputedly Eritrean. The cultural identity and collective memory of contemporary Asmara is, due to its history, complex, fascinating and, at times, counterintuitive for foreigners. Asmara boasts one of the world's finest ensembles of early twentieth-century architecture and the Eritrean authorities are seeking to have it declared a UNESCO World Heritage Site, even though one might find it difficult to reconcile renewed efforts for the preservation of this architecture with its dubious colonial associations. Cultural heritage has to be viewed as a part of Eritrea's remarkable history of fighting for independent statehood: it is a national symbol. On the other hand, there is an undeniable social and economic crisis in Eritrea that architecture cannot solve, even if it is one in which architecture is involved.

Urban planning and architecture constitute two distinct elements of the Asmara bid, but heritage does not end at buildings. The *passeggiata*, the *Giro d'Eritrea* (bicycle race), Eritrean soccer and Asmara's cappuccino are prime examples of an adopted cultural legacy that is now a cornerstone of Asmara's social character, which is founded on a distinctive sense of place. This colonial legacy shapes the intangible cultural heritage, including practices, representations, expressions as well as the knowledge and skills of communities, groups and, in some cases, individuals. Our book examines past and current efforts to safeguard Asmara's urban heritage.

The UNESCO nomination makes a statement about more than just a few buildings in Asmara; it sheds light on how we treat heritage globally. In fact, as regards the inventory and preservation of modern heritage (that is both colonial and postcolonial, early to mid-twentieth century), Africa is currently referred to as a blank spot on the map of the world.

Peter Volgger and **Stefan Graf** examine the first main attempt to preserve the cultural heritage in Asmara, the Cultural Assets Rehabilitation Project (CARP). Governmental and intergovernmental cultural heritage organisations are urging the making of an inventory and the protection of significant instances of modern architecture in Asmara. While colonial narratives in the field of architecture provide the historical context within which one can (collectively or individually) identify one's own origins and sense of belonging, the ambition of our study of Asmara's colonial architecture is to offer a navigation aid within a highly conflicting sphere of interactions between local and international players, all part of a process of finding and asserting one's position in a globalised world.

Medhanie Teklamariam and **Edward Denison** argue that the Asmara Heritage Project (AHP) reflects a paradigm shift in the World Heritage philosophy. The content of the term cultural heritage has changed considerably in recent decades, partially owing to the instruments developed by the UNESCO. Cultural heritage does not end at monuments and collections of artefacts any longer. It also includes traditions or living expressions inherited from our ancestors and passed on to our descendants.

Demissie Fassil points out that architecture produced under Fascist colonial rule constitutes, by definition, a dissonant heritage: at the time it was designed as an expression of dominance. He begins his contribution with the official submission of the nominating dossier to the World Heritage List. He studies the branding and marketing of Asmara as a tourist destination and explores the ways in which certain parts of the colonial heritage have been institutionally reconfigured to heighten their visibility for global tourist consumption. He uses the case of Asmara to illustrate the repackaging and revitalisation of colonial architecture into a sanitised and decontextualised environment – an international tourist space.

Royal Royal
STOP

MAPPING THE PAST FOR THE SAKE OF THE FUTURE
The Cultural Assets Rehabilitation Project (CARP)

Peter Volgger

Drawings: Stefan Graf and Arno Hofer

"Why destroy Asmara?", Naigzy Gebremedhin asked. Asmarinos are likely to agree with Gebremedhin, the former Director of the Eritrean Cultural Assets Rehabilitation Project (CARP) and co-editor of *Asmara: Africa's Secret Modernist City*,[1] who claims to have made his peace with the fact that Asmara's architecture was originally erected under a fascist regime. Indeed, the issue does not seem to be whether to conserve Asmara, but how to. But even this question is not easy to answer. In many post-liberation states a memory boom has taken place and the number of sites of memory has increased remarkably, in tandem with the transformation of identity narratives and political changes in society. In contrast, the case of Eritrea serves as an example suggesting that transnationalism does not only operate in opposition to nationalism; it can also work to reinforce it in terms of a cultural nationalism.

This essay points to one of the most significant preservation steps in Eritrea over the past decades and also to significant gaps in this attempt. For a critical decolonisation project involves contesting dominant narratives and hegemonic representations, producing counter-narratives and counter-maps, searching for unheard voices and digging in social and psychological soil to allow critical analysis to grow.

A Rationalist building on Harnet Avenue
Source: K. Paulweber 2013

Preserving Asmara's Colonial Heritage

Making sense of the main rehabilitation project in Asmara – the Cultural Assets Rehabilitation Project (CARP) – is part of the diploma thesis of Stefan Graf and Arno Hofer. Their research in Asmara was made possible through a collaboration between the University of Innsbruck and the Department of Infrastructure in Asmara (Mr. Teklemariam). It was divided into two parts: mapping of previous and present conservation work in Asmara in order to identify relevant challenges, and theoretical framework for the preservation of Asmara's built heritage. This account of CARP is primarily based on the *Guide to the Built Environment*[2] and the book *Asmara: Africa's Secret Modernist City*. In Asmara they examined several changing strategies for the appropriation of the built environment, which was not interpreted as a timeless solitaire, but as an ongoing event that is subject to everyday interaction with the city dwellers. For this reason, they tried to document not only the ensemble of monuments, but also mixed narratives of past and present days, which have been constantly re-negotiated among national and international agents.

The preservation of Asmara's architectural heritage was first openly discussed after Eritrea's independence within the Asmara Urban Forum (1995). Eritreans began to question the logic of high-rise developments in the historical city centre. In the mid-1990s criticism reached a climax in response to a project comprising a series of glass towers on the south side of Harnet Avenue opposite the cathedral. Leading the opposition to this high-profile development was a group of former inmates of the Italian prison (now the Bank of Eritrea), which was scheduled for demolition if the plan was approved. What started as an impassioned response by a few to preserve a site of unique heritage value grew into an organised national heritage programme – the Cultural Assets Rehabilitation Project (CARP) – set up in 1997.[3] This initiative of the government and people of Eritrea sought to preserve cultural heritage, its aim being to establish a clear strategy, including the definition and formalisation of a Historic Perimeter (HP). The focus was placed on Asmara's architecture and during the project research over 850 buildings were documented, including the gathering of technical, historical and visual information. The perimeter was delineated to protect Asmara's historical city centre. Within this perimeter special regulations were to be applied to control the height and size of new buildings; the number of old buildings placed under protection is around 400.

In 1998 the municipality took drastic measures to save the historical integrity of the city centre and imposed a moratorium on new projects within the HP.[4] Seemingly coincidently, the very features of poverty, the patina of decennia of forced neglect of the building substance and a desperate lack of resources for building new structures are precisely what appears to have made Asmara interesting in the Western eye of the beholder. But why should this African city be of any interest to us? Was a universally valid contribution to architecture made here? And what is its value for the local community?

The Good, the Bad and the Challenges

To answer these questions, the first part of this chapter offers a general introduction to the political background to the appropriation of World Heritage values operating with World Heritage designation and the impact of these values on local communities. It is important to note that heritage values are one amongst a set of competing values: political, social, economic and cultural. They are defined within a meta-cultural framework, a discourse in which culture, however defined, speaks of itself or makes an exposition of itself. Although heritage, both tangible and intangible, is an important part of the narratives of all societies, the practice of preservation is complicated by diverse notions of value. Decisions about what to preserve, and what to develop, provoke questions such as: who is it of value to, of what value are we speaking in social terms, whose cultural identity places a value on what?

Every type of heritage is socially constructed and linked to the making and shaping of identities,[5] hence it is always invented (heritage as such has no meanings except those that are attributed to it).[6] It is not simply about the past, it is, vitally, about the present and future or, as Graham put it, 'the contemporary use of the past'.[7] The process of folding past conditions into present ones is selective; we can even create heritage by adding new ideas to old ideas. Heritage can be pragmatically re-used, ideologically re-appropriated or nostalgically embraced or, on the contrary, it can be fiercely contested. Robertson sees heritage as a code which regulates the links between culture and society on the one hand, and between communities and outsiders on the other hand, as well as the relationships between communities and the world as a whole. Such communities come in all shapes and sizes – large or small, defined or informal. At one (universal) level we are all part of the community, and heritage measures that serve the public good serve us all.[8]

Robertson's images and Appadurai's cultural flows place the primacy of worldwide agency in various cultural contexts, in which heritage does not occupy a separate position. City imaging – the collection, presentation and representation of cultural artefacts – is now a key component of the new global order.[9] Cities position themselves in a worldwide flow of images. While historical city centres vie with one another as unique sites, the images designed to entice tourists are often quite similar. Different cities often employ identical strategies to ensure that they will be acknowledged as world heritage cities. Referring to the somewhat vague UNESCO criteria ("masterpiece of human creative genius", "important interchange of human values") heritage is protected not by virtue of the function that it fulfils for a specific community, but rather owing to the value that it represents for the world community.[10]

For a long time, recognition was only accorded to sites that met universal canonical standards pertaining to masterpieces. As a collection of such masterpieces, and with its emphasis on architecture, CARP tried to fulfil the criteria of a list – World Heritage is first and foremost a list. Within the world heritage sector, people identify with a worldwide imagined community that has outgrown national limitations. World heritage consists of examples with a significant symbolic function for the state but, in a sense, there is no room in this universal viewpoint for culture as an exclusively national symbol, because consumption of this heritage is facilitated by the accessibility and well-conserved state of the objects.

The dossier of the *Asmara Architecture Exhibition* approaches visitors with the following introductory question: "Can the superlative 'Asmara – Africa's secret capital of modern architecture' still be topped? There are other well-known sites of early Modernist architecture, such as Tel Aviv, Israel, Miami South Beach, Florida, or Napier in New Zealand. However, the rich collection of early Modernist architecture in the city of Asmara, the blending of a variety of Modernist styles, the urban comprehensiveness of the historic perimeter, and the almost untouched, yet deteriorated, condition of the buildings is unique".[11] Phrases such as "unique buildings", "rich collection of Modernist architecture" or "capital of modern architecture" abound in public documents and on websites. There are "significant, binding words in certain activities and their interpretation [where] certain uses bound together certain ways of seeing culture and society".[12] The underlying sentiment is expressed in a number of phrases, with slight semantic variations, and some phrases have become standard reference.

However, conflicts over the meaning and value of heritage are inevitable, for the simple reason that cultural heritage functions on various levels: world, nation and community. Moreover, all too often good intentions must make way for hard interests, while the imagined community functions well as an ideal, but often on different levels. But what can architecture preservation projects tell us about local, national and transnational identity concerns? Since Anderson's landmark analysis, the effects of globalisation have brought new formations of 'imaged communities'[13] and nationalism where face-to-face interaction is no longer possible. Yet as in Anderson's account, heritage continues to be a key ingredient. "Theories of globalisation, transnationalism, and the wired world that emphasise their unboundedness and their unifying and universalising effects overlook the ways in which people reimagine community and nation and reassert local loyalties and identities even as they engage in global processes and inhabit transnational spaces", Victoria Bernal has claimed.[14]

In 2002, the Eritrean government launched CARP, which the World Bank financed through a $5-million development loan. Focused on the preservation of Asmara's Modernist architectural heritage, CARP generated much attention and support abroad, particularly after the addition of Asmara's so-called historic perimeter to UNESCO's tentative World Heritage List.[15] Christoph Rausch investigated the situation in post-liberation Eritrea, where the involvement of international actors (UNESCO, World Bank) was perceived as neo-colonial interference and Eritrea's cultural capital started to play a role as a national value only. Rausch criticised a "dictatorial Eritrean government [that] sustains ongoing conflict over its border with Ethiopia and endorses a radical policy of self-reliance, which endangers food security and causes massive emigration".[16] Indeed international actors and the Eritrean government pursued different interests.[17] On the one hand, there had been much pressure to encourage the development of Asmara as the capital city of a young nation. At the same time, there was a strong sense of the unique identity of Asmara and of the historical role played by Eritrean labour in its construction and evolution. The residents of Asmara – as featured in the documentary *City of Dreams*, in any case – seem proud to have appropriated a city, at long last, that was not intentionally designed for them.[18]

Some practitioners are concerned that the use of the past to fulfil the needs of the present is open to wilful political manipulation. There are indeed a number of cases that can be easily pointed out as cautionary tales.[19] Hence in a postcolonial reading any initiative on this topic should be based on a dialogue between former colonised and colonisers; this should be organised under the more neutral notion of shared heritage to challenge the seemingly dichotomous relationships between past and future, preservation and development, conservation and innovation in Eritrea.[20]

Blank Canvas and Colonial Rhetoric

Visitors to Eritrea are often unable to find a map of Asmara prior to their trip to the country. Steven McCarthy wrote about his experiences in his second report from Eritrea[21] and about the *Asmara City Map & Historic Perimeter* (2003), which was also our orientation tool during our fieldwork in Asmara.[22] After commenting on the graphical features of the map, McCarthy argued:

"As the World Bank-financed CARP project shows, cartography has long been dominated by those in power: delineations, labels, emphasis, relations, detail, scale and many other factors are determined by political, military and economic forces. The fact that both maps I refer to have a sizable blank rectangle where American base Kagnew Station once was, is oddly telling."

Kagnew Station was established in 1943 as a U.S. Army radio station. In the 1960s, as many as 4,000 U.S. military personnel were stationed there. In the 1970s, technological advances in the satellite and communications fields made the radio station at Kagnew increasingly obsolete. The Americans left Asmara in 1977, so the former military base was not off-limits for the map makers, the area having turned into a dense urban community; moreover Americans are not well regarded in Eritrea today.[23] There would be good reasons to include the station on the map as a testimony to the American presence in Eritrea.

McCarthy has pointed to another blank spot on the map: "For all its tourist-friendly detail, Denison and Ren's map fails to mark one of the most fascinating monuments in all Asmara, itself related to mapping's oldest tradition: the so-called tank graveyard. Easily a square-kilometre sprawl, this huge lot just west of old Kagnew Station is a teeming pile, sometimes four vehicles high, of rusty war detritus. Tanks, armored personnel carriers, trucks, cars, buses, plane parts, shipping containers, and more, are a testimony to Eritrea's victory over Ethiopia in its war of independence."[24] McCarthy clearly recognises the ambiguity of the official CARP map, which gathers Modernist cinemas and other iconic buildings – and tries to capitalise on them – but also reveals patches of blank canvas.

CARP itself can be seen as an undertaking that excludes large parts of the city, such as: Aba Shawl (the former indigenous quarter) and large residential zones in the south (Gheza Banda) or the former industrial area of the Italians' planned city, Medeber, which is yet another aspect of Asmara's rich hybridity. The huge Medeber market is the centre of Asmara's recycling quarter, where thousands of household and industrial items, which are scarce in Eritrea, are made out of recycled metal.[25] Also lacking are the Italian cemetery and the Asmara railway station; these are standard tourist sites that are a must for anyone who wishes to understand the lasting impact of the Italian presence in Asmara. Nevertheless, they are not indicated on the map.

Branching out into more ethnographic terrain, we can mention that the Italians colonisers adopted one of the native housing types, the round hut with a conical thatched roof (*tukul*), for their own use. Subsequently, they built entire quarters for natives out of them. Given the blanket use of this structure in disparate areas and for different populations, it is worth noting that the *tukuls* resulting from Italian occupation rather than preceding it are not displayed on the Asmara City Map.[26]

If we view maps as a manipulated form of knowledge and a form of empowerment, we can approach the practice of preservation from a new angle. Mia Fuller precisely identified CARP's main weakness when she claimed that "The making and unmaking of CARP have drawn some scholarly attention, but there has been next to no discussion of parts of the city that lie outside CARP's, and the government's, areas of interest. And yet, examining what CARP's investigations obscured brings to light further ways in which Eritrea's official's stance converges with outsider's colonial nostalgia. For one, the city's 'historic perimeter', as identified by CARP and documented in its publications, corresponds alarmingly to what Italian planners included in the city's European and 'mixed zones' [...]. Today's delineation of what is valuable in Asmara, in other words, excludes the same as Italian colonisers did under the rubric of *quartiere indigeno* [native quarter], along with the growth it has seen since Italian rule."[27] In this way CARP's conception of the colonial conditions of modernity is based on traditional distinctions between European city/African city, civilised/uncivilised, ruler/powerless, specialist/layman, rather than on the historical conjuncture of modernity with the colonial enterprise; thus it perpetuates the binary code of the colonial city.

Indeed, some architectural critics have argued that binary methods of analysis are insufficient to fully address the complex urban conditions of cities whose formal development was profoundly determined by colonialism. They contend that presenting the morphology of colonial cities as binary is both inadequate and distorting. Therefore, a preserved Asmara should contain all the crucial parts of the colonial city in order to represent its key features: its extraordinary pluralism, a system of social classification that resembles neither the class structure of the European, nor the pre-colonial systems of colonised peoples (this means that none of these groups can return to its condition prior to colonisation) and the fact that interaction between those involved could not be prevented.[28]

A Romantic Approach to Heritage

Today, many heritage sites are a mixture of scientific conservation infused with nostalgia for the past.[29] A number of pertinent themes in the relationship between romanticism, beauty and the heritage experience can be highlighted. Historically, romanticism was about giving free rein to the experience of contradiction and paradox; the romantic feeling was characterised as involving opposites, sometimes simultaneously; sometimes one became the other and vice versa. This is one of the reasons why romanticism allied itself with tourism: it became a vehicle for the aestheticisation of the exotic other and still is today.[30] In the case of Eritrea, a society that was stagnating as a result of economic and political processes has rebelled against globalisation (and the resulting marginalisation) by re-inventing itself and presenting itself as a heritage location in terms of restorative colonial nostalgia. In the romantic tradition, everything is heritage in this location and conservation of the past can easily become a raw material that guarantees a decent future, just as glass and metal once did with colonial modernity.

The aim of CARP was to prepare the ground for international tourism in Asmara. The project's managers calculated that potentially there would be financial aid and touristic development for their small African country in the future but only if those voices in favour of heritage increased in number and influence. Accordingly, direct appeals for assistance were frequent in the catching 2005 documentary *City of Dreams*, regularly shown on the occasion of the exhibition, in which "Naigzy Gebremedhin guides through his city as a charismatic protagonist-narrator".[31]

Heritage in Africa is increasingly being employed as a vehicle for development and the desire to make heritage pay is palpable. From the beginning CARP portrayed Asmara as *bella Asmara*, an urban idyll and a safe city. Some practitioners will argue that the past was already being used for the benefit of the present before CARP started and will point to tourism. Cultural heritage has long been used to develop local tourism opportunities that are deemed to be sustainable and are designed to generate income for local communities.

New Approaches beyond CARP

Although romanticism tends towards monumentalisation in terms of a timeless and untouchable ensemble of architecture, CARP and the Municipality of Asmara agreed that the best interests of the capital's historical centre would be served if it was allowed to "evolve in tune with its tangible and intangible cultural heritage rather than be subjected to destructive pressures for major redevelopment.[32] Asmara is seen to require an approach that supports complementary developments elsewhere in the wider city to enable it to meet the new and expanding needs without compromising the historic core."[33]

However, if we look at contemporary Asmara, a few questions need answering. What is Asmara today? Is it an African city with a European core or a European city in the Horn of Africa? Whose heritage is this anyway? A specific European reading of the city would involve a strong relationship between the historical centre and the overall identity. But there is another point of view outside the Eurocentric discourse.

Today, the overriding objective as regards the city centre is to preserve its spatial and functional characteristics, and this is described as part of the land-use strategy for the Greater Asmara Area (GAA). The *Town Plan of the Mezzèdimi Firm* (1972–1973) constituted the last comprehensive plan for the city of Asmara; it described and drew the situation of the city in the first half of the 1970s by tracking urban development, as well as social, economic and demographic changes from the end of the Italian colony until the late 1960s; it also defined the direction of development over the following three decades. Mezzèdimi's Master Plan expressed the close relationship between urban scale and architecture that has always been crucial in Asmara's urban culture. But during the Derg administration (1974–1991) the city of Asmara continued to expand without a plan. In order to start new planning one had to wait until 1998, when a meeting of the Planning Committee outlined a strategy for the urban development of Asmara Town and its satellite villages. This was the first planning group that produced guidelines for the development of Asmara Town, and the first outcomes were visible in 2005.[34]

Currently the way things are done is leading to a decentralisation of housing that is very unfortunate for the future of the historic perimeter. Giving priority to a functional, vibrant city centre over the fantasy of a correctly conserved one is the only way to stop ongoing decay.[35] A transformation in the scale of historical sites and in the required conservation strategies has led to new territorial approaches to heritage properties, such as the Historic Urban Landscape (HUL). The new goal is to develop a projective analysis for Asmara that goes beyond utilising the built environment solely as a commodity for tourism and to pamper nostalgia. In future, the collective memory of Asmara could be engaged by promoting a redevelopment of the historic perimeter within the city.

More recently, the Asmara Heritage Project (AHP) was launched in March 2014. On 1st February 2016 the Asmara Heritage Office submitted an application to the headquarters of UNESCO's World Heritage Centre in Paris to have the capital city of Eritrea recognised as a World Heritage Site.[36] The essential insight of this new submission is that cultural heritage does not end at monuments and collections of artefacts. It also includes customs or living expressions inherited from our ancestors and passed on to our descendants, such as oral traditions, performing arts, social practices, rituals, festive events, knowledge and practices concerning nature and the universe, or the know-how and skills needed to produce traditional crafts. In contrast to the CARP approach, the Asmara Heritage Project marks a shift away from purely historical and architectural layers of cultural significance towards an increased appreciation of the fact that social and community values underpin all heritage.[37] Unlike CARP it encompasses the blank spaces on the map mentioned above and defines three different zones: the historic perimeter, a buffer zone and the cultural landscape.

Conclusion

CARP brought mixed experiences and results. Many things were done, and much was achieved in terms of mapping and creating a foundation for further work. However, more concrete results did not materialise and some of the expectations were not met. For these reasons, a new initiative, the Asmara Heritage Project (AHP) is currently being implemented. If its application to UNESCO is successful, it will not only lead to Eritrea's first World Heritage Site, but will also contribute to making the World Heritage List a fairer representation of heritage sites from around the world and from different time periods. This would ensure that the public good that is heritage is sustainably protected for generations to come.

Notes

1 Denison Edward, Ren Guang-Yu, Naigzy Gebremedhin, *Asmara – Africa's Secret Modernist City*. London: Merrell Publishers Ltd, 2003 & 2006.

2 Denison Edward, Ren Guang-Yu, Mebrathu Abraham, Naigzy Gebremedhin: *Asmara – A Guide to the Built Environment*. CARP: Asmara, 2003; CARP also undertook similar work for the port city of Massawa, a work which culminated in the publication of *Massawa: A Guide to the Built Environment*, 2003; helped delineate Asmara's historical perimeter, which is an area covering 4 km^2 at the centre of the city; laid out guidelines for the preservation of the historical perimeter; put together another set of guidelines on how to erect new buildings within the delineated perimeter, and strongly recommended that Asmara's historical buildings be maintained before it is too late, with the utmost specialised care (*Asmara: A Guide to the Built Environment*, 2003, p. 8, pp. 14-21).

3 Naigzy Gebremedhin: *Asmara, Africa's Secret Modernist City*. Prepared for the African Perspectives: Dialogue on Urbanism and Architecture, The Faculty of Architecture, TU Delft, 2007.

4 Idem

5 Sabine Marschall, "The Heritage of Postcolonial Societies" in Brian Graham and Peter Howard (eds.), *The Ashgate Research Companion to Heritage and Identity*. Burlington: Ashgate 2008 (Ashgate research companion), pp. 347-364.

6 Eric Hobsbawm and Terence Ranger (eds.): *The Invention of Tradition*. Cambridge University Press, 1983.

7 Brian Graham; G.J.Asworth and J.e.Tunbridge, *A Geography of Heritage. Power, Culture and Economy*. London: Arnold, 2002, p. 2.

8 Roland Robertson: *Globalisation: Social Theory and Global Culture*. Sage Publications: London, 1992, p.34.

9 Arjun Appadurai, *Modernity At Large: Cultural Dimensions of Globalisation*. Minneapolis: University of Minnesota Press, 1996, p. 31.

10 Anja B. Nelle, "Urban intervention and the Globalisation of Signs. Marketing World Heritage Towns", in Marlite Halbertsma, Alex van Stripriaan and Patricia van Ulzen (eds.), *The Heritage Theatre. Globalisation and Cultural Heritage*. Cambridge Scholars Publishing, pp. 73-93.

11 See the dossier of the *Asmara Architecture Exhibition* http://www.asmara-architecture.com/Dossier_engl.pdf [3-4-2014], p. 1.

12 Raymond Williams, Keywords. A Vocabulary of Culture and Society, quoted in: Marx Aldenderfer, "Editorial: Keywords", *Current Anthropology 52* (4) 2011, p. 487.

13 Benedict Anderson: *Imagined Communities. Reflections on the Origin and Spread of Nationalism*. London: Verso, 1983.

14 Victoria Bernal: Eritrea Goes Global. Reflections on Nationalism in a Transnational Era. *Cultural Anthropology 19*, no. 1, 2004, pp. 3-25.

15 Eritrea signed the World Heritage Convention in 2001. The Historic Perimeter of Asmara and its Modernist Architecture, as the extent of the Italian colonial capital is known, was placed on the Tentative List for Eritrea in 2005.

16 Christoph Rausch: *Modern Nostalgia: Asserting Politics of Sovereignty and Security in Asmara*. Washington and Brussels, 2011.

17 Christoph Rausch: *African Heritage Challenges. Development and Sustainability*, CRASSH (Centre for Research in the Arts, Social Sciences and Humanities), 2015, in: http://www.crassh.cam.ac.uk/events/25667[5-4-2016].

18 Naigzy Gebremedhin 2007, pp. 18-19.

19 see: https://en.wikipedia.org/wiki/Cultural_Assets_Rehabilitation_Project [5-4-2016].

20 Johan Lagae: Colonial today, *ABE Journal* (3) 2013, p. 1.

21 Steven McCarthy: *Mapping Asmara. Steven McCarthy examines the way maps represent Eritrea's capital city, Asmara – from architectural gems to military legacy*, in: http://www.eyemagazine.com/blog/post/mapping-asmara [5-1-2016].

22 The authorship of this 2003 map is credited to the Municipality of Asmara and Eritrea's Cultural Assets Rehabilitation Project (CARP), and names Edward Denison and Guang Yu Ren as designers.

23 Steven McCarthy recalls the detailed maps that former US soldiers stationed at Kagnew Station created, in: http://kagnewstation.com/maps/kagnew/index.html [5-1-2016].

24 Idem

25 Dennis Rodwell: *Conservation and Sustainability in Historic Cities*. Oxford: Blackwell Publishing, 2007, pp. 174-175.

26 Mia Fuller: *Moderns Abroad. Architecture, cities and Italian imperialism*. London and New York: Routledge, 2007, p. 83.

27 Mia Fuller, "Italy's Colonial Futures: Colonial Inertia and Postcolonial Capital in Asmara", *California Italian Studies*, 2 (1), University of California, Berkeley, 2011, p. 10.

28 Brenda S. A. Yeoh, *Contesting Space in Colonial Singapore. Power Relations and the Urban Built Environment*. Singapore University Press, 2003.

29 "Gebremedhin is well aware that the voices of nostalgia now urging to conserve relics of a bygone era in Asmara increased in volume because of the widespread publicity that the highly visual, but ardently informative exhibition – primarily based on the elaborate analysis provided by Gebremedhin's book – was able to generate in the West. And, in fact, Gebremedhin and his collegues at CARP – part of the International Cooperation, Macro Policy and Economic Coordination Department of the Eritrean government – must have calculated that if only these voices increased in number and powerful influence, they potentially meant financial aid and touristic development for their small African country in the future". In: *Why destroy Asmara?*, http://reviewc.nl/why-destroy-asmara/ [5-12-2016].

30 Russel Staiff, *Re-imagining Heritage Interpretation. Enchanting the Past-Future*. London and New York: Routledge, 2014, p. 65.

31 *Why destroy Asmara?*, in: http://reviewc.nl/why-destroy-asmara/ [5-12-2016].

32 Groys, Boris. "The City in the Age of Tourist Reproduction", *Art Power*. Cambridge: MIT, 2008, pp. 101-110.

33 Dennis Rodwell 2007, p. 176.

34 Belula Tecle-Misghina, "Asmara urban history and development", *Rivista L'architettura delle città. The Journal of the Scientific Society Ludovico Quaroni*, n. 3-4-5/2014: *The City in the Evolutionary Age*. Rome: Edizioni Nuova Cultura, 2014, pp. 99-111.

35 Almli Ingrid Rundhaug: Asmara – Balancing Conservation and Development, Norwegian University of Science and Technology (NTNU), Faculty of Engineering Science and Technlology, Department of Civil and Transport Engineering, 2011, in: http://ntnu.diva-portal.org/smash/record.jsf?pid=diva2percent3A458087&dswid=-4299 [5-12-2016].

36 Edward Denison, *Modernist architecture in Asmara, Eritrea. Africa Research Institute – understanding Africa today*, in: http://www.africaresearchinstitute.org/event/9-september-event-modernist-architecture-in-asmara-eritrea [5-3-2016].

37 Kate Clark (ed.), *Capturing the Public Value of Heritage: The Proceedings of the London Conference, 25–26 January 2006*. Swindon, UK: English Heritage, 2006.

19
15
58
25
32
40
9
37
35
55
28
17
31
33
30
29
34
20
4
27
14
5
3
22
11
13
12
1
36
26
21
51
48
10
47
41
2
6
7
46
8
54
16
43
18
50
39
52
53
44
42
49
45
38

56

23

57

1890–1935

1	State Palace
2	Regional Government Offices
3	Government House
4	Post
5	Denden Club
6	Department of Water Resources
7	Ministry of Education
8	Ministry of Finance, Customs Police
9	Department of Urban Development
10	Department of Family Planning
11	President's Office
12	Government Office
13	Guard's House
14	Tax Office
15	Prison
16	Hamasien Hotel
17	Albergo Italia
18	Africa Pension
19	Faculty of Engineering
20	University Testing and Training Center
21	Italian School
22	St. Mary's Catholic Cathedral
23	Degghi Selam
24	Synagogue
25	Greek Orthodox Church
26	Asmara Theatre
27	Dante Cinema
28	former Piazza Italia
29	Shops and Apartments
30	Shops and Apartments
31	Shops and Apartments
32	Shops and Apartments
33	Commercial Bank of Eritrea
34	Casa degli Italiani
35	French Embassy
36	PCS Internet Café
37	Bank of Eritrea
38	Nigerian Ambassador's Residence
39	Mufti Headquarters
40	Apartments
41	Apartments
42	Apartments
43	Villa Roma
44	Villa
45	Villa
46	Former Sudanese Embassy
47	Villa
48	Villa
49	Villa
50	Villa
51	Villa
52	Villa
53	Villa
54	Villa
55	Electricity Station
56	Medeber Market
57	Railway Station
58	Store

77
64
112
125
153
98
139
122
103
147
130
115
93
129
104
92
116
101
131
60
102
62
79
88
97
113
114
118
89
117
87
99
100
78
107
91
106
105
74
59
124
121
141
110
86
80
109
63
111
144
258
136
85
69
81
134
83
66
135
97
145
68
138
84
67
146
133
157
151
150
149
132
148
152
140
142
143
72

1935–1942

59	Ministry of Education
60	Ministry of Health
61	Ministry of Justice
62	Office for Immigration
63	Ministry of Trade and Industry
64	Ministry of Health Regional Office
65	Ministry of Land, Water and the Environment
66	Ministry of Public Works
67	Attorney General's Office
68	National Union of Eritrean Women Office
69	Regional Law Court
70	Mariam Orthodox Cathedral
71	Kulafa al Rashidin Mosque
72	San Francesco Church
73	San Antonio Church
74	Selam Hotel
75	Red Sea Pension
76	Mai Jah Jah Fountain
77	Stadium
78	Cinema Impero
79	Cinema Capitol
80	Cinema Odeon
81	Cinema Roma
82	Cinema Hamasien
83	British American Tobacco Group
84	World Bank
85	Dutch Embassy
86	Polish Consulate
87	Falletta Apartments
88	Minneci Apartments
89	Offices and Apartments
90–96	Shops and Apartments
97	Bar Zilli
98	The Market
99	Shops and Apartments
100	Shops and Apartments
101	Bar Crispi and Apartments
102–121	Shops and Apartments
122	Bar and Office
123	Market Stores
124	Bank of Eritrea
125	Vegetable Market
126	Shops and Offices
127	Shops and Offices
128	Fish and Vegeatable Markets
129	Shops and Offices
130	Apartments
131–144	Apartments
145–151	Villas
152	Fiat Tagliero
153	Soap Factory
154	Garage
155	Silicon Factory (south of the map)
156	Petrol Station (south of the map)
157	Spinelli Store

162
179
178
168
177
182
180
187
171
174
185
175
172
161
163
191
159
165
188
169
160
186
167
184
190
183
189
164
166

From 1942

158	Municipality
159	National Museum
160	Amasoira Hotel
161	Bristol Pension
162	University of Asmara
163	Ibrahim Sultan School
164	Semaetet School
165	Theological School
166	Barka School
167	Denden Junior School
168	Kidane Meheret
169	St. Michael Church
170	Evangelical Church
171	Shops and Apartments
172	Shops and Apartments
173	Shops and Apartments
174	Shops and Apartments
175	Shops and Apartments
176	Shops and Apartments
177	Shops and Apartments
178	Shops and Apartments
179	Shops and Apartments
180	Shops and Apartments
181	Shops and Apartments
182	Shops and Apartments
183	Shops and Apartments
184	Apartments
185	Apartments
186	Villa Gracia
187	Villa
188	Villa
189	Villa
190	IRGA
191	Asmara Swimming Pool
192	Bowling Alley

CARP Buildings

CARP forsaw three categories of preservation for the buildings and neighbourhoods within the perimeter: buildings and neighbourhoods that would be under complete preservation and no changes would be possible; buildings and neighbourhoods that would be under partial preservation and changes to the interior would be possible, and buildings and neighbourhoods in the third category which would be under selected preservation, meaning that certain important elements, such as doors and windows, would be preserved if permission was given.

The buildings were published in the book *Asmara. Guide to the Built Environment* with images, short descriptions and locations outlined on maps. This guide intended to bring Asmara's built environment to a broader audience, including Eritreans and foreign tourists.

We made a periodication of the buildings mentioned by CARP: the first period was chosen from the beginning of the colonial enterprise until 1935 when an enormous boom took place in Asmara; the second comprises the period from 1935 to 1942 when Italy had to give up its colonial ambitions. CARP also placed some buildings from the post-Italian period on to the Watch List which are simply dated post-1942.

On this page all the buildings that CARP categorised and published are shown. It is plain to see that some of the buildings lies outside the historic perimeter.

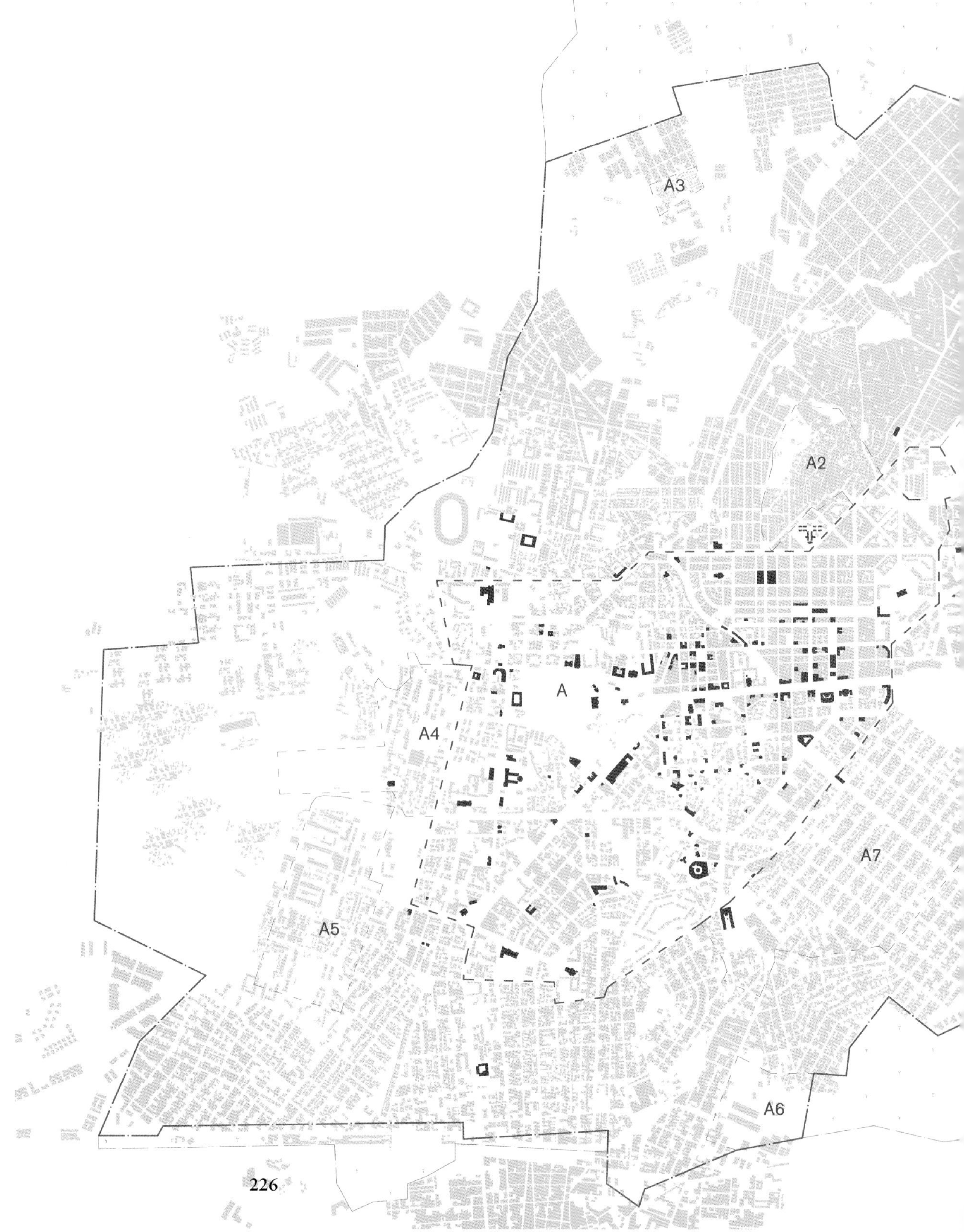
A3
A2
A
A4
A7
A5
A6

Asmara Heritage Project (AHP)

A Historic Perimeter

A_1 Railway Station
A_2 Aba Shaul
A_3 Agdos
A_4 Italian Cemetery
A_5 Tiravolo
A_6 Gheza Banda
A_7 Godaif

B Buffer Zone

C Natural Belt

Satellite Photo:

Greater Asmara Area (GAA) with

the Asmara Heritage Project (AHP) Area

and the Cultural Assets Rehabilitation Project (CARP) Area

Source: Bing Maps

SCORCIO. SALA. BA

ARCHITECTURE AS IMAGE
Photo Essay

Edward Denison

Image is everything. Images depict versions of reality as much as they lay the grounds for deceit. Images frame the external gaze, clarifying and obscuring in equal measure. In architectural terms, the projection of image transcends the material object, fixing it in space and time, while leaving it permanently open to interpretation. Images are as vital in a building's conception as they are in retaining its memory.

For Asmara, the projection of architecture as image has always been vital. In Asmara images range from the utopic to the nostalgic. In the early twentieth century the architects charged with designing Africa's Modernist city exploited the power of image by projecting a futuristic metropolis of glass and concrete populated with elegantly attired Europeans driving sleek automobiles along spotless streets by day and sipping cocktails and waltzing on rooftops at night. Image was everything.

In the early twenty-first century, Asmara's image is cast backwards not forwards, ensnaring in an Orientalist trap all those for whom Asmara elicits reminiscence. Since the publication of Edward Said's seminal thesis in the 1970s, the Orientalist's partial gaze has been a subject of intellectual curiosity. Eritrea at that time was engaged in a struggle for independence from its neighbour Ethiopia and closer than ever to achieving its objective, unaware that this would in reality take many more years and entail further incalculable misery. The protracted struggle for national self-determination, which saw Eritrea experience two separate phases of colonisation before arriving belatedly among Africa's postcolonial nations, was instrumental in determining how the mod ernist city of Asmara would come to be viewed from within and from outside.

Piazza Roma archive detail
Source: Asmara Archive

Following liberation in 1991, Eritrea emerged as the world's youngest nation with a capital city that appeared almost as it had done half a century earlier when Allied forces displaced the jewel in the crown of Mussolini's fanciful Roman Empire in Africa. As an authentic early Modernist urban landscape replete with all the trimmings – interiors, cars, bars and cafés – Asmara stimulated considerable interest around the world. Coinciding with the end of the Cold War and the dawn of the internet age, images of a complete Modernist city embalmed from another – more glamorous – era were revelatory. Asmara's image was swiftly enshrined and interpreted as memory: architecture as nostalgia. Small wonder that of all the labels pinned on Asmara by global commentators, the one that seems to have stuck is Art Déco – a retrospective (and in this case erroneous) appellation rooted in nostalgia.

In the twenty-first century, Asmara's Modernist image is its heritage. After several initiatives since independence to promote and preserve the architecture, an application for the city's inclusion on the UNESCO World Heritage list was submitted in 2016. For outsiders, especially Europeans, the familiar image of urban civility cast by the fading chic of an Italian strain of modernism from before the nuclear age appears highly seductive, not least because temporal distance has helped to diminish its fascist connotations. However, behind this superficial image lies a more complex narrative that challenges the enduring dominance of Eurocentric modernism.

During Eritrea's struggle for independence, Asmara became an object of love and longing that found various forms of cultural expression. Songs like the 1956 *Asmeretey* set the tone for depicting Asmara as the symbol of what was lacking and what was desired by Eritreans – freedom. Throughout the thirty year war of liberation, Asmara became synonymous with the final act of liberation. It came to be seen as the ultimate prize, whose capture would end a century of foreign rule. Artists, painters, sculptors and writers used their various talents to praise its beauty and mourn its fate. "How is the most beloved? How is the cradle of the family? Have they damaged its beauty? I miss Asmara, the retina of my eye," opined one song. Asmara's central role in Eritrea's struggle for national self-determination was not confined to Eritrean cultural outputs. The renowned Australian writer and author of *Schindler's Ark*, Thomas Keneally, who visited the areas liberated by the EPLF in the late 1980s, acknowledged the indissoluble bond between Asmara and the universal pursuit of liberty when entitling his novel *Towards Asmara*.

Much as the seductive image of Asmara's Modernist architecture appeals to global audiences for the way it elicits memories of a bygone age, this image is as false and fanciful as the stylised renderings by Italian architects in the 1930s.

The real image of Asmara belongs to those to whom the city belongs – not Europeans, not Italians, but Eritreans. For Eritreans and their nomination to UNESCO, this point is obvious and fundamental. It remains to be seen whether or not the global public and the international heritage industry are willing to concede such a fact or if they would prefer instead to continue feasting on fiction.

The drawings of some of Asmara's buildings from the Asmara Archive. On the following pages the buildings are shown in their natural neighbourhoods.
Source: Asmara Archive

View of the Kitkat bar

Pallazzo Mazzetti

Apartment house on Munich Street

TELEPHONE

الخطوط الجوية
بوابة افريقيا

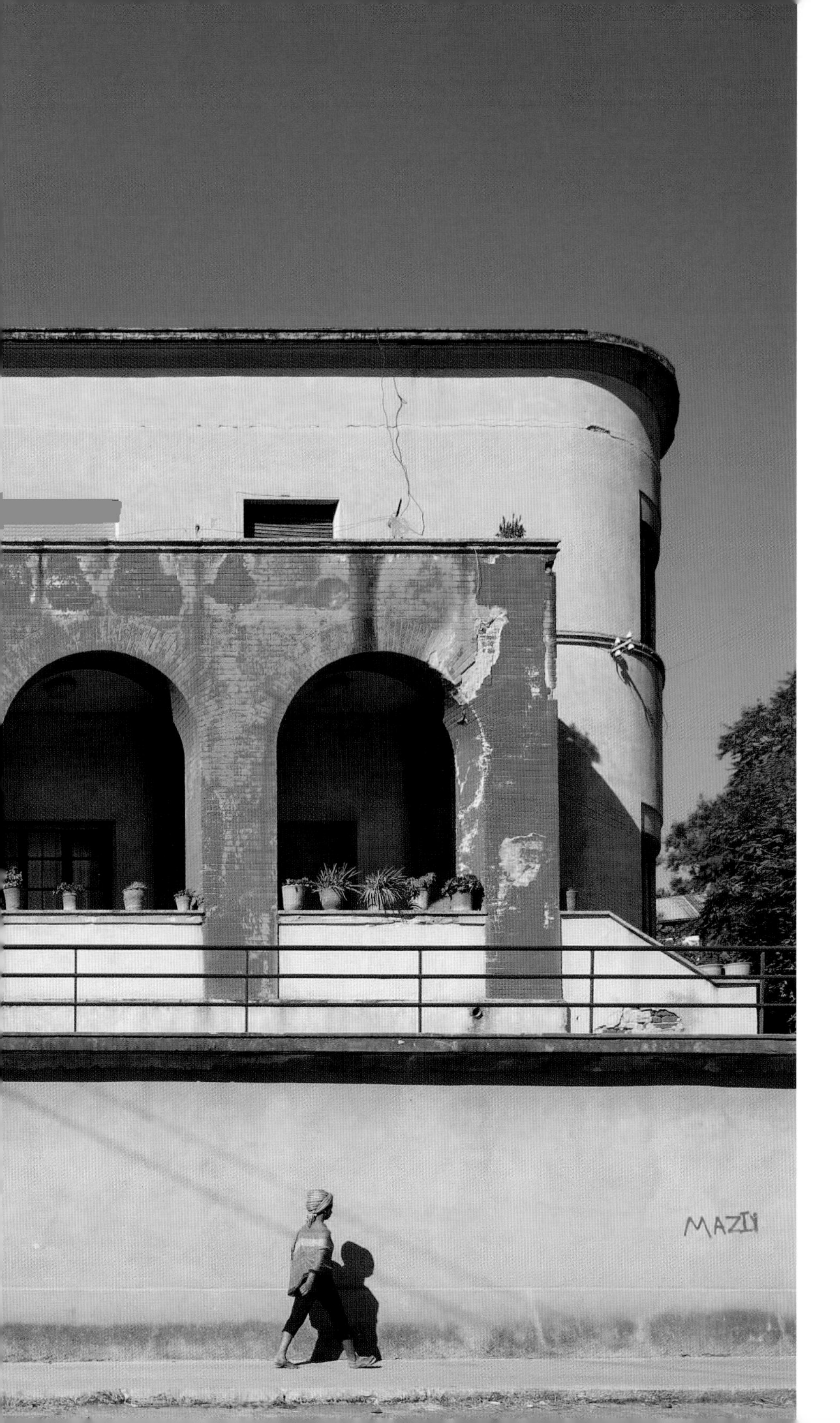
MAZIY

MOTIVO ESTERNO
SCHIZZO PROSPETTIC

THE ASMARA HERITAGE PROJECT
Heritage Preservation: Past, Present and Future

Medhanie Teklemariam and Edward Denison

The Asmara Heritage Project (AHP) was established in March 2014 under the auspices of the Administration of the Maekel Region (Municipality of Asmara). The creation of an office dedicated to managing Asmara's world-famous urban heritage continues an enduring aspiration among Eritreans since independence to research, promote and safeguard the nation's unique cultural assets. Over the last quarter of a century, successive initiatives from national and international organisations have contributed to furthering the understanding of Asmara's unique heritage.

Since the mid-1990s, Eritrea has faced major challenges with respect to conserving its cultural heritage assets, but it has also enjoyed considerable success. In 2006, Massawa's Old Town, the Modernist City of Asmara and Kidane Mehret Church in Senafe were all nominated on the World Monuments Fund's Watch List of Endangered Sites. Consequently, Kidane Mehret Church was completely restored in 2007 following donations from a private Eritrean donor in America, and the German and French Embassies in Asmara.[2] In 2008, the Darbush Tomb in Massawa was also successfully nominated on the Watch List. In 2009, the European Union in Eritrea provided a €5 million grant to establish the EU Heritage Project, with the aim of restoring Capitol Cinema and the city's main market – Mieda Eritrea – and undertaking a range of other capacity building initiatives. Although the buildings were not restored, rehabilitation design was conducted and staff training in various skills was completed, including an archival management study.

Piazza Roma archive detail
Source: Asmara Archive

The Asmara Heritage Project builds on the experiences of the initiatives stated above and draws on the knowledge and expertise of individuals and organisations around the world to submit the Modernist city of Asmara for nomination on UNESCO's World Heritage List. The preparation of the Nomination Dossier and associated studies (including an *Integrated Management Plan* (2015), *Conservation Master Plan* (2015); *Planning Norms and Technical Regulations* (2015); *Disaster Risk Management Plan* (2015); *Infrastructure Study* (2015); *General Report of Historic Buildings* (2015); *Cultural and Natural Heritage Proclamation* (2015); and *Socio-Economic Study* (2014)) began in 2013 with the aim of establishing the institutional framework and capacity to safeguard and manage the unique heritage site of Asmara in perpetuity. This article aims to provide a summary of the activities and responsibilities of the AHP as a work in progress.

The Asmara Heritage Project (AHP)

The Asmara Heritage Project (AHP) is responsible for managing the urban heritage of Asmara. This includes day-to-day activities, such as conducting research, data collection, and undertaking surveys as well as communicating with state parties and international organisations, such as foreign embassies, UNESCO, potential donors and other stakeholders. The AHP's organisational structure is designed to fulfil three primary objectives; the preparation of:

— the *Nomination Dossier* for UNESCO World Heritage Listing (WHL)
— the *Integrated Management Plan* (IMP)
— and the *Conservation Master Plan* (CMP)

Three different Sections – Archive and Documentation; Research; and Mapping & GIS – are responsible for conducting the necessary studies for achieving the Asmara Heritage Project's objectives.

The Inventory of the Historic City of Asmara

The priority in undertaking the conservation and rehabilitation of Asmara as a heritage site in the long-term and for compiling the UNESCO Nomination Dossier in the short-term was the production of a comprehensive city-wide survey to identify the city's heritage assets. The inventory of historical buildings, squares and urban spaces was the most ambitious and comprehensive study ever undertaken in Asmara. The principal goal of the inventory was to create a clear picture of Asmara's extant physical and social conditions and to provide the AHP, Department of Construction Development (DCD) and other related departments with the necessary information to administer and monitor building activities and to manage future development so as to prevent any negative impacts on the historic urban landscape. The inventory is an accurate, up-to-date, and comprehensive information system that helps to establish appropriate levels of protection and to define the necessary interventions so that public and private agencies have clear and unambiguous grounds on which to conduct their work. The foremost application of the inventory is in the establishment of the Conservation Master Plan, which provides a framework for conserving the urban and architectural heritage in the different protection areas based on typology, architectural and spatial value, historic context, state of conservation and physical and functional characteristics. In addition to refining and improving the task of protecting Asmara's architectural and urban heritage, the inventory also adds significantly to understanding the characteristics and values of different heritage assets and to raising awareness of these qualities more broadly.

The survey conducted provides empirical evidence of the current physical features of buildings, open spaces, squares and utilities. This included evaluation by surveyors in the field and assessments in the office. The information that was collected included the overall architectural quality of the buildings and open spaces; the types of transformations; and the overall state of repair. Architectural quality was assessed on both the presence and abundance of architectural elements and consistency with the historic urban fabric. The status of each subject was classified qualitatively using the following criteria: very good, good, bad and ruined. The inventory was instrumental in constructing a Geographical Information System (GIS) used in the management of issuing building permits and monitoring works to buildings, infrastructure and public spaces. It will also support the preparation and the evaluation of more specific and detailed conservation policies and strategies. The inventory was not merely intended to document the extent of Asmara's urban and architectural heritage, but also to document lesser known structures and spaces in order to help develop and implement a truly comprehensive urban conservation strategy. The AHP has collected data on more than 4,300 historical buildings and is in the process of inputting this information into a tailor-made database management system that will be instrumental in the effective long-term management of Asmara as a heritage site.

Asmara Heritage Project Management Database (AHPMD)

The AHPMD was developed to manage the vast quantity of information collected by the AHP, including over 4,300 buildings, 257 roads of varying sizes, and thirty-eight open spaces and plantation layers, most of which are located in the core and buffer zones of the proposed World Heritage Site (see Fig.02).

In addition to recording and collating data from the inventory, the AHPMD also incorporates the extensive Municipal Archive, which has been scanned and digitised in a process, taking teams of trained archivists many months. By the end of 2015, a total of 50,867 documents had been scanned. These documents provide invaluable evidence relating to the date of construction of buildings, original function and ownership, the architect's name and other supporting documents. The archive also provides a fascinating insight into Asmara's unrealised potential through a wide range of unbuilt projects (see Fig.03). The AHP intends to make this archival resource available to the public to promote knowledge, protect the original documents, and generate revenue.[3]

Definition of Asmara's Historic Perimeters

In recent decades, a wider and more complex notion of heritage in urban contexts has emerged that goes well beyond the notion of monument or masterpiece, to include the historic city in its entirety, particularly those parts of the urban fabric that have retained a certain integrity in the way they encapsulate peculiar societal values through time.

Any conservation approach should be based on a clear identification of the heritage values to be preserved. In the case of a historic city, this should address all the elements of urban heritage that find their expression in the morphology and spatial organisation of the historic urban fabric: not only the monuments or the prominent buildings, but also the street patterns and the open areas that give form to the public space, the different forms and types of building of residential, commercial, religious, recreational and industrial activities, as well as all of the various artefacts that can be defined as tangible urban cultural heritage. Consequently, the delimitation of the proposed World Heritage Site of Asmara is the first step towards the establishment of an appropriate and effective set of protection measures and rehabilitation programmes, and creating the conditions of a proactive policy of urban conservation and rehabilitation. The following considerations are therefore critical:

— The delimitation of the proposed World Heritage Site is to be consistent with the Statement of Outstanding Universal Value (SOUV), taking into consideration the Historic Urban Landscape (HUL) recommendation proposed by UNESCO (2011).
— The proposed historic perimeter must encompass the urban areas that the Urban Conservation and Rehabilitation would be applied to preserve and valorise the Outstanding Universal Values of the historic urban fabric and its buildings whilst improving liveability and promoting the socio-economic conditions of the city.

— Different levels of protection and/or possibilities of transformation will be provided depending on the level of integrity of the urban fabric to be assessed through appropriate tools and at different scales of intervention.

The conservation approach is therefore not intended to freeze Asmara in its present state, but rather create the conditions through which the city can develop and thrive, while retaining and enhancing the heritage values through the implementation of appropriate interventions, policies and guidelines based on the accurate identification and evaluation of all the components of the historic urban landscape (HUL).[4]

Operational Criteria and New Boundaries

The criteria for the delimitation of Asmara's historic perimeter are consistent with the criteria for its inscription and the SOUV based on the following characteristics highlighted in the *Nomination Dossier* and *Conservation Master Plan*: site and landscape as formative characteristics, subsequent phases of urban development, consistency of anchor buildings and urban nodes, persistence of street patterns, continuity of functional role and cultural significance, conservation approach with different degree of protection. Based on these elements and the urban morphological analysis, the proposed World Heritage Site boundary was defined with different degrees of protection measures in the Core, Buffer and Protected Zones. The identification of the historic perimeter is not merely based on aesthetic criteria, but also on the accurate analysis of the evolution of the urban fabric and its structure. This includes evidence based on archival documentation (historic cartography and iconography) of the components that have persisted or have been transformed, particularly over the past five decades.

Three distinct boundaries have been identified and designated according to the significance of architecture, urban form and layout, cultural and historical heritage values, and the natural environment. The nominated property has a Core Zone, Buffer Zone (which encircles the Core Zone by a certain radius), and an outer Protected Zone which skirts the Buffer Zone to the north and to the east to protect the views of the city in relation to the natural setting and the backdrop created by the edge of the escarpment.

a. Nominated Property (Core Zone)

The international movement in both architecture and urban planning developed rapidly in the early twentieth century, corresponding with Asmara's development as Africa's Modernist City. Consequently, it is important to refer to the city as a product of a modern planning process throughout the first half of the twentieth century, from the first master plan by Oduardo Cavagnari in 1913 (see Fig.05) to the competition-winning 1938 plan by Vittorio Cafiero (see Fig.06), combined with a variety of architecture, specifically Rationalist, from the mid-1930s (see Fig.07).

The Cultural Assets Rehabilitation Project (CARP) first defined Asmara's first historic perimeter, but this was based mainly on architectural criteria. The AHP's revised boundary expands the historic perimeter to boundaries that more accurately reflect the combination of an urban planning process and modern architectural features. The Core Zone[5] comprises Asmara's historic urban centre developed during the years of Italian occupation from 1889–1941. The boundary limit of the Core Zone to the north extends up to Afabet Street and encompasses the area of Abbashaul which is designated as Special Area 1 (SP1). To the east, the Core Zone includes the railway station and St Mary's Cemetery in the northeast. To the south, it encompasses Denden Camp, which is also designated as a Special Area (SP2), and includes San Francesco Church and Santa Anna Secondary School. To the south east, it includes the neighbourhood of Gheza Banda and to the west it incorporates Orrota Hospital as well as the Italian and Martyrs' Cemeteries. The total area of Core Zone is 484.4 ha.

b. Buffer Zone

The Buffer Zone[6] surrounds the nominated property and follows various physical and natural features. The boundary of the Buffer Zone incorporates Hazhaz and Mihram Chira neighbourhoods to the north and incorporates the old *tukul* settlements that are designated within the Core Zone as SP1. To the east, it incorporates the Asmara–Massawa Road and includes the Asmara Bus Company, Catholic Boarding School and Lagetto Night Club. To the south, it goes down up to Sawa Road and encompasses the Asmara Brewery Factory, extending to the Office of the Ministry of Agriculture. To the west, it includes Denden Camp as well as the Forto Area which are designated as SP2, extending up to the depot of scrub materials. The total area of the Buffer Zone is 1,157.2 ha.

c. Protected Zone

One of the many unbuilt projects contained in the Municipal Archive
Source: Asmara Archive

The Protected Zone[7] is an area that is delineated and preserved from encroachment of various urban development activities from within the Buffer Zone as well as agricultural development outside the Protected Zone. The flora, fauna, history and culture of the protected area, towering peaks, dramatic

gorges, sheer cliffs, gently rolling hills, spectacular cliffs, rocky stones, and diverse pattern of plant life all combine to create distinctive characteristics and backdrop to the designated area. Furthermore, the number of important archaeological remains around the original village of Arbate Asmera adds to the richness of the landscape. The Protected Zone encircles the eastern and northern perimeters of the Buffer Zone. It is delineated to protect the green belt of the escarpment edge which provides an important setting to the natural beauty to the city. The boundary limit of the Protected Zone to the north extends to the mountain of Akria. To the east it encircles the eucalyptus plantation and zoo of Bet Ghiorghis and the national Semaetat (Maryrs') Park. The total area of the Protected Zone is 767.5 ha.

Conclusion

The UNESCO World Heritage List is intended to reflect the world's cultural and natural diversity of outstanding universal value. Despite a Global Strategy launched in 1994 to redress imbalances in representation – notably in favour of "Europe, historic towns and religious monuments, Christianity, historical periods and 'elitist' architecture"[12] – there still remains an acute shortage of African sites and sites from the modern era. The Modernist city of Asmara is an outstanding example of a colonial capital that bears witness to the universal encounter with modernity in the twentieth century and consequent postcolonial experiences. If its application to UNESCO is successful it would not only be Eritrea's first World Heritage site, but would also contribute to the necessary process of making the World Heritage List a fairer representation of heritage sites from around the world and throughout time.

Notes

1 CARP was funded by a World Bank loan. Upon the project's conclusion in 2007 CARP was given a positive appraisal by the World Bank, specifically in "linking culture with education"; supporting "the role of the private sector and the community in cultural conservation"; "successfully demonstrating the value of investing in cultural assets"; being a "unifying force in post conflict societies", and "building community social capital in a conflict environment by promoting national identity and tolerance" (*CARP Implementation, Completion and Results Report*, The World Bank Report No. ICR0000708, 30 January 2008, pp. 23-24).

2 See: www.wmf.org/project/kidane-mehret-church

3 The design of the survey forms and the digital database were developed using postgress GRE and SQL software to define the fields of information and standardise the format of photographs and drawings. All photographs are recorded in high resolution format and site plan drawings are saved as AutoCAD files.

4 The Historic Urban Landscape (HUL) is an urban area understood as being the result of historic layering of cultural and natural values and attributes, extending beyond the notion of historic centre or urban ensemble to include the broader urban context and its geographic setting (UNESCO Recommendation, 2011). This introduces a notion of conservation that is not limited to physical restoration but also concerns the management of the urban transformations so as to preserve and ensure the vitality of heritage values.

5 A core zone is a nominated property which includes within its borders all the attributes which render it to be recognised as being of Outstanding Universal Value and which meets the conditions of integrity as well as authenticity for inscription on the World Heritage List (UNESCO).

6 Paragraph 104 of the Operational Guidelines (2015) state that for the purposes of effective protection of the nominated property, a buffer zone is an area surrounding the nominated property which has complementary legal and/or customary restrictions placed on its use and development to give an added layer of protection to the property. This should include the immediate setting of the nominated property, important views and other areas or attributes that are functionally important as a support to the property and its protection. The area constituting the buffer zone should be determined in each case through appropriate mechanisms. Details on the size, characteristics and authorised uses of a buffer zone, as well as a map indicating the precise boundaries of the property and its buffer zone should be provided in the nomination. Today, the World Heritage Committee gives special attention to the proper management of the buffer zone and even broader surroundings of the site, which is also reflected in the 2011 *International Recommendation on the Historic Urban Landscape.*

7 Regarding the boundaries of protected areas, the Operational Guidelines state: "The delineation of boundaries is an essential requirement in the establishment of effective protection of nominated properties. Boundaries should be drawn to ensure the full expression of the Outstanding Universal Value and the integrity and/or authenticity of the property. For properties nominated under criteria (i) – (vi), boundaries should be drawn to include all those areas and attributes which are a direct tangible expression of the Outstanding Universal Value of the property, as well as those areas which in the light of future research possibilities offer potential to contribute to and enhance such understanding."

8 *Operational Guidelines for the Implementation of the World Heritage Convention*, UNESCO, World Heritage Centre, July 2015, paragraph 120, p. 23.

Nur Boutique
PUPA

THE FUTURE OF THE PRESENT
Rebranding Fascist Architecture as Heritage in Asmara

Fassil Demissie

To the pitiful highland elites, Asmara represents everything: their pride and their identity. Eritrea is Asmara and Asmara is Eritrea. Everything else outside that Italian built city is just an ugly place inhabited by uncivilised peasants. Why people fall so much in love with a city that represents Eritrea's darkest history of Italian fascism, Italian Apartheid, Italian Nazism and Italian dehumanisation of the Eritrean people is mindboggling.

Sahay Erican[1]

As group pasts become increasingly part of museums, exhibits and collections, both in national and transnational spectacles, culture becomes less what Pierre Bourdieu would have called a habitus (a tacit realm of dispositions) and more an area for conscious choice, justification, and representations, the latter often to multiple and spatially dislocated audiences.

Arjun Appadurai[2]

A building from the 1930s on Harnet Avenue
Source: K. Paulweber 2013

Introduction

On Monday February 1, 2016, Hanna Simon, Eritrea's Ambassador to France and Permanent Delegate to UNESCO, officially submitted the nomination dossier under the title *Asmara: Africa's Secret Modernist City* to the UNESCO World Heritage Centre in Paris, France.[3] The nomination dossier and all the supporting documents had been under preparation for some time by international consultants and functionaries of the ruling party, People's Front for Democracy and Justice (PFDJ), in accordance with the operation guidelines for the implementation of the World Heritage Convention.[4] The official submission of fascist architecture constructed during between 1935–1941 as heritage to UNESCO is part of a strategy of the new PFDJ state to legitimise its history by appropriating Italian colonial heritage in the aftermath of the Eritrea formally succeeding from Ethiopia on April 24, 1993. If Asmara and its colonial built environment is to stand as a symbol of national belonging and serve as a major source of hard currency for the national budget, the transformation of the city centre through tourism became a top priority for new government.

I began this brief narrative with the official submission of the nominating dossier, *Asmara: Africa's Secret Modernist City*, to the World Heritage List because it crystallises a number of interlocking issues. The assembling of the nominating dossier to rebrand the crumbling fascist architecture in Amara as heritage as well as the considerable technical and legislative resources that have been initially deployed with World Bank funding reflect an emerging social relationship to insert Asmara into the globalisation process.[5] By globalisation, I am referring to the process of market expansion and the flow of international capital, tourists and commodities that will make Asmara a specific destination site for global tourist consumption. The designation of the city centre as a heritage site by the Cultural Assets Rehabilitation Project (CARP) is a discourse that enables certain urban features of Asmara built during the Italian fascist period (cathedrals, service stations, palaces, residential flats, cafés, cinemas and administrative buildings, etc.) to be incorporated as historic and heritage into the World Heritage List and institutional system. These edifices of fascist architecture comprise building types selected by CARP are identified as heritage whose circulation globally depend on rebranding practices that create and commodify the inner city of Asmara as a space of global tourist consumption. On the other hand, the commodification of the inner city of Asmara as heritage excludes those spaces and memories with a complicated and multi-layered history. Indeed, the social history of these spaces and the lived experiences of people in these indigenous quarters provides a counter narrative to the mythology of the ruling party and raises critical questions

Ambassador Hanna Simon (r) presenting the official application for nomination of Asmara as a World Heritage city to the Director of the Heritage Division and UNESCO World Heritage Centre, Dr. Mechtild Rössler (second from the right)
Source: http://www.tesfanews.net, retrieved May 1, 2016

about the nature of Eritrean history, national identity, belonging and heritage.[6] Since the succession of Eritrea from Ethiopia in 1993, newspapers accounts, scholarly monographs, films, international exhibitions, catalogues and coffee table books have been published about the built environment of Asmara, extolling the beauty of modern architecture and its local idiom expressed in eclectic styles such as rationalism, Novecento, neo-classicism, neo-Baroque and monumentalism. This body of literature reflects a particular nostalgia and an appreciation for the architecture that came to be the dominant marker of Asmara under Italian fascist rule. Indeed, the discourse of this nostalgic narrative was imbedded in tropes that suggested Asmara that is a Secret Modernist city, a Frozen City despite the passage of time and a City of Dreams waiting to be discovered by global tourism. Long before this mundane campaign to rebrand Asmara's fascist architecture to global tourism, Rausch has noted that:

> *[the] appropriation of Italian colonial heritage serves to assert the newly won Eritrean national sovereignty...the Eritrean government fundamentally depends on references to Italian colonialism in inventing its national tradition...it is...difficult to establish cultural differences with the enemy Ethiopia that reaches [sic] further back than the experience of colonialism.*[7]

This brief reflection on the rebranding of Italian fascist architecture and the desire to transform Asmara into a global tourist space began to take shape with the establishment of CARP in 1996 with the mandate to map and delineate the historic core under the advice of international experts, creating an investment incentive to attract global capital through tourism.[8] Heritage preservation of fascist architecture in Asmara is rooted in the practice of selective highlighting of the colonial built form while erasing the violence, brutality and racism of Italian colonialism.

Unlike other colonial powers in Africa, Italian fascism in East Africa has not been thoroughly studied. Indeed, as Sean Anderson[9] had noted, the end of Italian colonialism led to the erasure from scholarly and public attention "Italy's ties to fascism and pyrrhic military campaigns throughout North and East Africa". It was only in the last thirty years or so that serious efforts have been made to trace and analyse the grim realities of Italian colonialism both by Italian and non-Italian scholars. Equally, the historical memory of Italian colonialism and its fascist markers in Eritrea was expunged carefully from Italian national history, memory and everyday life[10] and Italian colonial archives remained closed for a long period. Even postcolonial Eritrea is entangled and trapped in the Italian colonial matrix despite the ruling party's rhetoric of national liberation.[11] Frantz Fanon has aptly noted that colonialism was never simply content with imposing its grammar and logics upon the "present and the future of a dominated country." Colonialism was also not simply satisfied with merely holding the colonised people in its grip and emptying "the native's brain in all forms and content". Rather, "by a kind of perverse logic, it turns to the past of the oppressed people and distorts it, disfigures and destroys it."[12]

The Italian colonial project in East Africa was fraught with difficulties from the very beginning. In the original Italian plans, Eritrea was expected to become an outlet for the colonial settlement of destitute Italian farmers as well as a gateway to further expansion southward to Ethiopia. As the only European country with a diminished capacity to project its imperial power after its humiliating defeat both at the Battle of Dogali (1887) and later at the Battle of Adwa (1896) by Ethiopia, Italian colonialism began to take shape in Eritrea on a very shaky foundation. Although Eritrea was strategically located in the Horn of Africa, it never enjoyed the status of Ethiopia in Italian colonial imagination. As Anderson aptly suggested, "Eritrea was originally discounted for its lack of materials, easily extractable resources and cultivable lands". Indeed, modern architecture in Eritrea "never enjoyed the highly regarded status of Italy's *La Quata Sponda* (Forth Shores) as Libya or the *Capitale dell'Impero* (Capital of the Empire) like Addis Ababa.[13]

During the early 1930s, Italian colonial ambition to annex Ethiopia began to accelerate and Asmara emerged to be the critical staging site; many Eritreans were conscripted into the Italian colonial army to take part in the military campaigns against Ethiopia. To facilitate Italian colonial ambition, Italian East Africa (AOI), the acronym for *Africa Orientale Italiana*, was created by Mussolini in 1935 which divided the region into six governorates: Eritrea, Amhara, Shoa, Harar, Galla-Sidamo and Somalia, each under the authority of an Italian military governor, answerable to the Italian viceroy who represented the Emperor Victor Emmanuel. As Diane Ghirardo has noted, "Officials believed that ultimately AOI would serve as a breadbasket for the homeland if it could achieve agricultural autonomy, thus reducing Italy's dependence on foreign resources. They dreamed about rich import of grain, meat, vegetable oils, cotton, coffee, wood, wool, rubber and minerals."[14]

The period saw significant increased Italian colonial settlement and, as Stefano Bellucci suggests, some 200,000 workers were available to work in infrastructure in AOI between 1935–1939[15] – a period that also saw significant construction of buildings in Asmara to house the burgeoning settler population. In the early 1930s Asmara was still a small town of 18,000 inhabitants and from 1935 onwards, the Italian population skyrocketed, peaking at 75,000 in 1940.[16] This sudden demographic growth reflected Asmara's political and strategic significance as the main operational and logistic headquarters for Italian fascist military aggression against Ethiopia. In preparation for this colonial war, the fascist government began a major urban development and infrastructural programme to meet the growing needs of Italian colonisation of Ethiopia. Given the pace of economic, social and military activities of the fascist government, colonial urban planning became an important spatial strategy aimed at entrenching both social and geographic divisions of the local population while at the same time establishing racial domination. In this context, architecture and urban planning began to play a central role in conveying and establishing the totalitarian imperial dream of the fascist regime[17]. After the invasion of Ethiopia, the Italian government issued a body of race laws aimed at enforcing strict racial segregation in the Empire.

The origin for conserving Italian fascist architecture for purposes of heritage in Asmara came in the aftermath of Eritrean succession from Ethiopia. Although the creation of history of the new Eritrean state is a process which started to take shape with the launching of the guerrilla movements, the issue assumed a new urgency both during the war and after Eritrea's succession.[18] Packaging and rebranding fascist architecture both for heritage and national identity became an urgent task for the new state in Eritrea.

Rebranding Fascist Architecture

Over the past decade, scholars working in the field of the built environment have pointed out the significance of the built environment and iconic buildings in particular as the cultural objects of cities par excellence.[19] Geographers such as David Harvey[20] as well as sociologist Zukin[21] have shown the link between the built environment and the centrality of cultural process in understanding urban change in contemporary cities. Given the importance of tourism, cities across the world have begun a campaign to brand their fixed and non-transportable built environment for global tourism. The rebranding of fascist architecture in Asmara stands at the nexus of the globalisation process and local actors who to seek to market the city as a desirable destination for global tourism. According to Destination Marketing Association International, an international network with more than 600 convention and visitor bureaus in more than twenty-five countries:

> A brand is more than a name, logo, or slogan and it is not built only through advertising. Genuine brands are the result of a comprehensive strategy that encompasses the entire experience from visitors' and prospective visitors' point of view ...Brand names are well known but similar, like supermarkets, car dealership, and fast-food restaurants. The distinguishing factor that sets a real brand apart from others is its set of distinctive characteristics and its experience ... You get to be a brand only when your consumers (visitors) say that you are distinctive.[22]

The succession of Eritrea created the necessary political and social conditions for rebranding fascist architecture as heritage with the creation of CARP. Given the absence of local experts in heritage, the new state had to rely on international experts to identify, classify and organise heritage and preservation issues in Eritrea. With funds provided by the World Bank, the first inventory of the colonial built form in Asmara began in 1997 within the delimited 4 km^2 of the city centre as the historic core. One of the main strategies developed by CARP was to use the colonial built environment, particularly that constructed during the fascist period as a specific place-based identity of the city. According to Greenburg, urban branding is about constructing and shaping an "urban imaginary" understood as a "coherent, historically based ensemble of representations drawn from architecture and street plans of the city...".[23] Rather than telling conventional stories, the rebranding of Asmara is geared to reshaping and manipulating history, consistent with the official story of the ruling party. Indeed, the complex and contested nature of the city's social history, its variegated people and their narrative has been homogenised and standardised in favour of the official narrative of the state.

As the former Minister of Information Ali Abdu noted, “This is [a]... priority for us, along with other programmes...The past is very important in order to build the future.”[24] While the Minister did not explain why the colonial past was important to build Eritrean’s future, it is very clear that Eritrean identity, its territorial boundary and the legitimacy of the new state is closely linked to Italian colonial presence in the country. Indeed, the production of Asmara as a heritage space is not somethings that is given, but has to be produced by the state. As Christoph Rausch indicated, “Eritrean Officialdom has colluded in fostering outsider colonial nostalgia, accepting international funding toward preservation of the colonial build heritage, all while manipulating this heritage’s value for national sentiment and ultimately, ruthless domestic control.”[25]

The creation of CARP by the state to bundle, name, market and regulate the urban landscape of Asmara and the application to World Heritage List is linked to make the city knowable and recognisable as an authentic heritage destination. While CARP was a lead agency with the responsibility for conserving and restoring Italian colonial heritage, it did not have the financial resources to transform the city centre. With the very limited power it received from the state, CARP was involved in the production of an essentialised urban landscape placed in the service of creating a tourist destination within the city centre. The intent to demarcate the inner city is to give coherence to those architectural buildings that were selected by CARP: gas stations, government buildings, and churches, etc. CARP also cordoned off areas of the city that had been the sites of community life for ordinary working-class Eritreans of all ethnic groups. While the initial work of CARP received support from the state, intergovernmental infighting and rivalry between and among key players in charge of the city’s conservation project, as well as the direct involvement of the country’s president in the work of CARP, finally led to the demise of CARP.[26]

As CARP’s work began, it became clear that certain areas of the city and memories that did not fit into the official version of Eritrean history were excluded from heritage consideration. Thus the homogenised and essentionalised past that privileges Italian presence is now promoted as heritage in Asmara. Like all other urban spaces designed to promote tourism, the branding and marketing of Asmara as a tourist destination is particularly silent about issues related to shared history and heritage prior to Italian colonial rule. For those involved in CARP’s work, the question on how to represent Italian colonial history and its atrocities, the history of multi-ethnic and multi-religious communities, andthe role played by Eritrean soldiers during Mussolini’s campaign to invade Ethiopia with Asmara as a launching pad does not figure in their historical narrative. Clearly, the rebranding of Asmara reflects a carefully crafted image of the city designed to promote tourism without its complicated history. As Fuller has suggested, the desire for attachment to the colonial past, "...provides them [Eritreans] with a claim to a long-standing cosmopolitanism", one tethered to colonialism and erasure.[27] Reacting to the rebranded architecture of Asmara, Professor Raimund Rütten noted that, "I was quite upset and shocked about what was presented about Asmara.... How could it come to such thoughtlessness and such unprecedented absence of historical awareness? I think about the imperial megalomania of fascist Italy and its forced colony Eritrea, at least since the 1930s gateway for the war of aggression and conquest of the fascists against Abyssinia being subjugated to its overseas territory; about the bombardments from the air, about the technologically superior air force, about the large-scale use of poisonous gas against the civilian population in Abyssinia; etc."[28]

In the Arcades Project, Walter Benjamin treated the built environment as compressed microcosms of the social world, reflecting hidden relations of power.[29] The hegemonic power in Eritrea is carefully rebranding Asmara as heritage for the last two decades. Part of this effort is closely linked to the need to maintain the politically and socially constructed Eritrean identity and at the same time use fascist architecture to sustain a mythology of Eritreaness outside the intersecting historical currents that has made and remade the region. Despite the Orwellian repression and the closing of political space, ordinary Eritreans do reimagine history beyond the crumbling fascist architecture of Asmara and continue to contest its structured symbolic significance.

Notes

1 "Eritrea: Asmara's Great Architectural Heritage in Danger", in: http://asmarino.com/news/4436-eritrea-asmara-s-great-architectural-heritage-in-danger, accessed May 10, 2016.

2 Arjun Appadurai, *Modernity at Large: Cultural Dimensions of Globalisation*. Minneapolis: University of Minnesota Press, 1996.

3 Eritrea is the first African state to submit Italian fascist architecture as national heritage to UNESCO.

4 The template for this dossier was published in 2001. See Edward Denison, Guang Yu Ren and Naigzy Gebremedhin, *Asmara: Africa's Secret Modernist City*. London: Merrell, 2001. Edward Dension and Guang Yu were hired as design and architectural consultants by CARP while Naigzy Gebremedhin, the Director of CARP, and his replacement Gabriel Tsegai were forced to leave CARP. According to a number of sources they had to flee the country for their life.

5 In 2005, the Historic Perimeter of Asmara and its Modernist Architecture was placed on UNESCO's Tentative List. The extent of this perimeter encompasses the colonial planned areas of the city but excludes the organically developed indigenous quarters.

6 Eritrean nationalist organisations have invented a previously unknown Eritrean history and identity prior to Italian colonialism. See Jordan Gebre-Medhin, *Peasants and Nationalism in Eritrea: A Critique of Ethiopian Studies*. Red Sea Press: Trenton, NJ, 1989.

7 Cited in Mai Fuller, "Italy's Colonial Future: Colonia Inertia and Postcolonial Capital in Asmara", *California Italian Studies*, 2 (1) 2011.

8 Eritrea before the colonial period had no common identity prior to its incarnation as Italian Eritrea. However, the sixty years of Italian colonial rule have led various groups to join new movements in the name of a new notion of community. Three of Eritrea's nine ethnic groups straddle its border with Ethiopia. The largest group is made up of Tigrinya speakers, who constitute about 50 per cent of the Eritrean population and have historically been major players, indeed an integral element, in all of the Ethiopian empires. Patrick Gilkes, "National Identity and Historical Mythology in Eritrea and Somaliland", *Northeast African Studies*, vol. 10. Iss. 3, 2003.

9 Sean Anderson, *Invisible Colonies: Modern Architecture and its representation in Colonia Eritrea, 1890–1941*. Ph.D. Dissertation, University of California Los Angeles, 2006.

10 Giovanna Trento, "Madamato and Colonial Concubinage in Ethiopia: A Comparative Perspective", *Aethiopica: Journal of Ethiopian and Eritrean Studies*, vol. 14, 2011, p. 186.

11 Like the colonial matrix, the EPLF which has renamed itself the People's Front for Democracy and Justice (PFDJ) has assumed absolute control of the state and created a vast Orwellian state apparatus to control the lives of Eritrean people both inside and outside the diaspora. For an insightful analysis of this process, see Tekle Woldemarian, "Pitfalls of Nationalism in Eritrea", in David O'Kane and Tricia Redeker Hepner (eds.), *Biopolitics, Militarism and Development: Eritrea in the Twenty-First Century*. New York: Berghan, 2009.

12 Sabelo J.Ndlovu-Gatsheni, *Coloniality of Power in Postcolonial Africa: Myth of Decolonization*. CODESRIA: Oxford, UK, 2013, p. 37.

13 Anderson, 2006, p.11.

14 Diane Ghirard, *Building New Communities. New Deal America and Fascist Italy*. Princeton: Princeton University Press, p. 91.

15 Stefanos Bellucci, "Italian Transnational Fluxes of Labour and the Changing Labour Relations in the Horn of Africa, 1935–1939", *International Journal on Strikes and Social Conflicts*, vol. I, no. 3, May 2013, pp. 161-174.

16 Giulia Barrera, "Dangerous Liaisons Colonial Concubinage in Eritrea, 1890–1941", PSA Working Paper, Program of African Studies, Northwestern University, 1966

17 Uoldelul Chelati Dirar, "From Warriors to Urban Dwellers: Ascari and the Military Factor in the Urban Development of Colonial Eritrea", *Cahiers d'etudees africanses* No. 175, 2004/3, pp. 533-574.

18 Patrick Gilkes, "Eritrea: Historiography and Mythology," *African Affairs*, 90, No. 361, 1991.

19 PB.Mackeith, *The dissolving corporation: contemporary architecture and corporate identity in Finland*. EVA – Finnish Business and Policy Forum: Helsinki, 2005.

20 David Harvey, "Monuments and Myth", *Annals of the Association of American Geographers*, 69, 362-81, 1979; *The Conditions of Postmodernity*. Blackwell: Oxford, 1989.

21 Sharon Zukin, *Landscape of Power: from Detroit to Disney World*. Berkeley: University of California Press, 1989.

22 Brand Strategy, Inc. 2004. *The Brand science guide for destination research: The handbook to help convention and visitors bureau tourism research for destinations*. Brand Strategy, Inc. http://www.destinationmarketing.org, accessed May 12, 2016.

23 Miriam Greenburg, "Branding Cities: ASocial History of Urban Lifestyle Magazine", *Urban Affairs Review* 36, No. 2 (November), 2000 pp. 228-262.

24 World Monuments, Fall, 2006, p. 29. The Minister has since fled his country and is now living in an undisclosed location.

25 Cited in Mai Fuller, "Italy's Colonial Future: Colonia Inertia and Postcolonial Capital in Asmara", *California Italian Studies*, 2 (1) 2011, p. 9.

26 According to WikiLeaks, the former US Ambassador to Eritrea, Ronald McMullen, indicated that the Eritrean President dismantled CARP because it failed to mention his name in one of its published works. http://asmarino.com/articles/1581-asmaras-crumbling-buildings-let-the-pictures-speak-part-ii5

27 Mai Fuller, 2011, p. 11.

28 Dossier: Asmara Africa's Secret Capital of Modern Architecture, Exhibition, Berlin 2006, p. 11. http://asmara-architecture.com/Dossier_engl.pdf (retrieved May 15, 2016)

29 Walter Benjamin, *The Arcades Project*. New York: Belknap Press, 2002.

PART II

POSTCOLONIAL EXPERIENCES

This book is not limited to an exploration of Asmara's colonial past or to a re-reading of its colonial history defining the relationship between former colonisers and colonised. The second part analyses another exclusive term: the *bella Asmara* — image as an illusory location of authenticity, the impossibility of a romantic return, namely, to that symbolic home or of the recovery of an authentic culture. We end up with a fragmented portrayal of cultural in-betweenness, often represented in literature, film, theatre and new media, which magnifies the amount of contact that a subject has with various cultures. By working with an interdisciplinary and intercultural cartography of the colonial sphere, we could draw literary, cinematic and alternative maps that may become potential testimonies to other histories, permitting us to reach out beyond existing critical modalities. How are new media used to consolidate desired place-narratives? When dealing with creative works, we must step over that critical threshold based primarily on accepted historical factors, as well as what one assumes is based on authorial intentions.

The second part of this book discusses the migration of people and images as one of the main factors that affect and shape cultures in the contemporary world. In particular, it identifies the common, global context in which a wide array of discourses, cultural and social productions of Asmara are finding expression. What is the role of Asmara outside Eritrea? This chapter will concentrate on the tension between the construct of a totalising, or panoramic, account of Asmara and the desire to tell the particular experiences of an individual character. What role is played by Asmara in Italian postcolonial discourse? Simultaneously, critical disturbance and problematics that are usually located elsewhere, in the Other, are brought home to probe the local and institutional complacencies of Italian studies and their particular understanding of cultural, historical and critical modalities.

First Chapter

TRACING POSTCOLONIALISM

This book seeks to counter the dominant representation of Italian colonialisation by examining the role of Asmara in the postcolonial and contemporary periods, highlighting the legacy of colonialism along with new social and cultural developments, and new media. The collection of essays foregrounds the work of scholars from different fields by theorising and comparing postcolonial conditions, and recasting debates in cinema, literature and postcolonial studies. Postcolonialism is presented not as a rigid category but as a lense through which questions of postcolonial geography, subjectivity and historiography can be addressed. By working with an interdisciplinary and intercultural cartography of the colonial sphere, we could draw literary, cinematic and alternative maps that may become potential testimonies to other histories, permitting us to reach out beyond existing critical modalities. The focus is on the material and cultural geographies of Italian colonialism and the role that Asmara played in this transnational cultural landscape. We argue that an understanding of colonialism and postcolonialism should take into account the following argument: one of the main Italian routes to postcolonialism (after the almost complete suppression of the Italian colonial past from the collective national memory and from the public sphere) is to be found in film, literature and new social movements. The aesthetic categories used to read and define the relation between colonial past and postcolonial present are linked with the relations between Italy and its former colonies in Africa, taking into account the anomalous situation brought about by the processes of suppression to which the Italian colonial enterprise has been systematically and strategically subjected.

From this perspective, this section signals the urgency of (re)opening and problematising the closed reading of Asmara, which was/is specifically intended for self-representation and representation of the Other. The postcolonial perspective engages Asmara in several ways. In this sense, the book repositions colonial history and its legacy at the centre of the debate on contemporary Asmara. This can involve a closer reading of texts qua texts to discover embedded codes or rhetorical shapes and to examine literary constructions. It can also imply a study of the history of images of Asmara. Thanks to their interdisciplinary expertise, our contributors have discovered and explored the conceptual temporalities and spatialities of postcoloniality.

Indeed postcolonial theory, as applied to the analysis of architecture and urbanism, serves to reveal underlying colonialist relations, to pinpoint latent self/other dichotomies and their derived binaries, to disclose the practices of romanticising, othering, essentialising and appropriation inherent in colonialist discourse, and to indicate how architecture reflects these. This chapter also warns against the danger of an essentialising position that presupposes a clearly defined Asmara aesthetic. Contributions to the book address the many representations of Asmara, developing an analysis of the different forms taken by the national and international appropriations of Asmara's architecture after the country's independence in 1991. More specifically, the aim of this section is to investigate how the imaginary around Asmara has been expressed in Italy through artistic practices such as literature, music and the performing arts.

In her piece, **Cristina Lombardi-Diop** considers the work of contemporary postcolonial artists, video-makers and writers who are engaged in presenting images of Asmara as a colonial capital as they emerge through memories and personal stories. In particular, the author examines visual and textual narratives by Bianchi and Scego, Brioni and Sibhatu, Dell'Oro, and Lucarelli, identifying a common effort in their work to bring traces of colonial history to the surface, a critical activity she defines as a form of postcolonial archaeology. In contemporary Italy, Lombardi-Diop argues, the colonial capitals of *Africa Orientale Italiana* (Asmara, Addis Ababa and Mogadishu) have not disappeared; they are still present in the multiple insertions of colonial ruins within the contemporary Roman cityscape and in the memories of the new generations of Ethiopians, Eritreans and Somali who have settled in Rome as part of Italy's postcolonial diaspora.

Rino Bianchi and **Igiaba Scego** demonstrate that architecture provides a powerful tool to mediate between colonial history and postcolonial memory. As such, Bianchi's photo essay not only draws attention to the need to unravel the individual histories underlying the production and development of particular buildings and sites over time, but also to the need to engage in memory work. In the book *Roma negate. Percorsi postcoloniali nella città* (2014) Rino Bianchi and Igiaba Scego undertake a historical and geographical, cross-cultural journey, combining Scego's writing and Bianchi's photos. The aim is to give back to Africa the voice that was erased by Italians, reconstructing an often omitted past in the middle of Rome. The authors try to fill the gaps in the memory of Italian colonialism by describing monuments and places, recovering generally ignored or removed meanings.

Rebecca Hopkins shows how contemporary writers Erminia Dell'Oro and Elisa Kidanè, who were born and raised in Asmara, and eventually migrated to Italy, have drawn on utopian discourses about Asmara promulgated by the Italian colonial regime and culture in the 1920s and 1930s. Eritrea in general, and Asmara in particular, were then portrayed as a new, ideal society whose future was full of possibilities (for Italians, the Italian regime and sometimes the local inhabitants). Dell'Oro and Kidanè have highlighted a problematic aspect of such a colonial utopian discourse: the imagined racial harmony between Italians and Eritreans. Using postcolonial theory, this essay argues that both writers transform these colonial utopian discourses about Asmara by imagining postcolonial spaces that echo the new, ideal and future aspects of the colonial imaginary of the city, while envisioning alternative social orders that reject the historical reality of racial segregation and exploitation.

In January 2008 the Eritrean capital of Asmara witnessed a theatre production that did not sit easily with the cultural imaginary of the country. Performed by a group of university graduates (rather than the well-versed artists in government employment), Beyene Haile's Weg'i Libi, or Heart-to-Heart Talk, caused a stir among the local art-loving community in that it challenged the common ingredients of Eritrean theatre. Difficult to understand, with no clear plot or clear-cut message, it nonetheless drew crowds during the two weeks of its performance run, largely because it allowed audiences to participate in the intellectual flânerie presented on stage. **Christine Matzke's** contribution provides an interpretation of the play, along with an outline and contextualisation of its production process, using material she collected in autumn 2008 and spring 2010.

Although Italian cinema in the postcolonial period has not manifestly dealt with the colonial past, this repressed past does re-emerge through the recoding of space that this cinema visualises. **Linde Lijunenburg's** essay deals with colonial spaces in popular Totò films, which conveyed Italy's trauma caused by the failed colonial enterprises, the country's anxiety surrounding the theme of the lost war, and the subsequent echo of the colonial narrative.

Moreover, it looks at Totò's characters' relationships with women, detecting in them a displacement of the trauma of the lost war and lost colonies.

Chris Keulen photographed the *Giro d'Eritrea* twice – in 2004 and 2009. His 2009 visit won the third prize in the Sports Stories category of the 2010 World Press Awards. Eritrea's passion for cycling is one of many lasting influences of Italian colonial rule. Italians brought cycle racing to Eritrea and it has become a national passion; in the 2015 Tour de France, Eritrean cyclist Daniel Teklehaimanot wore the King of the Mountains jersey. The Giro, the country's first multi-day cycle race, was first staged in 1946, although locals were not allowed to enter. The Giro was resurrected fifty-five years later, a symbol of the new-found confidence of a nation that had finally gained independence in 1991. Africa's oldest cycle race is a far cry from the televised sporting extravaganzas that we are used to seeing on TV. But a live telecast almost seems unnecessary since the roads are packed with spectators anyway. The event is a huge celebration in a country whose repressive regime gives its people little to cheer about.

Gianmarco Mancosu's essay describes how the visual legacies of Italian colonialism have been used in four contemporary documentaries on the Italian postcolonial landscape. He uses old visual material, called up to connect the colonial past with contemporary histories of mobility and, in turn, their peculiar relation with Asmara, which was conceived as the concrete reification of the fascist colonial myth. The first part of his essay investigates the relationship between the cinema and fascist colonialism, by looking at the activity of the *Reparto Africa Orientale Istituto Luce*, that took pictures and made footage of the Empire. The second part analyses specific documentaries in which multiple temporary dimensions are intertwined: by highlighting old representations of Asmara in current documentaries, the essay explores the tension between old centripetal images, which in the past attracted settlers to the colony, and current centrifugal images, which nowadays encourage Eritrean citizens to escape to Italy.

ROME – ASMARA
A Postcolonial Archaeology of Colonial Spaces

Cristina Lombardi-Diop

In his latest novel, *All Our Names*, the Ethiopian-American writer Dinaw Mengestu imagines the African postcolonial city as an invisible space, "a city that disappeared each night once the last inhabitant fell asleep."[1] (128). Much like Italo Calvino's invisible cities, the African city in the story, told by the protagonist's father, was once a real place. Its disappearance compels the people to keep the city alive in their imagination. The city exists as long as someone dreams of it each night. The work of salvaging the city from oblivion is intended in order to pass the image of the city on to the next generation. In line with the novel's title, this work implies naming all the names of those who have been unwilling victims of the wars of liberation and repressive militarisation of African postcolonial regimes. The uprooting of Isaac from his native village in Ethiopia in search of a pan-African utopia in Kampala leads to the inevitable encounter with the repressive brutality of Uganda's postcolonial urban life, where checkpoints are erected in the midst of shacks, half-burn piles of trash, and open latrine pits, "in a city that had clearly stretched its limits and was bursting at its seams."[2] The protagonist's journey is contrasted with the seemingly contained cityscape of the American Midwest, where the history of segregation looms at every corner.

Keeping alive visions of the colonial city in the present is also the task of Italy's contemporary postcolonial artists, video-makers, and writers who are engaged in the projects of making them emerge from the sites of their uncertain burial where they have been forgotten as a result of personal trauma, violent border wars, diasporic uprootedness, and historical negations. In this essay, I use the term postcolonial archaeology for this activity, that is, the excavation

Julius Caesar on the Fori Imperiali in Rome
Source: Courtesy of R. Bianchi

into the uneven ground of the present to bring to vision the multiple layers of colonial history. In contemporary Italy, the colonial capitals of *Africa Orientale Italiana* (Asmara, Addis Ababa, Mogadishu) have not disappeared, but they are hidden within the gaps of a vertically built Roman cityscape. Yet, by looking closely, one can find multiple inscriptions of their permanence among colonial ruins. As Daniele Comberiati notes, the colonial capitals of Italy experienced the type of cultural coexistence and clashes that characterise today's postcolonial cities. The uneasy cohabitation of different cultures and religions, the encounter between Africans and Europeans, Asian immigrations and multi-ethnic neighbourhoods are all the phenomena still visible in today's Italy.[3] The Italians built the colonial capitals in the image of fascist modern cities, yet their utopian and dystopian realities prefigured the urban landscape of the new millennium. Their modernity was already ahead of their time.

Re-imagining the modernity and future of the postcolonial capital necessitates the mediation – in the form of affective and mnemonic links – of the new generations of Ethiopians, Eritreans, and Somali that have settled in Rome as part of Italy's postcolonial diaspora. Igiaba Scego's Rome, for instance, is a denied city, "so inadequate for the present, completely imperfect." Rome keeps hidden "its secrets and unmentionable delusions." For Scego, a Somali-Italian writer born in the Italian capital, Rome is a city that never told her "the whole truth."[4] Her book, *Roma negata*, combines her semi-autobiographical reflections on the colonial past with photographic images by Italian photographer and reporter Rino Bianchi. Scego's affective narrative is told as she strolls the contemporary cityscape in search of the names and places that link Rome to colonial events and figures. The text is intended as an affective and cognitive operation aimed at uncovering both personal and historical data. In the photographic section of the book, Bianchi's images portray Somali, Ethiopians, and Eritreans placed in front of iconic buildings and monuments such as Cinema Impero, in the district of Pigneto. Their austere posture seems to mark the solemnity of such purposeful repossession of colonial history from the perspective of its African protagonists. The text-images signify that the whole truth can be revealed only by bringing to view the invisible traces of the presence of African Rome within its contemporary urban texture. The monuments and buildings that the people in the Bianchi's pictures occupy, monumentalise these sites again, ultimately re-signifying Rome's urban space: Ponte Amedeo d'Aosta, erected in 1939 to celebrate the eponymous Viceroy of Ethiopia, the African district of Rome, with such street names as Viale Somalia, Viale Libia, Via Tripoli, Viale Etiopia, and Piazza Capena, where the Axum Obelisk once stood, all stand as a reminder of the continuing links that the present entertains with the past. Scego explores their contextual colonial references, literally filling the gaps and creating a new Rome as the peninsular capital of the empire. In this act of postcolonial archaeological reconstruction, the complexity of Rome's stratified present materialises in one poignant moment in her narrative, when Scego evokes the image of the unnamed bodies of Eritrean migrants drown in the Mediterranean in the attempt at reaching Europe. She links their unburied bodies to the bodies of *Ascari* – the Eritrean soldiers enlisted in the colonial troops – left buried but unnamed at the margin of the African battlefields.[5] Like in Mengestu's climatic scene, when Isaac buries the corpses of the young African soldiers and attempts to name them all, Scego's critical archaeology consists in the act of unearthing bodies, names, and places.

Today, Mussolini's Rome and its visible national monuments and architecture stand in a reversal relation to colonial cities such as Asmara and Addis Ababa. In the fascist conception, building the colonial capitals involved remaking Italian modernity in the image of a classical antecedent, that is, imperial Rome. In this process, the exterior of Africa had to be conceived as an empty space to be filled with the very notion of a new civilisation. In building Asmara, "racial, sexual, and economic divisions evolved through the mediation of this Italian city's image."[6] The heavy investment in the urban development of a new Asmara, fascist, modern, monumental, white, rational and Mediterranean, was planned according to modern criteria. Such criteria, which applied to all of the newly constructed towns of the empire of *Africa Orientale Italiana*, including the capital Addis Ababa, envisioned the re-organisation of space along racial lines. The racial zoning of the Italian colonial towns was not a prerogative of Mussolini's regime. Pre-fascist Asmara had already been partitioned according to racial lines. The 1908 *Piano Regolatore* of Governor Salvago Raggi envisioned three distinctive residential areas, the first area for white Italians and other Europeans, the second area for assimilated and mixed populations of Eritreans, Egyptians, and Indians, and the third area reserved exclusively for the colonial subjects. Starting in 1935, when a series of public works began in preparation for the war, and in the span of six years, Asmara underwent a tumultuous growth. The Italian population grew from 3,000 to 55,000 residents, while the Eritrean population grew from 20,000 to 45,000 residents.[7]

The process of building a segregated society from the ground up required constructing a "new matrix of meaning" and a new "set of visual and textual codes"[8] embedded in the constant dialectics between exterior and interior, colonialism and modernity. Considered as spatially chaotic and disorganised, primitive and devoid of history, the spaces where the Italians built the colonial cities were meant to minimise contact between them and the imperial subjects.[9] Making space for the Italians in new modern dwellings meant the forced eviction of native citizens from their homes and their relocation.[10] New native villages (such is *Il Villaggio Azzurro* and the Acria area), lodged the military forces of the *Ascari*, heavily recruited among the Eritrean male populations.[11] The modern city, instead, was meant for the Italians alone. In the imperial visions of Addis Ababa, urban planners and architects envisioned public works that would reproduce almost entirely the organisation of native Italian spaces, the *piazza* and its church, the post office, and the Fascist Party headquarters. The imperial planning of Asmara brought to the development of segregated districts, such as Amba Galliano, built as residential areas for the Italian military high ranks and the government employees.[12]

Segregation and labour exploitation are a lingering legacy of colonial practices in today's urban capitals. The imagination of postcolonial writers and migrants has not remained immune to the lingering traces of such practices. Caterina Romeo has shown as the exploitation of black women by white female employers is made central in the writing of postcolonial women's writers such as Ingy Mubiayi and Gabriella Kuruvilla – a situation that puts into question the effectiveness of the legacy of Italian feminism in today's Italy. "In the social and public spaces of contemporary Italy," according to Romeo, "symbolic space in literature has historically been constructed as a white space."[13] Spatial segregation also appears, albeit often unnamed, in contemporary literature set in Asmara. The narrator of Erminia Dell'Oro's *Asmara addio* reconstructs the isolated and self-absorbed life of the community of Asmara's *vecchi colonialisti* from the early 1930s onwards: "It was the Asmara of white people, and on Corso Mussolini, later renamed Corso Italia, at that time no Eritreans would been seen passing by. They would rather stay in Ambasciaul, on the outskirts of Asmara, surviving in their misery of centuries."[14]

In Carlo Lucarelli's *Albergo Italia*, set in pre-fascist Asmara, the perimeter of the town is delimited by the Italian military camps, and the *Carabinieri's* presence in the native district of Ambasciaul is described as an oddity and incursion.[15] The public spaces of Viale Mussolini, the *Cattedrale*, the *Corso*, the *piazza* and the modern *villette* with their small gardens in Dell'Oro's recollection are separated from the white mosque and the indigenous market square. The Italians socialise among themselves in the *circoli*, playing cards and organising dancing contests. Interactions between the Italians and the native *Asmarini* occur most often in the domestic interiors; female domestic servants socialise with the children of white families. Even the spatial organisation of the domestic interior quarters is such that prevents sustained interracial contact. Female domestic servants are given their own room, such as is the case with Mafrasc and Abeba, the two sisters working at the service of *famiglia* Conti. While Mafrasc has covered the walls of her own room with posters of famous American actors such as Rita Hayworth and Tyrone Power, her sister Abeba, whom has internalised the existence of racial barriers at the moment of their dismantling following the war and the loss of the colonies, decides to take the posters down and purposely avoids mingling with the Italians, "because we were white, we were the masters, and we were therefore different."[16] The novel records a gendered division in racial attitudes: at the opposite spectrum of Abeba's budding nationalism and racial pride is the perceived behaviour of Eliseo, a male domestic worker, "servile and slightly fearful," "submitted and grateful."[17]

In the interviews with Eritrean women from Asmara who moved to Rome as domestic workers in the 1960s and 1970s, the spatial organisation of the domestic space in the residences of the affluent Roman families where they live replicates and brings to visibility the experience of racial and social segregation of colonial Asmara. Such segregationist practices linger in their memories. They describe with uneasiness their living space, a small room next to the kitchen, under the constant surveillance of the *signora*, while the assigned daily tasks replicate the separation of dirt from purity, one of the key metaphors of racial segregation in the Italian colonial imagination.[18]

The conflation of colonial and postcolonial temporalities features predominantly in the documentary *Aulò: Roma postcoloniale*, directed by Simone Brioni and written by Brioni and Ribka Sibhatu, poet, writer, and scholar of Eritrean origin.[19] The documentary script is based on the original text *Aulò! Canto-poesia dell'Eritrea*, a collection of lyrics and prose poems originally written in Tigrinya and translated by the author into Italian.[20] Through the *Aulò*, a form of Tigrinya oral narrative, Sibhatu narrates her personal story of imprisonment, and eventual exile to Ethiopia, France and then Rome, establishing an intimate and affective connection not only between Asmara and Rome at present, but also between Asmara's colonial past and the Eritrean diaspora in Rome. The documentary expands upon Sibhatu's original 1993 text by the same title, emphasising the work's cultural translation from official history to personal story, and from text to visual narrative.[21] The documentary effects this process of transformation from orature to literature by inserting shots of the poet's handwritten work in many languages (Amharic, Tigrinya, Italian, French, and English, to be exact)[22], being inscribed on to a blank page. As Alessandro Triulzi has argued, the use of orality and other forms of non-verbal expression such as graffiti, wall posters and paintings, music, and dance are all signs of "a new grammar of urban communication"[23] unfolding in the ex-colonial capitals of independent Africa, embracing neither tradition nor modernity understood in the colonial sense. Such forms counteract the urban decay of postcolonial cities, articulating the expression of vernacular and popular realities in the face of neo-colonial relationships of state power and the encroaching of urban poverty, by rethinking memory as a counteractive activity. As a privileged "site of memory,"[24] the coexistence of layers of cultures and memories in the life of postcolonial African cities makes possible the invention of multiform, multilingual, and multimedia expression proliferating in the midst of their chaos. Such proliferation of multiple traditions and creative sources counteracts the signs of authoritarian order that urban segregation imposed on African colonial cities.

In the case of Brioni and Sibhatu's *Aulò*, voice and sign, maps and buildings, silences and music all contribute to make Rome a postcolonial African city, where past and present are continuously relinked in spite of their spatial and temporal disjunctions. Similarly to Bianchi and Scego's *Roma nascosta*, the documentary expresses a form of postcolonial archaeology that makes Rome the ideal locus of postcolonial memorialisation. "By rethinking the history of some historical places and monuments of Rome, Ribka [Sibhatu] highlights one of the main meanings of *Aulò* in Eritrean culture, namely its role as a memorial. Thus, Ribka argues that Eritrean oral poetry has the same function of monuments in a Western context."[25] In the evocative poetic rendition of Sibhatu's orature in the form of the *Aulò*, Rome becomes the instantiation of a colonial temporality that has never been interrupted. Similarly to Bianchi and Scego's use of architectural iconic images combined with personal narratives, the documentary places voice, images, and text, personal and political statements, and monumental Rome and fascist Asmara in a contiguous relationship. In one key sequence, Sibhatu recites an *Aulò* composed by her uncle as both a prayer for salvation from and invective against Mussolini's racial policies while standing in front of the *Vittoriano*, the iconic monument of post-Unification and fascist Rome, marking the inscription of colonial monumentality in the texture of the national capital. In excavating the multiple layers of colonial elements that cohabit in the urban texture of Rome, Sibhatu simultaneously reconstructs her own family genealogy, using the city as a palimpsest of her own exilic life. Hence, the work of postcolonial archaeology rejects the monumentalisation of the colonial past as frozen in ahistorical celebrations. Its active transformative power inverts the inevitable linearity by which Rome supposedly provides the matrix for the existence of modern Asmara. In a reversal of historical sequencing, Asmara is no longer *la piccola Roma*. It is rather Rome that imitates and resembles a greater Asmara. As the invisible city in Mengestu's story, both Rome and Asmara are thus kept alive by this continuous work of remembering and imagining.

Notes

1 Dianaw Mengestu, *All Our Names*, Reprint Edition. New York: Vintage, 2015, p. 128.

2 Mengestu, op. cit., p. 64.

3 Daniele Comberiati, "Quando le periferie diventano centro. Le identità delle città postcoloniali", in Daniele Comberiati (ed.), *Roma d'Abissinia. Cronache dai resti dell'impero: Asmara, Mogadiscio, Addis Abeba*. Cuneo: Nerosubianco, 2010, pp. 75-90.

4 Igiaba Scego, "Roma negate", in Rino Bianchi and Igiaba Scego (eds.), *Roma negata. Percorsi postcoloniali nella città*. Rome: Ediesse, 2014, pp. 13-136, p. 13. All translations from Italian in this essay are are my own.

5 Scego, op. cit., p. 40.

6 Sean Anderson, *Modern Architecture and its Representation in Colonial Eritrea: An In-Visible Colony, 1890–1941*. Burlington, VT: Ashgate, 2015, p. 14.

7 Giulia Barrera, "La città degli italiani e la città degli eritrei", in Giulia Barrera, Alessandro Triulzi, and Gabriel Tzeggai (eds.), *Asmara. Architettura e pianificazione urbana nei fondi dell'IsIAO*. Rome: Istituto Italiano per l'Africa e l'Oriente, 2008, pp. 12-27.

8 Anderson, op. cit., p. 9.

9 See Mia Fuller, *Moderns Abroad: Architecture, Cities, and Italian Imperialism*. Oxon: UK, Routledge, 2007 and, more specifically, chapter 9.

10 Richard Punkhurst, *The Ethiopians: A History, Hoboken*. NJ: Wiley-Blackwell, 2001.

11 Barrera, op. cit., pp. 14-15.

12 See Mia Fuller, op. cit., and Sabrina Marchetti, *Le ragazze di Asmara. Lavoro domestico e migrazione postcoloniali*. Rome: Ediesse, 2011, pp. 73-75.

13 Caterina Romeo, "Racial Evaporations: Representing Blackness in African Italian Postcolonial Literature", in Cristina Lombardi-Diop and Caterina Romeo (eds.), *Postcolonial Italy: Challenging National Homogeneity*. London and New York: Palgrave, 2012, pp. 221-238, pp. 230-231.

14 Erminia Dell'Oro, *Asmara addio*. Milan: Baldini & Castoldi, 1997, p. 22.

15 Carlo Lucarelli, *Albergo Italia*. Turin: Einaudi, 2014, p. 82.

16 Dell'Oro, op. cit., p. 129.

17 Dell'Oro, op. cit., p. 130.

18 See Marchetti, op. cit. For an analysis of the meaning of hygiene in the social space of the colonies see Cristina Lombardi-Diop, "L'Italia cambia pelle. La bianchezza degli italiani dal Fascismo al boom economico", in *Bianco e nero. Storia dell'identità razziale degli italiani*. Milan: Le Monnier-Mondadori Education, 2013, pp. 67-116.

19 Ermanno Guida, Graziano Chiscuzzu, and Simone Brioni, *Aulò: Roma postcoloniale*. HDV, ITA 2012.

20 Ribka Sibhatu, *Aulò. Canto-poesia dall'Eritrea*. Rome: Sinnos Editore, 1993.

21 For a detailed analysis of the documentary see Simone Brioni, "Across Languages, Cultures and Nations: Ribka Sibhatu's Aulò", in Patrizia Sambuco (ed.), *Italian Women Writers, 1800–2000: Boundaries, Borders and Transgression*. Madison; Teaneck: Fairleight Dickinson University Press, 2014, pp. 123-142.

22 Brioni, op. cit.

23 Alessandro Triulzi, "African Cities, Historical Memory and Street Buzz", in Iain Chambers and Lidia Curti (eds.), *The Postcolonial Question: Common Skies, Divided Horizons*. London: Routledge, 1996, pp. 78-91.

24 Triulzi, op. cit., p. 81.

25 Brioni, op. cit., p. 133.

CINEMA

IMPERO

ROME DENIED
Postcolonial Paths in the City

(Roma negata. Percorsi postcoloniali nella città)

Rino Bianchi and Igiaba Scego

Photography is not a neutral medium. In the period between the second half of the nineteenth century and the 1930s, it played a key role in the Italian colonial Empire constitution. For the entire duration of the colonial experience, explorers, priests, travellers, anthropologists, military, traders, photographers, technicians and government officials produced a multitude of images of Africa which were widespread in Italy in the form of postcards, posters, printed magazines, newspapers, films, newsreels, or, in the case of private photographs, remained locked in a drawer, shown only to close friends – often igniting the curiosity of children and grandchildren. Although different, all these images helped to build a favourable public image and legitimise the colonial enterprise. Italian colonialism, albeit belatedly and logistically less organised than English and French, was no different from that implemented by the European states in the use of visual aids for the construction of its domain.

The camera, combined with the typewriter, became a symbol of modernity and technological superiority for Europeans in accompaniment to the occupation of territories. The documentation created with the camera often preceded the military conquest, providing a catalogue of places and people to colonise. The black woman, photographed in each pose, played a central role in the construction of the imaginary Italian colonial empire, becoming a symbol of Africa where the white-black relationship between man and woman is symbolic of the relationship between the imperialist nation and the colony: the man is the one that projects fertilising masculinity, and the woman is the one who benefits from this. Not only in photographs but also in movies, postcards, advertisements, posters, as well as in stories and songs, black women were associated with the conquest of virgin lands, represented as sensual beings, available to the domain of the Italian man. Combining African femininity with the naturalness of the African continent through photographs justified the colonial possession of African women, the so-called *madamato* phenomenon. Many in Italy, thanks to the massive spread of postcards, dreamed of the breasts firm and pointy of Abyssinian, or the slender body of Somalia.

Roma Denied: Postcolonial Routes in the City is a text that establishes itself as a durable project since it narrates and brings the metabolisation of history, a historical moment often removed. This double narrative, composed of words and photographs, brings out stories of great humanity, seeking to attack and subvert the collective imagination and vision colonialist who still resists, using the same medium (the camera) used to justify and to accept colonial enterprise. Women appear proud and not at all in alluring poses. Confident men, with their strong look and challenge seem to get out of the frame. In this way both people, children of the colonised, regain possession of those places that have always belonged to imaginary Italian colonialism.

Roma negata. Percorsi postcoloniali nella città is a book project by the Somali-Italian writer Igiaba Scego and photographer Rino Bianchi. The paper traces the urban and global, historical and geographical, cross-cultural journey that Rino Bianchi and Igiaba Scego undertake in the book *Roma negata. Percorsi postcoloniali nella città* (Ediesse 2014), effectively combining word and image. Scego's writing and Bianchi's photos give back to Africa the voice that was forgotten or erased by Italians, reconstructing an often omitted past. The authors fill the gaps and the voids in the individual and collective memory of Italian colonialism in Africa through stories, documents, texts, and autobiographical and literary references. In this fascinating journey between past and present, monuments and places more or less known are described through an estranged perspective, recovering generally ignored or removed meanings. This path allows us to resume the relationships that bind Italy to Africa, and to move towards a common recognition.

110

Termini

AVIATORE
TRVPPE LE GVIDAVA

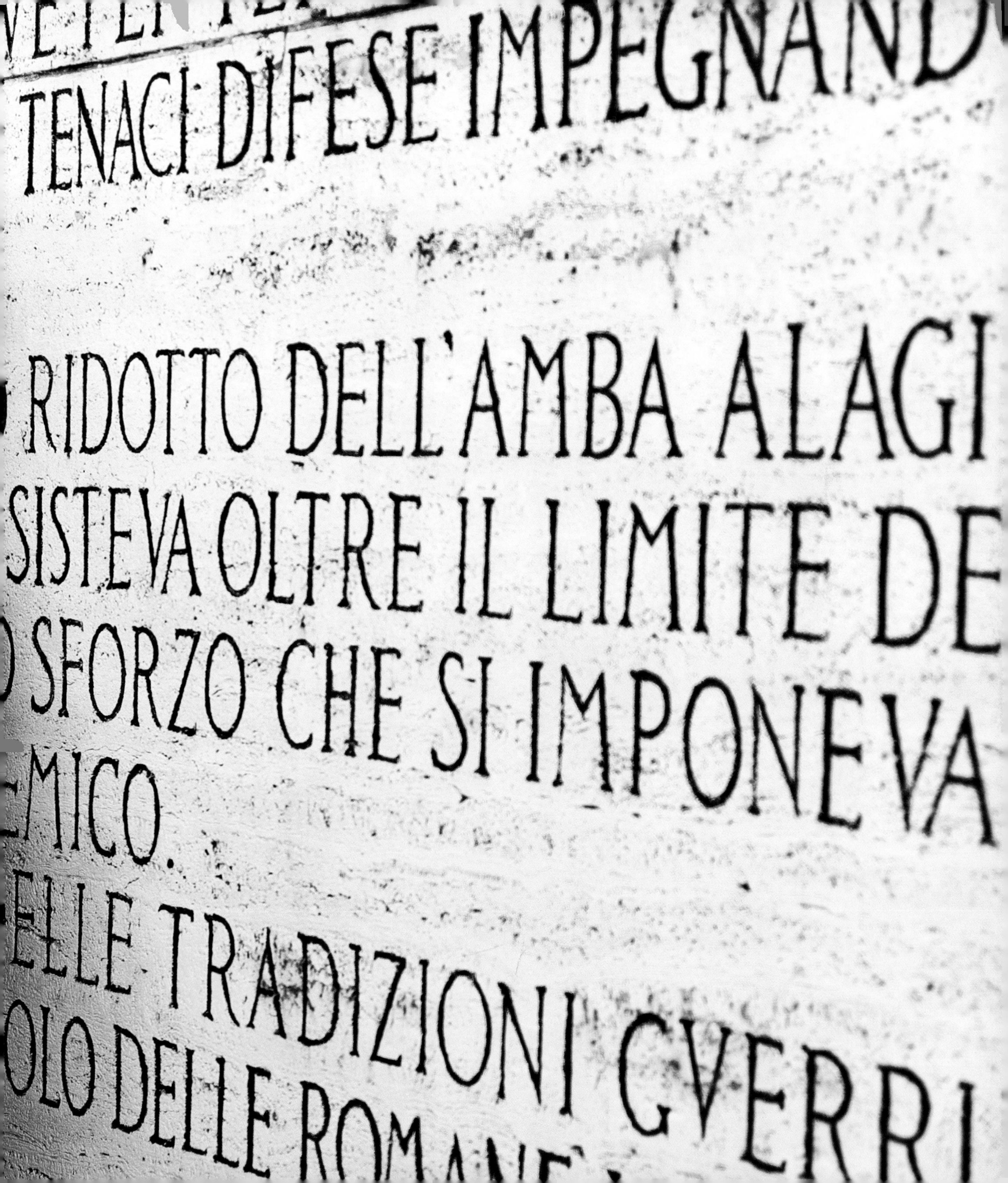

TENACI DIFESE IMPEGNAND

RIDOTTO DELL'AMBA ALAGI
SISTEVA OLTRE IL LIMITE DE
SFORZO CHE SI IMPONEVA
EMICO.
ELLE TRADIZIONI GVERRI
OLO DELLE ROMANE

POSTCOLONIAL UTOPIA IN ERMINIA DELL'ORO AND ELISA KIDANÉ

Visions of an Ideal Society in Asmara and Beyond

Rebecca Hopkins

Introduction

Like other Italian colonies in Africa, Eritrea – and particularly its principal city Asmara – was the locus of a utopian discourse disseminated in colonial texts during the fascist period.[1] Two contemporary writers, Erminia Dell'Oro and Elisa Kidanè, who were both born and raised in Asmara and eventually migrated to Italy, invoke this discourse as they transform it by imagining their own postcolonial utopias.[2] That is, Dell'Oro and Kidanè use the discourse of the colonial power (i.e. utopianism) but radically rework it to express something new. In particular, while the writers' postcolonial utopias appropriate colonial utopianism's emphasis on the future possibility of a new, ideal society in Asmara,[3] they critique the colonial project at its heart by imagining societies that redress the social injustice instituted by colonialism. In various poems by Kidanè, Asmara is the site of this postcolonial utopia while in Dell'Oro's novel *Asmara, Addio* (1988) the postcolonial utopia is located outside of Asmara on a mythical island that acts as an inverse mirror image of the city. In both cases, Asmara provides the context not only for postcolonial resistance but for a discursive continuity between the Italian colonial and postcolonial periods.[4]

Utopia in Italian Colonial Texts

Scholars have noted the sense of living on the threshold of a new epoch that characterised Italian fascism.[5] Articulating this as a form of utopia, Charles Burdett speaks of fascism's "rhetoric of anticipation" and the vision of a "new world" in writings on the Italian colonies.[6] Although he does not

The square in front of the mosque in Asmara
Source: K.Paulweber 2013

speak of Eritrea specifically, Burdett's observation upholds in this case too. Many texts, including articles in newspapers that were mouthpieces of the Fascist Federation in Eritrea, such as *Il corriere eritreo*, *Il quotidiano eritreo*, and *La nuova Eritrea*, as well as the well-known *L'azione coloniale*, describe the rapid evolution of a new Asmara. A 1937 article in *Il corriere eritreo* depicts Asmara as "moving forward on a path of progress and development".[7] Similarly, Alberto Pollera's 1932 piece *Eritrea* and his 1933 *Vita fascista in Eritrea*, published in the key colonial newspaper *L'Oltremare*, portray a new and idealised city rife with modern buildings, avenues, cinemas, banks, restaurants, stores, and villas with lush gardens. The new nature of the city in Pollera's texts goes hand in hand with the concept of the city's *avvenire* or future orientation and an "Eritrea of tomorrow ... marching toward a greater destiny".[8] Cesare Fraccari also uses the term *avvenire* to describe Asmara, stating that "the city ... will certainly become a model city", and that "the new history of Eternal Rome is on the march forward".[9] Likewise, other texts of the 1930s by the well-known colonial writers Renzo Martinelli, Orio Vergani and Mario Dei Gaslini express this image of a new and idyllic Asmara, whose *avvenire* is evident in its architecture and urban planning.[10]

In such texts the future promise of the new city coincides with the myth of social harmony, a key feature of many utopias.[11] In Pollera's piece *Eritrea* the future Eritrea is set against an idyllic Asmara where the different races mix harmoniously, forming a unified, happy whole. Thus social harmony here implies racial harmony. Similarly in a piece from *Il quotidiano eritreo*, Asmara, a city of "new life", is described as a "a meeting point between distant races... people from black Africa... and salesmen and travellers arriving from the western cities".[12] In *Vita fascista in Eritrea*, Pollera's "vision... of an Eritrea of tomorrow" is prefaced by the vision of the "happy union of Europeans and indigenous who seize every opportunity to show a perfect symmetry of sentiment" in the city space.[13] These harmonious relations, which are a key objective of the indigenous policy operating in many colonies at the time,[14] are also evident in a 1931 article in *Oltremare* as it speaks of the need to generate "reciprocal trust that moves the indigenous closer to the cause of civilisation and progress", as well as to "move the indigenous as close as possible to us [Italians], offering him even collaboration".[15] A key colonial figure, Maurizo Rava, in Eritrea (1927) invokes these indigenous policies as he calls for the local people to participate in Eritrea's future progress.[16] Echoing this, a 1932 article in *Oltremare* describes Eritrea as a "centre from which Italian civilisation radiates... as a land of example and training, as a meeting point of genuine contact with the people"[17]. Dei Gaslini imagines Asmara's *avvenire* in terms of the "need to call the natives to collaborate with the redemptive work of the land and progress", while Enrico Cappellina's novel *Un canto nella notte* 1925, set in colonial Asmara, imagines the city as the site of future promise not only in the new life accorded the hero in Asmara, but in the new enlightened path that he shows to the native character, Medin, whom he apparently civilises.[18]

Dell'Oro's Island of Future Possibility

This emphasis on a new city of future possibility is echoed in Dell Oro's novel in two points. First, the narrator's family leaves an increasingly tense political situation in late 1930s Italy for the promised land of Eritrea and specifically Asmara.[19] This myth of a promised land is linked with Asmara as a place of future possibility, depicted from the point of view of the narrator's mother: "The past was already far away and the future spread out before her feet like a multi-coloured rug sewn by the queen of the thousand and one nights" (55-56). Second, the narrator describes the new Eritrea and the new era that her family finds in Asmara upon their arrival in the 1930s, evident in the new villages, bridges, dams, buildings and avenues (34-35). This utopian rhetoric of the new and future possibility is appropriated in the frame story, set in Modok, an idyllic island off the coast of Eritrea, and a postcolonial utopian space of sorts. The island, described as the most beautiful island in the Red Sea, figures at the end of the novel as the place where the author travels upon her return to Asmara (having left for Italy in the late 1950s). The principal feature of the island is that it is home to thousands of birds who lay their eggs there. When the narrator visits this island at the end of the novel, the birds have returned, but have not laid their eggs, and as such there is the hope of new life, a rich metaphor that recalls the "rhetoric of anticipation" noted by Burdett and also Ernst Bloch's idea of utopia as "anticipatory consciousness", a vision of the "Not-Yet". Moreover, this island constitutes a realm of possibility, something that Asmara, slowly deserted due to the migration of Italians back to Italy after the dissolution of the colony in 1941, can no longer offer.[20] Indeed, when the author leaves for Italy in the 1950s, Asmara is a place without a future (197; 208). Upon her return some years later, the city is once again described as a place where the colonial paradise has been transformed into a hell (219; 224; 235) as political strife dominates the landscape due to the struggle for independence. Thus, the island of Modok acts as an inverse mirror image of the dystopian city of Asmara of this time.

In acting as this inverse image of Asmara of these later periods, Modok appropriates the rhetoric of future possibility that characterised Asmara in the 1930s. The postcolonial utopian space of Modok, however, transforms a key component of that earlier colonial discourse: the myth of racial harmony. Transformation describes how postcolonial writers "tak[e] the dominant language and us[e] it to express the most deeply felt issues of postcolonial social experience".[21] Likewise, the term postcolonial utopia is employed by Ralph Pordzik, Lyman Tower Sargent, and Bill Ashcroft, who imagine a world tradition rather than a strictly Western one and a tool that offers a "representation of both the past and future as seen by others besides the settlers and the exploiters".[22] While Dell'Oro is from a white Italian family, as is her narrator, she does indeed offer a view of the past and future that challenges the dominant colonial discourse.[23] To this end, the island of Modok is described in the novel as the place where "the birds are the masters" (125). This aspect of the island subverts the power dynamic inherent in colonial (and postcolonial) relations – relations upon which the white Italian "golden ghetto" (89) of Asmara in which the narrator is raised, and the new utopian Asmara of the 1920s and 1930s are founded. In this way, Dell'Oro's postcolonial utopia can be considered a critical utopia: a "vision of possibility that effects the transformation of social life", "a desire in the act of imagining...that can be at once oppositional and visionary". To cite Zygmunt Bauman: "'Any utopianism worth the name must engage in a significant polemic with the dominant culture'".[24]

The postcolonial utopian space of Modok challenges the connection between the utopian space of a new Asmara and the myth of harmonious race relations as Dell'Oro is clearly critical of the race relations in both city and home space. She notes that the new Asmara was predicated upon the fact that "the indigenous were docile" (34). Indeed, Dell'Oro suggests that the obedience of the natives, who are described as they "smiled at the new times" (35), makes this new utopian city possible. Telling of the problematic nature of this myth of racial harmony is the preceding passage that describes the violence of Italian conquest of this time, including the use of lethal gas on the native peoples of East Africa. Dell'Oro's polemic is also evident in the novel's descriptions of the happy relations between the black servants and the narrator's family. From Turù to Mahasciò, Rigbè and Elias the narrator's golden ghetto in Asmara is largely built upon her and her family's perception of harmonious relations with black workers, yet Dell'Oro reveals that such a utopia is possible because of an external group that is ultimately excluded from that utopia and yet whose exploitation is necessary to its construction.[25] The narrator reminds us that this was an "Asmara of whites, and on Corso Mussolini... Eritreans were not to be seen. They stayed in Abbasciaul, in the suburbs of Asmara, to survive in their centuries-old misery" (22). Thus, the novel shows that the utopianism of the city hinged not only on racial segregation, but on a racial inequality driven by problematic labour relations: "there were hordes of Eritreans trained for construction work and they were a huge resource for the Europeans because they cost nothing and worked from sunrise to sunset" (22). Underscoring this form of social injustice, the novel presents the story of

Abeba, a young black servant who worked for the narrator's family and was thought to be disagreeable and hence is rebuked by the narrator's family as "she now seem[ed] like the master" (129-130). Yet, in hindsight, the narrator realises that this tension was due to the fact that "we were the Whites, we were the masters" (129). The island utopia of Modok challenges this dynamic as it is a space where birds are the masters rather than the Italians. Thus, this island is not merely a dream of personal re-birth in an ahistorical paradise, as has been suggested by some scholars, but a utopian vision of future possibility for Eritrean society and one that indeed engages with colonial history.[26]

Kidanè's New African Society

Kidanè's poem *Eritrea* (2004), set in Asmara, draws a connection between utopia and the hope of the Eritrean people for a free nation, as she too imagines a new society that redresses the injustices of colonialism. The speaker wanders the streets of Asmara searching for the hope she saw in the city on the day Eritrea became an independent nation, May 24 1991. She finds that hope along with utopia, a vision of a new Eritrea, in the people of Asmara: "I observe the face of my people: a mix of hope and utopia. I hear the beating of determined hearts to not give up, and I find intact the faith of my people forced to relive a pain that they thought was by now unrepeatable."[27] Here utopia and hope are different concepts – in the note to another poem[28] Kidanè underlines the impossibility of utopia – and yet one accompanies the other. Both hope and utopia are a remedy of sorts to the ancient pain still palpable in the city, a pain that refers to the long, arduous struggle for independence, yet also alludes to the city's colonial past, a theme taken up in other poems. For example, *Utopia africana* imagines Mother Africa as giving birth to "a new creature by the name Utopia" where utopia refers to the vision of a new Africa that mends the damage incurred in past tragedies. These past tragedies in *Un canto nuovo*, *L'Altra Africa* and *Non rubateci il sogno* are unquestionably tied to colonialism.[29] Similarly, *Un canto nuovo* describes the"new song, just as the hope that is new" that the speaker "dreams of" for Africa, as the continent is once again "on its knees before the latest powerseeker". *Non rubateci il sogno* speaks of a dream that threatens to be crushed as in the past when the continent was exploited, borders confused and hope destroyed: "You extracted primary, secondary and tertiary material and more. You imported corruption and exported dignity, you ruined projects and destroyed hope but please do not rob us of this dream."

While hope and utopia are distinct concepts i*n Eritrea* they seem to be one of the same in other poems. Indeed, for many scholars, utopia is "the expression of hope construed not...only as emotion..., but more essentially a directing act of a cognitive kind".[30] In these cases, postcolonial hope is key to the vision of future possibility in the form of a new African society, particularly as that vision transforms the myth of the new Asmara of colonial utopian discourse. In *Donna, non piangere*, the project of building the future of a new Eritrea is tied to the hope Eritrean women have nourished over the years while in *...e mi sorprende* the speaker marvels at the hope of the people of Africa, in the "courage to dream a future for their people". Finally, in *Un millennio* Kidanè's dream of a new African society is a longing for a "more just world" that "lovers of hope" dare to imagine.[31] This vision of a new just world, also alluded to in *Eritrea*, contrasts notably with the utopian colonial vision of a new Asmara (as exposed by Dell'Oro) where white privilege depended on black servitude. Thus, Kidanè's dream of a new African society, and in one case a new Asmara, casts a dark shadow on the utopian myths of a new Asmara of racial harmony that was promulgated in colonial texts of the fascist period and that masked a brutal reality of segregation and oppression.[32]

In sum, this article has shown a vital aspect of these two women's texts: while the personal memory of the writer – acting via the mythologising lens of migration – surely contributes to each text's vision of an idealised Asmara and external spaces, so does collective memory. The collective memory here addressed is that shaped by the utopian discourse of a new, future-oriented, and ideal Asmara that was propagated by the fascist regime via both cultural forms and official discourse. Yet, this article has also shown that Dell'Oro and Kidanè transform this discourse as they envision new uses for it: their idyllic Asmaras and spaces beyond ultimately stage a harsh critique of the colonial project.

1 See Charles Burdett's theory of utopia in other colonies, "Italian Fascism and Utopia", *History of the Human Sciences*, vol. 16, no. 1, 2003, pp. 93-108; "Italian Fascism, Messianic Eschatology and the Representation of Libya", *Totalitarian Movements and Political Religions*, vol. 11, no. 1, 2010, pp. 9-10, p.14.

2 For transformation: Bill Ashcroft, *Postcolonial Transformation*. London: Routledge, 2001. For postcolonial utopia see Bill Ashcroft, "Critical Utopias", *Textual Practice*, vol. 21, no. 3, pp. 411-431; Lyman Tower Sargent, "Colonial and Postcolonial Utopias", in *Cambridge Companion to Utopian Literature*. Cambridge: Cambridge University Press, 2010; Ralph Pordzik, *The Quest for Postcolonial Utopia*. New York: Peter Lang, 2001.

3 For utopia as a good society: Ruth Levitas, *The Concept of Utopia*. Syracuse: Syracuse UP, 1990, p. 4 or for an ideal society, see Joyce Oramel Hertzler, *The History of Utopian Thought*. London: Allen and Unwin, 1922, p. 269, cited in *Levitas*, op. cit., p. 19. For future orientation of colonial utopias: Burdett, "Italian Fascism and Utopia", op. cit. (note 1), p. 96, 100 and "Italian Fascism, Messianic Eschatology and the Representation of Libya", op. cit. (note 1).

4 For continuity in other texts: Sandra Ponzanesi, *Paradoxes of Postcolonial Culture*. Albany: State University of New York Press, 2004; Uoldelul Chelati Dirar, Silvana Palma, Alessandro Triulzi, Alessandro Volterra (eds.), *Colonia e postcolonia come spazi diasporici*. Rome: Carocci, 2010; Jacqueline Andall and Derek Duncan (eds.) *Italian Colonialism*. Bern: Peter Lang, 2005; Cristina Lombardi-Diop and Caterina Romeo (eds.), *Postcolonial Italy*. NY: Palgrave Macmillan, 2013.

5 Roger Griffin, Modernism and Fascism: *The Sense of a New Beginning Under Mussolini and Hitler*. NY: Palgrave Macmillan, 2007, p. 221.

6 Burdett, "Italian Fascism and Utopia", op. cit. (note 1), pp. 96, 100, 101 and "Italian Fascism, Messianic Eschatology and the Representation of Libya", op. cit. (note 1), pp. 9-11, p. 14. See also utopia as "anticipatory consciousness" in Ernst Bloch, *The Principle of Hope*. Oxford: Basil Blackwell, 1986, in Levitas, *Concept of Utopia*, op. cit. (note 3), pp. 86-87.

7 Arturo Planca, "Nuovo volto di Asmara", *Corriere eritreo*, 5 August 1937. Translation is mine.

8 Alberto Pollera and G.Brunetti, "Eritrea", *Asmara: Cicero*, 1932 and Pollera "Vita fascista in Eritrea", *L'oltremare*, July 1933. Translation is mine.

9 Cesare Fraccari, *Viaggio in Africa Orientale: visioni, sogni, realtà*. Milan: La Prora, 1937, pp. 33, 42. Translation is mine.

10 Renzo Martinelli, Sud, *Rapporto di un viaggio in Eritrea e in Etiopia*. Florence: Vallecchi, 1930 p. 77, 93-95; Orio Vergani, *La via nera*. Cernusco sul Naviglio: Lampada, 1949 (1938) p. 9; Mario Dei Gaslini, *L'Italia sul Mar Rosso*. Milan: La Prora, 1938, pp. 29, 35, 75.

11 For social harmony in utopia: Jennifer Burwell, *Notes on Nowhere*. Minneapolis: Univ. of Minnesota Press, 1997, p. 54; Ashcroft, "Critical Utopias", op. cit. (note 2), p. 414.

12 "Asmara...ad occhio nudo", *Il quotidiano eritreo*, 18 August 1935. Translation is mine.

13 Pollera, "Vita fascista in Eritrea", op. cit. (note 8).

14 For indigenous policy: Barbara Sorgoni, *Parole e corpi*. Napoli: Liguri, 1998, pp. 141, 182-192; Angelo Del Boca, *Gli Italiani in Africa Orientale: La caduta dell'impero*. Rome: Laterza, 1982, pp. 239-241.

15 Arturo Nigra, "La nostra capacità assimilatrice nelle colonie", *Oltremare*, no. 9, 1931. Translation is mine.

16 Maurizio Rava, *L'Eritrea*. Rome: Libreria del Littorio, 1927, pp. 9-11, 63-65.

17 "Il viaggio di SM Il Re in Eritrea", *Oltremare*, 22 September, 1932. Translation is mine.

18 Dei Gaslini, *L'Italia sul Mar Rosso*, op. cit. (note 10), pp. 35, 75; Enrico Cappellina, *Un canto nella notte*. Bologna: Cappelli, 1925, pp. 2-3, 52. Translation is mine.

19 Erminia Dell'Oro, *Asmara, Addio*. Milan: Baldini & Castoldi, 1997 (1988), p. 58. Translations are mine.

20 Bloch, *The Principle of Hope*, op. cit. (note 6) in *Levitas, Concept of Utopia*, op. cit. (note 3), pp. 86-87.

21 Ashcroft, Postcolonial Transformation, op. cit. (note 2), p. 5.

22 Tower Sargent, "Colonial and postcolonial Utopias", op. cit. (note 2), p. 213.

23 Loredana Polezzi "Mixing Mother Tongues: Language, Narrative and the Spaces of Memory in Postcolonial Works by Italian Women Writers", *Romance Studies*, vol. 24, no. 2, July 2006, p. 153. Note that Dell'Oro speaks from the point of view of coloniser and colonised. I would underscore the same complexity of the novel.

24 Ashcroft, "Critical Utopias", op. cit. (note 2), pp. 418-419. Zygmunt Bauman, *Socialism: The Active Utopia*. New York: Homes and Meier, 1976, p. 47, in Ashcroft, "Critical Utopias", op. cit. (note 2), p. 419. See Joanne Lee, "Revisiting Italy's Colonial Past: Journeys through Memory in Erminia Dell'Oro's Asmara, Addio and La Gola del Diavolo", *The Italianist*, vol. 29, 2009, pp. 454-55, for the critical vein of the island.

25 For this aspect of utopia see Burwell, *Notes on Nowhere*, op. cit. (note 11), p. 66, and Tower Sargent, "Colonial and Postcolonial Utopias", op. cit. (note 2) p. 204.

26 See Polezzi "Mixing Mother Tongues", op. cit (note 23) for this other view, pp. 153-155.

27 The setting was confirmed by the author in a personal email. Elisa Kidanè, *Orme nel cuore del mondo*. Verona: Raggio, 2004. All translations of Kidanè are mine.

28 Elisa Kidanè, *Parole clandestine*. Verona: Suore missionarie comboniane, 2008, p. 10.

29 Elisa Kidanè, *Fotocopia a colouri*. Verona: Nuovastampa, 1999; *Orme nel cuore del mondo*, op. cit.; *Ho visto la speranza danzare*. Verona: Suore Missionarie Comboniane, 1995.

30 Bloch, *The Principle of Hope*, op. cit. (note 6), p. 12, in Levitas, Concept of Utopia, op. 00 cit. (note 3) p. 87; Bill Ashcroft "The ambiguous necessity of Utopia: Postcolonial literatures and the persistence of hope", *Social Alternatives*, vol. 28, no. 3, 2009, p. 8-9.

31 Kidanè, *Ho visto la speranza danzare*, op. cit. (note 29); *Fotocopia a colouri*, op. cit. (note 29).

32 For segregation: Del Boca, *Gli Italiani in Africa Orientale: La caduta dell'impero*, op. cit (note 14) pp. 232-251; *Sorgoni Parole e corpi*, op. cit (note 14), p. 142.

IATA
ACCREDITED AGENT
AGENTS FOR
Red Sea Air
Lufthansa
EGYPT AIR
Yemenia
WESTERN UNION

TRAVELLERS OF THE STREET
Flânerie in Beyene Haile's Asmara Play *Weg'i Libi*

Christine Matzke

Preliminaries: Rumours into Research

During a visit to Eritrea in September 2008 my curiosity was aroused by repeated references to a Tigrinya-language play staged in January of that year. The play, *Weg'i Libi*, or *Heart-to-Heart Talk*, had been written by novelist and public figure Beyene Haile (1941–2012), and had played for a two-week run to packed houses in one of the capital's main theatre venues, Cinema Asmara. This in itself was unusual. Never the most popular form of entertainment in Eritrea, drama as staged performance is in relative decline, with theatre artists increasingly working for the national broadcasting station, Eri-TV, or the ever-growing digital film industry. In Eritrea, it is not possible to go to the theatre regularly.

Very quickly it became clear to me that Asmara had witnessed a theatre production that did not sit easily with the usual cultural imagery in Eritrea. For one, it was performed by a group of university graduates rather than the well-versed artists of the PFDJ Cultural Affairs, one among several official bodies which largely determine cultural discourses today and under whose remit cultural work usually comes. Prior to 1998 the capital had hosted a good number of fairly independent amateur theatre groups, but in the turbulent aftermath of the latest Eritrean-Ethiopian war (1998–2000), this had changed. Striking, too, was the fact that *Weg'i Libi* was still being talked about nine months after the performance, at a time when the state-sponsored festival of *Hade Meskerem*, September 1st, the Beginning of the Armed Liberation Struggle, was being celebrated in the capital. The gist of it all was that the

Flaneurs on the streets of Asmara
Source: S.Graf 2015

play was genuinely fascinating but largely incomprehensible; that it seemed to defy or at least differ from locally common approaches to theatre arts, and that it seemed thereby to be setting new standards. This was indeed news in a place where due to a variety of circumstances such theatre as exists tends to be rather predictable.

In this chapter I trace the production history of *Weg'i Libi* before offering a short critical reading of the play in performance. I do so by relating the external topography of Asmara to the internal topography of the play, and by looking at the resultant metaphorical potential regarding the future of Eritrea. Drawing on interviews with the playwright, Beyene Haile, and the director of the play, Abraham Tesfalul, in September 2008 (plus a number of informal conversations with audience members and people working in the cultural field), my analysis is largely based on an unreleased full-length video of the show and an English version of the play, *Heart-to-Heart Talk*, translated by the author himself. I also had access to a shorter version of his translation, abridged by Abraham Tesfalul, which matched the production staged and from which all in-text quotations are taken.[1]

Working the System: Insights into the Production Process of *Weg'i Libi*

In 2006, Beyene gave the playscript to a senior officer in the PFDJ Research and Documentation Department who thought it might merit performance. However, the script was returned from Cultural Affairs because nobody knew what to make of the play. At the time, there were still students at the University of Asmara, so a group of young people got together to discuss and rehearse the play; Beyene occasionally joined them in discussion. The driving force behind the idea was Abraham Tesfalul, then a graduate assistant in the Department of Eritrean Literatures, who was familiar with Beyene's distinctive style as he had edited one of his novels.

The group had the intellectual capacity to deal with such a difficult text, but they lacked theatre expertise and the performance did not really take off. They also had no budget and no access to a theatre space; and life itself often interrupted the rehearsal process as people graduated, went for National Service and had to be replaced. (In fact, Abraham Tesfalul was compelled to stand in for one of the actors called for National Service shortly before the opening night as it was impossible for anybody else to take the part.)

The group initially discussed and rehearsed the whole play, but when they first showed it to selected members of the PFDJ Cultural Affairs – a common procedure, as no group can stage a play without having had it screened by an official body – they realised it was far too long and did not work on stage. About half of the play was cut, much to the chagrin of Beyene. The group also realised that something had to be done about their lack of funding and theatrical resources; and they invited director and filmmaker Mesgun Zerai (*Wad Faraday*) to join them. As one of the participants explained: "We wanted to access Cultural Affairs. We wanted to penetrate their office. We wanted him [*Wad Faraday*] as a support for the Cultural Office. He did not really help us with the play". Finally the group received the assistance they had been asking for. They were allowed to rehearse and perform in Cinema Asmara, with Demoz Russom, official stage designer of the PFDJ, constructing the naturalistic set and painting the backdrop.

In many ways, the play remained an amateur production, especially in terms of acting and directing. However, the success of the group is not to be underestimated, especially when one considers the following: first, they managed to mount a show in times when initiative of one's own is not exactly encouraged and when all forms of cultural production have to go through some form of government assessment prior to public viewing; second, the play goes against many theatre conventions in Eritrea and is difficult to understand. Yet the group managed to draw crowds, and the play ran successfully for a fortnight. Some people reportedly watched it several times; one woman is said to have taped the play on a dictaphone to listen to it at home. This all indicates that *Weg'i Libi* struck a chord, and that there is a hunger for new direction in the arts. This is also one of the key themes of the play.

Flânerie in Asmara: A Reading of the 2008 Production

It is very fitting that *Weg'i Libi* was staged in Cinema Asmara, and not in any other theatre venue in the capital. Cinema Asmara is located at the beginning of Godena Harnet, Liberty Avenue, where the play is set. Godena Harnet is Asmara's principal boulevard with bars, cafés, restaurants, shops, banks, internet cafés, cinemas and places of religious worship, many of which are extraordinarily beautiful examples of Modernist architecture. It is a space inhabited and shared by different groups of people from all walks of life and as such represents a microcosm of modern urban Eritrea. Godena Harnet is also a historical palimpsest mapped in space whose frequent renaming chronicles the history of the nation: Viale Benito Mussolini (1925–1941, during the fascist period of Italian colonisation when the avenue belonged to the Italian quarters of town and was off-limits to Eritreans), Corso Italia (1941–1952, under British Military Administration), Avenue Haile Selassie (1952–1974, under Ethiopia's Imperial Government), National Avenue (1974–1991, under the military Dergue regime which had ousted the Emperor) and, finally, Liberty

Avenue from the de facto independence in 1991 until today.[2] Godena Harnet thus constitutes the centre of Eritrea's social, historical and geographical topography, and as such serves as a key space for the public performance of self and social networks in Asmara.[3] As one of Beyene's characters puts it: "This street is the dance of life" (39).

In a real way, the play is an extension of the street life the audience has just left behind on entering the theatre venue. Even the stage set – with its fast food place opposite Cinema Asmara, the Ministry of Education to the right and the shoe cleaner's stall – is a mirror image of the street below. Both inside and outside Cinema Asmara, Godena Harnet is the space to see and be seen in, with everybody trying to look their most fashionable best. Particularly after working hours people succumb to the daily ritual of sitting outdoors and having tea and *paste* (cake) with friends. Others go on a *passeggiata*, greet acquaintances, walk on, meet someone else. This casual meeting, strolling and meandering on the main street is also the main movement in the play. If there is a plot or pattern of events in this drama than it is the recurring arbitrary encounter of the strollers. Images of the flâneur in Walter Benjamin's writings on urban modernity come to mind, to which Eritrean Studies scholars have also referred. However, I do not wish to concentrate on one particular theorist who wrote about flânerie in a specific, historically situated context; the Paris in the literature of Baudelaire, Poe, and Hugo. There also exists an ever-growing body of writing on flânerie in relation to other major, including African, cities of the world.[4]

No matter which spatial or temporal context, strollers exhibit a number of common characteristics, the most essential of which being the performance of meandering and looking on as detached observers of the urban multitude.[5] Flânerie in the Eritrean capital, however, shows two marked differences to other environments, both as a social phenomenon and in literary representation. For one, the flâneur in Asmara is not a lone individual who observes the crowd. On the contrary, flânerie on *Godena Harnet* has a deeply communal element to it since "the activity of strolling and looking"[6] is often done in a group or serves as a means to meet and engage with people. Secondly, the flâneur in Asmara is not solely gendered male.[7] Both women and men are seen walking down the main street engaged in the performance of flânerie, and they are accorded equal importance. No space portrayed in the play is out of bounds for either women or men.[8] Instead, the strollers exhibit a number of common characteristics also found in other contexts. I will focus on selected elements relevant to the play.

First, there is an interior/exterior quality to the strollers, their conversations and their movements. On Beyene's (and the actual) Godena Harnet this interior/exterior movement is mirrored in the in and out of cafés and the

The stage set: the fast-food place opposite Cinema Asmara to the left, the Ministry of Education to the right, with the shoe cleaner's stall in front
Source: © AVIE video print, 2008

crowd into which the strollers abandon themselves; it is also a dichotomy of exterior appearance and inner landscapes and feelings. Time and again the play encourages us to see beyond the outer façade: "Why not delve into the inner secret instead of looking at the surface of things. What is this street?" (39)

Second, the observing strollers are an integral part of the urban space they inhabit; they are constitutive of it, even if they appear to be outside this space as remote onlookers. Flâneurs are commonly seen as idle, but there is also a deeply creative – hence active – side to them because they watch and analyse their surroundings. As Keith Tester remarks in his analysis of Baudelair's flâneur: "the poet is possibly at his busiest when he seems to be at his laziest".[9] In the past flâneurs have often been associated with storytellers, journalists, and artists,[10] and these are all professions we also encounter in Beyene's play. There is the journalist (later known as Zahra) in conversation with the painter (initially introduced as The Pained, later known under his name, Bilen). We meet the company as dancers and singers; and we are also introduced to a poet (later: Walia) who leans on a palm tree throughout the play waiting for his love who never comes. Through the act of strolling, these characters begin to inhabit the street as an open space – both in the physical and the metaphorical sense – on to which they project their thoughts and ideas. On the one hand the city becomes an infinite canvas for their discussions; on the other hand it also engulfs and surrounds them like a closed room.[11] The characters are aware of the social, political and artistic frame they are moving in. This sets them certain limits, but they are not completely fixed. There is always room for negotiation; and most characters are concerned with broadening their space. Most of all, they are concerned with mapping and re-mapping, shaping and re-shaping, inventing and re-inventing the street, their lives and, ultimately, the nation they live in.

Initially the audience encounters a group of three friends having tea, the Short, the Medium and the Tall who are later joined by a fourth companion, The Woman. Eventually this group will be known as The Elders, which signifies their centrality to the play. In one of the self-reflexive moments that are characteristic of Beyene's text, the Short explains to his fellow Elders that the author "said we are the pillars of the play" (44). Richard Boon compares them to a chorus in Greek drama.[12] It is this group that initiates the deliberations which continue throughout the performance. Reminiscent of Modernist stream of consciousness,[13] the conversations we encounter are about the so-called larger things in life, though always emerging from a concrete moment on the street from which they draw their inspirations. The first conversation among the Elders, for example, is set off by the crying of a man, the sound of pain. While initially focusing on the man's bodily pain, the discussion quickly takes on a much more serious tone when it shifts from outer (physical) pain of one person to the inner pains of people and nations that remain unheard.

> THE TALL: Leaving aside what philosophers say, are we saying there is no one to listen to the pain of anxiety, pain of love, pain of yearning, pain of want, pain of debt, etc.? ... Do we know for sure the relationship between pain and beauty? ...
>
> THE SHORT: The so-called donor governments, when they help the so-called beggar countries, respond to the audible sound of hunger and not to the silent pain of thought. The beneficiaries do not recognise the pain of insufficient discovery, reflection, and creativity. (14)

Later on The Short also notes that: "We know our higher pain. Our pain is our vision" (27)

This gradual shift from exterior to interior and back again to the exterior world, but on a higher level – that is, from the bodily pain of an individual to the pains of a nation and from there to a new vision of society – does not occur sequentially, but is woven into other complex strands of the conversation and it is this in particular which makes the play difficult fully to understand. Other issues that surface are conceptions of and the need for love; the position and value of art and philosophy; the relation of Eritreans inside and outside the country, and of the past to the present. We also hear about the role of the journalist and other (creative) professions; the position of women; and the importance of traditions. Into this are woven complex intertextual references, from ancient Greek philosophy to Modernist literature. Often, the play is trying to do too much in too little time and space; it is overloaded and cumbersome and it is not surprising that the group had to cut half of the text. Yet the multitude of issues addressed also allows us, as readers and spectators, to take and contemplate our personal pick of issues and topics emerging from the play. It resembles the activities of the nineteenth-century flâneur who "could pick and choose where to play his game".[14] As audience we become part of the intellectual flânerie on stage.

This, I believe, was part of the reason why the play was so successful, also because there was none of the didacticism associated with some forms of Eritrean theatre and no obvious, clear-cut message. While the verbal exchanges often appear incoherent and baffling, they challenge us to re-establish our own form of meaning; they are engaging, provocative and potentially liberating. Intellectual engagement with the conversation on stage and beyond is already encouraged at the onset of the play when the audience is invited to:

> Please philosophise sometimes even while sitting on your chairs. This will help life not to be inundated by routine talks. Get to practice saying: Why? Where can it be? Starting from when? Who and who? What for? Instead of sipping life like diluted coffee with tiny cups, it is better to gulp it down thick and strong. Life without the spice of thought is stale. (4)

In the end, it all seems to point to the search for new directions and meanings. The various strands of the play eventually come together in one of the main motifs of the text, the repeated debate around columns, statues and pillars. There is a certain inconsistency in the way these three terms are used in the English translation, but generally columns have a slightly negative connotation while pillars are more positive. In the case of statues it varies,[15] and in the introduction to the play, Beyene presents these as "the perfect likeness of the individual in such a way as to reflect what he [sic] potentially could be in looks, personality, and wisdom". The Elders "also agree to build a statue representing the perfect state of the country. They believe that each citizen will be able to model his/her actions to enhance through his actions the perfect state."[16] Columns, on the other hand, are those who stand on the street without moving, such as the poet fruitlessly waiting for his love; but they are also the stubborn elements of society, the obstacles to progress. As the Elders complain:

> THE WOMAN: Do you think that it is only on the sidewalk that people stand like columns? The number of column-like blocks of persons standing on the way of all progress is not small. Those column-like persons who stand in the way of history, art, work, etc. are innumerable. (42)

What is called for instead are people, ideas and works of arts that do not calcify the status quo but lead to new departures.

> THE TALL: I say let not our country turn into a column. How can one bear the sorrow? ... Let it not be! Let not a country turn into a column! Let not people be turned into columns. Let not all the travellers of the street turn into columns! (44)

For Godena Harnet, both in the play and outside the theatre doors, is a street that moves and is in a constant flux. It is here where not just an individual goes in search of him- or herself, but, in microcosm, an entire nation. As Zahra, the journalist explains: the author "is telling all spectators that they are on the road of becoming. He is saying that the statues will become humans when they are set on the street of becoming" (47). Godena Harnet "is not a street that one can be through with" (53) – not in the play, not on the road, and not when you have left the country. Godena Harnet is the passage through life, and we are all asked to look for new, more appropriate ways of walking.

Notes

1 Beyene Haile, "Heart-to-Heart Talk", unpublished manuscript, October 2005, pp. 112. Beyene Haile, "Heart-to-Heart Talk", abridged by Abraham Tesfalul (2007), pp. 61. AVIE (Audio Visual Institute of Eritrea), *Production of Weg'i Libi*, January 2008, unpublished DVD, 2008. Recorded interview with Abraham Tesfalul, Asmara, 7 September 2008. Recorded interview with Beyene Haile, Asmara, 8th September 2008. I wish to thank Richard Boon for his invaluable comments on earlier drafts. This article was initially published in a longer version in *New Theatre Quarterly*, vol. 27.2, 2011, pp. 176-188.

2 Mebrahtu Abraham, "Historical Analysis of Asmara's Street Names", in CARP (The Cultural Assets Rehabilitation Project) (eds.), *Asmara: A Guide to the Built Environment*. Asmara: CARP, 2003, pp. 54-67.

3 Cf. Magnus Treiber, *Der Traum vom guten Leben. Die eritreische warsay-Generation im Asmara der zweiten Nachkriegszeit*. Münster: LIT, 2005, pp. 75-79.

4 Walter Benjamin, *Charles Baudelaire. Ein Lyriker im Zeitalter des Hochkapitalismus*, ed. and with an afterword by Rolf Tiedemann. Frankfurt: Suhrkamp, 1974. Walter Benjamin, "Paris, die Hauptstadt des XIX. Jahrhunderts", in *Illuminationen. Ausgewählte Schriften 1*, selected by Sigfried Unseld, Frankfurt: Suhrkamp, 2001, pp. 170-184. Franz Hessel, *Ein Flaneur in Berlin*. Berlin: Das Arsenal, 1984. Sarah Nuttall, "City Forms and Writing the 'Now' in South Africa", *Journal of Southern African Studies*, vol 30.4, 2004, pp. 731-748.

5 Petra Kuppers, "Moving in the Cityscape. Performance and the Embodied Experience of the Flâneur", *New Theatre Quarterly*, vol. 15.4, 1999, pp. 308-317 (310).

6 Keith Tester, "Introduction", in Keith Tester (ed.), *The Flâneur*. London: Routledge, 1994, pp. 1-21 (1).

7 For a critique on the invisibility of the flâneuse see Janet Wolff, "The Invisible Flâneuse. Women and the Literature of Modernity", *Theory, Culture & Society*, vol. 2.3, 1985, p. 37-46. Aruna D'Souza and Tom McDonough (eds.), *The Invisible Flâneuse? Gender, Public Space, and Visual Culture in Nineteenth-Century Paris*. Manchester: Manchester University Press, 2006.

8 Treiber, op. cit., indicates that as a social phenomenon women's flânerie somewhat differs from that of men in that they cannot, or do not wish to, frequent all places accessible to men after strolling.

9 Tester, "Introduction", op. cit., pp. 2-3.

10 Mary Gluck, *Popular Bohemia. Modernism and Urban Culture in Nineteenth-Century Paris*. Cambridge, MA: Harvard University Press, 2005, p. 78.

11 Walter Benjamin, "Die Wiederkehr des Flaneurs", in Franz Hessel, *Ein Flaneur in Berlin*, op. cit., pp. 277-281 (278).

12 Richard Boon, "'Neither Peace nor War'. The Role of Theatre in Re-imagining the New Eritrea", in Reuben Makayiko Chirambo and J.K.S. Makhkha (eds.), *Reading Contemporary African Literature. Critical Perspectives*. Amsterdam: Rodopi, 2013, pp. 421-437 (433).

13 Ghirmai Negash, "A Great Novel in a 'Small' Language. Representations of the African Intellectual in the Eritrean Novel Tebereh's Shop", *Research in African Literatures*, vol. 40.3, 2009, pp. 1-15 (4)

14 Zygmunt Baumann, "Desert Spectacular", in Keith Tester (ed.), *The Flâneur*, op. cit., pp. 138-157 (146).

15 I believe that there is also a word play going in the Tigrinya original that does not translate into the English text. It has to do with the word *andi* (pillar) and its various roots. *Andä*, the prefix to a noun, signifies "the pillar of", such as *andämariam*, meaning "the pillar of St Mary". The sixth root of *andi*, on the other hand – *enud* – signifies "depressed" and "confused". I leave further clarifications to mother tongue speakers of Tigrinya.

16 Beyene Haile, "Heart-to-Heart Talk", 2005, p. 2.

ar Lilli

FIAT
FIAT
TAGLIERO

GIRO D'ERITREA
Photo Essay

Chris Keulen

Cycling is to Eritrea as football is to the Netherlands. Every weekend, thousands of amateurs zoom along isolated roads through the desert and over mountain passes. With 4.8 million inhabitants, the country counts 500,000 bicyles. Eritrea's passion for cycling is one of many lasting influences of Italian colonial rule. The country's first multi-day cycle race was staged in 1946, although locals were not allowed to enter. The Giro was resurrected fifty-five years later, a symbol of the new-found confidence of a nation which had finally achieved its independence in 1991. Africa's oldest cycle race is a far cry from the televised sporting extravaganzas that Europeans are used to seeing on TV. But a live telecast almost seems unnecessary. The roads are packed with spectators, who seem to escape from the daily life sufferance from a suppressive regime. The event is a huge celebration in the country: about one-third of the country's entire population follows the race – a world record.

Chris Keulen (Netherlands, 1959) photographed the giro twice. In 2004 for his African cycling book *Hete glassplinters, le tour d'Afrique* (2008) and in 2009 for *GEO* Germany. The tour of 2009 has a special place in Eritrean cyling history. It was the first international contest on Eritrean ground and has been included in the calendar of the International Cycling Union (UCI). Keulen's 2009 visit won third prize in the Sports Stories category of the 2010 World Press Awards. For Keulen, who is not a sports photographer, it was the second time he won a prize in the World Press Photo competition. In 2000 he won first prize in the Sport Stories category with his series of the Tour du Faso.

See also: www.chriskeulen.com

Poster from the movie *Totò nella luna*
(Director: Steno, Italy 1958)

Source: Alberto Anile. I film di Totò (1946-1967): la maschera tradita. Le mani, 1998

LA PICCOLA ROMA
The Female Characteristics of Unoccupied Spaces in Totò Films

Linde Luijnenburg

"*Io sono un corpo, e per vivere qua sopra ho bisogno di una corpa*",[1] shouts Totò's character *il cavaliere* Pasquale da Poggio Mirteto out to an extraterrestrial creature in Steno's *Totò nella luna*, 1958. Alone on the moon for the rest of his life, he demands a woman to keep him company, but he is offered a man. When the extraterrestrial changes the male companion into a female, Pasquale is content. "*Con una cosona così, io starei tutta la vita su Marte, su Saturno, anche su Mercurio!*"[2] He then tells her with a fatherly tone that since she is young and innocent, he will explain her everything about *cosare*.[3] "*Fidati di me, vedrai. Cosa oggi, cosa domani, da cosa nasce cosa.*"[4] They walk over the moon into a undiscovered space. In the background we hear cheerful music, the lens zooms out and the light fades out: end of film. Pasquale's gendering of the words *cosona* and *corpa* emphasises the importance of her being female. It is the trope of the man in need of a subordinate woman in order to cope with his own insecurities and fears. This seemingly generic film, however, can provide us with information about Italian immediate post-World War II popular culture, and more specifically (and more metaphorically) about the Italian imagery of Asmara.

Not only Asmara in Eritrea, as has predominantly been the focus of this volume, but also *Asmara in Italy*, its representation and imagery in Italian culture in the postcolonial/neo-colonial epoch,[5] provides space (double meaning) for a visual analysis and for reflection, as it can bring to light the gendered and patronising undertones often prevailing in descriptions of the city and its population and, on a more abstract level, of (former) colonised spaces and its inhabitants, both in Italian literature, journalism and in cinema.[6] Unravelling the underlying trope of *la piccola Roma* (Mussolini's never nationally refuted name for Asmara) as female (passive, beautiful, victimised, etc.) and subordinate (*piccola*, female) in popular culture, could bring us closer to an acknowledgment, and as a result of that a renegotiation, of neo-colonial narratives that keep hegemonic relationships and systems in place on a global scale.[7] More specifically, it could trigger discussions surrounding disputable descriptions of Asmara presented in this volume, such as The Sleeping Beauty, a gendered and Orientalist label, as stated in the introduction.[8]

Central to this chapter is the representation and the imaginary of Asmara in a metaphorical sense: I focus on the colonial spaces in Italian cinema, symbolising Italy's trauma of the failed colonial enterprises, an anxiety surrounding the theme of the lost war, and a consequential echo of the colonial narrative. With colonial spaces I refer to Italian filmic spaces in which one can recognise a projection of a colonial desire, a colonial nostalgia and/or trauma, and/or a fear of the unknown through the camera lens, and/or through the behaviour and/or the words of (some of) the characters.[9] I am particularly interested in the medium of cinema, because of its visual (imaginary) characteristics. As Ponzanesi and Waller point out, both postcolonial studies and cinema studies "are deeply involved with questions of representation, and they have much to offer each other concerning the forms and legacies of epistemological violence and the role of aesthetics in reshaping the human *sensoriam*".[10] Moreover, Italy has a strong relationship to cinema, both in terms of its international fame and acclaim (especially between the mid-1940s and the mid-1970s) and in terms of its national popularity in the immediate post-World War II period.[11] As Duncan suggests, '[C]inema is (...) conceptualised as the cultural crucible of Italian national identity'.[12]

The corpus of the films analysed here is based on the actor playing its protagonist: Antonio De Curtis, better known as Totò. He occupies an iconic position in Italian cultural heritage and has become a symbol of Italian immediate post-World War II comedy cinema and theatre. Totò became a brand in itself, with his name always appearing in the title of the film, followed by a reference to a specific filmic genre.[13] In most of his films the purpose is exactly to parody specific filmic genres, such as the *maciste* and the Spaghetti Western.[14] Therefore, his films are an indication of fantasies and imaginaries of stereotypes and places among Italian viewers. As Brunetta argues, referring specifically to Totò films, '[Italian comedies of the immediate post-World War II period] – with their double entendres and parodies of everyday life and situations – touched upon important aspects of Italian life. They tended to focus on common attitudes and contradictions, and they offered a remedy to the overwhelming challenge faced by the ordinary man during the post-war period.'[15] Since Totò films still occupy a significant position in Italian (film) history, analysing these films can provide us with cultural codes and narratives that were and are registered by a broad audience, and that both at the time and today are seen as typically Italian.[16] This is significant specifically in the context of the 1950s and the 1960s; as Patriarca states, these decennia in Italy are relatively underinvestigated by historians, despite the fact that they have been essential for the reconfiguration of the dicourse around the concepts of race and *Italianness* in post-fascist and postcolonial Italy.[17]

The focus is on three films: the aforementioned *Totò nella luna*, *Totò sceicco* (Mario Mattoli, 1950), and *Tototarzan* (Mario Mattoli, 1950 – not a typing error). These films are all set in an undefined non-Italian space, and all those spaces have a specificity in terms of the stereotypes and projections one might expect: the moon before mankind had ever set foot on it (*Totò nella luna*), the jungle (*Tototarzan*), and the desert (*Totò sceicco*). What lies at the heart of architectural colonisation, central in this volume, is the occupation of space – not merely a (violent) physical taking over of that space, but a projection and appropriation of it in order to shape it into one's aesthetic norms and tastes. Therefore, the projections and desires by the filmic characters to violate, change and appropriate these places and spaces, specifically refer back to Italy and/or its capitol Rome. Since there is no one without an other, and no copy (*la piccola Roma*) without its original, the focus here will be just as much on *la grande Roma* (Italy), to take the analogy further, as on the other spaces.

Tototarzan

Presented as a parody of the American Tarzan series, *Tototarzan* begins with heavy drums and a camera shot on a group of elephants seen from a frog perspective, who elegantly walk through the jungle without touching anything.[18] In the next shot, we see Italians in safari outfits fighting their way through the plants, while their Black servants carry their possessions, leading the way and knowing their way through the jungle.[19] The contrast between people who belong and intruders is immediately emphasised: the latter are fully protected by their clothes and reveal an intrusive behaviour of trying to violate and master a land (the plants) and a people (treating them as servants) whereas the former, less protected by clothes, carefully walk through the land they seem to know well. In the middle of the jungle, the servants refuse to go further since they are about to enter the kingdom of the White Monkey. "*Maledetti, falli camminare!*", shouts one of the Italians angrily slapping his hands around, since he does not speak their language and does not know what is going on. One of the servants warns them in Italian that the White Monkey rapes all women he encounters at night. Puwar points out that woman's bodies commonly feature in allegories of the nation. "Within different forms of nationalism, the land of the nation is itself visualised in a female form that is beautiful, plentiful and worth dying for. (…) Women's bodies act as a border between nations but it is men who normatively defend this border in combat. So often territories are defended in a sexual language; the rape of women becomes the absolute assault on national land and character.'[20] Read in this context, *Tototarzan* starts with a strongly Orientalist, and thus feminised, imagery of the jungle (the drums and the elephants) followed by the threat of the Italian intruders symbolically raping the country through demolishing, intruding, and trying to master it and its inhabitants, and the White Monkey literally raping its women. The Italians demonstrate a degenerating undertone with respect to the metaphorical female land – *la terra*, a female word – and the women who happen to be around: they are presented as possible victims of the Italian men.

The colonial discourse on racial binaries is present as well.[21] The visual difference between the Black people living in the jungle and the White Italians is empathised through the abovementioned differences: The Italians are here presented as White. As the leader of the expedition explains, they are not afraid of the *White* Monkey, since he is the son of a famous Italian explorer in that area, the subtext being that he is "one of us". The intention of Italians is to bring the son back to "*il mondo civile*".[22] The monkey is interpreted by Totò, and he is brought back to Italy, where he continuously deconstructs the values of modern society, criticising rules, questioning how certain animals and people are treated, and denying the necessity of technology. At one point in the film, he becomes a military soldier, but fails to see the necessity, gets hurt, and concludes that civil society is not better than the jungle.

Towards the end of the film, Totò is back in the jungle together with a woman he brought from Italy, when a group of Italian women present themselves with tennis rackets and lamps, hoping to bring him civil society: an echo of Italian missionaries who went to Africa in order to *educate* the people.[23] Revealing the obsessive nature of forcing modernity on to Totò, the narrative of the advanced modern world is ridiculed in this film up to a certain point.[24] *White* and *male*, Totò's nature (monkey) part has to be eliminated in order to maintain the narrative of the White superior male dominator, so that the superiority complex of the White male (-like) colonisers can continue to exist.

A similar deconstructionalist attitude is presented through a group of women in the film who choose to go native, dressed in revealing clothes, living in the countryside and idolising Totò Tarzan in their *campo tototarzanista*, following the Tarzan fantasies as presented in American series. As Puwar points out, imperial women were often contrasted against natives through ways of clothing and education in order to construct a necessary difference: other women were presented as "still in a state of nature".[25] Choosing this path, the *tototarzaniste* challenge the binary distinction between women of civil society and women of nature, criticising normative hegemonic conceptions of, in this case, Italian femininity. A group of angry nuns demonising them, and an arriving radio station presenter asking Totò what he thinks of the civilised world illustrate the problems the *tototarzaniste* will face with being accepted in society. The anarchist characteristics of Totò's comedy as described by Faldini deny the White men their power.[26] He, the *White* <-> *monkey* refuses any help, brings a woman back from Italy who does *go nature*, and keeps three Italian White men imprisoned in a cage in his treehouse in the jungle, turning the White man into a spectacle. However, Totò has a slave as well: his good friend the real monkey. The narrative of the subordinate nature of monkeys is kept intact, as Totò, being half man, is still the boss of his monkey friend.

Totò nella luna

In *Totò nella luna*, Pasquale's son-in-law Achille (Ugo Tognazzi) turns out to have a rare substance in his blood since his biologist father raised him between monkeys.[27] This rare substance allows Achille to travel through space, and it is discovered by the US government. The rest of the plot is based on (good natured and democratic) American secret agents and an (evil spirited and aggressive) German private team chasing Achille in order to convince him to go into space on their behalf. However, through a complicated slap-stick mix-up between two *cosoni*, exact copies of Pasquale and Achille that are put on earth by extraterrestrials to prevent actual humans from arriving on the moon, it is Pasquale who is brought to the moon, with the *cosone* copy of Achille. He is forced to stay there for the rest of his life.

Just like the English word *space*, the Italian *spazio* refers both to a (un-) defined area, and to outer space. Pasquale remarks in the opening scene that he does not understand the need to occupy space since it is simply air.[28] Empathising the obsessive nature of the German and American need to occupy the moon through the contrasting lack of interest by Achille and Pasquale, the film's plot reflects Patriarca's affirmation that Nazi Germany served as a point of comparison in order to diminish or deny Italian forms of racism (and in this context, desires of colonialism) in the 1950s, whereas the US functioned as such in the 1960s. The film is set in the 1950s, which explains the good nature of the Americans, versus the evil nature of the Germans. Despite this nuance, both Germans and Americans are presented as a contrast to the Italian characters, who are interested only in women (as illustrated in the final scene of the film, described in the introduction of this chapter). *La luna* in Italian is female, which stretches the metaphor of the female body as a nation state to conquer and desire into space. Indeed, in this film, too, the language is gendered and sexualised. Achille and Pasquale are focused only on obtaining

Poster from the movie *Totò nella luna* (Director: Steno, Italy 1958)

Source: Alberto Anile. I film di Totò (1946-1967): la maschera tradita. Le mani, 1998

women. The film thus denies an Italian active interest in occupying (female) nation states, colonisation (and, as a consequence, an active role in racialising people) whereas the Italian characters search to occupy women's bodies. On the one hand, the film ridicules the obsessive need to occupy space, convenient in a context where the Italians had just lost the war and their colonies. On the other hand, it reconfirms the abovementioned trope of the (in this case, Italian) man in need of a subordinate woman in order to cope with his insecurities and fears, echoing the necessity to 'occupying land' trope on a micro cosmos scale.

Totò sceicco

Parodying the Rodolfo Valentino film *Il figlio dello sceicco* (George Fitzmaurice, 1926), and in the second act *Atlantide* (Gregg Tallas, 1949), *Totò sceicco* emphasises the fantasies surrounding the sheik character of the time, visibly non-Italian and other, and the Orientalist mesmerising effects of the desert that make one lose her/his mind. The film is set for the most part in an undefined Northern African country. After he cannot take the jealousy towards his girlfriend Lùlù anymore, Gastone (Aroldo Tieri) decides to enroll in the foreign volunteers. His butler Antonio (Totò) is ordered to get Gastone back, but he ends up in the rebel's army. Since their sheik is deceased, the rebels decide to dress Antonio up as the sheik. Everybody falls for it. In the second act of the film, having found Gastone and having escaped the rebels, Antonio enters a world under the ground, named *Atlantide*, where the queen falls in love with him, but has a deadly kiss. Just on time, he escapes, together with Gastone, who becomes crazy when standing in the sun. After some trouble, they arrive, back home safely.

Totò's comical mastering of *l'arte di arrangiarsi* demonstrates an adaptation to whatever situation offers itself: he belongs to one army if he is wearing the sheik's clothes, and later changes sides when he meets Gastone. Illustrating the random division between two groups of people, and possibly echoing the Italians changing sides during World War II, Totò's ambivalence also refer to the ambiguous position of Italy as south of Europe and north of the Mediterranean, as White and Black (or, *metticcio*, as Greene argues),[29] as the "starting point of Africa."[30] In the film, Antonio's only real interest is again, in women, suggesting that he is self-centred and interested not in occupying space, but in winning over women, in an indirect way sustaining the *italiani brava gente* myth. Moreover, the Orientalist clichés of Arab people as animal-like (cruel and stupid as they fall for Totò's trap) and the desert as a dangerous and mesmerising place, are reconfirmed in this film.

Towards a Postcolonial Reading of Post-World War II Italian Cinema

Other spaces in Italian film, which we could metaphorically interpret as *la piccola Roma*, provide information about *la grande Roma*, since we can register a projection of Italian narratives on to the spaces and cultures encountered by Italian characters. In the films analysed here, Totò's characters reveal a conflictual relationship with the colonial narrative. On the one hand, openly trying to occupy land is ridiculed by Totò's characters' counterbalancing this obsession with disinterest. He never takes his military tasks seriously, ridiculing its assumed importance. On the other hand, this overt rejection of occupying land and of military power as something to aspire to suggests a coping mechanism for the trauma of the lost war and the lost colonies, presenting the Italian as aloof and uninterested in occupying new colonial spaces to begin with. In this light, Totò's characters displace traumas exactly through dissociating themselves from these active colonisers and/or soldiers. This interpretation fits the *italiani brava gente* myth, preventing an acknowledgement of the Italian imperial enterprises. The films might have offered the ordinary man a remedy, as suggested by Brunetta, but not on the long term.

Moreover, we can confirm Ponzanesi's affirmation that "[gender plays a crucial role] in the rearticulation of difference at a global level".[31] Both *la terra*, often presented as divided by feminised nation states, and *la luna*, are presented as subordinate spaces desirable to violate/rape, occupy, and appropriate. The Italian characters in the films project concepts of femininity at a smaller scale on to women, who therefore become victim to their anxieties (in some cases, literally of rape). It is Totò's role in the films to question the obsessive behaviour towards occupying the female land, and the accompanying Orientalist and/or racialising thinking in terms of Black<-White (natural<->cultured), but the women's bodies on which Totò's characters project his desires parallel the obsession with occupying land.

In today's Italy there is a discrepancy between on the one hand a substantial body of academic texts in which the Italian colonial past is analysed in detail and Italy's postcolonial paradox is discussed, and on the other hand a strongly racialising, feminising and diminishing narrative about other cultures and countries stemming from the imperial narrative that was never disputed on a national scale, and that continues to exist in newspapers, on TV, and in politicians' debates. There are temptations outside of academia in order to challenge these discrepancies: in the past decade a large amount of interesting documentaries and books in which Italy's colonial past and its relationship to the former colonies is discussed, analysed and criticised.[32] Next to this, it would be useful to deconstruct popular media that belong to Italy's cultural patrimony.

Notes

1 I am a body [the Italian word for body is *corpo*, which is masculine, LL] and in order to live here I am in need of a body [female, LL]. All translations are mine.

2 With a cosona like this, I would stay on Mars, Saturn, and even Mercury for the rest of my life!

3 *Cosare*, literally translated "to thing" is a verb fitting for the plot of the film (even though Totò used the word in other films as well) since the fake human beings are referred to as big things, *cosoni*. Together, they could *cosare*. In this context, *cosare* means having sex.

4 Trust me, you will see. Some thing today, a thing tomorrow, and from one thing grows another.

5 The term neo-colonialism has been widely used to refer to any and all forms of control of the ex-colonies after political independence. The term was coined by Kwame Nkrumah, the first President of Ghana, in order to refer to the following mechanism: "Although countries like Ghana had achieved political independence, the ex-colonial powers and the newly emerging superpowers such as the United States continued to play a decisive role in their cultures and economies through new instruments of indirect control such as international monetary bodies, through the power of multinational corporations and cartels which artificially fixed prices in world markets, and through a variety of other educational and cultural NGOs (Non-Governmental Organisations)." Bill Ashcroft, Gareth Griffiths and Helen Tiffin, *Postcolonial Studies: The Key Concepts*. London, New York: Routledge, 2000, p. 146.

6 Gaia Giuliani and Cristina Lombardi-Diop, *Bianco e nero. Storia dell'identità razziale degli italiani*. Milan: Le Monnier, 2013.

7 By naming Asmara *la Piccola Roma* Mussolini appropriated space that up until this day is seen as the place where the human species comes from, since one of the oldest hominids was found in Eritrea by Italian scientists. This species represents a possible link between Homo erectus and Homo sapiens. Hence, by suggesting that Asmara (and, what it stood for symbolically, the Horn of Africa) is a small Rome, Mussolini enlarges Roman history all the way to the beginning of the human species, symbolically making the citizens of Rome the first people; the people.

8 When I use the term Orientalism or its adjective in this article, I refer to Edward Said's theorisation of those two concepts in his *Orientalism* (New York: Vintage Books, 1978): "The Orient is an integral part of European material civilisation and culture. Orientalism expresses and represents that part culturally and even ideologically as a mode of discourse with supporting institutions, vocabulary, scholarship, imagery, doctrines, even even colonial bureaucracies and colonial styles", p. 2.

9 Angelo Del Boca, *Italiani brava gente? Un mito duro da morire*. Vicenza: N.Pozza, 2005; Ruth Ben-Ghiat and Mia Fuller, *Italian Colonialism*. New York: Palgrave MacMillan, 2005; Jacqueline Andall and Derek Duncan, *Italian Colonialism: Legacy and Memory*. Oxford and New York: Peter Lang, 2005; Patrizia Palumbo, *A place in the sun: Africa in Italian colonial culture from post-unification to the present*. Berkeley: University of California Press, 2003.

10 Sandra Ponzanesi and Marguerite Waller (eds.), *Postcolonial Cinema Studies*. London and New York: Routledge, 2012, p. 2.

11 D'Amico mentions the massive amounts of Italian visitors to the cinema in the immediate post-World War II period. Masolino D'Amico, *La commedia all'italiana: il cinema comico in Italia dal 1945 al 1975*. Milan: Il Saggiatore 2008.

12 Derek Duncan,"Italy's Postcolonial Cinema and Its Histories of Representation", *Italian Studies*, vol. 63, 2008 (2), pp. 195-211, 196.

13 The term genre is highly problematic, as it closes a specific group of, in this case, films, down. Moreover, according to traditional Italian film history there is a strong binary distinction between genre films and auteur films. Elsewhere, I challenge this simplification. In my opinion, a definition kills per definition. This is why I do not call Totò's films a genre, but a brand.

14 The maciste film type was parodied in *Totò contro Maciste* by Fernando Cerchio (1962), and the Spaghetti Western in Totò Western in *Tutto Totò* by Daniele D'Anza (1967). By challenging and mocking the rules of film genres, Totò is questioning binary thinking in terms of closed-down genres.

5 Gian Piero Brunetta, *The History of Italian Cinema. A Guide to Italian Film From its Origins to the Twenty-First Century*. Princeton and Oxford: Princeton University Press, 2003, p. 115.

16 When looking for Totò films on Youtube, I found a large corpus of his films not only recently uploaded, but watched by tens of thousands of people. In the comment section I found nothing but positive comments (something rather rare on Youtube), such as "*totò uno dei più grandi attori del mondo*", "*divino@*", "*Totó e un anti-depressore. un Bacionecal nostro Totó*" for *Totò: L'imperatore di Capri*, and "*Che Film..., veramente elettrizzante. E poi Totò è sempre Totò..., 'ke grande!*" for *Totò d'Arabia*.

17 Gabriele Proglio refers to Totòtarzan in a very similar context, inviting scholars to investigate Totò's films in relation to echoes of Italy's colonial past. Cfr. Gabriele Proglio, "Memorie di celluloide in controluce. Politiche del ricordo, rimozioni e immaginari del colonialismo (1945–1962)", in Valeria Deplano and Alessandro Pes (eds.), *Quel che resta dell'impero. La cultura coloniale degli Italiani*. Milan, Udine: Mimesis Edizioni, 2014, pp. 317-329.

18 Silvana Patriarca, "'Gli italiani non sono razzisti!': construzione dell'italianità tra gli anni Cinuqanta e il 1968", in Gaia Giuliani (ed.), *Il colore della nazione*. Milan: Le Monnier, 2015, pp. 32-45, 33 and 45.

19 In this article, I capitalise Black and White when referring to a culture, ethnicity or group of people. Lowercase black or white are simply colours. For a plain explanation, see Lori L.Tharps' piece on this issue: "The Case for Black With a Capital B", in *The New York Times*, 18 November 2014, http://www.nytimes.com/2014/11/19/opinion/the-case-for-black-

20 Nirmal Puwar, *Space Invaders. Space, Gender, and Bodies out of Place*. Oxford: Berg, 2004, pp. 26-27.

21 Gaia Giuliani (ed.), *Il colore della nazione*, op. cit.; Gaia Giuliani and Cristina Lombardi-Diop, *Bianco e nero. Storia dell'identità razziale degli italiani*, op. cit.; Jennifer Guglielmo and Salvatore Salerno, *Are Italians White? How Race Is Made in America*. New York: Routledge, 2003.

22 The civil world. The real reason, the leader explains, is to get the money the White Monkey will inherit from his ancestors.

23 Ruth Ben-Ghiat and Mia Fuller, *Italian Colonialism*, op cit., Introduction.

24 As written elsewhere in this volume, Italy lost World War II and as a consequence, during the Treaty of Paris in 1947, all its colonies. There have never been wars of independence in the Italian colonies that would have questioned the colonial narrative in Italy. Therefore, Italy occupies a specific position as a former European colonising country. Ruth Ben-Ghiat and Mia Fuller, *Italian Colonialism*, op. cit.; Jacqueline Andall and Derek Duncan, *Italian Colonialism: Legacy and Memory*, op.cit.

25 Nirmal Puwar, *Space Invaders. Space, Gender, and Bodies out of Place*, op. cit., p. 27.

26 Faldini talked about this in a television interview. See https://www.youtube.com/watch?v=7GGOvs2syx8, last visited on 13 May 2016.

27 As in the case with Tototarzan, contact with monkeys (nature?) has a particular influence on characters.

28 "*Tutto questo perché? Per conquistare lo spazio. Ma che se ne fanno nello spazio? Che cos'è lo spazio? È niente! È aria! Conquisti l'aria! Apra la finestra e conquista l'aria*!"

29 Shelleen Greene, *Equivocal Subjects: Between Italy and Africa. Constructions of Racial and National Identity in the Italian Cinema*. New York: Continuum 2012. See also Jennifer Guglielmo and Salvatore Salerno, *Are Italians White? How Race Is Made in America*. New York: Routledge, 2003; Gaia Giuliani (ed.), *Il coloure della nazione*, op. cit.; Gaia Giuliani and Cristina Lombardi-Diop, *Bianco e nero. Storia dell'identità razziale degli italiani*, op. cit.

30 The *questione meridionale* (Gramsci) has brought forth this north-south division within the country, echoing the concept of the Global South from within. See also John Agnew, "The Myth of Backward Italy in Modern Europe", in Beverly Allen and Mary Russo (ed.), *Revisioning Italy. National Identity and Global Culture*. Minneapolis: University of Minnesota Press, 1997, pp. 23-42.

31 Sandra Ponzanesi, *Paradoxes of Postcolonial Culture Contemporary Women Writers of the Indian and Afro-Italian Diaspora*. Albany: State University of New York Press, 2004.

32 Documentaries include *Asmarina, Voices and Images of a Postcolonial Heritage* (Alan Maglio and Medhin Paolos, 2015), *Aulò: Roma Postcoloniale* (E.Guida, G.Chiscuzzu and S.Brioni, 2013), and *Blaxploitation* (Fred Kuwornu, 2015). For an updated list of literature, see Maria Grazia Negro, *Il mondo, il grido, la parola*. Florence: Cesati, 2015. See Gianmarco Mancosu's chapter in this volume.

ASMARA, THE PAST IN THE PRESENT
Echoes of Italian Colonialism in Documentaries on Mobility

Gianmarco Mancosu

Non so se ti chiami Ciccirilli o Zazzà, sei nata in Asmara e sei un fior di beltà
Fanciulla asmarina sei più bella per me, e ogni giorno alle tre suono e canto perché mi ricordo di te.
Asmarina Asmarina di bellezza sei regina, a vederti da lontano casca quello che ho in mano…

In the lyrics of this song, written in 1956 by Pippo Maugeri, the attractive girl who astonishes the singer is identified as Asmarina: this trope transposes the meaning of the word *asmarina* from a name to the adjective that describes a peculiar beauty by evoking the exotic-erotic attractiveness that both Eritrean girls and the city exerted in Italian colonial culture.[1] Such ambivalent attraction was imbricated in representations of the conquest of black women originated within colonial discourses, and also in the metaphoric sexual conquest of the African landscape which was described as awaiting Italian virile action.[2] However, the arising interest in Maugeri's song is not exclusively related to a generic exotic attraction, but it specifically addresses the legacy and the privileged position that Asmara had in Italian mass culture. Images of Asmara resounded well beyond the Italian East Africa by representing an enduring form of *esotico nostrano* which unfolded its attractiveness through representations based on the reformulation of Italian colonial desires.[3]

This transposition of meaning in relation to the *piccola Roma*, and the ways through which this process can be traced in contemporary representations

Film stills from the film *Asmarina*, 2015

about mobility in Italy will be focused by analysing two examples of the present-day flourishing documentary production. The documentary has established itself as one of the most thriving Italian artistic forms over the last decade by addressing changes that are refashioning Italian society.[4] This production reshapes forms and genres, and it actively conveys new meanings of Italianness by encompassing in this category both subjects and social groups previously depicted as marginal and not matching an alleged and monolithic image of national identity.[5] The selected documentaries, namely *Aulò. Roma Postcoloniale* (Brioni, Guida, Chiscuzzu, 2012)[6] and *Asmarina* (Maglio, Paolos, 2015),[7] both deal with personal histories in which mobility and colonial memory interlace by fixing a peculiar gaze on the Italian postcolonial landscape in its interconnected geographical poles.

The imbrication between memories and mobility will be explored from a peculiar perspective which aims to assess to what extent the use of old visual material, mainly found footage, pictures, and audio records produced by the *Istituto Luce*, displaces time and spaces relate the colonial experience of mobility. The use of both still pictures and found footage will be regarded as able to engender a peculiar historical link between the colonial past and the lack of social awareness about its legacies which the documentaries try to address.[8] Accordingly, stylistic choices of the directors will be approached as complex strategies aiming to generate narratives and counter narratives within the discursive space each documentary produces.[9]

According to Bill Nichols, the use of old footage in documentaries helps in the process to bridge past and present by reworking both spatial and temporal dimensions of the audience's experience;[10] such a theorisation will sustain the investigation of Asmara's representations as heterotopia, where spaces and times are juxtaposed, offering new ways to link memories of the colonial past with current issues related to fluxes of people, hybrid identities, social inclusion or exclusion. The concept of heterotopia, as coined by Michel Foucault in 1967,[11] will be useful in explaining the use and the re-signification of the images of Asmara within selected documentaries. Unlike what happens in the case of utopia, described by Foucault as a site with no real place and in which society presents itself in a perfected form, heterotopias are places that do exist, a kind of effectively enacted utopia characterised by the juxtaposition of apparently antithetic elements. These antithetic elements in both documentaries are broached in the dialogue between still pictures, found footage, and several stories of mobility. The colonial rhetoric that both *Aulò* and *Asmarina* evoke and challenge is mainly related to the fascist *Istituto Luce*, whose production was regarded as the most powerful tool to envision imperial myths throughout Italy and in Africa.[12]

Envisioning Fascism's Empire Myths

The peculiar images of the Italian East Africa produced by the *Istituto Luce* had a pivotal role in defining fascist imperial imaginations that both *Aulò* and *Asmarina* deconstruct. Italian fascism used non-fictional cinematography to educate Italians toward its own political goals by establishing in 1924 the *L'Unione Cinematografica Educativa – Luce*, which soon centralised the production of newsreels and documentary films.[13] During the Ethiopian war, a structure of the *Istituto Luce* was established in order to produce and spread visual representations of the colonial campaign both in Italy and in Africa. The *Reparto Foto-cinematografico Luce Africa Orientale* was specifically appointed by Benito Mussolini in September 1935 in order to testify to the Ethiopian war.[14] The way in which propagandistic content was both produced and diffused reveals the discourse that underpinned the fascist colonial ideology, fuelling a racist image about African otherness.

Not only the visual production, but also the diffusion of the cinema in the Horn of Africa, had to reproduce the physical and social segregation between Italian colonisers and colonial subjects. The rules that organised the cinematographic experience under the fascist empire were organised according to racial principles, such as the differentiation of shows addressed either to Italian or to African audiences.[15] In 1938, there were seven movie theatres that counted 7,680 seats in total in Asmara; these theatres were divided in three categories according to their prestige, and the best theatres, such as the Impero, the Teatro, and the Excelsior, were reserved for high-class Italians who were able to watch the most recent films. On the other hand, the cinema Hamasien was reserved for a native audience only.[16]

The construction and exaltation of fascist values were used to justify the new hierarchy upon which the Empire should be based: in this context, the colonised were shown as primitive, backward, but at the same time able to acknowledge Italian's supremacy, and to accept their own new role as subjected people. This degradation of African otherness is a pivotal feature in understanding how *Istituto Luce's* production refashioned images of national identity: Africans embodied the disvalues for the new fascist man, and the Italianisation of African landscapes was a recurring theme to justify the Italian civilising mission. In particular, images about the urban dimension can be regarded as the mirror of the acting fascist civilisation which transformed so-called underdeveloped villages in westernised cities worthy of being inhabited by Italian colonisers.[17]

Colonial Memories and Postcolonial Landscapes in Italy

This peculiar construction of African alterity by the *Istituto Luce* seems to resound in some present-day representations of migrants coming to Italy.[18] Both *Asmarina* and *Aulò*, in distinctive ways, try to overtake these images by dealing with the re-evaluation of a peculiar form of aphasic colonial memory[19] in order to counter the inadequacy through which Italian society has, or perhaps has not, conceived the legacies of colonial past. The relation between a huge Italian city and the experience of mobility of the Ethio-Eritrean community is the core of *Asmarina*. The film gives an insight into the Habesha community living in the area of Piazza Venezia in Milan.[20] By adopting a polyphonic structure and meta-discursive narratives that simultaneously connect and displace space and time, the documentary expounds how the old colonial interaction reverberates within several experiences of mobility to Italy starting from the 1950s.

A more direct effort to engage in the relation between the colonial past, subjectivity and hybrid identities in Italy is offered by *Aulò. Roma Postcoloniale*. More than a documentary, *Aulò* is a part of a bigger transmedial project that is composed of different products, such as books, documentaries, poetry, academic investigation, and sound tracks. This project addresses how legacies of Italian colonialism can still influence the perception of the African *Other* in Italian society, and how the presence of colonial traces is tangible in Italian buildings and streets. In *Aulò*, the vicissitudes of the Eritrean-born writer Ribka Sibathu are used to analyse both the postcolonial landscape of Rome and the Italian level of awareness about its colonial past. The title *Aulò* refers to a specific kind of oral poetry that was used for different purposes in pre-colonial Eritrea: Ribka, throughout the documentary, proclaims different *aulòs*; these poems set the pace for each section by connecting Ribka's vicissitudes to the traces of Italian colonial history. The whole documentary revolves around the research of colonial legacies in the city of Rome and in its inhabitants, who are interviewed on the seashore of Ostia.

The Past in the Present

Both in *Asmarina* and *Aulò* the directors, by using found footage, still pictures, and audio recordings, actively promote a discursive space in which they develop intertwined narratives and counter narratives by aiming to involve the audience in the process of reassessment and deconstruction of a monolithic idea of Italian identity. In the initial sequence of *Asmarina*, a moving camera pans over old photographs in a way that makes them seem to come alive.[21] These still photographs, which portray marriages, school classes, and children, are used to begin the journey through space and time, and to give faces and bodies to the memories of mobility unfolding throughout the documentary. This introductive part is useful to conceive Asmarina as a family album in which still pictures, songs, and chronicles describe both social and cultural experiences of the Habesha community in Milan. If these first sequences of Asmarina offer a very intimate point of view, the following ones unfold in an unsettling way. In particular, an old member of the *Archivio Nazionale Reduci Rimpatriati dall'Africa – ANNRA* talks about the beneficial contribution of Italian colonialism in Africa. This positive interpretation is shown by using very old still pictures: these photographs, which call to mind the official pictures taken by the *Istituto Luce*,[22] portray the infrastructures that Italians had built in Africa, and some urban landscapes described as civilised since they were *Italianised*. By using old pictures as evidence, the returnee's voice offers an authoritative and positive understanding of the Italian colonial presence there. After this unsettling prologue, the vicissitudes of the Habesha community are presented as more intimate and lively. Personal memories are awakened through the use of both still pictures and old songs, as it happens with the song *Asmarina* that gives the film its title.

The pivotal role of photography is not limited to the awakening of memories, since it helps to fill the vacuum between the experience of the old mobility related to the Italian colonial conquest, and the long process of integration in Italy. Still pictures can be regarded as diegetic elements: they guide the viewer towards a film's political aims, relating to the complex and often contradictory historical process of integration with regards to past colonial interaction. In Asmarina, still official photographs are metaphorically juxtaposed with the family album of the Habesha community. The construction of this peculiar and metaphorical juxtaposition works, according to Rosenstone, as a "kind of commentary on, and challenge to, traditional historical discourse",[23] where the adjectives *traditional* and *historical* can be contextualised and conceived as able to reproduce the idea of the *Italiani bravi gente* who had a positive impact in Africa.[24] If the older pictures are used by the directors in order to reproduce the myth of the *brava gente*, the more recent visual memories of the Habesha community overturn this rhetoric by creating an interpretative framework that shifts the meaning of the Italian colonial presence in a specific counter narrative. Old pictures produced during the Italian presence in East Africa are no longer evidence testifying to civilised activity, since they are located in a persistent dialogue with the more recent photographs depicting how colonial interaction originated and fashioned the embodied stories of mobility between Africa and Italy which *Asmarina* develops.

This mechanism of juxtaposition between old material recalling the colonial past, and current postcolonial subjectivities can be traced also in *Aulò. Roma Postcoloniale*. According to Simone Brioni, one of the directors, *Aulò* addresses new forms to counter the amnesia of the colonial past and the negative representation of immigrants in the Italian media.[25] The documentary unfolds its strong connection with African oral narration, and this peculiar feature contributes in expounding multiple narrative levels.

The main character, the poet Ribka Sibhatu, acknowledges she came to Rome since Italian colonialism left relevant traces both in her family and in the whole Horn of Africa. These traces are evoked not exclusively in Ribka's words, but also through some old pictures showing the Italian buildings in Asmara. The pictures are interconnected with several sequences, usually shot using fixed wide angles which focus on several monuments in Rome. This contiguity between Asmara and Rome is asserted throughout the whole documentary: if Ribka clearly states she wants "*colourare Roma coi profumi e i colouri dell'Eritrea*", on the other hand the *piccola Roma* is shown in its massive and enduring Italian traces. To show the Italianisation of Asmara, the directors use still pictures, mainly focusing on buildings such as the Cinema Impero, the Fiat Tagliero, and many others shops and signs with Italian names. The use of old pictures is something conceived as verifiable and concrete[26] which overtly challenges Italian aphasia about the colonial past.

The colonial rhetoric is clearly evoked in a sequence in which the voice of Benito Mussolini giving a speech intertwines with postcards and still pictures produced during the fascist invasion of Ethiopia with a clear racial meaning.[27] The fascist racist propaganda, however, is both engaged and challenged by the words of Ribka, who emphasises the interaction between Italians and Eritreans as well as the oppression and racism. Ribka, by challenging this colonial rhetoric, embodies the diegetic aim of the directors, who try to convey a different meaning to some physical places in both Rome and Asmara which are regarded more as places of interaction than spaces of separation.

Heterotopic Asmara

Both in *Asmarina* and *Aulò*, the use of different visual sources aims to displace the temporal dimension of the viewer, who is invited to recognise what Bill Nichols defines "the paradoxical status of moving images": the present time of the audience, while it watches images recalling Italian colonialism, becomes past, or prologue, to a common future that in the discursive space of documentaries is embodied by Ribka, or by the Habesha community in Milan.[28] This relocation of time is unfolded by using a complex structure of visual sources: both interviews, old footage produced by the *Istituto Luce*, and personal records are used to awaken personal memories, and to stimulate the audience's reflection on the historical roots of present-day issues. Such manipulation of the old images places the viewer in a different relationship to the film from that of viewers watching the original several decades earlier[29] by developing a suspension of the flow of time that contributes to a questioning of the silence on the colonial past.

The peculiar practice that displaces the time of the viewer – by interlacing narratives and counter narratives engendered by archival material – is also entangled in the process that displaces spaces in which postcolonial interaction is conceived. In Asmarina, both the voices of the Ethio-Eritrean community and still pictures reframe the meaning of colonial contact by inviting the audience to consider both *le cose brutte e le cose belle* within this experience.[30] The city of Asmara is described as both a place of colonial interaction and as a place to escape from. A refugee in the last part of the documentary tells of his farewell to Asmara: while he was leaving, he was aware that this could be the last time he would see his birthplace. In a very similar way, a section of *Aulò* focuses on the history of some refugees whose stories connect the Italian colonial presence to their current condition. If old still photographs depicting Asmara give the idea of a massive Italian influence, this presence is interpreted as the historical underpin of the political situation that is pushing Eritreans to escape from their country. In this process of representing and contesting a given historical meaning of the city, the directors work against, as well as with, the still pictures and found footage: they rescue these from oblivion by refashioning their former propagandistic use in the effort to connect colonialism with current mobility issues.

Both in *Asmarina* and *Aulò*, the city of Asmara is simultaneously the place of an enacted utopia, the space of a postcolonial interaction, and a dystopia characterised by totalitarianism and oppression. However, such contrasting dimensions do not seem to have different temporalities: the enacted utopia in Asmara is both evoked by the old still pictures and by the several voices who assert to be willing to go back there. The interaction between Italians and Eritreans happened both during and after the formal colonialism, and it is also dislocated in Rome and Milan, as is shown throughout the documentaries. The dystopian Asmara emerges both in the memories of colonial racism and in the description of the current situation.

Such images of the Eritrean capital resonate with Foucault's elaboration of the concept of heterotopia which is capable of "juxtaposing in a single real place several spaces, several sites that are in themselves incompatible," such as the colonial myths, the social space Italianised and racialised, and the political situation that forced people to leave Asmara to reach Italy. According to the sixth principle through which Foucault describes heterotopia, it has a function in relation to all the space that remains. This specific feature unfolds between two extremes poles: the creation of a space of illusion that exposes every real space and in which human life is illusory and, at the other pole, the creation of another real place that is as perfect and well arranged compared to the jumbled space in which everyone lives.[31] The Italian colonial space evoked in the selected documentaries simultaneously accommodates these disjunctive experiences by covering imperial segregation, the interaction between Italians and Africans, the dismantling of the Italian presence, and the hard situation which pushes Eritreans to leave their country. Furthermore, heterotopia helps to conceptualise the "often overlooked intersection of time with space" through which the re-signification of the representations of Asmara is conveyed, allowing the dialogue between old and new visual narrations of the city to unfold.[32]

In *Asmarina* and *Aulò*, Asmara emerges as counter site that stands in opposition to a peculiar established meaning that is both evoked and challenged by the use of found footage, still pictures, and old sounds. Accordingly, Asmara can be conceived not as a traditional utopic space, since it was not merely an unreal space ideally constructed as a perfect projection either of colonial myths or the promised land in which migrants aim to return to. Rather, it seems a suspended space connecting different times and spaces, an enacted utopia in which all the other "real sites that can be found within the culture are simultaneously represented, contested, and inverted."[33] Such juxtaposition has been proposed as a pivotal element in the proposed work: by reworking space and time to assess the link between colonialism and present-day mobility, both documentaries try to dismantle hidden aspects of colonial legacies that echoed in representations focusing on the relationship between Italianness and mobility.

Notes

1 Sandra Ponzanesi, "Beyond Black Venus: Colonial Sexual Politics and Contemporary Visual Practices", in Jaqueline Andall and Derek Duncan (eds.), *Italian colonialism. Legacies and Memories*. Bern: Peter Lang, 2005, p. 176; Loredana Polezzi, "Il pieno e il vuoto: Visual Representations of Africa in Italian Accounts of Colonial Experiences", *Italian Studies*, vol. 67, 2012, pp. 345-357.

2 Federico Caprotti, "The Invisible War on Nature: The Abyssinian War (1935–1936) in Newsreels and Documentaries in Fascist Italy", *Modern Italy*, vol. 19, (2014), pp. 305-321.

3 The category of the *esotico nostrano* (familiar exotic, translation mine) has been used by Mario Isnenghi in analysing recurring themes in Italian colonial literature, see Mario Isnenghi, *L'Italia del fascio*. Florence: Giunti, 1996, p. 216.

4 Michela Ardizzoni addresses those topics and states that the recent documentary production testifies a new form of *cinema d'impegno*, Michela Ardizzoni, "Narratives of Change, Images for Change: Contemporary Social Documentaries in Italy", *Journal of Italian Cinema & Media Studies*, vol. 1, 2013, p. 317.

5 Anita Angelone, Clarissa Clò, "Other visions: Contemporary Italian documentary cinema as counter-discourse", *Studies in Documentary Film*, vol. 5, 2011, pp. 83–89.

6 Simone Brioni, Ermanno Guida, *Graziano Chiscuzzu, Aulò. Roma Postcoloniale*. Rome: Kimerafilm, 2012.

7 Alan Maglio, Mehdin Paolos, *Asmarina*. Italy, 2015.

8 On the relation between old propagandistic footage in present-day films about migration, Derek Duncan observed that "the newsreel footage intimates a historical link, yet also provides dramatic evidence of the lack of suture in terms of historical knowledge". On the impact of colonial season in Italian culture: Derek Duncan, "Shooting the Colonial Past in Contemporary Italian Cinema Effects of Deferral in 'Good Morning Aman'", in Cristina Lombardi-Diop, Caterina Romeo (eds.), *Postcolonial Italy. Challenging National Homogeneity*, New York: Palgrave Macmillan, 2012, p. 117.

9 Brian Winston expounds the process of narrativisation by defining documentary as "the narrativised recorded aspects of observation received as being a story about the world". Brian Winston (ed.), *The Documentary Film Book*. London: Palgrave Macmillan, 2013, p. 24.

10 Bill Nichols, *Blurred Boundaries. Question of Meaning in Contemporary Culture*. Bloomington and Indianapolis: Indiana University Press, 1994, p. 4.

11 Michel Foucault, "Of Other Spaces: Utopias and Heterotopia", lecture given to *Cercle d'Études Architecturales* in March 1967, translated by Jay Miskowiec, in *Architecture, Mouvement, Continuité*, vol. 5, 1984, pp. 46-49.

12 Ruth Ben Ghiat, *Italian Fascism's Empire Cinema*. Bloomington and Indianapolis: Indiana University Press, 2015; Barbara Corsi, "Istituto Luce. Inventario generale dei documentari e dei cinegiornali a soggetto colonial", in Giampireo Brunetta, Jean Gili (eds.), *L'ora d'Africa del cinema italiano 1911–1989*, Rovereto: Rivista di studi storici – Materiali di lavoro, 1990, p. 119.

13 Ernesto G. Laura, *Le Stagioni dell'aquila: Storia dell'Istituto Luce*. Rome: Ente dello spettacolo, 2000.

14 Gianmarco Mancosu, "L'Istituto Luce nella guerra d'Etiopia", in *War films: interpretazioni storiche del cinema di Guerra*. Milan: Acies, 2015, pp. 211-223.

15 Archivio Centrale dello Stato (Rome), group Ministero della Cultura Popolare, folder 115, file "Ufficio Stampa e Propaganda in AOI – Reparto fotocinematografico Luce", file n. 2493, 1936. On the topic, see Salvatore Ambrosino, "Cinema e propaganda in Africa Orientale Italiana", *Ventesimo Secolo*, vol. 1, 1990.

16 Archivio Storico Diplomatico Ministero degli Affari Esteri (Rome), group Eritrea, folder 1008, file "*Commissione per lo spettacolo – cinematografi*", sub file. "*Disposizioni per le proiezioni dei film*", document 48028, 1938.

17 Federico Caprotti, "The Invisible War on Nature: The Abyssinian War (1935–1936) in Newsreels and Documentaries in Fascist Italy", op. cit., p. 311; Gianmarco Mancosu, "L'impero visto da una cinepresa. Il reparto foto-cinematografico Africa Orientale dell'Istituto Luce", in Valeria Deplano and Alessandro Pes (eds.), *Quel che resta dell'impero. La cultura colonial degli italiani*. Milan and Udine: Mimesis, 2015, p. 275.

18 Francesca Locatelli, "Migrating to the Colonies and Building the Myth of 'Italiani Brava Gente'. The Rise, Demise and Legacy of Italian Settler Colonialism", in Ruth Ben Ghiat, Stephanie Malia Hom (eds.), *Italian Mobilities*. London and New York: Routledge, 2016, p. 147.

19 The term *aphasia* can be translated as speechlessness. As Dietmar Rothermund argues when discussing the contemporary post-imperial memory, the aphasic memory metaphorically refers to the social inability to find the adequate expression to articulate past experiences, and this may happen when there is no social framework available which permits the formation of collective memory. Dieter Rothermund (ed.), *Memories of Post-Imperial Nations. The Aftermath of Decolonization 1945–2013*. Cambridge: Cambridge University Press, p. 5.

20 As observed by Anna Arnone, "Habesha denotes the people from the plateaus of Ethiopia and Eritrea where Semitic languages coming from a common Ge'ez root are spoken and where mostly Tewaheldo Orthodox Christianity is practised, and other cultural practices such as certain ways of preparing coffee and particular foods are shared"; see Anna Arnone, "Talking about Identity: Milanese-Eritreans describe themselves", *Journal of Modern Italian Studies*, vol. 16, 2011, p. 526. In *Asmarina*, some scenes relate to how the interviewees conceive the term Habesha.

21 Robert Rosenstone, *History on Film, Film on History*. Harlow: Pearson Longman, 2006, p. 72.

22 See also: Silvana Palma, *L'Italia coloniale, Storia fotografica della società italiana*. Rome: Editori Riuniti 1999; Angelo Del Boca, Nicola Labanca, *L'impero africano del fascismo nelle fotografie dell'Istituto Luce*. Rome: Editori Riuniti, 2002.

23 Robert Rosenstone, *History on Film, Film on History*, op. cit., p. 9.

24 See Angelo Del Boca, *Italiani, brava gente? Un mito duro a morire*. Venice: Neri Pozza 2005; Silvana Patriarca, *Italianità. La costruzione del carattere nazionale*. RomE-Bari: Laterza, 2010, pp. 217-218.

25 Simone Brioni, "Migrant Stories and Italian Colonialism: A Report on Two Documentaries", *The Italianist*, vol. 33, 2013, p. 322.

26 Bill Nichols, "The Question of Evidence, the Power of Rhetoric and Documentary Film", Brian Winston (ed.), *The Documentary Film Book*, op. cit., p. 33.

27 The speech was given in September 1938; Benito Mussolini stated "*gli imperi si conquistano con le armi, ma si mantengono con il prestigio*", see Newsreel D041401 'Il Duce a Trieste. La giornata – Il Duce nel Veneto 1938', http://www.archivioluce.com/archivio/, accessed 18 June 2016.

28 Bill Nichols, *Blurred Boundaries. Question of Meaning in Contemporary Culture*, op. cit., p. 117.

29 Robert Lumley, "Amnesia and Remembering. 'Dal Polo all'Equatore', A Film by Yerevant Gianikian and Angela Ricci Lucchi", *Italian Studies*, vol. 64, 2009, p. 135.

30 These words ("Let us consider both the good and the bad things") are used by the Italo-Eritrean Michele Lettenze in the first sequences of the documentary.

31 Michel Foucault, op. cit., pp. 48-49.

32 Maurizio Marinelli uses the concept of heterotopia in analysing the Italian colonial presence in the Chinese city of Tianjin, see: Maurizio Marinelli, "Italy and/in Tianjin", in Jacqueline Andall and Derek Duncan (eds.), *National Belongings. Hybridity in Italian Colonial and Postcolonial Cultures*. Bern: Peter Lang, 2010, p. 68.

33 Michel Foucault, op. cit., p. 47.

Second Chapter

A GEOGRAPHY OF MEMORIES

Most urban research that sees itself as part of postcolonial studies in fact concentrates on excavating histories and legacies of colonialism. It is often said that this favours a particular (Western) interpretation of the city at the expense of a more indigenous one. Thus it can be argued that Asmara is more of an outsider's than an insider's label. Discussions about Italian colonialism and memories are often problematic because they focus nearly exclusively on the memories of Italians – thereby perpetuating the self-centredness that shaped and restricted the colonial viewpoint. In Asmara, but in a different way compared with other African cities, we find odd juxtapositions of something unique and different – beyond colonialism – with continuities from the colonial era. Postcolonial research names the cultural, political and linguistic experiences of former colonised societies by including voices, stories, histories and images from people traditionally excluded from European/Western descriptions of the world. The influence of postcolonialism on cultural geography and everyday practices can be traced back in work on imaginative geographies and geographies of identity that challenge the fixities of nationalism as well as colonialism.

Following our thematic strategy in the contributions to this book, we would like to consider recent intersections between cultural geography and postcolonial studies, and explore the significance of indigenous practices and memories so as to give Asmara a local voice. This section develops a "memory-scape, the historical consciousness of the wretched and the dominated [which] rewrites our present and challenges the hegemonic forms of memory when it produces different ways of translating the experience of time"(Hartog).

The city, as Roland Barthes puts it, speaks to its inhabitants, we all speak our city, the city where we are, simply by living in it, by wandering through it. Indeed, colonialism and its effects are at the centre of this part of our book, inspired by stories of people who grew up in Asmara. These people might speak about Italian schools that functioned as a social and cultural space where the performative dimension of belonging and attachment was deployed, or about the indigenous quarter on the hill known as Aba Shawl.

Navigating the city, we compile spatial sentences that begin to make sense. Slowly, we learn to make the spaces of the city speak. Drawing on personal experience, **Alemseged Tesfay** offers a reading of the urbanscape's geographical and mental maps, the moorings of its imagination. It examines the models of urban order and discipline that the Italian colonial administration attempted to impose on Asmara. It describes the ways in which Eritrean women and inhabitants who grew up in the former indigenous quarter experienced the city and shaped the pattern of their own lives with their social significance and political implications in the context of a postcolonial African city. These different subjects had participated in the same history, but in a subordinate position.

All around the colonial city grew the other Asmara, which is hardly mentioned or talked about. It is the other Asmara, where indigenous working-class residents mixed with the poor lived, founded their families and raised their children. **Tekle Woldemikael** grew up in the working-class indigenous part of Asmara in the early 1950s and 1960s. He uses his own memories of the area to describe the lives of children, families and communities who lived there. The working class adults he knew in the 1950 and 1960s, who lived in the indigenous Asmara, worked in, around and on the periphery of the Modernist Asmara as railroad workers, shop assistants, day labourers, maids and servants, artisans, teachers, hawkers, small-scale shopkeepers, craftsmen, and traders/merchants in the informal indigenous markets of the city.

Sabrina Marchetti and **Domenica Ghidei Biidu** introduce Eritrean migrants who remember their youth in little Rome. The memories of Eritrean women who migrated to Italy in the 1960s to 1970s testify to the importance of the Italian acculturation that they received during their youths in Asmara. The city is indeed remembered as a little Rome, a place where the previous colonial presence was evident not only in the city's architecture, but also in the opportunities to establish relationships with Italian people and to access what was considered to be the authentic Italian culture. This contribution describes these memories, exploring the role of Italian cultural influence in Asmara after the end of the official colonial rule.

A SHORT NOTE ON ABA SHAWL

Alemseged Tesfay

One cannot speak of Asmara's unique heritage without giving due credit to the zone that helped it acquire its exalted status. For on the hill to the northeast overlooking the very heart of the city, the Campo Cintato, were the cluttered houses, the narrow alleys, the mud huts and the *tukuls* – the living quarters of the indigenous population. True, none of these will claim the architectural worth that Asmara's historical perimeter is now famous for. But Campo Cintato would be bereft of the culture and colour that Eritreans have given to it if the central role played by Aba Shawl in its construction and preservation is not considered worthy of a parallel treatment. Aba Shawl and Campo Cintato still retain their respective original forms; they still complement each other.[1]

Prior to Italian occupation, the hill on which Aba Shawl is constructed was known as Gnbar Aba Awts. It was a thickly forested, uninhabited wilderness of cypress trees and thorny bushes where wild wild animals roamed at will. The first settlement began on the eve of the Italian arrival when a feudal lord, Kentiba Desta, from the neighbouring powerful village of Tse' Azega, brought his family and troops to set up camp and to establish a fiefdom at the top of the hill. Kentiba Desta had a vassal from Tigrai in Ethiopia, a man of wit and abilities who helped him in administrative chores. The latter had a horse called Aba Shawl which was also the vassal's battle cry.[2]

The name Aba Shawl thus comes from the man and the horse that, in the fulfillment of the vasall's administration duties, had become ubiquitous. With the growth in population in Italian times, Aba Shawl expanded enough to create extended administrative districs, such as Geza Banda (Habesha),

View of Aba Shawl
Source: K. Paulweber 2013

Haddish Adi, Geza Berhanu and new adjacent settlements like Edaga Hamus, Edaga Arbi, Mercato, Kidane Mehret, etc. But the honour of having been the original hub of Eritrean urban settlement, indeed, of having set a trend for the urbanisation of future Asmara, incontestably goes to Aba Shawl.

If the houses of Aba Shawl were cluttered and crowded, the rooms in every house were swarming with family members, visitors, renters and even passersby. The legendery Aba Shawl hospitality, still in many ways retained by Asmara residents, was bred of necessity, of the habit of sharing which a life of proximity and common needs brings about. The famous joke that Aba Shawl children who reach out to scratch an itch in their sleep always end up stroking a sibling's body part attests to how half a dozen of them slept in a small room crammed one on top of the other. One had to learn self-respect towards the rights of siblings and self-defence whilst jostling for space in this jumbled existence. And one did.

It was the neighbourhood though that left a lasting imprint on the culture and character of Asmara. People shared everything; above all they shared their secrets. In rows of housing where cardboard, corrugated sheets or porous walls were the only partition between families, there could be no privacy. Every rustle, cough or grunt was audible on the other side. Every spousal spat or financial difficulty soon found its way to every household in the row and far beyond. There was therefore no point concealing one's likes, especially in the face of an alien ruler. A culture of openness thus evolved and common solutions were sought for common problems. Sharing, materially and spiritually became the norm. Street safety evolved into a community concern, as did child discipline and education.

Small and large self-help groups banded together to form associations (the *ekub*), today the most common form of grassroots organisation in the whole country. Patron saint's days and religious holidays also grew into more than mere pious gatherings to provide large forums for discussion. The third and fourth generation of original Aba Shawl residents, wherever they may be today, still retain and nurture the associations they inherited from pioneering ancestors. The practice of arbitration and the settlement of disputes within the neighbourhood and inside these associations prevailed over police intervention and court adjudication, a much later development.

It was, above all, a egalitarian community where district chiefs, judges and native officers of the colonial administration freely mixed with less fortunate subjects – small peddlers, grave diggers and butchers – with mutual respect devoid of class antagonism and acrimony. Every Eritrean ethnic group was represented in Aba Shawl, as was every religion. Not only Eritreans, but also Ethiopians from Tigrai, Gonder, Shoa and even the faraway Oromo land were warmly accepted and integrated. Many, like Aba Shawl himself, attained prominence, fame and wealth and their descendants, albeit intermarried and assimilated, can still be identified.

Inclusiveness and tolerance to ethnic, religious and cultural diversity, traits that Asmara still holds dear as its special heritage, were bred in Aba Shawl. It is significant and a great credit to the zone that in spite of all the disparity in faith, class and ethnicity, it never registered any home-bred strife or sectarian violence. On the contrary, its role in abating potential dispute is near legendary. For example, in February 1951, at the height of the dispute between Eritreans advocating union with Ethiopia (mostly Christian) and those vetting for independence (mostly Muslim) armed violence flared up and raged for one whole week throughout Asmara. It is the only time in the whole history of the city that such a major incident has ever taken place.

Characteristically, Aba Shawl had its own reaction and solution to the internecine killings that followed. When marauding unionists invaded the district to attack Muslims wherever they could find them, Christians saved their neighbours by camouflaging or concealing them. When armed Muslims came to predominantly Muslim areas to persecute Christians, Muslims returned the favour by protecting their Christian friends and neighbours. Aba Shawl suffered amongst the least casualties and it was at the forefront of the popular move that ended the strife and brought back peace and reconciliation to the entire city.

With all its unlit narrow streets, blind alleys, and dead ends, Aba Shawl has all the characteristics of a ghetto. In fact, recent Tigrinya literature uses the word *shawl* to mean ghetto. Its inhabitants insist that this is a misnomer. True, Italian colonisers used Aba Shawl to confine natives to a restricted area; to ward them off the territory that they had reserved for themselves. It was therefore a ghetto in the sense that it resulted from a policy of discrimination and exclusion similar, say, to the Jewish ghetto in the European capitals of earlier centuries. But the discrimination came from a colonial master with a different political system, religion, morality and culture. The mass confinement of Eritreans to Aba Shawl and other subsequent zones was a physical phenomenon. It could in no way establish the spiritual superiority of the European coloniser. Nor could a European culture and set of beliefs penetrate the established customs and religions of an old society. It is not surprising therefore that no subculture of undesirable traits developed at Aba Shawl or the other similarly restricted areas throughout the country. The Italians set up modern government, effective administration, and introduced up-to-date technology to an essentially traditional African setting. But the dominant culture was what the natives took to Aba Shawl and what they brought back when they came to Campo Cintato as artisans, masons, surveyors, accountants, junior clerks, household servants and daily labourers whose land, toil, sacrifice and acquired skills form an integral part of the Italian architectural finesse that Asmara has to offer.

From start to finish, Italian culture stayed superficial. First, Eritreans were too deeply rooted in their respective customs and faiths to fall for the alien norms and beliefs introduced by the coloniser. For example, the Italian mission to Catholicise Eritreans failed to make headway beyond the few pockets where they managed to convert mainly Orthodox Christians. Orthodox Christianity itself had entered Eritrea in the fourth century AD. Islam had found its first converts when the prophet Mohammed was still alive in the mid-seventh century. These were thus religions that had coexisted side by side for centuries, too entrenced for European missionaries to penetrate easily.

But, equally significant, was the fact that the Italians did all they could to insulate themselves and their culture from extension to their colonies' subjects. Eritreans were denied modern education beyond the fourth grade; their access to modern technology was limited by design to the rudimentary skills the masters were willing to share for their won expediency: with the advent of fascism, Eritreans were required to obtain a permit to enter the Campo Cintato. The outcome of this policy of conscious discrimination and aloofness was that European culture in Eritera largely remained a culture confined to an enclave. The trickle effect it had on zones like Aba Shawl, barely 2 km away from the hub of the Italian presence, although significant in instilling a feel for urbanisation, industrialisation and modernity in the minds of the populace, could not alter their traditional ways, faiths and senses of worth and identity. Eritreans thus did not succumb to a culture of alienation and depression, or of anger and hatred that their circumstances would otherwise have imposed on them. Rather than harbour resentment and antagonism towards the modernity and relative affluence in the European sector which stood in sharp contrast to their own crowded existence, natives of Asmara adopted an attitude of acceptance, even a sense of ownership of the city that was evolving in their very midst, with much of their own labour. Ultimately, Eritrean love and pride for the beauty and dignity of Asmara was to form one of the bases for the upsurge of nationalism that was to see the country achieve full independence a century after the city became its recognised capital.

Aba Shawl's role in all of these developments has been pivotal. Its bond with Asmara's historic perimeter is such that one could not have existed without the other. The preservation of Asmara's rich architectural heritage cannot be imagined without the local sense of attachment and ownership first established at Aba Shawl. In short, just as Asmara would lose its lustre, beauty and attraction without the preserved European environment, it would have similary lost its culture and essence without Aba Shawl's indigenous and, indeed, jealous guardianship and protection of its heritage.

In the 1960s, during the illustrious tenure of Mayor Haregot Abbay, Aba Shawl was marked for destruction and urban reconstruction.[3] Its residents were notified to that effect and provided with choices for an alternative outside of the district. The outpouring of grief, anger and indignation that ensued was alarming in ist immediacy and overwhelming it its scope and intensity. Reconstructing Aba Shawl to suit the demands of urbanisation and improve its amenities, a need long overdue, was not in itself objectionable. But the resettlement of its founding residents would eliminate the tradition of inclusiveness and tolerance that has always been its hallmark, a wealth that Asmara as a city also inherited. Aba Shawl was particularly revered for providing shelter to the poor and downtrodden. A development that would alienate and rendert the deprived and unfortunate would almost amount to an act of cruelty.

Perhaps a song by the popular singer of the time, Alamin Abdulatif, summarised the mood and reaction to the proposal in his, until now, highly emotionally charged song, *Good bye Aba Shawl*. Some of its lyrics follow:

> "Good bye, Great Aba Shawl, / Selam before your destruction, / The Mother of the poor, / The guardian of orphans. / Let me sing of Great Aba Shawl before its demolition / ... Great Aba Shawl that reared me ... / ... Great Aba Shawl, Mother of my youth."[4]

Mayor Heregot did not carry out his plan, partly because of the public outcry, but maybe also because of the heavy costs that the endeavor was likely to incur on the finances of the Municipality.

Aba Shawl lives on, in many places in its old, original form. The few asphalted streets crossing it are still fed by the narrow alleys of a century ago. Neither have the few villas, rows of modern houses and one-storey buildings totally done away with the crammed shacks that gave to Asmara many of its personalties and luminaries. Famous historical figures – freedom fighters, politicians, bureaucrats, soldiers, artists, footballers and wits – learned their respective trades in this melting pot. Young poets and playwrights still visit the Aba Shawl *sewa* houses[5] and neighbourhoods in search of characters and originality in down-to-earth humour and local wisdom, elements still not in short supply.

Indeed, Aba Shawl has a magical hold on Asmarans in general, but mainly on those who lived and grew up there. This year, 2015, grandchildren and great grandchildren of the pioneers of Aba Shawl, most of them living elsewhere in Asmara and far away in the diaspora, are in the final stages of reestablishing and revitalising their ancestral Aba Shawl Association. It is a self-help gathering intent on the preservation of the culture of inclusiveness and tolerance of their neighbourhood.

Aba Shawl's inclusion in the historic perimeter of Asmara is therefore deeply rooted in the psyche of the city. The need to restructure and modernise it cannot be put into question.[6] Asmara's further growth as a cosmopolitan capital will surely demand this, as it has for a while now. But, how to accomplish this without destroying the social, cultural and psychological balance that is based in Aba Shawl will remain a challenge for urban planners and decision makers. One thing is clear. The possible recognition of the Asmara historic perimeter as a World Heritage site will be incomplete if the indigenous culture, as embodied and represented by Aba Shawl which helped preserve it, is not included in that recognition.

Notes

1 Aba Shawl represents an important part of Eritrea's history and is one of the oldest districts of Asmara. This area was a part of the indigenous zone during the colonial phase; it was part of the so-called unplanned city which is characterised by ist unsystematically built-up houses and narrow phatways. The urban development plans of the colonisers were affected by a policy based on racial segregation. The Eritreans who lived in the area of the later European zone before the Italians came were to a large extent forced to move into the indigenous quarters, which resulted in Aba Shawl becoming the area with the highest population density of the city. See: Peter Volgger and Stefan Graf, "City as a Palimpsest – Re-Mapping Asmara" (section 1.3 in this book).

2 According to Yishak Yosief "… the hill and the whole area around it known as Cherhi Aba Shawl today were originally called Gmbar Aba Awts and Shawl was in fact the name of a horse, whose owner had been appointed as a sanitation monitor of the area owned by the Italian administration. The man used to boastingly call himself Abu Shawl (implying he was the owner of Shawl). He had built a hut on the hill and the residents would look up to it and say, "that's Abu Shawl's house," and over time the name stuck throughout the whole neighbourhood…" See: Yishak Yosief, Zanta Ketema Asmera, *History of the City of Asmara*. Adis Ababa, 1993.

3 Belula Tecle-Misghina, "Asmara, an urban history", *L'Architettura delle città, UNESCO-Chair Series – The Journal of the Scientific Society Ludovico Quaroni*. Rome: Edizioni Nuova Cultura, 2014 pp. 101-102.

4 "… I sang this farewell song because I felt sorry for the people of Aba Shawl who lived in love and harmony. To me, destroying Aba Shawl meant destroying the long-standing cultural ties, value systems and social fabric of the inhabitants. I felt sorry for the broken hearts and shattered dreams of the young lovers and old acquaintances of that place. Of course, I was not against developmental projects in general but I felt that it should not have been done at the expense of the poor and the needy that were left homeless and uprooted following the demolition project. Fortunately, the demolition work stopped right near my house…" Alamin Abduletif was quoted as thus by Sophia Tesfamariam in her article, see: Sophia Tesfamariam, *Taking in the sights and sounds of Abba Shaul* (2009), in: http://www.dehai.org/archives/dehai_news_archive/jan-mar09/0367.html (14.11.2015)

5 During colonialism *sewa* houses run by women were associated with prostitution, although the Italian administration attempted to separate prostitution from the *sewa* business. *Sewa* houses were meeting points. Drinking *sewa* together allowed people to share common problems or thoughts. In the postcolonial period people used to sing in the *sewa* houses because songs were the most widespread form of political expression. See: Francesca Locatelli, "Beyond the Campo Cintato: Prostitutes, Migrants and 'Criminals' in Colonial Asmara (Eritrea), 1890–1941", in: Francesca Locatelli and Paul Nugent (eds.), *African Cities. Competing Claims on Urban Spaces (Africa-Europe Group for Interdisciplinarity Studies III)*. Leiden and Boston: Brill, 2009, p. 243.

6 Asmara is suffering from a water shortage. To increase the water supply of Aba Shawl it is therefore advisable that Asmara constructs more dams and upgrades parts of the existing system, especially old equipment that causes leakages and other operation trouble. However, the existing dams have a large unused hydraulic potential which should be more than sufficient to provide the Aba Shawl district with potable water. Aba Shawl is today dependent on water delivered by trucks, but this is not an economically or environmentally friendly solution in the long run. Aba Shawl is located close to the city centre and its existing water network; therefore, it should be possible to install a water distribution network for the district.

View of Aba Shawl

Source: K.Paulweber 2013

UNDER A SHADOW OF A COLONIAL CITY
A Memory of Childhood in Indigenous Asmara

Tekle Woldemikael

The city of Asmara and its Modernist architecture have received worldwide attention and recognition. This essay describes the neighbourhood in indigenous Asmara, where I grew up, under the shadow of one of the most modern African cities, with buildings, streets and infrastructure that were shaped by the innovative European Art Déco style of architecture of the early twentieth century (circa 1910 to 1940).[1] Around this Art Déco city grew the indigenous Asmara – the hardly noticed and talked-about Asmara. The indigenous Asmara served as the home of the indigenous cheap labour on the periphery of metropolitan Asmara. As Haile Bokure put it, Asmara during Italian colonialism "... was [a] segregated city with separate living quarters and shopping centres for the natives and colonial masters alike." According to Haile Bokure, the apartheid system in Asmara and elsewhere in Eritrea "created a deep mark in the Eritrean psyche which is a moving force in mass uprising culminated in armed struggle that claimed the lives of generations of Eritreans."[2] I was born and raised in the other Asmara, the indigenous Asmara, where the local lower, working, emerging middle classes (by local standards) lived, established families and raised their children. I will provide a short glimpse of this other Asmara, the life I lived in the 1950s and early 1960s. The indigenous lower-, working- and middle-class families I knew worked within and around the Modernist Asmara as factory workers, office help, guards, elementary school teachers, day labourers, maids and servants, artisans and craftsmen, street vendors, shop keepers, traders/merchants in the indigenous markets of the city and sources of unskilled cheap labour.

View of Aba Shawl
Source: S.Graf 2013

Home

I spent my early childhood and boyhood in a mixed (by local standards) working- and middle-class neighbourhood, known by its popular name Gheza Kenisha, in the 1950s and early 1960s. Its official name was Zoba Saba. I was born in a small room that had a shared bathroom and kitchen and a small cemented courtyard connecting the two. There was a big window on the side of the door that opened to the courtyard. Everything was enclosed except the small room which served as an all-purpose room for sleeping and dining and as an outlet to the outside world. The room had two opposite doors; one door opened to the street and was used for getting in and out of the room and the other door connected to the small courtyard, kitchen and bathroom. We shared the courtyard, the kitchen and the bathroom with another family who lived in a small room like ours – the configuration of their room was similar to ours. In fact it seemed that the two rooms were part a double room with a door in the middle connecting the two rooms. It was a crowded home with two families in two adjacent rooms, with each family consisting of three children.

We had electricity and piped water in the courtyard that included a water tap and a water basin beneath it. The room had a light bulb hanging from the ceiling. We did not have electric blackouts, except on rare occasions. But I remember there was a constant shortage of water. Every week a water truck sold water around the neighbourhood, filling wooden barrels (locally known as Bermil) and/or big, empty steel drums (locally called *Fisto*) which were utilised for the storage of water inside the courtyard or rooms. When the water shortage became severe, people in the neighbourhood bought water from the local wells which were sold in small quantities from vendors who delivered water in canvases (called *ghirba*) loaded on donkeys. The neighbourhood was kept clean and the trash was collected by garbage truck every week. The Asmara Municipal guards penalised those who threw garbage on the street. Up to the late 1950s there was a public health clinic that was open everyday for half a day; a medical doctor visited and examined sick people once a week, but was discontinued from giving services in the late 1950s.

Although there were regular utility services, such as electricity and garbage collection, not every resident of Gheza Kenisha had access to these services. The quarter had a few feeder roads and those who received services were those along the lines of the feeder roads. A significant portion of the homes in Geza Kenisha were small cottages, built crowded over one another on steep hills that lacked modern facilities, including electricity, water, and bathrooms, and were only accessible by foot.

My father served in the Italian colonial army during World War II and after his demobilisation, he decided to settle in Asmara, seeking a better life for himself and his family. He brought his young bride to the city and first settled in Gheza Berhanu and later moved to Edaga Arbi, both part of poor and crowded quarters of indigenous Asmara. I suspect my parents moved to Gheza Kenisha because it had a relatively good reputation for being an education-oriented, stable, safe neighbourhood to raise a family. In addition, Gheza Kenish was a quarter of the city where the Eritrean Evangelical Church established its central office, an evangelical church (Wengelawit Betekristian), a school, a printing press, and a clinic and training of nurses and midwives.[3] Around this institution, the adherents of the Eritrean Evangelical Church (often known as *Kenisha* (an Arabic word for a church) established their home and raised their children in proximity to the church and school. While Gheza Kenisha was quite an indigenous residential neighbourhood, the other indigenous neighbourhoods of Abashawl, Hadish Adi, Gheza Berhanu and Edga Arbi were noisier with a lively night-life. These quarters served multiple functions, including homes for workers and their families, cheap rental places for single people – some of them prostitutes – places of entertainment and drinking bars (*Enda S'wa*) for men.

My family rented a room in Gheza Kenisha from the son of a respected indigenous dignitary, a ranking ex-Italian soldier who inherited a property comprising several rows of rental rooms. Stories had it that these rooms were rented to several Italians before us. Amanuel Sahle confirmed that Italians rented rooms in Gheza Kenisha. He wrote, "When I was a little kid, my mother used to tell me that Italian soldiers lived in Geza Kenisha in rented houses. Just like the indigenous people."[6] One piece of evidence pointing to the fact that Italians lived there was a stray cat which came to us with the room since its owner had abandoned it without much plan for its future. We were told the cat's name was Moochi. We adopted Moochi and after its death from old age we replaced it with another cat and also called it Moochi. After that, all the cats we owned were called Moochi. We left the room and rented a nearby bigger room in the same neighbourhood – but with more space for our growing family of two adults and four children. In 1960,we grew to a family of six children and moved to Geza Banda Talian (Italian). This time my family moved to a house which we built on a plot of land they had bought the year before.

Periphery

We had limited contact with the other Asmara, the Italian section of Asmara, where the houses were big and spacious, and clean wide boulevards contained trees. There were also courtyards, two- and three-storey houses featuring beautiful gardens, and brightly lit shops with clean streets and glass windows. The colonial Asmara did not belong to us. Although Geza Kenisha seemed a safe neighbourhood, there was a widespread fear of crime, especially of theft at night. During the night all homes were locked using padlocks and wooden bars. Every night the police walked through the neighbourhood in pairs, patrolling the streets. We, the children, were warned not to venture out of the neighbourhood and to be careful of child kidnappers who abducted children and sold them across the Red Sea.There was one story of a lost child from my neighbourhood; the child was never found. That story sent chills down our young spines.

Most of the families were working class who were financially unstable. Many of the men were in and out of jobs. When they could not find jobs, they left their families in the neighbourhood and went looking for jobs in other places, mostly in Ethiopia. Out of the four families in my row of rental rooms, two of the four fathers left in search of work and economic opportunities in Ethiopia. One went to Dessie (the capital of the Wollo province) and the other left for Addis Ababa (the capital of Ethiopia) to never return. While the women were housewives, the men worked in and around the modern city. The fathers worked in the surrounding firms, factories, modern and local markets (*souks*) and shops in informal marketplaces and work stations (*Medeber*, which literally means a station/a centre) and as street vendors. They made a living in and around the European part of Asmara as day labourers, factory workers, taxi and truck drivers, teachers, office clerks, guards, small merchants, traders, carpenters, employees in the nearby train station (known as *Ferrovia*), milk factory (locally known as *Enda Eche*) and glass factory (locally named as *Enda Merengi*).

Although most of the women were housewives, some were employed as domestics working in Italian homes, as cooks, nannies, cleaners and/or live-in servants. They were referred to as *Gual B'dama* (Gual Madama), a name given to them as the daughters of their Italian female boss (Madam), who hired and supervised them.[5] There are least two types of *Gual B'damas*, those who stayed in their work for the whole week and came home on weekends and those who would go to work early in the mornings and return in the evenings. They often rented rooms for themselves and/or their children who stayed there while their mothers worked. It should be noted that some of the children were half-Italian, a product of illicit and sometimes forced sexual encounters between Italian male bosses and their female workers, concealed from their wives.

Notes

1 Amanuel Sahle, *The Asmara Few People Knew The Napoli of Africa?* on June 08, 2002. https://groups.yahoo.com/neo/groups/italo-eritrea/conversations/topics/3383 accessed 09/26/2015.

Edward Denison, Guang Yu Ren, Naigzy Ghebremedhin, *Asmara, Africa's Secret Modernist City*. Merrell Publisher, 2003.

Jochen Visscher (ed.) and Stefan Boness (contributor), *Asmara: The Frozen City*. Berlin: Jovis, Mul edition July 1, 2007.

Haile Bokure, *OH ASMARA!* (poem) posted on Fri, 27 Mar 2015 23:24:43 -0400 in Dehai.org http://www.dehai.org/archives/dehai_news_archive/2015/mar/0483.html, accessed on 09/26/2015.

Natasha Stallard, "Only in Asmara, Eritrea", An Urban Guide to the Middle East N.D. http://brownbook.me/only-in-asmara/ accessed 09/26/2015.

Sean Anderson, *Modern Architecture and its Representation in Colonial Eritrea: An In-visible Colony 1890–1941*. Farnham, Surrey, England and Burlington, VT: Ashgate Publisher, 2015.

2 Giulia Barrera, "The construction of racial hierarchies in colonial Eritrea: The liberal and the early fascist period (1897–1934)", in Patrizia Palumbo (ed.), *A Place in the Sun: Africa in Italian Colonial Culture from Post-unification to the Present*. Berkeley: University of California Press, 2003, pp. 81-117.

Haile Bokure, *Asmara During the Last Decade of Italian Rule*, ND in http://www.meadna.com/businessper cent20page/Commentaryper cent20pages/asmara-last.html, accessed 09/27/2015.

3 Karl Johan Lundstrom and Ezra Gebremedhin, *Kenisha: The Roots and Development of the Evangelical Church of Eritrea 1866–1935*. Trento, New Jersey: Red Sea Press, 2011, pp. 321-322.

4 Amanuel Sahle, Loc Cit. p. 2

5 This is different and should not be confused with what Julie Barrera and Ruth Iyob described as *Madamato* or *Madamismo*, institutionalised sexual relationships between Italian men and local women. See Guilia Barrera, *Dangerous liaisons: colonial concubinage in Eritrea, 1890–1941*, Ph.D. Dissertation, Northwestern University, 2006. And Ruth Iyob "Madamismo and Beyond: The Construction of Eritrean Women", *Nineteenth-Century Contexts*, vol. 22, 2000, pp. 217-238.

St.
116-5

GROWING UP IN THE SECOND ROME
Eritrean Migrant Women Remember their Childhood in Postcolonial Asmara

Sabrina Marchetti and Domenica Ghidei Biidu

This article is based on autobiographical narratives collected through in-depth interviews with eleven Eritrean women who migrated from Asmara to Rome in the 1960s and 1970s.[1] What keeps together the story of these women is the fact that, once in Italy, they have all been employed as domestic workers in Rome – one of the very few employment positions Eritrean women could have access to, even though educated. The large majority of these women have mentioned, during the interview, their frequentation of Italianised environments already during their childhood and youth in Asmara, where not only the architecture and the infrastructure of the city powerfully evoked the Italian presence, but it was also possible to become acquainted with the small – yet powerful – community of Italians and their lifestyle that remained in Eritrea after the end of the colonial time.

It is important to notice how this was a very specific period in terms of postcolonial relations between Italy and Eritrea. On the one side, about 10,000 Italians still lived in the country, predominantly concentrated in the city of Asmara, where they maintained a central role in economic, cultural and social matters.[2] On the other hand, these are the years in which the bond with Italy is increasingly represented in positive terms with the purpose for Italians to neglect their responsibility in terms of colonial atrocities and for Eritreans to emphasise their opposition to the federation with Ethiopia.[3]

The repetition of the slogan "Asmara, the second Rome" – taken from Mussolini's colonial propaganda – is a classic trope of the discourse enhancing the privileged relationship between Italy and Eritrea. This slogan was part of the Fascist rhetoric describing Eritrea as Italy's *Colonia Primogenita* (First-born Colony), i.e. the first, as well as the most trustful and loyal to the

View of a rebuilt quarter in the north of Asmara
Source: S. Graf 2013

colonial power amongst all colonies. However, the use made of this slogan by Eritreans does not go without ambiguities. On the one hand, the slogan evokes the idea of similarity between Asmara and Rome and, as we said, it is thus used to reinforce the idea of a privileged bond between Italy and Eritrea. In this sense, it mainly refers to Mussolini's effort to construct the Eritrean capital as a miniature of Rome, particularly through the development of Modernist architecture in Asmara.[4] On the other hand, it is important to highlight the biased meaning of the same slogan: this idea of alikeness does not immediately imply a cultural or political equal condition for Eritreans vis à vis Italians. From this perspective, Asmara's being second to Rome means to be inferior to it. Therefore, Asmara is relegated to a subordinated position in this emphasis on its similarity to Rome.

By taking the same perspective, we are looking here at memories of interviewees about their childhood and adolescence in Asmara when, although racial laws where no longer in place, Italians still played an hegemonic role in the economic and cultural life of the city, as its white elite. Institutional racism was not recognised, let alone problematised. In fact, the conversations and common activities that interviewees remember as products of a Italo-Italian cultural contamination will be actually seen as a form of contamination with a fundamentally hierarchical character. This is due to the fact that it was a contamination taking place between subjects in asymmetrical power positions, with the absorption of one's practices as a model with normative implications rather than an equal cultural exchange.

This asymmetry in the Italian-Eritrean relationship is also present in this article in many ways. On the one hand, it finds expression in narratives in which interviewees talk about the authority given to Italians in postcolonial Asmara and the respect given to them. When recalling these encounters, interviewees reveal a struggle for power to win recognition and the dependency on that recognition.[5] On the other hand, it must be taken into account that although the two authors – one Eritrean and one Italian woman – have carried out the analysis of the interview material together, this material was originally gathered by Sabrina Marchetti who is an Italian researcher; thus, at least partially, her interactions with interviewees might have been affected by the same layered historical and psychological aspects of coloniser-colonised relationships. In the case of interactions between Italians and Eritreans, this necessitates that the former negotiates the historical denial of recognition of the abovementioned reciprocal dependency. In fact, as always in the case of oral history and ethnographic research, the narratives here analysed are not simply memories of the past, but also the result of the interaction between interviewee and interviewer,[6] as well as of the analysis process.

"There were many Italians in Asmara"

After the end of Italian colonialism and during the time of the participants' youth, the city of Asmara still presented an enduring presence of Italian culture in its language and food. Urban premises testified to the Italians' architectural and infrastructural influence on the town. For some that had access to more Italianised circles, and churches, schools and leisure facilities – such as bars, cinemas, theatres, and shops – can be seen as the location for encounters and cultural contamination. Contrary to what was happening in Asmara under colonial rule, when the city centre and the Italian quarters of Asmara were forbidden to Eritreans, in the 1950s and 1960s some Eritreans lived in the same neighbourhoods as Italians. In fact, one interviewee, Azzeza, born in Asmara in 1957, says to have been acquainted with Italian culture and language long before her arrival to Italy because of the encounters she had with Italians in Asmara's public space. She remembers:

> There were many Italians in Asmara. Many children spoke Italian, in Asmara. And we are quiet [people]... In Asmara you can hang around with everybody. [...] There were many Italians... There were the Italian priests... Everyone spoke [Italian]. We were already used to Italians in our country. Here [in Italy], it was not the first time [we met them].

In this statement, Azzeza is trying to downplay the shock of her migration by emphasising her familiarity with the Italian community of Asmara. In her view, the Italian presence was pervasive and created a positive cultural mix. However, from her words we also understand that the peaceful coexistence of these different groups was possible only thanks to the quiet and friendly attitude of Eritreans. Which is to say that the coexistence between the two groups was only possible due to the privileges that Italians had in economic and cultural life, and thanks to Eritreans' attitudes of acceptance and submission to this.

The same perspective is reinforced when interviewees describe Italian authority as based on the Eritreans' incorporation of feelings of respect towards them.[7] This, in our view, is in line with the social positioning of the colonial times. These sentiments are well expressed by Semira, a woman born on the outskirts of Asmara, who later migrated to the capital to work as a domestic for an Italo-Eritrean family. When talking about Italians in Asmara, she explains:

> We gave a lot of respect to foreigners: Italians were very respected.

And why?

> I don't know… This is the way it was – I don't know how to explain… We had a lot of respect for foreigners. Above all for Italians. I believe that they were better off [in Eritrea] than in their own country. Actually, they said it [themselves]. They said so because there they gave orders, they were very respected and they always came first.

Here Semira is depicting the general attitude of those Asmarians who were born in the aftermath of Eritrean colonisation and who belonged to Italianised environments where Italians were always put first. In her view, the authority of the Italians in the town, together with the Eritreans' attitude of acceptance, might explain why some Italians decided to remain in Asmara after the end of colonialism and why for many years one could still find a small but vivid Italian community living there. Another example of spatial propinquity between Italians and Eritreans can be found in the words of Mynia, born in Asmara in the 1950s, who lived in the area known as the Italian quarter.[8] She remembers:

> I knew them [Italian guys], [many] with an Italian father and an Eritrean mother. In the area where we used to live, there were many of them. […] I knew some of them because we used to live next to each other: one was a driver, the other worked at Enel.[9] Some of them were studying, some were working in a bank, others ran small shops.

For Mynia the neighbourhood is the place for contact between Eritreans and Italians, and also Italo-Eritrean youngsters. Mynia is stressing the familiarity with them, the spontaneity of their encounters and their mixing. Propinquity is taken by Mynia as a concrete example of the easy contact between the two differently racialised groups.

A neighbourhood relationship is also described by Madihah, a woman born in Asmara in 1950. She remembers the everyday meetings with her Italian neighbours as not only occasions of physical interaction, since they shared a common courtyard, but also as occasions for the transmission of a culturally specific knowledge. In Madihah's memories, the preparation of traditional Eritrean coffee was accompanied by nostalgic conversation between Italian migrants and by language exchange:

> They spoke our language, and we spoke Italian with them. […] We chat while making coffee. […] There was a nice courtyard, so we made the coffee there.
>
> SM: In the home of these Italians?
>
> Yes. When the professor came back home, we made coffee. It was nice.

From these words, the semi-private space of a courtyard is the location for Italo-Eritrean cultural encounters in which Madihah's family seems to have a positive and peer-to-peer interaction with their Italian neighbours: they equally exchanged not only practices related to food – with Italians preparing traditional Eritrean coffee – but also language, with the quite exceptional aspect being that Italians were interested in learning the Tigrinya language.

However, in line with Anthony King's[10] view of urban propinquity in colonial spaces, we believe that the closeness described by Madihah was largely possible only thanks to the fact that some forms of colonial hierarchies were still at play. In fact, neither Mynia nor Madihah mentions a relationship of true friendship with Italians, but always one of superficial acquaintance. This meant that colonial divides were not overcome in the most intimate sphere. Moreover, in both excerpts one can find some reference to the higher class status of Italians who held jobs in the commercial, industrial and education sectors – a legacy of their colonial position as rulers of the country. This high-class status strikingly contrasts with that of Mynia and Madihah, if one considers that these girls belonged to recently urbanised Eritrean families that, from other parts of the interviews, we know to have been in a condition of economic hardship which demanded these girls abandon their studies to find jobs.

Thus, the social distance between the two groups coexisted with a sense of closeness, familiarity, and acquaintance. This illustrates how, as in postcolonial Asmara, it was the rigidity of the social positions inherited from the past that allowed different groups to enter into close contact with each other, at the same time maintaining the distance which protected the (former) colonisers from actually intermingling with (former) colonised people.

"We knew all the songs, everything"

Between the 1950s and the 1970s, Italian mass-media products such as newspapers, magazines, films and music were also circulating in Asmara.[11] If during the time of colonialism the diffusion of cultural items, especially films, to colonial audiences had been part of an explicit strategy of Italian hegemony,[12] after 1941 this process took a different shape. Rather than being top-down promoted by the colonial administration, Italian culture was something that belonged to the white elite and to which only some Eritreans had (or wished to have) access.

Women's magazines in particular used to circulate in the city of Asmara among people that read Italian. Among them are also Eritrean interviewees, such as Luisa and Luam who grew up in a pretty Italianised environment because they lived with their mothers in the Italian homes where they worked (as in the case of Luisa) or because a step-family member was of Italian origin (as in the case of Luam). This is the way Luisa remembers the newspapers and magazines that she shared with other Eritrean girls who, like herself, spoke Italian and attended Italian circles:

> *There was Famiglia Cristiana – you might know it – then there was Gioia which still exists, there was Topolino, La Settimana Enigmistica; and then those small magazines about [pop musicians like] Pooh, Gianni Morandi, Ranieri, things like this. And the fotoromanzi. And there was also this 2Più that was a magazine about sexuality that for us at the boarding school was 'the top'!*

Other often remembered Italian magazines are the *fotoromanzi* in which famous actors and actresses were portrayed in a sort of photographic novel. These were extremely popular in Italy during that time, and therefore also amongst the Italian diaspora in Eritrea which emulated what was happening in the homeland. It is important to notice that for Eritrean and Italian youngsters in Asmara, this women's press was a fundamental source of information on the modern and emancipated lifestyle of women in Italy. In fact, women's press of the time was not only rich in articles about fashion and house decoration, but also in sexuality, politics and science.[13]

Along similar lines, Luam also remembers other items of Italian popular culture – music, films, etc. – that she absorbed in her encounters with the Italian elite of Asmara. She says:

> *I saw all the Italian films coming out, like [those with] Giuliano Gemma, Ciccio and Franco, Bud Spencer…All these films. The Westerns of the 1970s: all of them. […] So I wouldn't miss one Sunday. Saturday or Sunday. I wouldn't miss one, when we were young. At 2 pm we went in and at 4 pm we came out, and we went on to the Italian Club for dancing.*

Again, in Luam's words, one can see the importance of spaces of intermingling and contamination between Italians and Eritreans. This connects to another dimension of the circulation of Italian culture in Asmara, which related to the image of pop stars who populated the imaginations of the Eritrean youth and spoke to them about "how Italy was". In Luisa's words:

> Italy for me was Italian films: all the films by Fellini, Pasolini; Italian poetry; Italian songs: Pooh, Gianni Morandi, Patti Pravo [laughs], Gigliola Cinguetti, Mina! For me, this was Italy. […] Living in Eritrea, the Italo-Eritrean

Cover of the book *National Belongings* by Jacqueline Andall and Derek Duncan
Source: Sabrina Marchetti (permission: Il Chinchingiolo)

> community was so concentrated on Italy that... All those things...[...] I felt like I knew Italy, even though I had never been there, because of [all] these films. Together, these statements give a description of how the Italian Club's dancing hall, and Italian cinemas, locals and bars were all spaces of cultural contamination for some Eritreans who, for different reasons, lived in close contact with the Italian elite. However, it is important to notice again how these social activities only took place in locations that referred to the Italian community, thus we can more often seen in these gatherings moments of cultural assimilation with the Italian model than of true exchange between Italians and Eritreans.

Another important issue has to do with the fact that these different cultural items have been very important in conveying a gendered dimension of Italian identity in a way that was strongly influenced by the glamour of the then booming Italian cinema industry, in which both black and white female beauty icons had different yet central roles.[14] This thus also, in some ways, offers a model of femininity typified by the contrast between black and white images and thus by extension Italian vs. Eritrean models in relation to gender, sexuality and eroticism.

Conclusion

These are some of the features describing what it meant for Eritrean migrants in Italy to have been raised in the postcolonial city of Asmara, where public and private spaces were imbued with the cultural presence of Italians. This presence was not without some normative implications and, in fact, it positioned Italian cultural practices (including consumption habits, lifestyle, etc.) in a position of authority towards other groups' cultures. The contacts which took place in the public space of Asmara had their influence on the configuration of postcolonial relationships between Eritrean migrant women and Italian society. Narratives from the interviews with Eritreans offer us an example of the way in which colonial discourse was comprised of a complex intertwining of intimacy and authority, proximity and distance. The ambivalence of these intricate forces is partially explained by the abundance in colonial discourse of gendered metaphors related to kinship as a way to affirm social hierarchies.

The hierarchical cultural contamination with Italy also revolved around several cultural products and consumption goods that were accessible in Asmara. We have seen in particular the role of consumption of mass and popular culture as part of the dynamic of the culture-contact situation in Asmara. This confirms how mass and popular culture is a fundamental gear of the legacy of colonial systems in shaping a normative relationship between former colonised and colonisers, with the continuing spread (and thus absorption) of Italian culture after the end of the official domination.

In conclusion, the contacts which took place in the public space of Asmara bore influence on the configuration of the postcolonial relationship between Eritrean migrant women and Italian society. In several key points in this relationship, respect and subservience towards Italians is clearly discernible, as well as idealisation of Italy and Italian people and the belief in the affinity and closeness between these two populations.

Notes

1 Interviews have been collected by Sabrina Marchetti in Rome between 2007 and 2008.

2 Luigi Bottaro (ed.), *Gli italiani in Eritrea. Esploratori, missionari, medici e artisti*. Asmara, 2003; Mattia Sforza and F. Luzzi (eds.), *La scuola italiana di medicina di Asmara. Rievocazione di un'opera di italianità in Africa (1941–1961)*. Rome: Arcuri, 1978.

3 Giampaolo Calchi Novati, "National identities as by-product of Italian colonialism. A comparison of Eritrea and Somalia", in Jaqueline Andall and Derek Duncan (eds.), *Italian colonialism. Legacy and memory*. Oxford: Peter Lang, 2005; Tekeste Negash, *Eritrea and Ethiopia. The federal experience*. Uppsala: Nordinska Afrikainstitutet, 1997.

4 Paola Gaddi (ed.) 2003. *Glimpses of Asmara Architecture*. Asmara: Liceo Guglielmo Marconi, 2003; Eugenio lo Sardo (ed.) *Divina geometria: Modelli urbani degli anni Trenta: Asmara, Addis Abeba, Harar, Olettà, Littoria, Sabaudia, Pontinia, Borghi*. Florence: Maschietto&Musolino, 1995.

5 Fanon 1952, op.cit. and Memmi 1957, op.cit.

6 Alessandro Portelli, "Across the line: Neri e bianchi nella storia orale", *Zapruder: Storie in movimento*, vol. 18, 2009, pp. 106-115.

7 Frantz Fanon, *Black Skin, White Masks*, op. cit.; and Albert Memmi, *The Coloniser and the Colonised*, op. cit.

8 This is the area called Amba Galliano which was built for the Italians during the colonial time.

9 Italian state company for electric energy provision (Enel is an acronym for *Ente nazionale energia elettrica*).

10 Anthony King, *Urbanism, colonialism, and the world-economy: Cultural and spatial*. New York/London: Routledge, 1990.

11 Luigi Bottaro (ed.), *Gli italiani in Eritrea. Esploratori, missionari, medici e artisti*, op. cit.

12 Ruth Ben-Ghiat, "The Italian colonial cinema: Agendas and audiences", in Ruth Ben-Ghiat and Mia Fuller (eds.), *Italian colonialism*. New York: Palgrave, 2005, pp. 47-56.

13 On Italia female press see Ermanno Detti, *Le carte rosa: Storia del fotoromanzo e della narrativa popolare*. Scandicci: La Nuova Italia, 1990; and Maria Teresa Anelli, *Fotoromanzo: fascino e pregiudizio. Storia, documenti e immagini di un grande fenomeno popolare (1946–1978)*. Rome: Savelli, 1979.

14 Stephen Gundle, *Bellissima: Feminine beauty and the idea of Italy*. London: Yale UP, 2007; Sandra Ponzanesi, "Beyond the Black Venus: Colonial Sexual Politics and Contemporary Visual Practices", in Jacqueline Andall and Derek Duncan (eds.) *Italian Colonialism: Legacies and Memories*. Oxford: Peter Lang, 2005, pp. 47-56.

Third Chapter

CITY AND MIGRATION

The creation of new images of Asmara leads us to the next mirror, upon which Asmara generates an image of itself, considers itself and projects itself outwards. This mirror is Eritrean migration. In the course of the thirty-year war for independence from Ethiopia, hundreds of thousands of Eritreans were forced to leave their country. Today, an estimated third of all Eritreans live scattered across the Middle East, North America, Australia, Europe and Northeast Africa. The history of Asmara is indeed a history of migration: its documents, artefacts, images and ideas have been dispersed across a fragmented world. Just as in the colonial years, Asmara's architecture is again entangled in geopolitical transformation on the global stage. The cancellation of the variable safety distance between the colonial centre and the colonised periphery creates a gap that has to be bridged at the expense of migrants. We follow Eritrean migration by presenting the narrative of *bella Asmara* and its transformation along the trajectories of migration. Migration creates a location for transformation (transgression, suspension) along diverse spatial and temporal dimensions. Moving beyond colonialism definitely involves, quite literally, moving: coming to grips with diasporic understandings of Asmara. The presence of migrants in Italy since the late 1980s has commonly been seen as a key factor in prompting some revival of interest for the nation's own colonial past. The section starts with a few reflections on how the absence of a decolonisation process might influence contemporary attitudes towards African immigrants in Italy and how migration has contributed to the elaboration of an Italian identity as well as to its deconstruction in the socio-political debate.

Annalisa Cannito's transdisciplinary project, *In the Belly of Fascism and Colonialism*, deals with the intersection between Italian historical colonialism and racism in contemporary Italy. It conducts a critical analysis of the present Italian colonial matrix of power; this is achieved through the reflections and critical engagement of migrant cultural workers, including the so-called second-generation migrants, who have an accurate perception of their postcolonial background, in order to acquire a non-Eurocentric genealogy of our European history. This project stems from the need to learn and understand the historical relationships between fascism, colonialism and capitalism, and how this history still shapes the present time.

Strolling through the refugee camps in Northern Ethiopia or certain neighbourhoods of the Sudanese capital Khartoum – in the footsteps of **Magnus Treiber's** ethnographic work – is a moving experience. Here refugees and migrants from Eritrea have opened up numerous cafés and teahouses, restaurants and cinemas (often in a makeshift manner) that carry the well-known names of their original counterparts in Asmara. Foreign environments, in which thousands of Eritreans live the harsh and precarious lives of refugees, have thus been renamed (in Khartoum) or the original environments have literally been rebuilt out of mud (in Shimelba Refugee Camp). Khartoum's Capri Restaurant will probably remind its Eritrean guests less of the picturesque Italian island than of Capri Pension, a family café in downtown Asmara that used to offer fresh juice and ice cream. Urbanites from Asmara connect these remembrances to various places and locations, and take the names and aesthetics of these places with them abroad. Far from home, a re-enacted Asmara keeps the collective memory alive and at the same time manifests the yearning for a better place elsewhere that may bring back childhood's lost happiness. The contribution draws on ethnographic fieldwork in Asmara (2001–2005), Shimelba (2007) and Khartoum (2009, 2011).

In her piece, **Hadas Yaron** describes and analyses the story of a young man who escaped Asmara and Eritrea and reached Israel, the country in which he currently resides. Israeli immigration policies have been designed to ensure that Israel remains a Jewish-majority state; contradictions and problems arise from this approach. Hadas wished to unravel how different places, including the city where the young man grew up and which he was forced to leave (Asmara), and the new ones he encountered (Jerusalem and Tel Aviv), coexist in his mind as part of a narrative of belonging, persecution and uprooting. Hadas Yaron also explores the notions of geography, space, politics and culture to which Asmara is connected, and the significance that the forbidden hometown and capital holds for the person living in exile.

L'oro
alla Patria
da Vita

IN THE BELLY OF FASCISM AND COLONIALISM

Annalisa Cannito

The investigation I carried out during the International Fellowship Program for Art and Theory in Künstlerhaus Büchsenhausen 2014–2015[1] is an extension of a trans-disciplinary project I started two years ago as part of my diploma at the Academy of Fine Arts Vienna. The title I had chosen at that initial point, and that continues to frame the research up to this day, is *In the Belly of Fascism and Colonialism*. The attempt here is to understand the visceral relation between these two historical phenomena, their enduring nourishment by oppression and violence, and present-day *necrocapitalist* practices. In other words, my interest is on the one hand to analyse historical colonialism and fascism, with particular reference to the Italian context, and their intersection with contemporary forms of *coloniality* and modes of *fascistation*. On the other hand, it is to endorse a de-colonial approach in all spheres of white-dominated societies (from education to politics, love, relations, work, etc.) through the thinking and critical engagement of activists and cultural workers that are precise regarding their postcolonial lineage and counteract hegemonic narratives given as natural and unquestioned. It is crucial to acquire a non-Eurocentric genealogy of our European history.

In this regard, I would like to mention the three people I invited as guests of the programme *Italian De-colonial Memory Politics* which I organised during my stay in Innsbruck in collaboration with the Künstlerhaus Büchsenhausen and the Italien Zentrum: Dagmawi Yimer, Antar Mohamed Marincola and Igiaba Scego (the latter unfortunately had to cancel her participation for personal reasons). Dagmawi Yimer, a documentary filmmaker based in Verona, was invited to present two of his movies: *Va'Pensiero – Walking stories* tells the story of two violent racists attacks in Milan and Florence, the latter resulting in the killing of two men, Samb Modou and Diop Mor, by the hand of a fascist nostalgic affiliated with the extreme right political organisation called *Casa Pound*. *Like a Man on Earth* lends a voice to Ethiopian refugees living in Rome and through this provides direct insights into how the former Libyan government, with the support of Italy and the European Union, often resorted to brutal measures in efforts to control the immigration attempts made by people coming from different African countries.

Antar Mohamed Marincola was invited to read from his book *Timira – Romanzo meticcioi*,[2] written in collaboration with Wu Ming 2, with musical accompaniment from Maurizio Nardo. Timira is a hybrid novel that combines memories, documents from archives, and fiction. The novel covers seventy years of Italian (post-)colonial history from the beginnings of fascism to the end of the Cold War, and is written from the standpoint of a black Italian woman. Her Italian name is Isabella Marincola, Antar's mother; in Somalia, the country of her birth, she calls herself Timira.

Igiaba Scego was invited to present her last book *Roma negata*,[3] done in collaboration with the photographer Rino Bianchi, which is a journey through the city of Rome that aims to bring its suppressed colonial past back from oblivion. Here, Igiaba Scego describes highly symbolic places and tells of their colonial past; Rino Bianchi takes photos of them together with the heirs of this history.

The Belly of Fascism and Colonialism departs from and insists on an almost absent critical debate in Italian society on the impact of the colonial/fascist heritage on:
- contemporary migration flows;
- the racialised and gendered perceptions of the constructed representation of the *Other*;
- the ever-increasing restrictive racialised laws in the field of immigration policy;
- the violent racists attacks that have been occurring since the 1980s, which in many cases resulted in the murders of black people;
- the spreading of fascist ideology and organisations, especially among the youth, throughout the country.

In the Italian society, with reference to the colonial time, the rhetoric of the "short duration", "lacking economic productivity", "limited geographical extension", has been masked for more than a century as *colonialismo buono*, that means a "good colonialism," and the Italian colonialists as *brava gente*,[4] "good-natured people". People recall the time when Italians were there to build bridges, roads, schools, and churches as if they were well-intended works to modernise the countries and help local communities. These works were carried out because it served the wealth of the colonisers and was a greater benefit for the motherland. With the construction of roads and bridges, for example, the transport of material was facilitated and the time needed shortened. Moreover, it was possible to have a more extended control on broken ground, difficult to be accessed by the military vehicles.

Because of Christian complicity in colonialism, churches were built to give spaces to the missionaries to carry out their work of evangelisation and civilisation of the populations considered wild and deprived of human values. The schools, first and foremost built for the education of the colonisers' children, the next generation of oppressors, were places of indoctrination where the superiority of western knowledge was imposed, both through the language of instruction and the subjects taught. The cultural heritage of local communities was completely concealed, as were their languages and their oral histories.

Italy started to fulfil its colonial imperialist ambitions from the nineteenth century, during more liberal governments, and expanded throughout the twentieth century, culminating in the most brutal atrocities committed during the fascist dictatorship of Benito Mussolini. Lands and people were appropriated by force in Somalia, Eritrea, Ethiopia, Libya and Tien-tsin in China. Occupations occurred also in Slovenia, Croatia, Albania and some Greek islands.

From the very beginning, the motive of colonial expansion policies is that of capital accumulation which leads the Italian regime to take possession of the land, resources and people of these territories. The genesis of the capitalist economic system – that is the system of over-production, exploitation, environmental destruction, impoverishment of the many and the enrichment of the few, privatisation of primary resources, land, bodies and minds – is to be found right in colonialism. Today, as in the past, the super-exploitation of the workforce of former colonies, as well as the extreme pollution and the devastation of fields, continues in the name of super-profits for companies and governments. The installation I presented at the exhibition at Kunstpavillon (Innsbruck) related to several historical and contemporary events connected with each other that I will contextualise here.

Modern Italy, as a unified state, had only existed from 1861. The unification brought with it a belief that Italy deserved its own overseas empire. The Italian Empire was created after the Kingdom of Italy joined other European powers in establishing colonies overseas during the Scramble for Africa. Initially it had been defeated in its first attempt to conquer Ethiopia during the First Italo-Ethiopian War of 1895–1896. In 1895 the Prime Minister Francesco Crispi ordered Italian troops to enter into the country, which resulted in a humiliating defeat for Italy at the hands of Ethiopian forces. The Battle of Adwa in 1896, one of the greatest defeat of the colonial troops in the history of European colonialism, become known as the "African's victory".[5]

The Second Italo-Abyssinian War occurred between 1935 and 1936 when Italy, under the fascist dictatorship of Benito Mussolini (who in his wounded pride wanted to revenge the earlier defeats), entered with its armed forces in Abyssinia and occupied it militarily for five years. During this war the League of Nations imposed economic sanctions on Italy, guilty of open hostilities against Ethiopia. On this occasion Mussolini made an appeal to national solidarity and claimed Italy to be an autarky. Consequently, some supplies of raw materials left office. The effectiveness of the sanctions, however, was diminished by the fact that they did not relate to oil and coal, which were essential to the Italian industry.

However, this act set off the resentment of Mussolini and consequently of the Italian population against the League and aroused waves of patriotism in the country and the Italianess myth. To overcome the economic difficulties resulting from the sanctions, the regime started a campaign called *Oro alla patria* (Gold to the Fatherland) in order to collect gold and other precious metals to finance the war against Ethiopia. In particular on the 18th December 1935 a very highly emotional ritual mass was established with the name *Giornata della fede*. The translation of *giornata* is "day", the word *fede* can be translated with the word "faith" as well as with "wedding ring". The main ritual took place at the Altar of the Fatherland in Rome and consisted of the donation to the regime of golden wedding rings and other objects. It was highly symbolic on many levels. With the request of the wedding rings the regime penetrated inside the institution of the family. The union between the population and the regime was sacralised. Christianity and nationalism were reinforced in the name of the sacrifice for the colonial campaign.

It was on the 9th May 1936 when Mussolini declared, from the balcony of his personal office called the *World Map Room*, the conquest of Ethiopia and the birth of the Italian Empire – one of the moments of major mass consensus during fascism. The nationalistic feeling of revenge was shared by Italian society as a whole. During the Ethiopian occupation, the fascist military commander Rodolfo Graziani was the author of the ruthless repression of the anti-colonial revolts. Because of all the atrocities committed, he earned the name of the Butcher of Ethiopia and the Executioner of Libya.

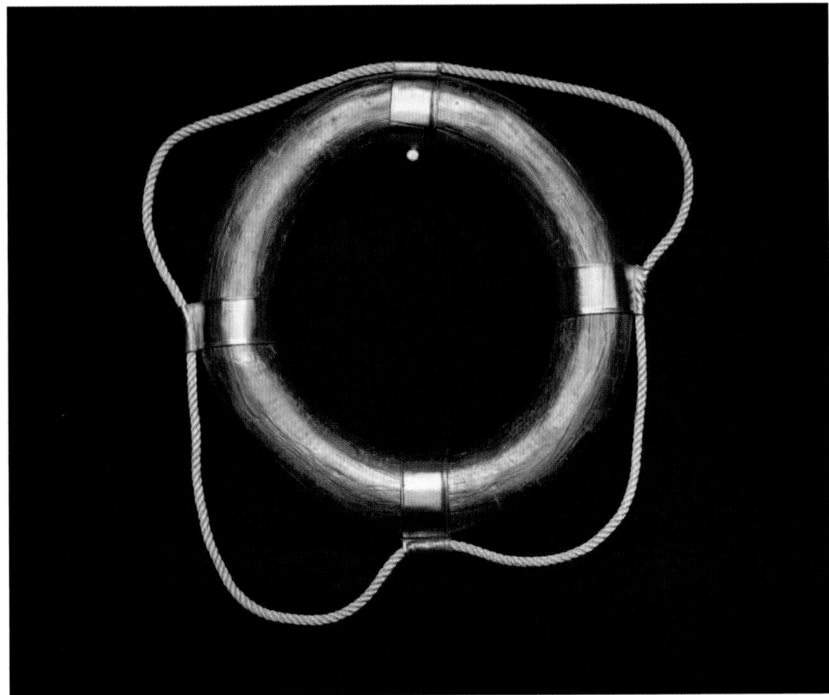

On p. 364: *L'oro alla patria* (Gold to the Fatherland), original postcard dating back to the 1930s (Italy).
On the left: *Lifesaver,* 2015, concrete/gold paint sculpture.
These photos are taken at the exhibition at Kunstpavillon, Innsbruck.
Source: A.Cannito

The movie *The Lion of the Desert* (1981) by the Syrian-American filmmaker Mustafà Akkad describes through accurate historical research the crimes and violence perpetrated by Italians in Libya between 1929 and 1931, led by General Rodolfo Graziani as well as the anti-colonial resistance led by Omar el-Muktar who fought the Italian occupation for more than twenty years. In Libya, Graziani ordered the use of chemical weapons such as mustard gas; destroyed plantations; poisoned water wells; decimated and burnt down villages; deported the entire population of Gebel in a concentration camp and executed most of the people; built a barbed wire fence 270 km long to isolate the Libyan partisans, and captured and publicly hanged el-Muktar.

The Italian authorities banned the screening of the film in 1982 because, in the words of the then Prime Minister Giulio Andreotti, the film "harms the honour of the army". This act of censorship lasted for almost thirty years. In June 2009, during his first official visit to Italy, Muammar Ghedaffi kept pinned on his chest the historic photos of the arrest of el-Muktar by the Italian colonial troops. On that occasion the private Sky television platform announced the screening of the film. Nevertheless, as Italian colonialism and its implications were kept in silence for many years, the event has not triggered a deep critical debate at the public level – in the following case rather the contrary.

In many Italian cities, streets, squares, theatres, cinemas recall our colonial past without any kind of contextualisation. Brutal generals are still celebrated as the saviours of the country. So here we enter the twenty-first century when a monument is built to rehabilitate fascism in the collective memory by gaining political control of a public space. In August 2012, in the small town of Affile, a monument was dedicated to the memory of Marshall Rodolfo Graziani. The memorial, strongly desired by the mayor Ercole Viri, has been built with public funds. On Affile's website Graziani is listed as one of the village's famous sons. An article dedicated to him states that "Graziani was able to direct his every act for the good of the Fatherland through his inflexible uprightness and scrupulous fidelity to duty as a soldier (...)". The words *Patria e Onore*, "Fatherland and Honour", a phrase that in the Italian political lexicon is closely associated with fascism, are engraved on the monument.

The building initially hosted relics from Graziani such as honour medals, pictures and other objects such as his half-bust, old newspapers articles and a street plaque bearing his name. After some interrogations the small historical archive museum was closed in order to clean up its image, upon request of the regional authority sponsoring the construction and the maintenance of the building. Nevertheless, since then, the memorial has been used as a meeting point for nostalgic fascists. Several events have been organised to celebrate Graziani by the association named after him, which includes the mayor as a member. After the inauguration of the monument, a small group of individuals quickly formed the *Anti-fascist Committee* in Affile which contested the memorial and the mentality it represented. Despite this and other actions against it, including a petition initiated by Igiaba Scego, the monument still exists. The story of Affile is paradigmatic of a more complex system of oppression, colonial amnesia and *fascistation* of conscience.

What is at stake here is also to unveil the covert way in which racist ideology is spread through politicians' speeches, assisted by the media, which say in tears that catastrophes such as the one dated October 2013 – where hundreds of people lost their lives crossing the Mediterranean – should not happen again and that they act in the name of justice, peace and freedom (the EU received the Nobel Prize for Peace in 2012). This while at the same time increasing exponentially borders control with security and deadly technologies whereby giving even more power to repressive Frontex, the European agency for external border control, and letting Europe becoming more and more an impermeable Fortress for non- European citizens.

Following the 2013 Lampedusa shipwreck, where most of the victims were from Eritrea, Somalia, Ethiopia (all three former Italian colonies), the Italian

Affile, Rodolfo Graziani memorial, 2013
Source: A.Cannito

government, decided to strengthen the national system for the patrolling of the Mediterranean Sea by establishing *Operation Mare Nostrum*. The Operation, which ran from October 2013 to November 2014, was managed by the Italian Military Navy in collaboration with Frontex. The military deployment included helicopters, airplanes, naval aircrafts, drones and many different technologies of surveillance, control and defence, such as those developed by the Spanish company Indra.

Some politicians' claims and actions are quite paradoxical. The day after that very Lampedusa shipwreck, the former Prime Minister Letta – during a speech held at the University of Siena – said that from that precise moment onwards all those dead bodies would acquire Italian citizenship. This was done in order to bury them in Italy, so as to save money for the transport of the corpses. Simultaneously, the survivors were criminalised and persecuted by the illegal immigration crime, defined by the dated Italian law *Bossi-Fini*.

Although the media have been mostly referring to *Mare Nostrum* as a humanitarian operation for the search and rescue of migrants, one of its hidden objectives was to actually prevent the migrants to arrive at the Italian coast by blocking the ships directly in Libya or intercepting them as soon as they left the North African cost. In this way, migrants could be identified directly on board and brought back to their countries of origin (the same countries from which they were escaping) through Libyan authorities. The migrants, once in Libya, are confined in detention centres with inhuman conditions, subjected to violence and abuses of any kind, as is well illustrated in the documentary by Dagmawi Yimer *Like a Man on Earth*.

Mare Nostrum (Latin for "Our Sea") was a Roman name for the Mediterranean Sea. In the years following the unification of Italy, the term was revived by Italian nationalists and later used by Benito Mussolini who wanted to re-establish the greatness of the Roman Empire by promoting the fascist project of an enlarged Italian Empire. He believed that Italy was the most powerful of the Mediterranean countries after World War I and created one of the most powerful navies of the world in order to control his *Mare Nostrum*.

When *Operation Mare Nostrum* came to an end, it was substituted by another border security operation called *Triton*, conducted by Frontex. In April 2015, a ship carrying migrants capsized in Lampedusa, resulting in over 1,000 deaths. Since then EU ministers have proposed doubling the size of *Operation Triton*. Instead of creating humanitarian corridors that could bring people legally and safely to Europe, they are fortifying repressive immigration policies, including the naval blockade in Libyan territorial waters and the creation of detention centres on the territory of Libya. That is, to dismiss the unstoppable political subjectivity of migrants and refugees, out of sight of the white privileged people living in European countries. The EU "humanitarian"-military operation is to push away the conflicts that these people bring with them, to deny it, to bury it in the desert sands of Libya, as well as at the bottom of the Mediterranean Sea. Conflicts that are a direct result of the Western capitalist system, the colonial past and its legacy. We are living in a regime of Necropolitics. The politics of regulation of death under global capitalism. In other words, the governmentality of death.[6]

Right-wing (and in many cases also leftists-masked) white superior policies are reinforced and perpetuated in institutional politics from the local to the European level. They are legal but not for this reason legitimate. At the same time, some people are made illegal and looted of the legitimacy of existence. Treated either as commodities (sources for super profit) or as dispensable lives (left to die). The survivors are continuously blackmailed and subjected to miserable living and working conditions without any right to appeal for a better situation. They are deprived of all citizenship rights and therefore made non-citizens. The hysteria around illegal migration is thus used to justify, among other things, increases in defence budgets (the latest example is the construction of a 175 km long steel barrier on the border between Hungary and Serbia) and spending on security technologies. While structural European violence acting through media, politicians and laws nourishes public opinion with hate against a constructed enemy, contemporary humanitarian interventions are launched by male white criminals in high offices. Europe, death's trafficker.

What is also necessary is to start to think about us, the natural white citizens of Italy and the EU, differently; to see that our privileges and hegemonic positions are an outcome of the fully brutally conducted processes of dispossession, exploitation, discrimination, death and subjugation. Processes that were carried out historically and that are presently reinforced and perpetuated.

The western states violate human rights, the same they claim to support. How many thousands of dead bodies should we count before politicians will take responsibility? How to face the brutality of us white citizens, who know what is going on but behave as if nothing is happening, or even promote "hate campaigns" through racist statements and actions? The *brava gente* over time get used to what they see and hear and do not argue and act critically, still believing in Europe – the recipient of the Nobel Prize for Peace on the one hand but the promoter of superiority with a talent to oppress on the other. Are we really able to get used to all this?

www.nelventredelfascismo.noblogs.org

Notes

1 http://www.buchsenhausen.at

2 Wu Ming 2, Antar Mohamed Marincola, *Timira, romanzo meticcio*. Torino: Einaudi, 2012.

3 Igiaba Scego, Rino Bianchi, *Roma Negata. Percorsi postcoloniali nella città*. Rome: Ediesse, 2014.

4 Angelo Del Boca, *Italiani brava gente?* Vicenza: Neri Pozza, 2005.

5 Ayele Bekerie, "The Significance of the 1896 Battle of Adwa", *Tadia Online Magazine*, 2013.

6 J.-A. Mbembe, "Necropolitics", *Public Culture*, vol. 15. no. 1, winter 2003, pp. 11–40.

Marina Gržini⊠, *From Biopolitics to Necropolitics, Lecture for Knowledge Smuggling!*, Belgrade, 12 January 2009.

1921
Ferovia Cheren

A CITY GOES ABROAD
Remembrance and Hope in Migration from Asmara

Magnus Treiber

Hundreds of thousands of predominantly young people left Eritrea in the last decade, many of them urbanites from Asmara, Eritrea's beautiful capital. These migrants fled an authoritarian government as well as economic crisis, but they have not been ready to forget overall positive experiences of childhood and youth back home. Refugees from Asmara actively remember various urban places and locations and take their names and aesthetics abroad. In the midst of migration's miseries, Asmara's re-establishment keeps up a collective memory and at the same time manifests the yearning for a better place elsewhere, which may bring back childhood's lost happiness. This article argues that Asmara urbanites did not leave without looking back, but literally took the city with them – in an aesthetic as well as moral way. Respective ethnographic fieldwork has been done in Asmara (2001–2005), in Shimelba (2007) and Khartoum (2009, 2011).

Passing Time in Shimelba

City Park had been closed for some time. Its owner apparently had moved on and no one else had taken over it. It looked run-down and abandoned, with branches blocking the way in and weeds dominating the surroundings. Without its name explicitly written on its veranda pillars, I would not have recognised that this small pavilion was copy and quotation of a large, clean and beautiful outdoor café in Asmara. There, City Park is located at the foot of Government Hill at the Western end of Godena Harnet, Liberty Avenue – a recreative oasis that merges the adjacent park with the busy downtown.

A bar interior in Asmara
Source: E. Lafforgue 2000

City Park, Shimelba Refugee Camp, Ethiopia
Source: M. Treiber 2007

Shimelba Refugee Camp was established in 2004, after a first refugee camp, Wala Nihibi, which originated from the border war (1998–2000) was moved further away from the border. Its first generation of inhabitants indeed built a town out of mud, drying bricks in the pitiless sun of Western Tigray, Ethiopia's Northern Region. Besides the usual rectangular farmhouses and picturesque round huts, someone had also rebuilt City Park to make this new and isolated place a bit more homelike. During my stay in Shimelba in August 2007 the constructor(s) apparently had already left – leaving a simple mud hut behind, but taking the idea elsewhere.

Shimelba's City Park lacked an adjacent park, but likewise opened up a way into the camp's downtown. Admittedly the main avenue here was sided by make-shift barracks, put together from mud bricks, corrugated iron and plastic sheets instead of Modernist Italian *palazzi*, but the number of cafés, bars, even restaurants and cinemas was remarkably high. And like City Park they carried telling names – at least to those who had come from Eritrea's capital. In Shimelba Asmara's Mask Place – a chic downtown bar – reappeared as a café and bakery, Sunshine Bar – which originally belonged to an expensive hotel – apparently became the camp's brothel house. The names of two make-shift cinemas – Hollywood and Diana – likewise referred to well-known bars in the Eritrean capital. Massawa Restaurant as well as Dolphin Café were reminiscent of Eritrea's seaside and major port – where urbanites once used to spend holidays and weekends.

Shimelba's Texas Café went beyond mere remembrance and hinted towards a more promising future in another world. *Everything you want is available* is written on the wall. Its carefully designed diner benches invite one to sit down and stay: their ostensible comfort, however, remained a *trompe-l'oeil*, it was simply dried and coloured mud – hard and uncomfortable. It matched well, that also the writing on the wall turned out to be an empty promise whenever I came in. Still, Texas Café also referred back to Eritrea. In the early 1990s a returnee from Germany opened a big restaurant outside Asmara, which became known as *inda texas* and specialised in wedding parties and weekend visits. Its owner, nick-named Texas, never appeared without a huge cowboy hat. Two decades later Texas stood for the lost hopes of those who had seen the world, but preferred to come back to their beloved and promising home country.

Despite plans to successively empty Shimelba the camp still exists and still hosts several thousand refugees, though less than before additional refugee camps opened their gates. Formerly strict regulations eased up to some extent. Permits to leave the camp (and even to move to Addis Ababa) are granted more often than before. In 2007 Shimelba's refugees felt like prison inmates – especially the younger generation. They had come with high hopes and found themselves trapped again, rendered into passive recipients of aid (basically a monthly ration of unground grain) and administrative decisions from above, opaque and unreliable. People sat around, got frustrated and became desperate to leave through one way or another. While resettlement to a third country was far from being a reliable option, keeping up morale posed a major problem. The majority of refugees were penniless – especially people from the countryside, who could not ask relatives in the global diaspora for money. Nevertheless Shimelba's bars were well-frequented in the evenings: although people did not spend much on drinks and food, they enjoyed entertainment and chatting. The loud bar music alongside Shimelba's main avenue indicated generational imbalance and the dominance of a youth who already tasted some of the freedom they once hoped to find.

Strolling through Khartoum

Tens of thousands of refugees have moved to the Sudanese capital Khartoum, mostly without valid papers or formal permits from the refugee camps in the vicinity of the Eritrean border in Eastern Sudan. Eritrean (and also Ethiopian) migrants – mostly young people, more men than women – started to settle in peripheral neighbourhoods such as Jiref, Sahafa or Daim. They have become an omnipresent part of Khartoum's social fabric, but remain bound to their ethnic niche and an unprivileged informal labour market. The so-called *habeshi* (Christian highlanders from both Eritrea and Ethiopia) are working

Capri Restaurant, Sahafa, Khartoum, Sudan
Source: M. Treiber 2009

as housemaids, construction workers, guards and rickshaw drivers. Sudan's economy, however, decreased since the independence of the South and the illegally employed immigrants have been among the first to suffer from the recurrent crisis. Thus it is more attractive to open one's own café or restaurant (although a – mostly inactive – Sudanese partner is usually required).

While the Eritrean capital was rebuilt from mud in Shimelba, Asmara here reappeared in the names of cafés, clubs and restaurants – and it enriched an already established diasporic infrastructure. Whereas Khartoum's Castello – in Asmara a fine Italian restaurant – was a well-known Habesha restaurant in the surroundings of various Ethiopian fashion boutiques and spice shops, Asmara Migib Biet did not comprise much more than a couple of plastic chairs and make-shift-tables under the shed of a large tree in Sahafa-Zelet. It may have been established by AMCE, children of Eritreans living in Ethiopia.[1] Eritrea Coffee House on the other side of the street also used to be a simple straw hut. Capri restaurant was located a bit further down the street. While another Capri could be found in Jiref – a simple tea and juice house – Sahafa's Capri was a real restaurant and well frequented by Eritrean migrants as well as Sudanese neighbours.

For Asmara urbanites, Capri is less an Italian island (incidentally very far off from current migration routes) but a famous juice house in downtown Asmara. Capri-Pension was a family place, especially on Sundays, when proud fathers used to invite their children to mixed juice and vanilla ice-cream. Therefore

Capri became more than just a name; it signifies a jointly remembered experience and symbolises good childhood. Of course, Khartoum's Capri restaurant was a much shabbier place with an outside area covered by plastic sheets, a public TV and a corner for traditional *Habesha* coffee, a dirty kitchen and a carambola room.[2] It served all kinds of Eritrean dishes – from *frittata* (scrambled egg) to *zigini* (hot stew), slightly depending on the current owner and cook – but certainly no ice-cream. More interesting than its menu was its outside decoration. Several paintings on a wall-covering cloth showed romantic island sceneries – perhaps Capri Island. More importantly, the wall itself was a painting which framed these pictures and consisted of red brick above and rough stone in black and white below. Remarkably it is this background that signifies Asmara itself.

The Wall of the Cathedral

It is not too difficult to recognise Asmara's cathedral (1923)[3] and its surrounding walls in this motif: red brick, built on a basement of rough stone in black, separated by thick white lines. Certainly the cathedral is most noticeable, but this particular motif may also be found elsewhere and does not necessarily represent Catholic or at least Christian symbolism. Well-known restaurants such as Cherhi (built in 1983 on the hill of Aba Shawl) or Castello (Alfa Romeo area) show the same motif and can be read as architectural quotations and tributes to Asmara's cathedral – Khartoum's Castello restaurant is even decorated with a wall-size painting of a church and campanile. Originally the cathedral's architectural style was common in Italy's Lombardy and other regions of rural Europe, where red brick was used. Some villas and hotels in Ethiopia, which date back to the Italian occupation 1935–1941, show it likewise.

In Asmara, however, this specific motif gained its own meaning. Here it stands for a very positively valued urban life, for freedom and leisure, get-together and sociability. In front of Asmara's cathedral wall, people used to sit and chat in pavement cafés or stroll up and down Godena Harnet, bumping into friends every few metres. Before the introduction of the mobile phone ten years ago, being on Harnet Avenue in the late afternoon was the easiest way to meet whomever one wanted to meet – even without any previous announcement. The Eritrean singer Alula Araya narrates in his song *Neahiteakle* (2015) how a man and a women fall in love with each other after an accidental encounter: the man had been in need of a coin for the telephone box opposite the cathedral. Urban life essentially happened in front of the cathedral; so, the architectural style of the cathedral walls became emblematic for urban life in Asmara itself.[4]

Fireplace, Shimelba Refugee Camp, Ethiopia
Source: M. Treiber 2007

Indeed, Shimelba's City Park does not only refer to its original in Asmara, it also quotes the wall of the cathedral (which the original does not). The little house in which Mattewos and his fiancée used to live during their time in Shimelba even had a carefully designed – albeit fake – fireplace in their sleeping room. It consisted of red bricks on rough black stone. No one who came from Eritrea's capital had difficulties in understanding this sign. Refugees from other places learnt to read it and made it their symbol as well – a symbol for a lost paradise.

Asmara as Experience and Ideal: Today, Tomorrow and Yesterday

Migration from Eritrea is full of crisis, perils, frustration and conflict – one must constantly reassure oneself. Leaving a world one knew and esteemed despite everything for a better future inevitably led to the poor and protracted reality refugees have to face upon arrival in Eritrea's neighbouring countries. Hope is easily lost after falling into this trap. Symbols help to construct identity, bundling individual and collective experiences, imaginations and interpretations; they mirror, produce and integrate meaning – and blur fundamental contradictions.[5] Life in Asmara – idealised of course and cleansed from the daily experience of dictatorship, poverty and insecurity – is remembered through symbols, effigies and names that give orientation, provide stability and make alien places familiar. Social life in Asmara has become a cultural value worthwhile to be extracted and saved from a home country associated with agony and injustice. It allows one to positively remember an otherwise lost childhood and destroyed youth – it helps to keep up morale in an unpleasant present situation and it holds hopes and imaginations of a good life to unfold elsewhere. Inherently it also contains a social utopia. While migration from below brings out human society's worst sides – rivalry, conflict, mistrust and jealousy – shared remembrance of a lost paradise also represents a vision of a seemingly ideal society.[6] That Asmara can provide moral and life-affirming orientation. While trying to leave, today's generation of refugees remains closely connected with Asmara and Eritrea – and inevitably the country's long and uneasy history. Present migration certainly writes on older traditions.[7] It is therefore not mere irony when young illegal migrants in Khartoum describe their poor living conditions as *kalayi gedli*, as second liberation struggle.

Far from Asmara, in Eritrea's northern Sahel mountains three decades ago, the poet Ararat Iyob dreams of the beloved city, which had to be left behind for the sake of Eritrea's liberation and promising future:

"Cathedrals and Minarets/appeal to the sky/call for Asmara's children/her pain echoes in the cracked streets/where childhood steps remain buried/waiting and waiting for another September."[8]

Notes

1 CARP was funded by a World Bank loan. Upon the project's conclusion in 2007 CARP was given a positive appraisal by the World Bank, specifically in "linking culture with education"; supporting "the role of the private sector and the community in cultural conservation"; "successfully demonstrating the value of investing in cultural assets"; being a "unifying force in post conflict societies", and "building community social capital in a conflict environment by promoting national identity and tolerance" (*CARP Implementation, Completion and Results Report*, The World Bank Report No. ICR0000708, 30 January 2008, pp. 23-24).

1 AMCE (pronounced *amiche*) is the abbreviation of Automotive Manufacturing Company of Ethiopia, a joint venture with Fiat in Addis Ababa, that assembles parts imported from abroad – therefore the nickname. Cf. Jennifer Riggan, "In Between Nations: Ethiopian-Born Eritreans, Liminality, and War", *PoLAR. Political and Legal Anthropology Review*, vol. 34, 2011, pp. 131-154; Magnus Treiber, "Trapped in Adolescence: The Post-War Urban Generation", in David O'Kane and Tricia R. Hepner (eds.), *Biopolitics, Militarism, and the Developmental State. Eritrea in the 21st Century*. New York: Berghahn, 2009, pp. 92-114.

2 Carambola is a regional version of billiard, played without cues.

3 Edward Denison, Guang-Yu Ren and Naizgy Gebremedhin, *Asmara. Africa's Secret Modernist City*. London, New York: Merrell, 2003, p. 110.

4 Magnus Treiber, "The choice between clean and dirty. Discourses of Aesthetics, Morality and Progress in Post-revolutionary Asmara, Eritrea", in Eveline Dürr and Rivke Jaffe (eds.), *Urban Pollution. Cultural Meanings, Social Practices*. Oxford: Berghahn, 2010, pp. 123-143; Magnus Treiber, *Der Traum vom guten Leben. Die eritreische warsay-Generation im Asmara der zweiten Nachkriegszeit*. Münster: LIT-Verlag, 2005. Cf. Walter Benjamin, "Paris. Die Hauptstadt des XIX. Jahrhunderts", in Walter Benjamin, *Das Passagenwerk. Gesammelte Schriften*, vol. V-1, Frankfurt: Suhrkamp, 1982, pp. 54-56.

5 Cf. Victor Turner, *The Forest of Symbols. Aspects of Ndembu Ritual*. Ithaca: Cornell University Press, 1967, p. 405.

6 Cf. Victor Turner, "Experience and Performance. Towards a New Processual Anthropology", in Victor Turner (ed.), *On the Edge of the Bush. Anthropology as Experience*. Tucson: University of Arizona Press, 1985, pp. 205-226; Magnus Treiber "Grasping Kiflu's Fear – Informality and Existentialism in Migration from North-East Africa", *Modern Africa. Politics, History and Society*, vol 1/2, 2013, p. 111-139.

7 Pierre Bourdieu, *The Logic of Practice*. Stanford: Stanford University Press, 1990, p. 333.

8 September is the first month of the Orthodox year and calendar; Ararat Iyob, "September in Asmara", in Ararat Iyob, *Blankets of Sand. Poems of war and exile*. Lawrenceville NJ, Asmara: Red Sea Press, 1999, p. 43; cf. Magnus Treiber, *Der lange Schatten der EPLF – Guerilla-Kultur, Wandel und Wissenschaft in Eritrea*, Working Paper 1. Felsberg: Felsberger Institut, 2014, p. 30.

טוטו
כשר
רפד רכב עמוס
בדאבל לוטו
עד
56
מיליון
פרסי המשנה גדלו
ב-50%!!!
פרס שני
1

ASMARINO IN JERUSALEM
Asmara from the Perspective of an Eritrean Refugee

Hadas Yaron

In his notes *Actes et paroles pendant l'exil* (1875), Victor Hugo describes his feelings and thoughts of being a person living away from France, forced into exile. He writes about his longings for Paris, describing the actual site and the city as a metaphor: "And yet he cannot complete these pages without saying that throughout the entire long night that exile brought about – Paris never left his sight, even for one moment. He noticed Paris. He, the one who has been in the dark for so long, has the right to notice it...".[1] As we shall learn, Hugo's words written at the end of the nineteenth century in Europe are still relevant today and not only for Europe and Europeans.

In this piece I wish to tell the story of Asmara from the perspective of an Eritrean man named "John" forced to leave his country and city and who is now living in Israel, among many other Eritreans who reached this country. This piece, therefore, is based on the details and analysis of one story, and has been written on the basis of different conversations I held with John over the years since he arrived to Israel. My aim is to unravel the spatial and temporal aspects of his narrative and trace themes in order to provide an insight as to what Asmara is for an individual who, for political reasons, are not able to visit Asmara and how the city continues to reside inside of him.[2]

John escaped Eritrea in 2007 through the country's border with Sudan. He escaped the military camp where he was detained. His detention, as is the case with many other Eritreans, was not based on a court's conviction and his penalty was not rated. He suffered torture before being forced to sign a confession for a crime of whose nature he was not informed. Escaping the

Israel's Little Asmara (2015), Eritrean refugees in Israel
Source: S. Caron, Paris

prison where he was held was complicated and put his life at great risk. But he fled since he felt he already had nothing to lose. He stayed for a while in a refugee camp in Sudan and then continued to Khartoum where he lived for about a year. People arriving at Khartoum – so I was told by many other Eritreans living in Israel – are exploring the way to reach the West, Europe or North America. Countries which are considered rich and developed received protection. Israel at the time was a new destination, easier to reach, and cheaper in price. John arrived to Israel in 2008. At this time many refugees from Eritrea and Sudan started to enter the country.

John spent much of his life in Asmara. He was born in a place not far from the city named Dekamehare. His father was not present at his birth while his mother left him with his grandmother and escaped to Nakfa. Both of his parents were members of the EPLF, so John and his sisters were reunited with their parents only after independence. After independence the family moved to Asmara. John is therefore the descent of the generation of nationalism and later himself became part of the generation of asylum.[3]

John explains that he already heard of Israel and Jerusalem in Eritrea. His grandmother visited Jerusalem twice as a pilgrim. She even brought oil from one of her trips that healed his infected ear. For him Israel was the Holy Land, associated with all the sacred places mentioned in the Bible and the New Testament, including Jerusalem, Nazareth, the Sea of Galilee and other sites. He even believed – so he told me prior to arriving in Israel – that most of the people living in the country are Christians rather than Jews. He first arrived at Be'er Sheva where he did not stay long and from there went to Tel Aviv. In John's mind, escaping Eritrea was first an ascent, but one which involved hardships. Therefore, he imagined in his mind that travelling to Israel meant reaching a better place, a safer place, a higher place. Yet, the encounter with South Tel Aviv and the area of the central bus station was rough. Drug addicts, prostitution, the neglect, filth, all of those things shocked him. He lived in a crowded shelter held by an NGO and tried to find out how he could lead his life in this new country. South Tel Aviv was perceived in his eyes as a no-man's land, with no clear rules and order. The first time he travelled to Jerusalem was just after he arrived during the Eastern (Phasika).

"How did Jerusalem seem to you?" I ask John.

"I arrived on Saturday; there were no cars. At first the city did not seem beautiful to me sice the entire city is made of stone, no colours… ". Although Jerusalem was not seen as chaotic as South Tel Aviv, it did not excite him as a holy place.

The encounter with Tel Aviv and Jerusalem and the way those cities appeared to him is very different from the image of Asmara he carries in his mind.

"Why is Asmara considered to be a beautiful city?" I ask him.

"Because of the Art Déco and the beautiful houses. The city is very clean in comparison to other cities in Africa. The city is safe, unlike Johannesburg; for example, you can go around freely, except for the military police who are searching for you...for those who left their base without permit..."

Asmara for John is a mixture of Africa and Europe – the product of the Italian colonial period, as he told me: "there were seven villages; they were united and a city was built in 1909–1910. The Italians actually built Asmara and the other cities..."

For this reason he considers Asmara to be a place in which one can find a more advanced culture than the rural areas of the country. The culture of Asmara for him does not overlap with that of Eritrea. Yet the colonial period in the city is not only remembered for its aesthetics. John also told me once that during the Italian period the main road in Asmara was restricted for whites only. This discriminatory policy reminded him, in fact, of his situation as a refugee in Israel since he cannot enter the interior ministry's office in Jerusalem through the main door but has to queue in a special line. Asmara was also a safe place, where order rules, since one was not afraid to visit the different parts of the city at different hours. Yet, the city has not been empty of fear. John told me that since Asmara has long and straight roads, he used to examine the street from beginning to end to see if there were any military police. One could be arrested even if he or she did not leave their base without permission.[4]

John was arrested and held in Asmara. But he spent also other much happier times in the city. He told me that for him Asmara "is Cappuccino, bicycle competitions...my favorite place was the Expo, a wide square where cultural events and games are held...". In fact John's family had ties to the city before he moved to live there with his parents. As a child he can remember he came to visit from time to time; the family owned houses in the city in different neighbourhoods. He remembers they used to watch Indian movies in the theatre.

"How did Asmara appear to you?" I ask.

"Beautiful, not big, rich..." In 1991 when John's parents returned, they moved to Asmara and lived in one of the neighbourhoods. Then he was sent to a boarding school and returned three years later.

"How were the years you spent in Asmara as a teenager?"

"Good years...we used to party, swim and walk... I stayed in Asmara even during basic training... it was a good time; we used to hang around, we had ID and we could drink wherever we wanted...even in prison I was held in Asmara."

For John, Asmara and Eritrea are the same since, as he told me, he spent most of his life in the country residing in this city. Asmara represents his family's history and his youth. For him, as he told me, the difficult thing is that he is not able to visit the city:

"I feel sad...I would have wanted to see what have changed for better or worse..."

John has lived in Israel and Jerusalem for the last few years. And yet, as in the case of Hugo, Asmara has not left his sight. He watches Eritrean movies filmed in Asmara in streets and places he is familiar with. In some of the films he can recognise the neighbourhood where he lived or the places where he used to spend time. In the films he says he can notice some of the changes which are not for the best: "the city appears much dirtier...". Yet, films are not a reliable representation he says since they are censored.

For John, Asmara is a symbol. The city symbolises his biography, and in particular the formative period and happy times before he had to leave the country and live in exile. Asmara represents in its good times order, cleanness, and belonging. A higher place, from which he descended when he went into exile. At first, his new home of Jerusalem could not compete with the beauty of Asmara. And yet at the same time Asmara represents his life in exile, the place he cannot return to since if he attempts to he would lose his freedom and even his life – a place has remained frozen in his mind.

Notes

1 Hugo V. (2010, 1875) *Ce que c'est que l'exil Binyamina*: Nahar (Hebrew), p. 75.

2 Riessman C H (2003) "Narrative Analysis", in MS Lewis-Beck, A Bryman and T Futing Liao (eds.), *The Sage Encyclopedia of Social Science Research Methods*, vol. 3 and Cohen A. (2008) "Stories from Refugee Camps", *Misgarot Media*, 2, 1-25 (Hebrew), pp. 1-25.

3 2015 [2009] Hepner, Tricia Redeker, "Generation Nationalism and Generation Asylum: Eritrean Migrants, the Global Diaspora, and the Transnational Nation-State", *Diaspora* 18 (2), pp. 184-207. Special issue, "Migrant Political Generations", edited by Susan Eckstein and Mette Louise Berg.

4 Bozzini D. (2011), "Low-tech surveillance and the despotic state in Eritrea", *Surveillance and Society* 9 (1-2), pp. 93-113

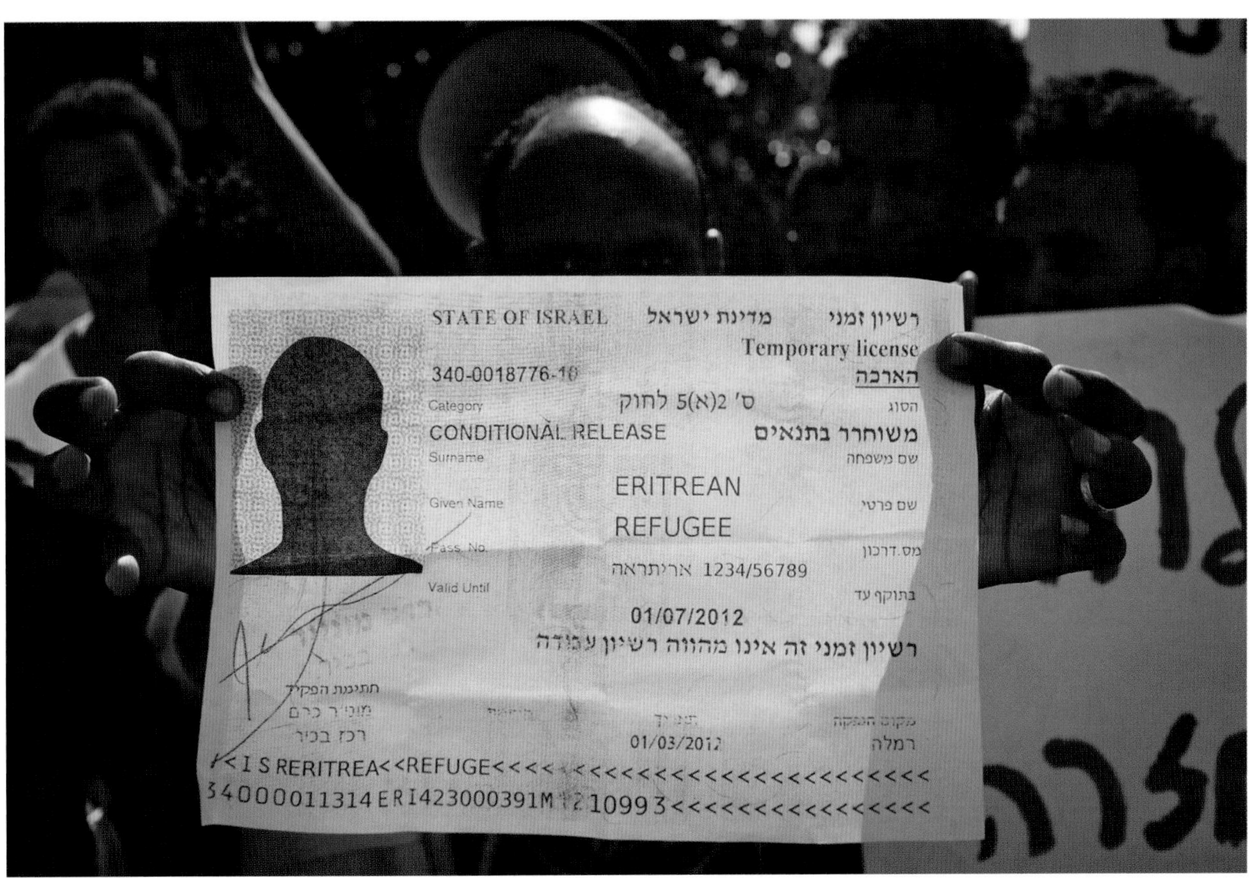

Eritrean refugee shows his document

Source: O. Ziv (www.activestills.org)

floreal
floreal

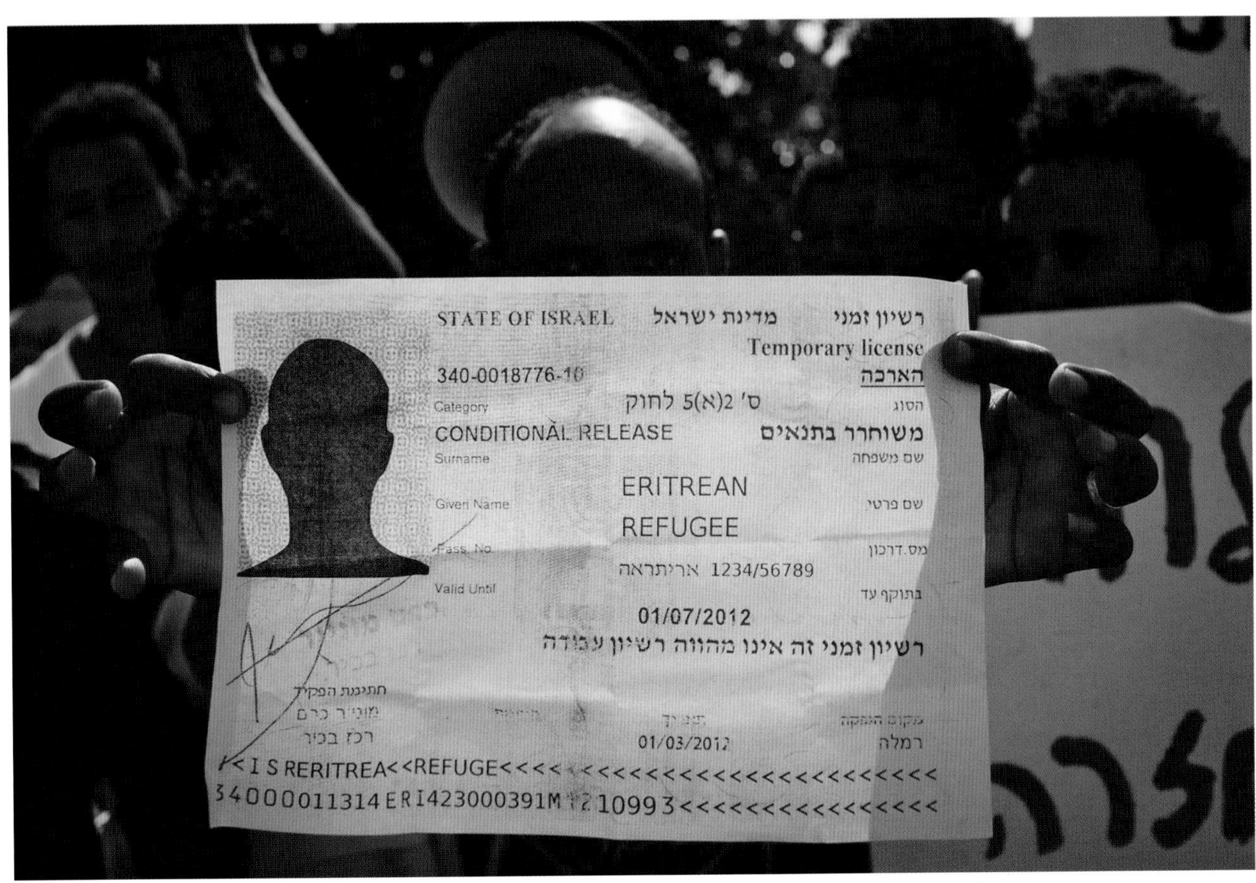

Eritrean refugee shows his document

Source: O. Ziv (www.activestills.org)

floreal
floreal

BAR INTERIORS IN ERITREA
Photo Essay

Eric Lafforgue

What do you associate with the name *Asmarino*? Although Asmarino means different things, the primary meaning is someone who is from Asmara or someone who knows the ins and outs of Asmara. An evening walk in Asmara and a stop for a gelato or a cappuccino in one of Asmara's bars is one of these ins, a must-do.

Bars and hotels can be labelled as paradigmatic spaces. Indeed Michel Foucault introduced the term heterotopia, pointing to various institutions and places that interrupt the apparent continuity and normality of everyday space. Because they inject alterity into the sameness and topicality of everyday society, he called these places hetero-topias – literally "other places".[1] Asmara's bars provoke events, both similar and contrastive, which simultaneously assert the sameness and the difference between contemporary Asmara and the city of the 1930s. It is, as Foucault maintains, the relational aspect of heterotopia that signifies. Magnus Treiber studied how youth in post-liberation Eritrea differentiated between clean and dirty bars and hangouts. Certain groups associated themselves with the clean spaces, which symbolise modernity, social exclusivity and comfort. Indeed Asmara's bars bring together a milieu of people who have a shared ideal of a lifestyle that they could afford under other circumstances; they simulate this in their spare time, often thanks to money that comes from family members living in the diaspora.[2] Anna Arnone's work explores the narratives of Eritreans in Milan who go to Eritrea on holiday and return from their vacation, and questions the impact of their imaginary of Eritrea as a place for leisure and tourism. The returnee is much more than a simple tourist since she/he also upholds a wider diasporic identity.[3]

1 Michel Foucault, "Of Other Spaces. Utopias and Heterotopias", *Architecture/ Mouvement/ Continuité* (*Des Espaces Autres*, March 1967), translated 1984 by Jay Miskowiec.

2 Magnus Treiber, "The Choice between Clean and Dirty: Discourses of Aesthetics, Morality and Progress in Post-Revolutionary Asmara, Eritrea", in Dürr, Eveline; Jaffe, Rivke (eds.), *Urban Pollution. Cultural Meanings, Social Practices*. Berghahn: Oxford, pp. 123-143.

3 Anna Arnone, "Tourism and the Eritrean Diaspora" in the special issue *Heritage Management and Tourism in Africa* edited by Boswell, R. and O'Kane, D., *Journal of Contemporary African Studies*, vol. 29, no. 4, 2011, pp. 441-454.

ICE
PURE
AQUA

RED SEA
HOTEL

NO SMOKING

NO
SMOKING

Fourth Chapter

ASMARA'S NEW IMAGES

In this chapter Asmara is viewed as a system of representation, where different ways of organising, clustering and arranging concepts and images lead to specific articulations of individual and national identities. However, the postcolonial approach may also imply a particular critique, one which emphasises the impact of colonialism not only on the society, culture and spatial form of Asmara but also on the way the city itself is understood and represented. While colonial narratives in the field of architecture provide the historical context within which one can (collectively or individually) identify one's own origins and sense of belonging, the ambition of our study of Asmara's colonial architecture is to offer a navigation aid within a highly conflicting sphere of interactions between local and international players, all part of a process of finding and asserting one's position in a globalised world.

In his widely-read book on nationalism, Benedict Anderson underlined the role played by print culture in establishing a national community: anonymous readers are connected through print, establishing a deep, horizontal comradeship that becomes the embryo of a nationally imagined community. The Eritrean diaspora of friends and kinfolk – pro-governmental patriots and anti-government Eritreans – has created networks that are maintained through new media, mutual visits and support. Thus the diaspora refers to a homeland which is shaped by the imaginings of a shared community, a long-distance nationalism as well as often mythical ideas of return. The way in which Eritreans abroad relate to Asmara both as a real and mythical place demonstrates its contested status within an imaged community. In cyberspace Asmara comes to stand in for Eritrea.

Victoria Bernal's contribution explores representations of Asmara on websites set up by Eritreans in the diaspora; these reveal the ways in which the city of Asmara offers a terrain for exploring and constructing Eritrean futures. The city comes to stand in for Eritrea, notably an Eritrea full of potential and on an upward course rather than one set in stone. While Asmara has often been viewed through the lens of nostalgia, this perspective is about the construction of Eritrean cosmopolitanism, as well as the prospects of new social formations and new kinds of belonging. Eritreans in the diaspora use the Internet as a transnational public sphere where they produce and debate narratives around culture, history and identity. The ambiguousness regarding location, both in the diaspora and in cyberspace, contributes to the construction of Asmara as a civic imaginary. In her work, Bernal introduces the ideal of linking engagement with homeland and a new dimension of citizenship that might be understood as emotional citizenship. Such transnational communities should not be essentialised, but nonetheless are subject to dynamic processes and struggles for identity.

Peter Volgger's contribution addresses representations of Asmara. The essay develops an analysis of the different forms of appropriation of Asmara's architecture that could be uncovered after the independence of the country. Transnational as well as national players hoped – and still do today – that Asmara would be transformed into an engine of national development. Ultimately, the essay's goal is to provide a theoretical basis conveying a sense of the multiplex in Asmara's history of the past few years. The author wishes to approach the making of architectural heritage from a new point of view, namely the interaction between (neo)colonialism, nationalism and globalisation. Architecture is viewed as a type of cultural heritage that has become as fluid as any other form of cultural capital. It is an activity capable of producing images, identities and memories. Progress can be reconfigured either as a perpetual process of returning to a shared heritage in terms of a restorative nostalgia or as a reworking of the colonial legacy in the light of contemporary concerns. Wall posters, paintings or graffiti are a grammar of urban communication that articulates vernacular and popular realities. While Asmara is best known for its colonial-era Modernist architecture, its historical and contemporary graphic designs also merit consideration. **Steven McCarthy** reveals that architectural signage, murals, billboards and posters in Asmara's urban environment play roles ranging from identification to commerce, and national pride to propaganda. Typography and lettering typically combine the Roman alphabet (formerly for Italian words, now mostly English) with Arabic and Ge'ez, an ancient Semitic script used when writing in the main indigenous languages: Tigrinya and Tigre. Although it accommodates a pluralism of languages and cultures, Eritrean visual communication is rhetorically subjected to the constraints imposed by an authoritarian regime.

Tanja Müller's essay deals with the Eritrean capital as an imagined place that once liberated would fulfil the wider promises of Eritrean independence. It is based on personal encounters with Eritrean refugees of the 1980s in Israel, Eritreans who lived through the liberation war either in Asmara or in the countryside, as well as Eritrean refugees who recently arrived in Israel. The way in which they relate to Asmara, as a both real and mythical place, demonstrates its contested status within post-liberation Eritrea. On the one hand, Asmara is a place of promise and aspiration, on the other hand it is considered by the ruling elite as an urban setting that distracts from the core values of the Eritrean nation-building process. Post-liberation Asmara has thus retained its status as a symbol of a better future, whereas lived realities in the city are characterised by alternating patterns of aspiration and despair.

Stefan Boness's essay portrays the hugely proud old men of the Eritrean capital Asmara who call themselves *Asmarinos*. In their European suits, classic hats and hand-made leather shoes, they enjoy their daily macchiato in one of the many coffee bars. In their youths, under Italian colonial rule in the 1930s, the *Asmarinos* were not allowed to enjoy such pleasures. The palm-lined Independence Avenue, with its almost surreal Italian landscape, was then called Viale Mussolini – it was totally off limits to the *Indigenos*. Today this dark side of the Italian occupation seems almost forgotten. The old *Asmarinos* are proud of the fact that they can still speak Italian and follow in many ways an Italian lifestyle – this is most visible in their dress code, reminiscent of Italian gentlemen of a bygone age.

65:55
1 - 0
A. MARCHESIN
ROBINHO
ATC
2
ATC
3

ASMARA ONLINE
The City as Contested Icon

Victoria Bernal

[D]oes one fall in love merely with the brick-and-mortar buildings that make up a city...? Do the other aspects matter more? You know...the unique sounds and smells; the way people talk, wave, and smile; the taste of a special treat from the corner store; the way a taxi driver looks at you if you slam the passenger door too hard? These are some of the intangibles that make up the vibes of a place, the spirit of a city; and Asmara, the city we Eritreans idealise and romanticise so much, may have a thing or two to teach us after all about the value of capturing this metropolitan spirit and use to build a better nation. (post on Awate.com, 12-11-11, first elipses added).

This paper explores representations of Asmara on political websites established by Eritreans in the diaspora to reveal the ways the city of Asmara offers a terrain for exploring, contesting, and constructing Eritrea's past, present, and futures. Websites such as Awate, Asmarino, and others form a dynamic online public sphere initiated by Eritreans in the diaspora that has been institutionalised over the past fifteen years as a vital component of Eritrea's transnational political field.[1]

While Asmara is often viewed by Europeans through the lens of an aesthetic nostalgia that casts the city as a time capsule, where exemplars of the architectural style of Italian fascism are preserved, to Eritreans Asmara represents something very different. The poster quoted above addresses this since it is stated that it is the spirit of the city that people love: "not the pseudo superiority inducing 'Italianesque' features of the city." As my title is meant to suggest, defining and claiming Asmara is as complex and contested for

Eritrean boys playing computer games
Source: Courtesy of E. Lafforgue

Eritreans as defining the nation itself. As the primal city of this small country, Asmara often stands in for the nation as a whole. In a predominantly rural society, Asmara represents the quintessential city. It is a city of bars and nightlife, and of teashops and cafés where friends linger to chat. Here people from various walks of life cross paths, not least among them the flaneurs and cosmopolites, proud of their urbanity. Asmara is also the national capital and the seat of power of the Isaias regime that has exercised a highly centralised control over the country since Eritrea's independence. It is noteworthy that Thomas Keneally's novel[2] paying homage to the EPLF guerillas is titled *To Asmara*: to take the city meant to take power in Eritrea. One of the most iconic images of Eritrean nationalism depicts the victory march of the EPLF guerillas into the city in 1991 at the end of the war and shows them being welcomed by elated crowds. Underlying that moment of unified jubilation, however, were the divisions between civilians and fighters, and between urban and rural Eritreans.

Eritreans increasingly have grown critical of President Isaias's regime and one-party rule under the People's Front for Democracy and Justice, the name taken by EPLF after independence. Online Eritreans can explore issues and voice critical perspectives that cannot safely be aired inside the country. Posters have begun to depict contemporary Eritrea in terms of a clash of cultures, particularly the culture of the guerilla movement as opposed to civilian Eritrean culture, notably that of Asmara. A number of posters contrast the easy-going, sophisticated, and life-loving *Asmarino* culture with the rigid culture of the fighters who spent crucial decades in remote areas, missing out on formal education and on participation in the conventional forms of Eritrean sociality that characterise civilian life. The Awate poster quoted earlier writes, "Needless to say, Asmara is now controlled by neo-communists who despise the *Asmarino* culture. The ethos from the mountains of Sahel [the remote area that was EPLF's stronghold] and streets of Asmara don't mesh well" (material in brackets added).

This poster, moreover, argues that in order for the opposition to succeed in overturning dictatorship Eritreans cannot afford to be "regional, provincial and parochial" but rather "familiar with and able to comfortably associate with diverse sets of people, culture and places." He goes on to say that this is no utopia or dreamland because Eritreans "already have such a place, such a state of mind, which can be claimed to belong to everyone, yet to no one; such a metropolis of diversity, variety and tolerance, where individuality and personality matter more than other tribal identities. That beautiful place is called Asmara." The spirit of Asmara, he says, is "dynamic, aspirational...and entrepreneurial, it is about diversity and flexibility." He goes on to discuss the personification of these values: the *Asmarino*. While *Asmarino* technically means someone from Asmara or living in Asmara, the *Asmarino* is a figure that represents Eritrean modernity, sophistication, and urbanity. For Eritreans, the city of Asmara is entwined with Eritrea's particular flavour of modernity exemplified by the *Asmarino*, rather than by a collection of buildings or a palm-lined avenue. An entry titled simply *Asmarino* on the website farajat.net that bills itself as the "voice of the denied" and presents news and critical analyses on Eritrean politics, opens with this line:

"As we grow up in Eritrea there used to be a perception...that everything that came from Asmara was the best" (posted 6-12-2004). The author goes on to say:

> *There was a strong belief that people from the capital city were good at everything. They talked better, walked better, sang better, played football and told jokes better compared to the rest of the people. And not surprisingly many found it as sort of a fashion to be imitating the Asmarinos...Asmarino was associated with sophistication. Asmarinos were seen as people in a class of their own. The Asmarinos themselves sort of believed that.* (ellipses added)

One of the first politically critical websites established by the diaspora chose *Asmarino* as its name. It is a name that not only asserts and claims Eritreanness, but a particular form of Eritreanness, one that is inclusive since people who were born or descended from all corners of Eritrea inhabit the city, and *Asmarino* also makes a claim to worldliness and broad-mindedness. This choice of name is the subject of criticism by someone posting on a lesser-known pro-government website, meadna.com. While the poster's politics stand in contrast to those quoted so far, his definition of an *Asmarino* is similar. He writes that term means more than simply someone from that city: "Asmarino carries other meanings such as elegant, smart, street savvy, someone that can adapt easily to any environment" (meadna.com 8-27-15). He then talks about the history of *Asmarino* heroism in fighting colonialism and Ethiopian occupation, and in helping to establish the liberation movements. He writes that "a lot of the *Asmarinos* you know growing up have passed to liberate Eritrea." Then he says:

> *Unfortunately, we have some Asmarinos who are, simply put, bad and they use the very name Asmarino to try to destroy what the good Asmarino's established...They have sullied the name Asmarino by using a website by the name Asmarino to try to defame Eritrea and by any means necessary to destroy the fabric of the liberators of Eritrea and I am sure many harbor the agenda of reversing our Independence.*

As this post illustrates, Eritrea's politics are bitterly contentious. For the writer of the opening post, however, it is the spirit of Asmara that offers hope of building real unity. Toward the end of the post he shifts toward a nostalgic tour of the city where places throughout the city are connected to memories of particular friends, family members, and inspirational teachers of the author's youth. He ends with "These are the flavours of Asmara that those who don't want to admit we already have a solid foundation to build upon cannot ignore." This post provoked many comments, almost all of them positive. One exception is a comment that objects to representing Asmara in terms of its centre and most desirable neighbourhoods rather than by "districts where the majority of Eritreans live." The commenter invokes the colonial history of the city when central Asmara was reserved for the Italians and British and argues that there was only "a brief period from 1958 to 1973" when life was good for "the few who...now remember Asmara...as *la dolchi* (*dolce*?) *vita*." (ellipses and spelling original) "The truth is", the commenter continues, the "majority has no access to the amenities and call it luxuries a city could afford...[the author] is just bringing or making a story he and most Asmara residents didn't live."

Asmara, as this last comment suggests, is first and foremost a city of Eritreans' imaginations, and the meaning of Asmara is more about the possibilities it suggests than about any harsh workaday realities experienced by people there. Asmara represents a certain lifestyle, not characterised by material luxuries so much as by peace and well-being. As the first writer argues, Asmara and *Asmarinos* represent a set of values and an orientation toward society that infused many people – even those who did not or could not even live in the city. Asmara is always more than a real city because it is freighted with all of these significances. Another commenter writes:

> *Thanks to HEGDF [the ruling party], gone are the days when the people of Asmara use to be like one family. All of the children of Asmara are scattered around the world; all what is left are lonely old people, children and the donkeys of HEGDF. The culture of Asmarinos has gone as well, to be replaced by the culture of SAHEL [the culture of the liberation front].*

Another commenter adds, "The culture of Asmara is highjacked by those street thugs of IA [President Isaias Afewerki] for now, but they can not take it away from us because it is inside of us." This way of thinking about the spirit and culture of Asmara is interesting because it allows them to transcend the city; the regime may physically control Asmara, its capital city, but the ideals of civic life and citizenship that the city symbolises cannot be captured and contained.

Eritreans represent Asmara, not only in the texts they post, but also in photos and videos they upload to websites. The examples I found suggest that the ways Eritreans see the city and the images they select to represent it stand in

contrast to the focus on aesthetics and preserved architecture from the past that are typical Western depictions of Asmara. A video titled *Tour of Asmara* and subtitled *A nice video showing how beautiful Asmara is as a city* was posted on the website asmarino.wordpress (not to be confused with Asmarino.com) on June 18, 2010. The video is shot from a moving car that is coming from the outskirts of the city (perhaps from the airport?) toward the centre of the city; it passes down palm-tree lined Harnet Avenue before heading on through the streets beyond it. The experience of watching the video is first and foremost the feeling of motion, the camera's eye never lingers on anything or anyone, but conveys the dynamic sense of city life through motion itself. Buildings are mere background, the action is from pedestrians walking and crossing the street in random places, and from streams of cars moving in different directions, punctuated by colourful yellow taxis and big red buses.

Eritrean men watching an international football match

Source: E. Lafforgue

The beauty to be observed here is not the lifeless beauty of the city's architecture which is hardly visible, but the inviting sense of possibility that emerges from all of the movement, the camera's freedom as it glides through the streets, and the hustle and bustle of people and cars animated by the myriad purposes of daily life. The city is alive.

A series of photos and another video offer a contrasting view. They focus on decay and destruction in Asmara. A series of photos appeared on Asmarino posted by AI staff (the staff of the website, AI is an acronym for Asmarino Independent) under the heading, *Eritrea: Cry My Beloved City* and subtitled *Asmara's Crumbling Buildings: Let the Pictures Speak* (12-8-14). The images show decaying walls, crumbing façades, cracked ceilings, trash, peeling paint, discoloured, stained, and faded exteriors, and walls marred by missing stucco or plaster with patches of underlying brickwork exposed. In photo after photo, few people are visible to enliven the scene in any way. In contrast to the video described above, this is an autopsy of an urban corpse, a city composed of wounds and scars. The photos convey the overall shabbiness of the urban environment, but more than that, a powerful sense of neglect, desolation, and abandonment. An upbeat song serves as the soundtrack, but does not detract from the sadness contained in the images.

The text that accompanies these photos begins, "Asmara has many a time been hailed as one of the most beautiful and cleanest cities in Africa," and then cites a website about its architecture as well as Michela Wrong's book about Eritrea.[3] It goes on to say that today, "Asmara is only a shadow and a skeleton of its former self. Asmara's acclaimed beauty and cleanliness is being reduced to a myth under the PFDJ gang in the face of increasing decay of its buildings, dilapidation of its infrastructure and fetid streets." In case the pictures don't speak clearly enough, this text makes clear that they are meant to stand as an indictment of the current government. Here the pride of Eritrea whose value has been recognised not only by Eritreans but has garnered international recognition is being allowed to disintegrate by those in power.

A video posted on *Asmarino* contains a different political indictment of the government. The video is titled *Eritrea in Pictures: Demolition of houses in Arbate Asmara on July 3, 2015*. It shows a series of images of houses being destroyed by bulldozers. One commentator notes that the EPLF, referred to by the author as "cavemen of the Sahel," "billeted themselves on the houses of the poor peasants of Eritrea for decades." He goes on to speculate that they were once squatters among people with little means."

Building on this theme, another comment includes this passage:

> *Nothing else in Eritrea was more glorified than the city of Asmara during the era of the ruthless ghedli [EPLF]. There were songs of praise sang for it and there were dramas played on stages depicting its beauty and glamour. At times, it felt that Asmara was what the ruthless ghedli was fighting for to liberate and it was true in many ways.*

The author goes on to say that when EPLF entered Asmara, "it took no time to get rid of its poor inhabitants," by abolishing rent controls and evicting people from government housing. He continues:

> *Ghedli had emptied the human and material resources of the countryside of Eritrea in its thirty years onslaught before it took over the cities of the country. And for twenty-four years, whatever was left hanging in the cities... is now either gone or decaying beyond recognition.*

In these last visual posts the desperate condition of Asmara comes to represent the desperate condition of Eritrea under the Isaias regime. Here the buildings are almost anthropomorphised as they come to stand for the deprivation and oppression of the Eritrean people. Rather than end on such a sad note, I draw some final words from *The Spirit of Asmara* post with which I began:

> *As we form alliances to topple the regime, and return the power to the Eritrean people, let us all ensure that the spirit of Asmara Shkor [sweet or darling Asmara] is part of what we do. It won't hurt to put on our Asmarino hats now and then, chill and relax a little, stop being so paranoid and uptight, welcome people who are different and think differently; add warmth to our handshakes and smiles; and learn to laugh at ourselves.* (material in brackets added)

Asmara, then, is not so much a city, but a civic imaginary. It is about the on-going construction of Eritrean cosmopolitanism and the possibilities of new social formations and new kinds of belonging.

Notes

1 Victoria Bernal (2014), "Civil Society and Cyberspace: Reflections on Dehai, Asmarino, and Awate", *Africa Today* 60 (2), pp. 20-36.

2 Thomas Keneally, *To Asmara, A Novel of Africa*. New York: Serpentine Publishing, 1989.

3 Michela Wrong, *I Didn't Do It For You: How the World Betrayed a Small African Nation*. New York: Harper Collins Publishers, 2005.

ASMARA
Image, Identity and Memory

Peter Volgger

Eritrea is a challenging place to think about the cultural geographies of memory in which to consider the relationships between public memory and cultural self-definition. Public memory in Eritrea is a volatile object, both the legacies of colonialism and the inequitable social and political outcomes of the present contribute to this volatility. This essay deals with the question of representation through images – the production of meaning through architecture. According to this view, meaning is constructed: it is a matter of invention or creation. Representation here is not a true reflection of reality, the discourse on imaging of the city goes far beyond simply trying to mirror accurately what exists.[1] Thus Asmara is viewed as a system of representation; it consists of different ways of organising, clustering, arranging and classifying concepts, and of establishing a triangular confrontation between culture, power and identity. In order to understand Asmara, we will need to explore reflection, images, imitation and the work of the imagination.

Consequently, our narrative of Asmara distances itself from reductionism. Instead, it considers a different type of colonial future, inherent in an unconcluded colonial past. It explores the relationship between modernism and the modernisation project expressed in architecture, intertwining these parts within the context of colonialism and decolonisation and looking beyond a simple history of buildings. Few colonial practices, despite the demise of that obsolete model of formal domination, have been effectively abandoned since decolonisation. Thus, an impressive pattern of continuity can be observed and today a nostalgic colonial rhetoric of modernisation is re-emerging. Mia Fuller wrote: "Asmara's physical continuities are the vehicle of complex local appro

Eritrean man sitting in front of a Ferrari flag in Asmara
Source: E.Lafforgue 2000

priations and rejections of the past, against a larger backdrop of aspirations for the future – a future that, appearances notwithstanding, is not linked to Italian colonialism."[2] Both local and international actors have been using the power of images and symbols to bequeath their stories about Asmara to the coming generations. Asmara's architecture has remained uncannily close to the Italian image. Image and identity often seem to be identical. How should we interpret this?

The Romantic Image of the City

Everywhere, colonial urban politics were mostly founded on a simulacrum: they focused on the valorisation and preservation of an image that was assumed to constitute the mythical origin of the town form, probably without any real historical precedent, creating an iconography where suggestion and imagination overlapped. A very good example of this is the construction of the *medina* during French colonialism. With the tourism industry, the colonial partition of the urban layout and demography lives on in former French colonies, resulting in the creation of a *medina* that is still marketed through an orientalising lens and is little more than an exotic spectacle.[3]

Indeed most former colonial cities retain obvious markers of their colonial past, mostly in combination with highly visible changes to what is left. "By contrast, Asmara's colonial architecture and urban layout are so unchanged today that they remain uncannily close to the Italian image in which they were designed".[4] Thanks to this Asmara offers a paradigmatic example of one of the key processes involved in the practices of representation. What stands before the traveller's eyes is a mirage. This is perhaps the most common topos used to express the illusion of waiting that, far from vanishing, brings us back the image of an unaltered city where time almost seems to have stopped in a dimension suspended between the evocation of a disappeared reality and the projection of a renewed imagery.

Asmara emerges out of the current debate as a prime example of modern colonial architecture that can still be investigated since most of the structures are well preserved. Many visitors are surprised by the illusion of a parallel universe offered by Asmara, one that can only be described in terms of "time stands still". The mere act of walking in the city of Asmara recalls a moment in Marcel Proust's *À la recherche du temps perdu*, in which the protagonist literally trips over uneven paving stones, leading to an obscure but powerful flash of remembrance of a past experience. In *Present Pasts*, Andreas Huyssen describes how people require memory discourses in order to comprehend the core structure of the world that surrounds them.[5] Imaging the city as a crossroads of memory, nostalgia and modernity recalls Andreas Huyssen's conception of present day Asmara as an urban palimpsest, where the city's spaces hold memories of what was there before. Huyssen also highlights our current obsession with colonising the past, drily mocking the insincerity of this trend: memory in the city has often been written over or erased, and he outlines how this effacement has created a strong desire for narratives of the past. Indeed, he claims that the "seduction of the archive" and its trove of stories of human achievement and suffering has never been greater. In much conventional urban conservation he finds potted histories nailing us to a censored version of the past, or to a past that is narcotic, careful to avoid any engagement with present furies. The romantic image of the city as a representation of a world that has already been imagined and actually preexisted the tourist's own discovery.[6]

Of course, the colonial period constitutes a key stage in the emergence of Eritrean modernism, and the colonial heritage demonstrates a broad range of responses to complex ideological and cultural conditions. Since the country gained independence in 1993, Asmara has generated a set of descriptive tropes, such as *The Forgotten City* (Street 1997), *The City of Dreams* (Ofori, Scott and Gebremedhin 2005), *The Frozen City* (Boness and Fischer 2006), *The Secret City* (Denison, Yu Ren and Gebremedhin 2007) or *Asmara Dream* (Barbon 2009). In most cases all these images are a combination of a romantic spirit of discovery and an exploration of the exotic, combined with political disillusionment with the present and the mechanisms of colonial nostalgia. Mia Fuller claims: "Dubbing the city's 'secret', which the book *Asmara: Africa's Secret Modernist City* did in 2003, suggests that it was forgotten and has now been rediscovered, as an earlier magazine article *The Forgotten City* had already implied [...]. Other portrayals, like the photography book entitled *Asmara, the Frozen City*, add to this aestheticising intimation of frozen time [...]. *Asmara Dream*, a book of hazy, 'timeless' images, further likens visiting the city to experiencing a dream-state [...]".[7] Hence, it is easy to create a set of clichés that reach into the micro-texture of Asmara: espresso machines, cappuccino, Cinquecento taxis and the daily *passeggiata* melt into a specific atmosphere.

Recognising Asmara's potential after the independence of Eritrea in 1993, Gebremedhin's first decision was to hire Edward Denison, a British photographer who had already travelled in Eritrea: "A big part of our work (...) was about getting (the modern heritage of Asmara) into the international domain: we gonna get the support of UNESCO, we gonna get the support of the World Monuments Fund. (...) So we sent out masses of e-mails to these organisations."[8] The book *Asmara, Africa's Secret Modernist City* literally reads like a call for support; it was meant to celebrate Asmara and prepare

An Asmara interior where Eritrean men meet for a Cappuccino
Source: E. Lafforgue 2000

it for capitalisation as a tourist destination. Its rhetoric, combined with the aesthetic appeal of the highly visual content, created the romantic image of Bella Asmara. Denison described the city as follows: "Asmara is, by any standard, not simply a most convivial city, well planned and executed; its physical character – its architecture and urban spaces – also reflects strongly a range of international influences."[9] He attributed the development potential of the modern architecture of Asmara to two features of the city that he perceived: a convivial city and a safe place to live. In this way, he emphasised the European character of the city.

Mia Fuller has described postliberation Asmara as a vehicle for complex local appropriations and rejections of the past – against the larger backdrop of the future – that is not linked only to Italian colonialism: "The photogenic representation [the icon of the Italian city] is the perfect snapshot of the past".[10] It is also the result of involvement by many local and foreign actors who have developed their own strategies for the appropriation of Asmara.

However, Asmara has totally changed in the past thirty years. Asmara has become Greater Asmara, one of the fastest growing cities in Africa. What is the relationship between the historic centre and the rest? The invention of a memory providing an alternative to the real stratification of historical events often involves the return to a fictitious figure through an authentic image. On the basis of this mystification (where the authentic overlaps with the real), a memory can be created that recognises the Asmara Style as a code for a universally decipherable and transmissible communication; the World Heritage Site thus becomes a paradigmatic event of aspiration.[11] Up against the necessity of protecting a traditional centre that results from the superposing of European imagery on an African city, and is a typically western legacy subject to preservation and valorisation, the site retains a glimmer of that inclination to change and balance that has always been typical of towns that have arisen on the edge of the desert. The neglect of a traditional (European) centre constitutes a natural reaction to the distortion imposed by European thought. This reaction has materialised in new spaces and relations that are able to reinterpret the alternation between the original conditions and the new ones. More importantly, we have tried to move beyond a perspective of Asmara authored solely by external viewpoints to start understanding Asmara's internal struggle to create its own identity. This is also where the metaphor of the mirror is pushed to its limits. Asmara is not merely represented in the mirrors held up to it by colonial modernities or national myths. Asmara does not merely reflect, it sometimes moves beyond this representation in an unexpected, surprising way.

The tensions between the formal and informal city, between architecture designed by architects and architecture built without any architects, have existed ever since modern urbanism began as the profession of town creation. But in the romantic representation of *Bella Asmara*, tension is absent. Svetlana Boym summarised the mechanisms of the romantic image: 'The twentieth century began with utopia and ended with [colonial] nostalgia. Optimistic belief in the future became outmoded, while nostalgia, for better or worse, never went out of fashion, remaining uncannily contemporary [...]. Nostalgia is a sentiment of loss and displacement, but it is also a romance with one's own fantasy.'[12] But simply put, it is the desire to come back to an idealised past.

Asmara as a National Symbol

In his paper of 2007, Gebremedhin argued why the colonial city should be preserved although it had deliberately been created as the abode of a fascist regime that wanted a place under the African sky for Italians and excluded Eritreans: "Eritreans, however, they have no quarrel with the buildings. They have instead successfully adopted the Modernist architecture of Asmara and reinvented its life space in their own manner. They cannot understand those who argue against such a bold and mature stance.'[13] After the independence war, Eritrean people saw their city as an expression of national sacrifice and thus an integral part of Eritrean nationalism. One Eritrean commentator voiced this clearly: "Asmara is our Jerusalem, the goal of our pilgrimage! *Bella Asmara* has become a symbol of Eritrea's newly won national sovereignty."[14]

After a brief period of opening up, Eritrea's government turned the cultural capital of Asmara into a static symbol of Eritrean nationalism. In turn, Eritrea's policy of self-reliance at all costs (including serious human rights violations) disappointed the World Bank's interest in post-conflict reconstruction and the concept of the shared heritage. The Eritrean government has been sustaining a conflict over its border with Ethiopia. In Eritrea, the capital city issue has always been inextricably connected to geopolitics and caught up in the border conflict with Ethiopia. The notion of new discovery should not obscure the fact that we are not simply dealing with a return to Italian architecture originating from the interwar period. Created in a laboratory of European Modernist fantasies, the colonial architectural heritage stands both for a timeless example of Modernity and for Modernity as a programme. Rabinow has argued that the colonies "constituted a laboratory of experimentation for new arts of government capable of bringing a modern and healthy society into being."[15]

Based on ideologies of progress and development through the organisation of urban space, the state developed the norms and forms of modernity. In her study (2007) Mia Fuller applied Rabinow's theories on Italian colonialism in Asmara and indicated how the Italian colonial government had relied on modern architectural practices: "The colonies served the colonisers as a 'laboratory' for testing modern techniques, which they regarded as being easier to realise in reference to the legal 'state of exception'. The laboratory paradigm had to be expanded, however."[16]

Asmara illuminates the urban transfiguration of the postcolonial dilemma – with Eritrean independence in 1993 raising fundamental questions regarding the country's past and its architecture. The protracted war had attracted the interest of numerous researchers, not only because of its implications for the redefinition of the geopolitical landscape of the Horn of Africa, but also because of the ways in which it had reorganised Eritrean society. The neither-peace-nor-war-situation in contemporary Eritrea has led to a less hopeful situation. Of course, national identity as perceived by a government is inherently tied to the image of a splendid cultural past. According to Wallerstein, a state can create a national culture through its monopoly of policies: "A national identity based on shorter-term political interest and the ideology of struggle emerged as the driving force behind most nationalist movements. Once independence was achieved, the glue that bound together the various groups no longer held."[17] The question of Eritrean national identity is intimately connected to its colonial architecture: "The Italian colonial period between 1890 and 1941 was a crucial moment in the definition of those social and political transformations which contributed to the formation of Eritrea as a nation."[18] Identities and aesthetics in today's Asmara still refer to colonial modernity. This is the way in which Asmara takes part in colonial nostalgia – a longing for a mythical golden age of (colonial) modernity. The constant propaganda invocing an image of Eritrea as a small country surrounded by mighty enemies (border conflicts) shows that for Eritrea's ruling clique the liberation struggle has not ended with independence. Indeed, the Eritrean nation stands above all.

Magnus Treiber documented young urbanites in Asmara, who have developed their own aesthetic ideas concerning a clean life, leading to quite different, even rivalling, urban lifestyle milieus. Engaged in a high Modernist mission, the government makes no distinction between physical and moral pollution. Plastic bags are forbidden, beggars and prostitutes are transferred to the countryside or to the military camp of Sawa. Features of architecture become features of the nation. The insistence on cleanliness, order and security in Asmara have led to a restrictive definition of urbanity and public space.[19] As Roland Barthes pointed out, "The obsession with cleanliness is certainly a practice of immobilising time".[20]

Christoph Rausch mentioned an example of a direct reference to the colonial order. During the Ethiopian occupation, many owners heightened the walls around their properties for safety reasons; this was a major, visible alteration of Asmara's street view. However, the global call for the preservation of Asmara's heritage has effectively provided the Eritrean government with the means to discretely exercise disciplinary power. An orchestrated press campaign was launched to reduce the height of walls around privately-owned houses: "Asmara is an open city, so walls should only be 1.20 m high. The 1938 master plan dictates this. (...) The government is now urging to abolish the walls."[21]

Mimicry and Urban Lifestyles

The concept of mimicry, as discussed by Homi Bhabha, is not as simple as it seems at first instance, but a complex one. My focus here is on the various ways in which mimicry operated not only during the colonial era – to mimic the whites became the ultimate destiny of all the racially distinguished people – but also how it has crept into postcolonial times. The older *Asmarino* – an urban *dandy* and *flaneur* – deals with the colonial past, this repressed past reemerges in the recoding of urban and neo-bourgeois space. Their stories are innocent or cunning but unique and entertaining with a lot of charm, their memories are very selective, including the *Regina Margherita* and many anecdotes about the Italian past. The *Asmarino* belongs to an imagined class in a non-hegemonic state, the subordinate subject's transgressive imitation of the dominant identity is very much evident in his self-production as a 1930s Italian coloniser. The urban *dandy*, functioning as a subject of transition, the past as well as the future, has historically also been a mode of expression of metropolitan subjectivity. He embodies a simultaneous identification and counteridentification with the dominant social imaginary. This kind of subversive dandyism Bhabha has termed *mimicry*. At the same time the *Asmarino* embodies the desire to introduce urban lifestyle in the city of Asmara.[22]

Thus the *Asmarini* imitate Italian bourgeois lifestyles and their rhetoric. Strong elements within the revolutionary forces are promoting the rationalisation of society in the name of progress. It is rationalisation – usually also conceived as the solution to problems of poverty and backwardness in the periphery – that provides the impetus for revolution. In this way, Eritrea exemplifies features of modernity that have already disappeared from the Western world; for example, political and economic modernisation in the city of Asmara are expressed within the spheres of culture and architecture. This results from an interest in the symbolic value that was attributed to architecture as a means of urban planning during the colonial period; this concept not only stood for the aesthetic aspect of modernism, but also for the plannability of social progress and the dawn of a new society. Furthermore, a naturalised belief in progress is being used against the influence of globalisation. Both the Eritrean government and transnational organisations (such as the European Union, UNESCO and the World Bank) have founded their problematic national sovereignty politics on colonial nostalgia. There is a belief in the capacity of cultural heritage to transform Asmara into a most modern city again. Boym would understand Asmara's architectural heritage as "institutionalised nostalgia" which is not opposed to modernity, but coeval with it: "Nostalgia and progress are like Jekyll and Hyde – doubles and mirror images of one another".[23]

World Heritage Site: Looking for Heritage, Looking for Modernity

The period of opening up to the world after independence also corresponded to a phase of internationalisation of Eritrea's territorial identity, in which the national imaginary was transplanted. During this period Eritrea was a field of experimentation both for national and transnational organisations; they tested new approaches to nation-building through cultural heritage and its representation. More generally, in the economy of nations preserving architectural heritage has become important in terms of global competitiveness and prestige; nations find themselves in need of exploiting their heritage to attract international investment. However, globalisation has made the idea of culture as a way of life located within definite boundaries increasingly problematic. Culture can no longer be understood solely in terms of locations and roots, but more as hybrid, creolised cultural routes in a globalised space. In particular, that which is considered to be local is produced within and by globalising discourses. These include global corporate marketing strategies that orient themselves to differentiated local markets.

At the same time, the paradox of heritage preservation in a global context is that investment in heritage may further encourage nationalist sentiment, often reinforcing a sense of superiority and therefore isolationist tendencies. Following the success of their independence struggles, nations have invoked nationalism and resorted to heritage preservation as a form of resistance against the homogenising forces of globalisation. For example, the policy of CARP (Eritrean Cultural Assets Rehabilitation Project), namely creating a global sense of shared heritage, led to the following governmental reaction: a radical policy of self-reliance in which the government crushed CARP's rallying call for global assistance. The Eritrean authorities have become increasingly apprehensive about foreign influence. Indeed globalisation is the third phase in the relationship between dominant countries and dominated ones; the search for, and the reconstruction of, identity have become paramount. Now that national independence has been achieved in Eritrea and the dust from the struggle against Ethiopia has settled, problems of national and community harmony have begun to surface.

Paradoxically, the Eritrean case leads us to a two-fold bond between the universalism of World Heritage and the national imaginary. In the specific case of Asmara, these two phases in attitudes towards heritage and tradition coincided, as Eritrea is one of the youngest nations in the world. However, the complexity of the international scenario and the multiplicity of possible narratives make divisions within Eritrean society and between government and civil society even deeper.[24]

The ambition to forge Eritrea's national identity through the revaluation of Asmara's colonial heritage coincided with an interest in colonial architecture in Africa among global heritage organisations. These argued that culture should be regarded as a direct source of inspiration for development; and in return, development should assign to culture a central role as social regulator. In the late 1980s the World Bank in Washington adopted a holistic approach to development and turned its attention to cultural heritage as a tool for what was called post-conflict reconstruction, poverty reduction or nation-building.[25] After the World Bank had terminated its loan to CARP in 2007, the European Union launched a follow-up national heritage programme. Five million euros were invested exclusively in the restoration of modern architecture in Asmara. The World Bank considered Eritrea a natural experiment (ironically, the same rhetoric had actually been used by the Italian colonisers) where this new approach could be tested. The entry on the historic perimeter of Asmara in the UNESCO World Heritage list even refers to an era when "Italian architects could [...] realise modern ideals."[26] The untouched historic heritage can reconstitute the blank canvas allegedly available to colonial architects in the past. According to Boym, "restorative nostalgia" manifests itself in the complete reconstruction of monuments of the past.[27]

What happens when a young, African nation state is forced to operate in the same global space as emergent transnational players? Generally speaking, Asmara's modern architectural heritage has been used instrumentally both by transnational organisations and the national Eritrean government. More specifically, the Eritrean government very strongly depends on the appropriation of Asmara's modern architecture as national heritage for the re-territorialisation of national sovereignty. This is also the case for international organisations, given their approaches to nation-building in Africa. World Heritage works as a meta-cultural code which regulates relationships between the parts and the whole, between individual communities and the world. Through their nomination – achieved thanks to their cultural heritage – Eritreans have gained a place on the world stage; globalisation is the extent to which the abovementioned relationships and systems have converged. At the same time, continued protection of the inherited image becomes the means through which the West periodically renews the original discovery. Somewhat paradoxically, for transnational organisations the appeal of Asmara's modern architecture appears to be flavoured with nostalgia, too.

Notes

1 Stuart Hall, "The Work of Representation", in Stuart Hall (ed.), *Representation: Cultural Representation and Signifying Practices*. Thousand Oaks, Calif.: Sage Publications, 1994, pp. 13-74.

2 Mia Fuller, "Italy's Colonial Futures: Colonial Inertia and Postcolonial Capital in Asmara", *California Italian Studies*, 2 (1), 2011, p. 5.

3 The capital of Rabat f.e. is a clear case in point, as the century-old town became literally surrounded by new French developments in less than a decade after the French take-over. The city centre was shifted away from the indigenous old town, which was literally bypassed by the new boulevards. In addition, the obvious contrast between the latter and the dark alleys of the medina, as well as that between the indigenous architecture and the straight lines of the *ville novelle*, reinforced the colonialist representation of the indigenous Maroccans as backward. See: Demerdash, Nancy Nabeel Aly, *Mapping myths of the medina: French colonial urbanism, Oriental brandscapes and the politics of tourism in Marrakesh*, Massachusetts Institute of Technology. Dept. of Architecture, 2009 in https://dspace.mit.edu/handle/1721.1/49723 (12.04.2015).

4 Ibid. Mia Fuller, *Italy's Colonial Futures*, op. cit. (note 2).

5 Andreas Huyssen, *Present Pasts: Urban Palimpsests and the Politics of Memory*. Stanford: Stanford University Press, 2003), pp. 5-7.

6 Ibid.

7 Ibid. Mia Fuller, *Italy's Colonial Futures*, op. cit. (note 2), p. 6.

8 Interview with Edward Denison, in Christoph Rausch, *Modern Nostalgia: Asserting Politics of Sovereignty and Security in Asmara*, Ph.D, University of Maastricht, 2011, p. 8.

9 Edward Denison, Yu Ren Guang and Naigzy Gebremedhin, *Asmara: Africa's Secret Modernist City*. London: Merrell Publishers Ltd, 2003, p. 50.

10 Mia Fuller, *Italy's Colonial Futures*. p. 6.

11 Ferdinand De Jong and Michael Rowlands (eds.), *Reclaiming Heritage. Alternative Imaginaries of Memory in West Africa*. Walnut Creek: Left Coast Press (Publications of the Institute of Archaeology), 2007.

12 Svetlana Boym, *The Future of Nostalgia*. New York: Basic Books, 2001.

13 Naigzy Gebremedhin, *Asmara, Africa's Secret Modernist City*. Paper prepared for the African Perspectives: Dialogue on Urbanism and Architecture, The Faculty of Architecture, TU Delft, 2007 in http://www.bk.tudelft.nl/fileadmin/Faculteit/BK/Actueel/Symposia [5-5-2015], p. 20.

14 Ibid.

15 Paul Rabinow, *French Modern. Norms and Forms of the Social Environment*, Chicago: The University of Chicago Press 1989, p. 289. See also: Nezar Alsayyad, "Culture, Identity and Urbanism. A Historical Perspective from Colonialism and Globalisation", in Tom Avermaete, Serhat Karakayali and Marion von Osten (eds.), *Colonial Modern. Aesthetics of the Past – Rebellions for the Future*. London: Black Dog Publishing, 2010, p. 80.

16 Mia Fuller, *Moderns Abroad: Architecture, Cities and Italian Imperialism*. London: Routledge, 2007, p. 144.

17 Immanuel Wallerstein, "The Nation and the Universal. Can There be Such a Thing as a World Culture?", in Anthony King (ed.), *Culture, Globalisation, and the World System*. New York: Palgrave McMillan, 1991, pp. 91- 106.

18 Francesca Locatelli, "The Archives of the Municipality and the High Court of Asmara, Eritrea: Discovering the Eritrea 'Hidden from History'", *History in Africa*, vol. 31, 2004, p. 469.

19 Magnus Treiber, "The choice between clean and dirty. Discourses of Aesthetics, Morality and Progress in Post-revolutionary Asmara, Eritrea", in Eveline Dürr and Rivke Jaffe (eds.), *Urban Pollution. Cultural Meanings, Social Practices*, Oxford: Berghahn Books, 2010, pp. 123-143.

20 Kristin Ross, *Fast Cars, Clean Bodies: Decolonization and the Reordering of French Culture*. Cambridge MA: The MIT Press, 1995, p. 73.

21 Christoph Rausch: *Modern Nostalgia: Asserting Politics of Sovereignty and Securita in Asmara*. Washington and Brussels, 2011, p. 14.

22 Homi Bhabha, "Of mimicry and man: The Ambivalence of colonial discourse", in *Homi Bhabha, The Location of Culture*. London and New York: Routledge, 1994, pp. 85-92.

23 Ibid. Svetlana Boym, *The Future of Nostalgia*, op. cit. (note 12), p. 23.

24 Nezar Alsayyad, "Consuming Heritage", in Sang Lee and Ruth Bergmeister (eds.) *The Domestic and the Foreign in Architecture*. Rotterdam: 010 Publishers 2007, p. 180.

25 James David Wolfersohn, "The Challenges of Globalisation: The Role of the World Bank. Address to the Bundestag, Berlin/ Germany: The World Bank Group 2001", in Rausch 2011, op. cit. (note 8), p. 5.

26 Tentative UNESCO World Heritage List Entry, Eritrea: The Historic Perimeter of Asmara and Its Modernist Architecture. UNESCO World Heritage Centre, in Rausch 2011, op. cit. (note 8), p. 5.

27 Ibid. Boym 2001

ናጽነትና ክብረትና

ASMARA'S GRAPHIC LANDSCAPE
The Contested Rhetoric of Posters

Steven McCarthy

Publicly displayed posters, scaled and placed appropriately, have a significant history of communicating to pedestrians, street vendors, passers-by, and inhabitants of slower-paced vehicular traffic. Messages ranging in topics from commercial, cultural, political and social give many urban areas a lively graphic vitality. Posters also contribute to a city's or region's style or sense of self with specific visual attributes, such as typeface, composition, colour and imagery. This paper is concerned with a series of nationalistic posters and other public graphic designs, like billboards and painted murals, observed in Asmara, Eritrea during March of 2013. Before the details and analysis of Asmara's graphic landscape are provided however, a bit of personal background is required.

My family lived in Eritrea, then part of Ethiopia, between 1967 and 1969 (I was eight to ten years old at the time) because my father, a civilian school administrator, was posted to the U.S. military base Kagnew Station. I even saw, and my father met, the Ethiopian emperor Haile Selassie on a couple of occasions. After Selassie (originally Ras Tafari – revered as god by rastafarians) was overthrown in 1974 and the Americans hastily exited, Eritrea was increasingly oppressed by Soviet-armed Ethiopia. After a lengthy war, Eritrea won its independence in 1993.

When I returned, forty-four years later, the context had dramatically changed. Free from Ethiopia, but shackled from within, Eritrea is essentially a police state, and is often referred to as "Africa's North Korea."[1] War hero and former leader of the Eritrean People's Liberation Front Isaias Afewerki is president –

a job he apparent likes these past twenty-plus years as no elections are held – implementing the constitution has been indefinitely postponed, and any opposition is jailed. A free press does not exist, the economy is in shambles and United Nations sanctions allege official ties to the Somali-based terrorist organisation Al Shabaab.[2]

About Eritrea, Amnesty International states: "Thousands of prisoners of conscience and political prisoners continued to be held in arbitrary detention, in harsh conditions. Torture and other cruel, inhuman or degrading treatment was common. Eritreans continued to flee the country in large numbers."[3] The U.S. Department of State "continues to warn U.S. citizens of the risks of travel to Eritrea."[4] Although the U.S.A. maintains an embassy in Asmara, it lacks an ambassador and is headed by a lesser position, a *chargé d'affaires*.

Every official indicator pointed towards abandoning my trip because of the personal risks, especially for an academic whose work involves politically and socially engaged artistic and journalistic inquiry, things that Eritreans are jailed for doing. Stories circulating locally from Minneapolis, St Paul's sizable Eritrean immigrant community, also painted a negative picture. When I gleaned information from non-U.S. sources, however, such as Dutch, British or Australian websites, the situation did not appear so dire. That Lufthansa flew bi-weekly flights from Frankfurt gave me added confidence. So when the Eritrean embassy in Washington granted me a tourist visa, I eagerly went to Asmara to conduct my visual research sponsored by my employer, the University of Minnesota. En route, I read Michela Wrong's excellent book about the history of Eritrea, *I Didn't Do It For You. How the World Used and Abused a Small African Nation.*[5]

This establishes a geo-political context for contemporary visual communications in present-day Eritrea. All of the graphic images I witnessed, with the exclusion of shop signs, product packages, corporate branding or other quotidian designs, were apparently government-sponsored; to express dissenting views would be to risk incarceration and torture. Three current graphic campaigns suggest, however, that Eritreans should have pride in their nation – as it is. The campaigns try to promote a sense of national identity: one using painterly illustration techniques that typically depict heroic figures and the flag, another employing photographs of people from Eritrea's nine ethnic groups, and the third a tourism advertisement.

I am an Eritrean...
I am proud.

The Fighters and Iconicity

A ubiquitous illustrated image of guerilla soldiers (Fighters is the term Asmarinos use) ascending a mountain and brandishing an Eritrean flag seems to re-enact the iconic World War Two photograph of American soldiers erecting the flag at Iwo Jima. Its triangular composition, view from below and rhetoric of collective action seem to suggest victory against overwhelming odds. French artist Eugène Delacroix's 1830 painting *July 28: Liberty Leading the People* – "a blend of document and symbol, actuality and fiction, reality and allegory"[6] – comes to mind for similar qualities. The Fighters image is aspirational and idealistic, and of course, propagandistic.

One such Fighters image is painted on metal and mounted to a building exterior on Harnet Avenue; another, drawn in graphite with only the flag in full colour, is in the lobby of the Cinema Roma. The image aspires to iconicity – consider how other nations have widely circulated icons of nationalism: Cuba's Che Guevara for example, and China's Mao Zedong whose likeness "has become a symbol of revolutionary culture. It is natural that he would be used on T-shirts or cups as a cultural logo."[7] American graphic designer Shepard Fairey's 2008 Obama Hope poster is another example, albeit one that emerged as designer-authored free speech.[8]

Nation-building through Posters

The photographic posters feature a variety of faces, as opposed to the singular mission of the anonymous Fighters, whose faces we do not see. Fit in standard street display furniture – often their metal frames are leaky or glass cracked – these posters depict a deadpan pluralism. The figures are dressed in indigenous clothing and are sometimes shown with animals. With Eritrea's multiple languages, cultures, histories, religions (primarily Muslim, Coptic Christian and animist), the posters attempt to show a common national destiny. All the posters share the words *I am an Eritrean. I am proud* typeset in the font Comic Sans, apparently without irony. In graphic designer circles, Comic Sans is widely reviled as amateurish, frequently inappropriate and aesthetically unsophisticated.[9]

These posters were designed as a series, as a promotional campaign for nationalism. They share a uniform size, full-bleed composition, a consistent slogan, comprehensive public placement and a reliance on photography. While the medium of photography denotes specificity, the images appear to depict representational members of various Eritrean ethnic groups (a woman with distinctive nose jewellery is most likely from the Tigre or Saho peoples).

Eritrea Simply
Magnificent....

While both the illustrated Fighter image and the ethnic group photo campaign are controlled, one-way communications typical of dictatorships – pro-government, nationalistic, propagandistic – unexpectedly progressive and incongruent themes emerge. The Eritrean guerilla soldiers image depicts women engaged in combat, and wearing revealing and gender-neutral apparel, especially considering the era (the 1960s through the early 1990s) and cultural mores of the geographic region. While many developed nations aspire to claims of social equality, this type of battlefield equality is rarely seen, and for traditional women to be seen in what are termed hot pants must have been a radical departure from social, and largely patriarchal, norms.

The poster series also has a progressive aspect. Plurality, especially in developed multi-cultural countries like the United States, France and the United Kingdom, is touted as evidence of racial, ethnic and religious acceptance. The reality, however, is occasional strife based on lack of tolerance, assimilation or understanding. The photographs of representatives of the nine Eritrean ethnic groups attempt to show both equality and difference, and togetherness and heritage. The first-person voice – "I am..." – provides for individuality in relationships to their own ethnic group and to national identity.

Eritrea Simply Magnificent

Another public graphic, a billboard near the intersection of Sematat and Harnet Avenues, departs from the overt rhetoric of nationalism and instead advertises Eritrea as a tourist destination. *Eritrea Simply Magnificent...* appears in script lettering over a full-bleed photographic image of an attractive young woman in Western apparel. In the background, palm trees, a beach and the blue sea beckon. The woman is holding what appears to be a green marker and is writing the slogan on the vertical plane of the billboard (backwards, apparently). The words are in yellow however, not green, with a black drop-shadow. She makes eye contact with the viewer, not her writing task. Another awkward element is the colours of the Eritrean flag – they appear to be created in Adobe Photoshop software on to the band of a hat sitting in the foreground, ignoring light and depth cues from the image. Although not as ridiculed as Comic Sans, Mistral, the billboard's script typeface (designed by Frenchman Roger Excoffon in 1953), has also suffered from popular use. Perhaps the billboard's designer chose it because it is also the logotype for Sandals Resorts International, a holiday tour company that operates in the Caribbean Sea. Unlike the specific references to Eritrea's nine ethnic groups as shown on the poster series, the woman on the billboard seems to represent the generically modern Eritrean as offered to international tourists. She is liberated, young, healthy, attractive, literate, trendy and worldly.

The poster series lacks visual and conceptual sophistication but seems to depict an authentic ethnic plurality. The Fighters mural embodies the national ideology of triumph through revolution and shows gender equality in a military context. These qualities, as mentioned earlier, can be interpreted as socially progressive. The *Eritrea Simply Magnificent...* billboard, while ostensibly leveraging contemporary media and fashionable cues, is the least progressive of the group. Its rhetoric is classic advertising: the bare-shouldered woman uses her body to sell a product (Eritrean vacation), the copy makes subjective, untestable claims (simplicity, beauty), and seemingly clever visual tropes lack believability (typography, image manipulation). The composite image seems less promotional of Eritrea as a tourist or even business destination, and more a statement about the quest for modern legitimacy.

Much of Asmara's commercial and civic signage is simultaneously typeset in the Roman alphabet (typically in English, a few still in Italian), in Arabic script and in Ge'ez, an ancient South Semitic language whose curvilinear characters resemble a less boxy Hebrew. Ge'ez is used to write Tigrinya and Tigre, Eritrea's main languages. That the billboard and the poster series use only English signals its role as an international language, and acknowledges the official role that English has in Eritrea.

Conclusion

All these examples operate as anonymous, one-way communications (I saw only one nationalistic mural attributed to an artist – Jacob Abraha). They are broadcast by a totalitarian government with no interest in a dialogue – compliance is the only option. While the goals of national identity, ideological aspiration and commercial enterprise might benefit most nations, only within the context of an open society can they be realised.

If the access, mobility, affluence, pleasure, simplicity and beauty promised by the enticing billboard are denied to the Eritrean people, why would tourists want to visit? Paralleling this notion, why is the country's pluralism locked into pictures of different ethnic groups but not recognised as part of a robust, divergent political discourse? And regarding the equality depicted in the Fighters image, why limit progress to past heroics when Eritreans deserve a brighter, freer, self-determined future?

Practically the only non-official, non-commercial, publicly displayed graphic messages that I witnessed in Asmara were obituaries. Austere in presentation, these black and white, A4-sized prints were written solely in Ge'ez and invariably featured a small grainy photograph of the deceased person. Many included a Christian cross. Fly-posted mounting was typically on utility poles, in shop windows or on community bulletin boards placed on Asmara's many stone walls. They serve as a vernacular reminder that, given the chance, *Asmarinos* would probably express their personal views on politics, culture and society. Then, their national identity would not be forcibly imposed from above, but would be an open dialogue about pluralism, ideology and progress. Unfortunately, graphic messages about the dead, by the oppressed, impose no threat to totalitarianism. Until Asmara's graphic landscape is opened to dissenting visual communications, the use of Comic Sans to build national identity is just a cruel joke.

Notes

1 Nathaniel Myers, *Africa's North Korea: Inside Eritrea's Open-air Prison* in http://foreignpolicy.com/2010/06/15/africas-north-korea/ (2010) (online 26 August 2015).

2 United Nations Security Council, *Security Council Imposes Sanctions on Eritrea over Its Role in Somalia, Refusal to Withdraw Troops Following Conflict with Djibouti* in http://www.un.org/press/en/2009/sc9833.doc.htm (2009) (online 26 August 2015).

3 Amnesty International, *Amnesty International Report* in https://www.amnesty.org/en/countries/africa/eritrea/report-eritrea/ (2014–2015) (online 26 August 2015).

4 U.S. Department of State, *Eritrea Travel Warning* in http://travel.state.gov/content/passports/english/alertswarnings/eritrea-travel-warning.html (2015) (online 26 August 2015).

5 Michela Wrong, *I Didn't Do It For You. How the World Used and Abused a Small African Nation.* New York: Harper Perennial, 2005.

6 Malika Bouabdellah Dorbani, *July 28: Liberty Leading the People* in http://www.louvre.fr/en/oeuvre-notices/july-28-liberty-leading-people (undated) (online 26 August 2015).

7 Maxim Duncan, *Granddaughter Keeps Mao's Memory Alive in Bookshop* in http://in.reuters.com/article/2009/09/28/idIN-India-42756920090928 (2009) (online 26 August 2015).

8 Steven McCarthy, *The Designer As... Author, Producer, Activist, Entrepreneur, Curator and Collaborator: New Models for Communicating.* Amsterdam: BIS Publishers, 2013.

9 Simon Garfield, *What's so Wrong with Comic Sans?* in http://www.bbc.com/news/magazine-11582548 (2010) (online 26 August 2015).

"UNTIL NEXT TIME IN ASMARA"
City of Aspiration, Despair and Ambition

Tanja R. Müller

My first encounter with Asmara goes back to the year 1984. I was on what would now be called a gap year, although less sophisticated; one simply went travelling. I had lived in Cairo for a couple of months and needed some money, and thus did what many then did: took the bus to Eilat in Israel to work in one of its hotels. In need of accommodation, I rented a room in the flat of an Eritrean who, like many of his fellow countrymen, worked in the construction industry. Mike, as he shall be called, had fled the Eritrean liberation war that was then in full swing, as he was essentially reluctant to get involved in politics of any kind, and wanted to join his sister who was living in Italy. At the time, his UN-issued laissez-passer papers allowed him to go as far as Israel. Israel then was not so much the destination of imagined democracy as it has been for a few years for contemporary Eritrean refugees, but the dead end of a long journey – in fact ultimately not too dissimilar from what it has become again more recently for the Eritrean refugees now stuck there.[1] Mike, during the three months I came to share a flat with him, instilled in me vivid imaginations of a beautiful city in the Abyssinian highlands, and when we eventually parted company it was with the words then common among Eritreans dispersed throughout the world: "Until next time in Asmara". In relation to Mike, who over the coming decade I lost touch with, next time never came – even if during my first visits to Asmara in the 1990s I kept looking our for his tall figure, and always expected him to somehow show up on the *passeggiata*, the routine evening walk on Asmara's main street, another of those Italian traditions that have survived in post-liberation Eritrea – including among many of the Tegadelti who at the same time try to re-calibrate the sprit of Asmara for their own purposes.

Eritrean men sitting at the Mai Jah Jah Fountain in Asmara
Source: S. Graf 2015

Thus not only for those outside Eritrea, but also for those who fought in the trenches as well as for those who are literally "children of the revolution", Asmara retained this mythical status of a place that once liberated would fulfil the wider promises Eritrean independence would bring.

One of the latter is Mehret, in whose life Asmara as a contested space in the Eritrean state-building project comes to the fore in exemplary fashion.[3] Mehret was one year old when her parents decided to join the Eritrean People's Liberation Front. Her mother took her to the liberated areas, where she grew up first in a children's home and later in the Revolution School. She finished schooling there after grade seven and was assigned to teach younger children. She always dreamed of being in Asmara, the city where she was born but had no memory of, and to continue her education. It was only after liberation that Mehret could finally complete secondary education, with the highest grades possible, determined to join the University of Asmara (UoA).

At the time, the expansion of secondary education and the re-opening of the UoA that had been closed and partly dismantled by Ethiopian authorities in 1990, was one of the priorities of the new Eritrean government – albeit with the narrow objective to mobilise new population groups into becoming skilled contributors to the PFDJ-led state-building project. For the UoA this produced a two-fold dynamic: On the one hand it was regarded as suspect by the ruling elite as an institution that would hinder rather than help to transfer the values of sacrifice of the liberation struggle.[4] On the other hand, graduates in subjects with clear benefits for the modernisation of Eritrea were regarded as vital for future economic success.

For Mehret, these potentially contradictory dynamics played out in her life in the following ways: after years of pleading her release from teaching duties with the Ministry of Education that, because of a vast shortage of teachers was reluctant to grant any release, she was allowed to join the UoA and graduated as one of the best students in her subject. She had a strong desire to "complete my Masters, and hopefully also Ph.D some day ... but I want to come back and live and work here, do something useful".[5] Mehret became a graduate assistant, first at the UoA then after its closure at the college in Mai Nefhi.[6] She expected to be sent for further education and each year was told to be patient. Eventually, after more than ten years of waiting, Mehret was sent on a scholarship to obtain a Masters degree from a respected University abroad. She completed her course of study successfully and returned to Eritrea and her teaching post – the sole person to do so from a cohort of five who were sent with her to study abroad, and she still hopes to continue with a Ph.D eventually.

Eritrean working on the beach in Tel Aviv
Source: S. Boness/IPON

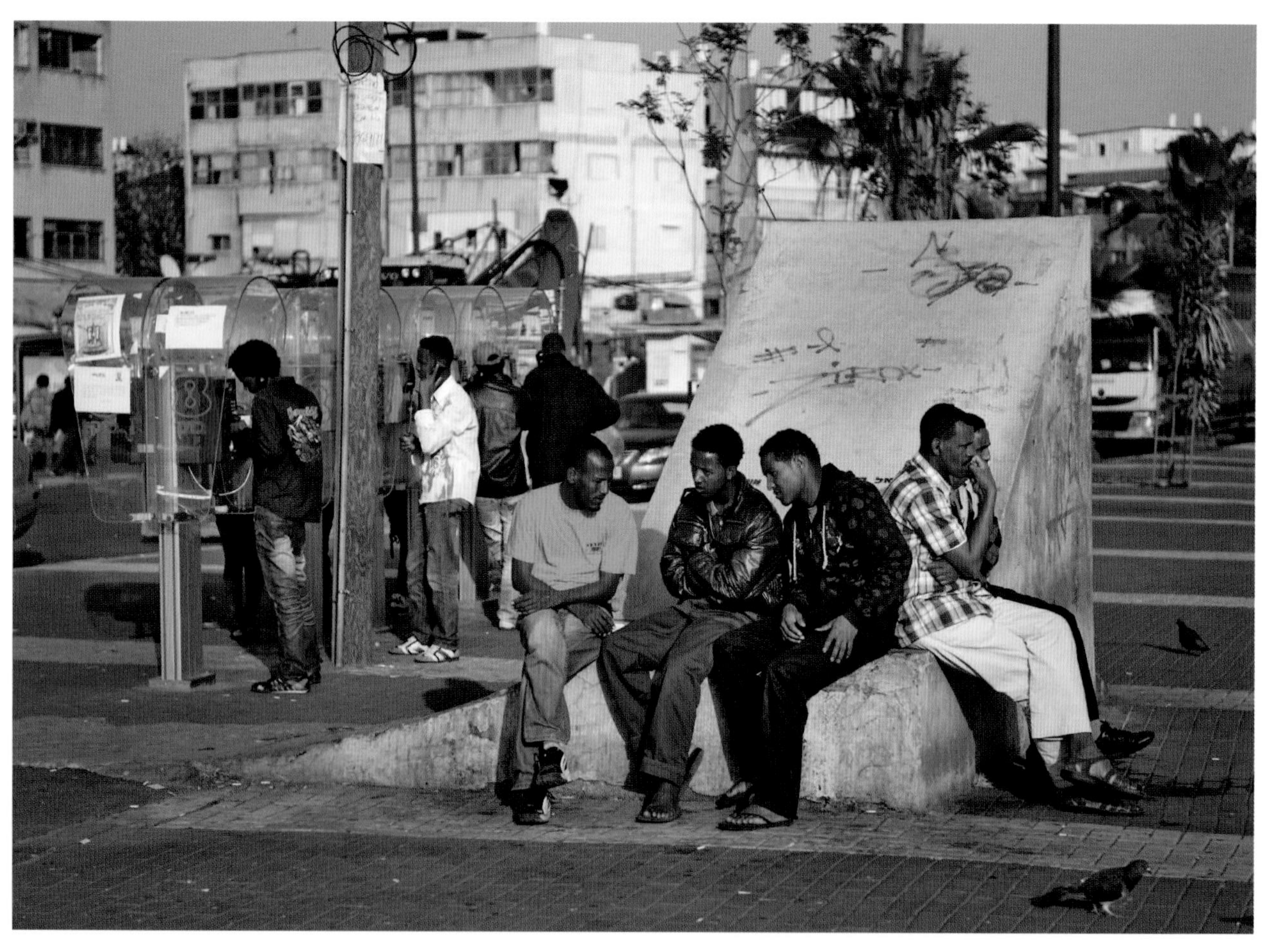

Eritrean men on the street in Tel Aviv
Source: S. Boness/IPON

When we jointly watched the video of her graduation ten years later she pointed out "all those with me there are not here now; I am the only one still in the country".[7] Mehret on a personal level is very content with having had the opportunity to gain a respected Masters degree, even if in the judgement of society at large her studies make little sense. She got a slight salary increase, but for people in her extended family and wider society, there are other expectations. "You go out and study, and this brings a lot of sacrifices as well", she says, in her case not having seen her young children for almost two years, "and once you come back, if there is no visible difference in your material condition, people do not understand that, there are a lot of expectations you cannot meet".[8]

Mehret's story is in many ways typical for life trajectories in post-liberation Asmara, for the fact that between realising aspirations or ambitions and despair the distance is rather small, even for those who are committed to contributing to the PFDJ state-building project with their professional expertise, as the following example demonstrates. One of those who is in Mehret's graduation video but is no longer in Asmara is Esther, who grew up in Asmara and started secondary school in 1991, the year of liberation.[9] She joined the third round of military service after school completion, but because of her excellent matriculation exams was called back after the summer months to start at the UoA from where she graduated with an engineering degree. Esther had worked for the public works in Asmara as a national service requirement, where most of the work was monotonous. She recalls, "even when there was no work at the office, you were not allowed to leave but had to sit there the whole day with nothing to do", which she really disliked, "but it has passed, it was only for one year, and I accept I should do some service".[10]

After graduation her main objective was to help her parents and siblings economically and eventually do a Masters. She successfully started her own construction company with her husband and they earned well by Eritrean salary standards. But in September 2005 a government proclamation resulted in the closure of all privately owned construction companies on diffuse charges of corruption in the sector that were never substantiated. This was followed by the arrest of many former company directors in April 2006. From then on, only government- and/or PFDJ-owned construction companies were allowed to operate and the PFDJ-owned import-export company became the only source permitted to import building supplies. At a meeting with Esther in October 2006 the family savings were running low but they were happy to only have been prohibited from working – with them at the time was a friend who had also owned a construction company and who had been imprisoned for some months, and one could see it had broken him in many ways. Subsequently,

Esther found employment at the state-owned Housing Bank where she worked until her husband secured a scholarship in Australia. He was allowed to leave and she secured the papers to eventually follow him with their children. In 2006, when she already anticipated that in the foreseeable future there would be little chance to work in her profession again in Eritrea, Esther said she really wanted to "contribute to the reconstruction of my country" and "in case the government changes I will come back to achieve this aim", but the longer the family has lived outside Eritrea the less likely that will become.[11]

The cohort of Mehret and her fellow graduates is not unusual in having a majority of its participants outside the country, and initially those who fled were often university-educated youth accused of unpatriotic behaviour after the general crackdown of 2001. In the initial years afterwards, Asmara became a place of frequent *giffas*, or round-ups – but also remained the location where people could hide from national service impositions undetected for many years. Over time, Asmara has on the face of it become a vibrant city again where cafés are full and people speak their minds, while generators everywhere are visible signs of economic hardship and power shortages not seen before.[12]

Returning to the beginning of this essay, while I never met Mike again, our encounter in 1984 made me return to Israel to conduct research among the new cohorts of Eritrean refugees there between 2010–2013.[13] I spent my last evening in Tel Aviv with an Eritrean friend at the opening of a photo-exhibition by Stefan Boness (who is also part of this volume), who has published photo-books on the architecture of Tel Aviv and Asmara respectively.[14] The exhibition at the Bauhaus Centre focused on the architecture of Tel Aviv, which, as my friend remarked, is in many ways similar to that of Asmara, so "we have come all this way to find a similar city" he joked.[15] My friend has meanwhile become one of the few who managed to secure papers to leave Israel, and now resides in a Western country, but his ambition of eventually being able to return to Asmara is very much alive. We parted that evening with the same words I had parted with from Mike by then almost thirty years ago: "Until next time in Asmara".

Notes

1 Tanja R. Müller, "Universal rights versus exclusionary politics: Aspirations and despair among Eritrean refugees in Tel Aviv", *Afrika Spectrum*, vol. 50, 2015, pp. 3-27; Hadas Yaron, this volume.

2 All names have been changed for reasons of confidentiality. The following is based on interview data collected between 2000–2015.

3 Tanja R. Müller, '"Now I am free'-Education and Human Resource Development in Eritrea: Contradictions in the Lives of Eritrean Women in Higher Education", *Compare*, vol. 34, 2004, pp. 215-229; Richard Reid, "Caught in the headlines of history: Eritrea, the EPLF and the post-war nation-state", *Journal of Modern African Studies*, vol. 43, 2005, pp. 467-488.

4 Interview, Asmara, 26 May 2001.

5 On the dynamcis around the closure of the UoA see Tanja R. Müller, "Bare life and the developmental state: implications of the militarisation of higher education in Eritrea", *Journal of Modern African Studies*, vol. 46, 2008, pp. 111-131.

6 Encounter, Asmara, 20 October 2011.

7 Interview, Asmara, 24 October 2015.

8 The following is based on interview data collected between 2000–2006 and via email and Facebook since.

9 Interview, Asmara, 5 November 2000.

10 Interview, Asmara, 20 October 2006.

11 Fieldwork diary, Asmara, October 2015. See also Tanja R. Müller, "Beyond the siege state – tracing hybridity during a recent visit to Eritrea", *Review of African Political Economy*, vol. 39, 2012, pp. 451-464.

12 Tanja R. Müller, "Universal rights versus exclusionary politics: Aspirations and despair among Eritrean refugees in Tel Aviv", op.cit.(note1); Tanja R. Müller, "From rebel governance to state consolidation – Dynamics of loyalty and the securitization of the state in Eritrea", *Geoforum*, vol. 43, 2012, pp. 793-803.

13 Stefan Boness, *Asmara – Africa's Jewel of Modernity.* Berlin: Jovis, 2016. Stefan Boness, *Tel Aviv – The White City.* Berlin: Jovis, 2011.

14 Conversation, Tel Aviv, 15 September 2013.

ASMARINOS
Photo Essay

Stefan Boness

The hugely proud old men of the Eritrean capital Asmara call themselves *Asmarinos*. With their European suits, classic hats and hand-made leather shoes, they enjoy their daily macchiato in one of the many coffee-bars. In their youth, under Italian colonial rule in the 1930s, the *Asmarinos* were not allowed to enjoy such pleasures. The palm-lined Independence Avenue with its almost surreal Italian landscape was then called Viale Mussolini and totally off limits to the *Indigenos*. Today this dark side of the Italian occupation seems almost forgotten. The old Asmarinos are proud they still speak Italian and follow in many ways an Italian lifestyle – most visible in their dress code, reminiscent of Italian gentlemen of a bygone age.

Opposite page: Ato Gebrehans Keleta
"I was an Italian cook at Rino Hotel. I left the work in 1950 because I was buying my own restaurant." "The Eritrean elegant dressing code is influenced by the Italians." "The Italians were very bad; they were not respecting our rights as workers."
Source: S. Boness

Next page left: Buru Tekle
"In 1941 I was participating in the war on the side of the Italians against the British Empire. But the British defeated us." "The Eritrean dressing system is completely influenced by the Italians."
Source: S. Boness

Next page right: Ato Eyasu Tlslasie
"Under the time of the Italian Empire, I was working in Italian politics administration." "Throughout Asmara there was bitter racial discrimination by the Italians." "Eritreans are influenced by the Italian dressing culture."
Buru Tekle
Source: S. Boness

Page 300: Abdella Salih
"I was working as a farmer in Elabered low land. This is an area were the Italians built up huge agricultural farms. A lot of the products were exported to Italy."
Source: S. Boness

Page 301: Berhe Dahle
"I remember that Asmara was classified into three zones: 1. Nationale: Italians only. 2. Mixed Zone: Italians, Arabs and Aihuds. 3. Indigini Zone: Eritrean people only."
Source: S. Boness

CONVERSATIONS

Interview

Peter Volgger Talks with Medhanie Teklemariam

Today, Asmara represents Africa's oldest Modernist architectural heritage. The current project to nominate Asmara for inscription on the UNESCO World Heritage list is the latest in a series of initiatives spanning two decades, starting with the Cultural Assets Rehabilitation Project (CARP, 2001–2007) and including the EU-funded *Heritage Project* (2008–2010). The most recent initiative, the *Asmara Heritage Project*, was formally established in 2014 by the Central Region Administration Region (Municipality of Asmara) in collaboration with the Ministry of Education with the aim not only of preparing the requisite Nomination Dossier, but also of drafting comprehensive plans to ensure the long-term managment and conservation of the city's heritage assets. The preservation of colonial architecture appears preferential to new architectural projects. We will analyse the aims and objectives of the *Asmara Heritage Project*, including its advisory body, and the methodological approach towards the UNESCO application, impelling a re-evaluation of Africa's architectural heritage internationally. Mr. Teklemariam, head of the *Cultural Heritage Office*, speaks about current and past efforts to safeguard this distinctive tangible and intangible heritage.

A view of the centre of Asmara
Source: S. Graf 2015

PV: Today we have the pleasure to speak with Mr. Medhanie Teklemariam, the coordinator of the Asmara Heritage Project. Asmara is famous for its nearly untouched ensemble of Italian colonial architecture. What do you think makes Asmara unique?

MT: I think when we talk about the uniqueness of Asmara, it is distinct through its buildings, generous tracks, public spaces, different religious buildings, different amenities and social services. I think when we look at Asmara from the point of view of the inhabitant, the pedestrian and the cyclist as well, it is a very convenient city. Is it unique because of its architectural and urban qualities. We can look at different places in the city – there are *favelas*, there are high-rise buildings, and there are different services in the city. When we look at it as a whole and in its entirety this has quite different characteristics and qualities. So, I think we will have to reserve this built heritage.

PV: Asmara has sometimes been considered a living museum of architecture. Other people described it, for example, as a frozen city, or a city of dreams... Do you believe such notions are accurate?

MT: I don't agree with the notion of Asmara as a living museum of architecture because the city is evolving culturally and economically; there is social development. When I look at it, this is not a frozen city. Maybe the current situation, the no war-no peace situation, might affect the economic development of the city. But the city is still in continuous development, so I do not agree with the notion of a frozen city. I think the city is a very ideal city, a very dynamic city. And I think that once the economic situation improves it will be even more dynamic and liveable.

PV: The status of UNESCO world heritage is one aim of the city. What advantages and disadvantages would this result bring?

MT: I think Asmara deserves World Heritage status because Asmara, as we know, is the result of experimental architecture from the twentieth century. So Asmara is bidding for UNESCO status and we are scheduled to prepare the nomination dossier and the nomination plans for 2015 or 2016. I think by listing Asmara as a World Heritage site would have several advantages. The city would receive publicity across websites and different magazines. Therefore, Asmara's rich architectural and urban treasures would be made public. This would be a real advantage because later on tourists from all over the world would be attracted to visit these treasures. Moreover, the city would benefit from the technical and financial assistance from UNESCO and the World Heritage Programme. In my opinion the advantages outweigh the disadvantages.

Maybe in the long run the city will be under pressure to cope with these expected local and international tourists. Perhaps this will be a disadvantage.

PV: Asmara is very famous for its iconic buildings, such as the Fiat Tagliero station, as well as cinemas, villas and so on. All those buildings were definitely ahead of their time, whereas Asmara's urban plan seems to belong to the nineteenth century and is often considered to be less important. What are your thoughts regarding this?

MT: I think the research which has so far been conducted emphasises the architectural aspect. However, Asmara's urban planning is not well researched and there are still a lot of things to come out. I strongly believe that when we look at Asmara, it is not just about the buildings; Asmara's beauty is on an urban level. I think we have to examine planners such as Odoardo Cavagnari, Guido Ferrazza, Vittorio Cafiero – the architects who designed and planned the city, who were all very ahead of their time in the introduction of a new planning concept. The mixed-use types for example: in other cities there are a lot of zoning separations, whereas in Asmara you can find any service within walking distance. You can find schools, post offices, government offices, cinemas, and theatres. All this concerns the urban plan which is crucial; if all services are not located in the right strategic location, then the singular building cannot overcome this shortfall. We have to investigate and conduct further research on the town planning aspect in terms of its innovativeness and dynamism for contemporary urban planning. I think we have to further investigate that.

PV: Europeans often think that the historical centre of a city is always a link to the identity of the city. Asmara's historic centre is very well defined but, on the other side, the city is growing and developing towards Greater Asmara. Overall, would you all consider Asmara nowadays as a European or an African city, or something between those poles?

MT: I think Asmara's city centre is very liveable and charming. A great variety of people visit the city centre. Therefore I believe the city centre is crucial for the identity of the city. Also because every *Asmarino*, every city inhabitant, has to visit the city centre for recreational purposes or to get the services he needs. Asmara is growing towards the Greater Asmara area because the city has to provide services outside the centre; if all services are clustered in the inner city then the centre will be destroyed. One of the strategies of the city administration is to expand the city towards the periphery to provide housing and industry in order to foster economic development. I think this development is not harming the city centre. The city centre of Asmara is quite different from other African cities. But still, Asmara is an African city – even though it shares some similarities with European cities. I think it preserves some of the European ideas and cultures within the living context of Asmara. We could say Asmara has both European and African characteristics.

PV: What is typical for the development of Greater Asmara? What are the greatest challenges there?

MT: Basically the challenges we are facing are the expanse and the growth of the city. When the city is expanding, you have to provide infrastructural services like roads, transport, water supply and sanitation. And you have to provide services like markets, recreational facilities, and educational facilities. When there is a massive new development towards the peripheral area of the city, the city administration is challenged to provide these services.

PV: Back to the centre of Asmara. The centre impresses with its beautiful streets, buildings, piazzas and has been protected with the so-called CARP programme. Now there is a new approach in developing CARP, which implies the addition of new zones. Could you please speak about this?

MT: CARP has conducted an inventory of historical buildings and has also defined the historic perimeter of Asmara. A new Asmara heritage project was just initiated and started this year. CARP emphasised the colonial settlements and the city centre and missed a significant part of historical buildings that are outside its historic perimeter. In the new proposal we included some other parts of the city as well. Another very important part that we included in the new drawn perimeter is Gheza Banda, the villa area, where the railway station is located. We extended the perimeter to include all the missing parts of the city. And another important area in the north of the city is Aba Shaul, the indigenous area. Historically this is area is very important; I think the entire city is part of its heritage and so it will be good and justified to include this northern settlements. In another part in the west we find the cemeteries, which are historically, and culturally a very important landmark of the city. CARP missed this part and it is proposed to be included in the new perimeter. We created a layer of zonings; first we proposed a core zone, then a buffer zone, because for the operational guidelines of UNESCO it is required to propose such a buffer zone. The light blue line is the proposed area for the buffer zone. Another zone we included in our planning is the green belt from the southwest to the east west of the city. So this will also be a protected area.

PV: The Eritreans appropriated the colonial heritage and established a positive relationship towards it. There is a continuing appropriation of the built environment. Can you give any good examples of this?

MT: I think one of the good things in Eritrea is that we Eritreans already inherited the tangible and intangible cultural heritage. When we look at the city, especially the Mekel areas, we see that during Italian colonial times there is segregation: there is a European zone, a mixed zone, an indigenous zone and an industrial zone. Eritreans were thus given the opportunity to meet with Italians and other ethnic groups like Arabs, Jews and Greeks. The Medeber area is a mixing point for different ethnicities to meet together and to exchange cultural, economic and social news. This is a very beautiful urban space for cultural exchange. Specifically, when the Italians left Eritrea, the Eritreans were living in the city belts. However, everything was built by the Eritreans; therefore they feel that they own and protect the city. I think if you felt hatred towards the buildings and the urban spaces, then they may have been demolished or destroyed. Look at other places! But in the case of Eritrea it is something very special: there is an appropriation of the buildings and the urban space.

PV: What does historic heritage mean for the identity of Eritreans today? Is there a linkage between nation and architecture?

MT: I think Asmara's and Eritrea's heritage is very important, because all Eritreans are proud of their identity. Separating Eritreans from this heritage means to deny them their identity. Their psyche is deeply rooted in their history and their cultural background. *Asmarinos* love their city, not only here, but also all over the world. So I think for the Eritrean identity it is very crucial. Especially during the liberation war, for the fighters on the field Asmara was the aim – the road led to Asmara. This is deeply rooted in the movement of liberation. The fighters have great respect for the history of Asmara. It is very important for the nation's identity.

PV: What is your personal vision for Asmara in ten or twenty years?

MT: Asmara will try to make itself very liveable. There will be massive restoration works and we will upgrade the infrastructure. And we hope that Asmara's architecture and urban planning will be recognised by the international community and will lead to a very positive image of Asmara, especially as a tourist attraction. The city will be very liveable and dynamic – that is my wish and my expectation.

Interview
Stefan Graf and Arno Hofer Talk with Magnus Treiber

Magnus Treiber holds a Ph.D in Anthropology from Munich University and received his *venia legendi* in 2016 from Bayreuth University, where he has also held a post as assistant professor. He taught at Munich, Bayreuth and Addis Ababa universities and is affiliated to the German Felsberg Institute. Since April 2016 he is a Professor of Anthropology at Munich University. For his dissertation he conducted fieldwork in Asmara between 2001 and 2005 and studied the urban life of young people in Asmara. Treiber investigated the way in which these young *Asmarinos* take possesion of the urban space within the constraints of harsh daily life. Another of his fields of interest is Eritrean emigration in different stages and stations between Eritrea and the wider world and the connection these people keep with Asmara. His main fields of interest are urban anthropology, migration, anthropological theory and methodology as well as political conflict in the Horn of Africa.

An *Asmarino* on his *passeggiata* through the city
Source: S. Graf 2015

Arno Hofer: Magnus, you are an ethnologist and an expert on Ethiopia and Eritrea. You have also lived for several years in Asmara. What makes Asmara so interesting from an ethnologist's point of view?

Magnus Treiber: The city is beautiful, you can simply fall in love with it; these are very subjective and personal reasons. Life there could be very beautiful; one could lead a very convenient life which marks a difference between other big African cities – or the whole world in general. An ethnologist is interested in everything – where people act, think and make. When it comes to Asmara it is interesting how people themselves think and invent their city and how this is reflected daily life.

AH: Asmara is fascinating, especially for its architecture. The architecture has been conserved for a long time because of unpleasant circumstances: warfare and poverty. That's why Asmara sometimes is called a frozen city – a city from a time machine. What do you as an ethnologist think of such a statement?

MT: The slogan *Frozen City* seems to be suitable but it also ignores the social processes and political changes that took place. The expression overlooks the people who live in this buildings which today seem unchanged. From a sociologist's point of view this expression is not suitable.

AH: In the past Asmara was always a melting point of different cultures, ethnicities and religions. Is this still visible in some quarters of the city? Or do land tenure and social class still shape the city today?

MT: First of all, it is possible to consider this from the point of view of old/existing urban research. The Chicago School discovered a laboratory in the city: a laboratory where social life and conflicts begin which are foreseeable. Something happens – you don't exactly know what – and you observe it. This is also possible in Asmara. Many residential areas were built by soldiers, auxiliary forces of the Italians or by different religious groups. This is why some quarters for a long time had a Christian or Muslim character. These quarters have changed over the passage of time. In some there was more capital and new buildings were built. So you can see the social differentiation in the development of the different quarters. City means differentiation but it also means enforcedly living together on a relatively small area. What you see today is that the traditional aspects of these quarters survived in large part, even if these are not so easy to define. The city expanded to the south, where a lot happened. Who pays for the houses there and who possesses them? Two groups which are of course privileged: the diaspora and high-ranked militarists. They express today's class relations.

Stefan Graf: We will talk later about the Eritrean diaspora. You mentioned the differentiation of the city quarters and the fact that Asmara is famous for its colonial centre. Is there an urban elite which identifies especially with the colonial heritage or is identification with the city centre more a general one?

MT: I don't see an urban elite which remembers the colonial times positively. Of course there is the Italian Club and the Italian school which try to maintain the Italian aspects of Asmara. But apart from that there is an urban habitus that is shared by many people. The colonial heritage is another story: the fascist interpretation of Italian culture as modern and future-oriented was perceivable for the Eritreans only as maids, servants and soldiers. And in the time before fascism Asmara was relatively small; the emphasis on Italian culture was not so present. Eritreans could only adopt Italian and urban culture after 1941 when the British demanded and promoted civil life with newspapers, political parties, labour unions; that is when an assertiveness – a national one but also an urban one – came to life. The urban assertiveness adapted a lot of Italian urban life – strolling through the city, being chic, and drinking coffee are part of it.

AH: This aspect of *italianità*, the culture that seems influenced by Italy, is perceivable in Asmara everywhere. We met many elderly gentlemen, dressed kind of glamorously with suits and walking sticks – some of them even greeted us in Italian. We called them urban dandies. Is there something similar in other African cities or is this a phenomenon specific to Asmara?

MT: You can also find it in other African regions. The phenomenon of the neat and chic urban townsman is always a mixture between colonial heritage and a regional story. You can compare this to the intellectual scene in the North African Arabic world from Casablanca to Cairo; there you can find similar things which are influenced in particular by French intellectuals. Also in Congo Brazzaville there are the clubs of sapeurs, who relate to a tradition of the exterior. It is a cultural aesthetics which mixed colonial and postcolonial aesthetics. In the 1960s sapeurs were young people denied the social recognition they wanted. So they aimed to gain social respect with elegant clothing. In South Africa there is a tradition of urban clothing which is remarkable. If you look at old family photographs you see that the people wear suits. There are no zulu skirts or things like that. James Clyde Mitchell described a dance from the copper belt in southern Africa – today's Zimbabwe – the kalela dance, which is performed only in European clothes, even white gloves. You can probably find similar things in Somalia, or at least you could. Today it may be different; you have to look around and make comparisons. Eritrea is a special case – on the basis of its history and regional circumstances – but it's not the only example.

SG: Aside from the colonial heritage, Asmara's cleanliness strikes the visitors right away. Also security; Asmara is a very safe city. You already wrote about it. One can imagine encountering European aspects within Africa. Can you really find Europe in Africa? To what extent is Asmara an European city?

MT: From an ethnological position this question is not relevant. You have two concepts – Europe and Africa – and we would have to examine these concepts first and see what we put inside before we evaluate what comes out. Cleanliness and safety are organisational problems and duties pertaining to local affairs, so there has to be a political will behind it. The other thing is the general acceptance of such a measure. In many cities you find a political will to keep the city clean but, nevertheless, people throw their waste on the streets, so the political will is broken. But in Asmara it is accepted because it is a prosecution of modernity that comes from the colonial period. Cleanliness means more than only clean streets, it also means safety and a clean life. Interestingly this is expressed with the word for white: *tsada*. *Tsada hiwet* means "white life", a clean, well-regulated life – a safe life. Morality is also meant by this which is part of the urban habitus. Eritrean townsmen are not ecologically conscious, but culturally the border – which has to be renegotiated within discourse – is the one between clean and dirty. This concerns the dirt in the streets but also relates to political and moral spheres; it is that which separates the urban from the rural dweller.

AH: We talked about the ethical dimension, now let's talk about the political dimension. Eritrea is one of the poorest countries in the world. We noticed posters with freedom fighters and films about the war for independence all over Asmara. Which role does the fight for independence play today?

MT: The presence of the war on independence in films, TV, music, theatre, festivals is an example of official commemorative politics. I did my research about family milieus and their spare time and I asked what kind of music young people listened to. They had a preference for Sudanese and Ethiopian music, *amharic* music. Why? Because it was not about war but about love. Here I saw a certain maturity among young people. Official media show the historic victory and this victory legitimises what happens today. The young, but also elderly people, understand what is covered by doing so: for relevant political questions there is only a historic answer. A historic answer was successful, but that does not mean that it is successful anymore. This crack is known and perceived, sometimes it is perceived as a nuisance and therefore suppressed. For some of the older people who were in the war, however, it has a nostalgic value. Some of them remember the good old times because there was a social sense of togetherness which does not exist anymore.

SG: Shortly after Independence an atmosphere of departure was apparent which – with reference to the building sector – stalled in the mid-1990s with a construction ban to protect the historic heritage. What do you think about the idea to renovate Asmara or to open the country for new flows of funds?

MT: The government cancelled a campaign for the renovation of parts of the city because they were afraid that rents would rise in renovated buildings and many people would have to leave the city. So the city stayed mixed in many parts, especially in the centre. This is a consequence of the former Ethiopian socialist regime. I think we are experiencing an awaiting period; possible investors are waiting to see what happens. In 1991 to 1993 there were plans to demolish parts of the centre to build something new. Should there be a political change and the chance to invest, I am sure there would be many investors. And then we would have to raise our voices to protect this area because I am sure there would be interest to demolish and modernise parts of the city centre.

AH: In our project we try to respond to the question of how Eritreans adopt colonial heritage, as well as which phenomena appear and which factors play a role. In your research you show how young people develop free spaces and describe different milieus. Can you tell us more about this?

MT: My research was about young people and how they arrange their free time, although their professionalism is shaped by mobilisation and the national service, while their familiar life is restricted. They have a few hours in the evening where they can find the life they would like to live, but this is not possible at the moment – although they can play-act it. They go to a chic establishment with no money and don't drink anything. Some save money and play and claim social ascent. Others promote a social togetherness and lust for life but have no more money for clothes and looking chic. They have to accept a certain stigmatisation to enjoy a certain milieu that others would consider dirty. Asmara is a conservative city – including the government, middle classes, families and religion. Others tried to escape these groups and seek religious liberation; they became pentecostal and broke with their families and the government. Unfortunately I don't have any insight into today's Asmara, most of my former informants immigrated.

AH: Today many Eritreans live in the diaspora all over the world and many try to leave this country. Nevertheless Asmara is a growing city. These are two opposing phenomena which shape the city. We talked about the war for independence and the atmosphere of departure after the war. This was used by many Eritreans in the diaspora to make investments. But this spirit soon abated. Can you tell us the reasons for this?

In 1991 the EPLF had won the war and took over the administration of the country to legitimise Eritrea two years later as a state and bring it into the United Nations. It was a very emotional time which reflected the hope for peace and a bright future. It was the same period in which people returned from Germany, building bigger houses and opening cafés. They established a lifestyle that the city was unfamiliar with. Educated young people could have attractive jobs and didn't think about leaving the country. What was overlooked however was that this volitional spirit of departure had something mythical about it. It was a political exaggeration which cancelled anything that could have overshadowed the prospects, the authoritarian tradition of the guerrilla itself. Returnees today see things clearer. Many things done by the government come from the times of the guerrilla. If the people – Eritreans, the diaspora and all the other observers – would have had more critical eyes then, things could have been changed. The shock happened in 1998 owing to the border conflict with Ethiopia and after 2001 with the ruptures we know: the detention of journalists and the abatement of the student revolution.

AH: Which relation do people in the diaspora have to Asmara? Is the city important to them and their identity?

MT: Yes, of course. Asmara is a symbol which stands for Eritrea. Eritrea is a rural country and the diaspora from the 1980s in Germany, Sweden, Switzerland or Italy has their roots in the city. They had the possibility to leave the country because they had a middle-class background. Asmara becomes a *pars pro toto*. At the same time, people in the diaspora have become frustrated and silent. Some of them go into opposition, but I think the majority has become quiet. This is because they want to return to Asmara for the holidays to visit their grandparents. Political identity and discourse have vanished in favour of social relatedness, aesthetics and romantics.

SG: Asmara stands in a certain way for Eritrea. What is the connection between Asmara and the countryside? Is there a reciprocal effect or does the city encapsulate itself? Is there migration within the city?

MT: Since the times of the DERG regime, Asmara has been a rigorously policed area. Migration to the city is only possible under certain preconditions; you need permission and a good reason to move to Asmara. The city as an overall global phenomenon is ambivalent. The state and political power stem from the city in their modern sense. But the city was always a place of upheaval, where intellectuals and students came from. So the city has to be controlled by the political power. Migration to Asmara is not so common, but commerce with the surrounding areas is very common. The countryside feeds the city which is why farmers, vegetable vendors and drovers come to the city. However, they only come to the market and never lay a foot on Godena Harnet. The urban dwellers – rich or poor – focus on their distinction and embody the urban habitus. They show the people from the countryside that they don't belong here.

AH: Could you give an evaluation of how Asmara will develop within the upcoming years? How will Asmara look like in fifty years? Or at least – how would you like Asmara to look in fifty years?

MT: How should I know?! I know from experts that if the city continues to expand like it is currently there will be water shortage and drought. The single houses with gardens where people from the diaspora and the military live need lots of water which isn't there, especially if Asmara keeps growing. These are ecological problems. Another threat is that the city centre is demolished and overbuilt by the new generation which does not have any connection to it. As an ethnologist, this should not be my problem if other people have another understanding, it should only be of my interest, what understanding they have. I don't have to intervene, but I would consider it a pity. Asmara is a beautiful city and I would be delighted if it was restored temperately. I conducted interviews with architects and urban planners who shared quite different points of view, some of whom were in favour of restoring the buildings but also building new houses in the city centre, while others wanted to make a museum out of the centre, allowing it to decline in order to build a new capital city of concrete and glass 40 km away. The capital that is awaiting to be built should be opposed politically and the building boom should be canalised. If you look at cities like Addis Abeba, the building boom did not lead to a good outcome. The historic perimeter is a treasure and could be a capital for tourism, thus rendering it profitable for Eritrea as a whole.

AH: Thank you very much for the interview.

TIGRINYA

Interview
Peter Volgger Talks with Christoph and Konrad Melchers

During the 1990s, German architectural historians were at the forefront of the re-discovery of Asmara and made this topic popular for a broader public with an exhibition at the DAZ (Deutsches Architekturzentrum) in Berlin. For the first time, the rich architectural heritage of the Eritrean capital Asmara has been introduced in an exhibition. The exhibition was curated by Naigzy Gebremedhin (former Director of Eritrea's Cultural Assets Rehabilitation Project, CARP) and Prof. Dr. Omar Akbar (Director of the Bauhaus Foundation Dessau) and was based on Denison's book *Asmara-Africa's Secret Modernist City* which focuses on the iconic buildings and created the *bella Asmara* image. The exhibition was criticised for not taking into account the racist aspects of urban planning. But, there are some other aspects to consider.[1]

Asmara exhibition in the Shedhalle in Tübingen, 2008
Source: C. Melchers

PV: The touring exhibition Africa's Secret Modernist City showcases the paramount examples of Modernist architecture in Asmara – both in pictures and models – and started a re-exploration of the spacial and architectural qualities in the capital Asmara, a striking sample of European urban architecture in the early twentieth century. How did your Asmara exhibition come about?

C&KM: In 2000, Naigzy Gebremedhin, the initiator and Director from 1998 to 2004 of the Centre for the Preservation of the Eritrean Cultural Heritage (CARP), visited us in Tübingen, Southern Germany. At this time the Institute for Foreign Cultural Relations (ifa) was exhibiting the work of architect Erich Mendelsohn in the Kunsthalle (art gallery) Tübingen. We took Naigzy to the exhibition and he became instantly excited: "This is all Asmara!" We knew the beauty of Asmara architecture through many visits. But we were not aware, as Naigzy was, of its extraordinary global value in terms of early Modernist architecture. By comparing it with Mendelsohn and Bauhaus architecture, Naigzy opened our eyes and we also became excited. That day it was decided with Naigzy to create an exhibition on the Modernist architecture of Asmara.

PV: And how did things move forward from there?

C&KM: Naigzy Gebremedhin had hired the writer and specialist in architecture photography Edward Denison and the architect Guang Yu Ren to assist him in producing a thorough survey of the urban development of Asmara, searching archives in Asmara as well as Italy and taking excellent photos of the buildings. The result was the seminal book *Asmara, Africa's Secret Modernist City*, published in 2003. This book comprises a summary of Eritrean history dating back to early human settlements several thousand years ago. The colonial policies of Italy are described in detail, in particular the segregationist, racist town planning of Asmara culminating in the rapid expansion of the city for the cause of the brutal war of aggression against Ethiopia in 1935/36 by the fascist Italian regime of Benito Mussolini. Extremely racist laws were enacted in 1937. The book also covers the British rule from 1941 to 1952, followed by the federation with Ethiopia, which was turned into an annexation in 1962. This caused an armed liberation struggle that succeeded in 1991, leading to the independence of Eritrea in 1994. This period is described as *Dormant Asmara*. Most Italian settlers left Eritrea and very little change occurred to the built environment. The final part of this historical analysis is devoted to the first ten thriving years after independence, marked by the creation of the historical perimeter of Asmara. Future tasks of urban planning and development were determined to take into account the legacies of colonial rule and thirty years of liberation struggle: poverty, disruption of society and deterioration of the built environment, all exacerbated again by the new border war between Eritrea and Ethiopia leading to a no peace-no war situation.

PV: Denison's book emphasises Asmara's beauty ...

Yes, in the second part of the book the most brilliant buildings of Asmara are described. These buildings comprise a unique ensemble of Modernist architecture in most classical styles representing all urban functions: government and administration, shops, markets, squares, banks, hotels, post office, factories, service stations, schools, university, cinemas, theatre, parks and fountains, cafés and bars, sports stadium, public bath, cathedrals, churches, mosques and synagogues, villas and apartments often mixed with shops and cafés.

PV: The book became the basis for the exhibition.

It was obvious that the book had to become the basis for the exhibition. There was no need to produce a catalogue; the book could be used as the catalogue of the exhibition.

PV: How did you receive the necessary support for producing the exhibition?

C&KM: With this wonderful book it was easy to find support. First we approached like-minded Eritreans in Germany with whom 4Asmara, Arbate Asmera, a project group of the Association to Promote Education and Journalism for Environment and Development, was established. Naigzy Gebremedhin accepted the invitation to be the honorary president and Edward Denison became an honorary member. It is worth mentioning that two Ethiopian architects in Berlin, Dawit Shanko, the founder of the LISTROS art gallery in Berlin, and Girmabiru Michael, supported the project group from the beginning. They all contributed greatly to the success of the exhibition. The first spokespersons of the group were Mekonnen Mesghena and Senayt Kesete, followed by Bisrat Kifle and Michael Tesfai.

PV: How important was the collaboration with professional institutions for your project?

The Bauhaus Centre in Berlin declined support, arguing that the Italian architecture in Asmara was not their concern. A different view was held by Prof. Dr. Omar Akbar, then President and Director of the Bauhaus Dessau Foundation. He showed great interest and instantly agreed to become curator of the exhibition together with Naigzy Gebremedhin. Omar Akbar commissioned one of his scientific assistants, Rainer Weisbach, to produce the exhibition.

PV: How was the exhibition produced?

C&KM: Rainer Weisbach, expert in Bauhaus and other classical Modernist architecture, had little knowledge of Eritrea. Therefore, Naigzy Gebremedhin wrote the first draft of the text for the panels. Both engaged in an intensive dialogue to develop short texts for twenty-four panels on complicated issues to be captured easily by visitors of the exhibition. The panels are combined in four topical entities: history of Asmara, international architecture and the functional city, Modernist architectural styles and impressions of Asmara through photographs. Edward Denison contributed the pictures of buildings. Almost no plans or architectural designs existed of buildings. Therefore we approached Professor Wolfgang Knoll, Stuttgart, who had developed a computer-based system for the production of reconstruction models using only photos of the buildings. Knoll produced seven fine models of outstanding Asmara buildings. Also part of the exhibition was the film *City of Dreams* by Ruby Ofori and Edward Scott, as well as fifty-two competition entries (drawings, poems and stories) submitted by school children from Asmara in 2004. At some venues seventeen framed photos by Edward Denison were displayed as well.

PV: What are the aims of the exhibition?

C&KM: The architecture of Asmara was barely even known to experts and historians of architecture. On a world map of ICOMOS showing places with significant classical Modernist architecture Asmara was not mentioned. Therefore, the exhibition wants to draw international attention to this cultural heritage and it is intended as support for Eritrea's endeavours to have Asmara classified as a World Heritage Site by UNESCO which will support the maintenance of this unique architectural ensemble. Furthermore the exhibition aims to contribute to the discourse and evaluation of classical modernism, the globalisation of modern architecture, the historic value of modern architecture, and the impact of modern architecture on urban planning. Already in 2001, CARP had managed to convince the Eritrean government to protect the entire city centre of Asmara as a national monument. On February 1, 2016, the Eritrean government filed the candidature of Asmara as world heritage with UNESCO.

PV: Where has the exhibition been shown?

C&KM: The exhibition opened October 2, 2006, at the Deutsches Architekturzentrum (DAZ) in Berlin. Since then it has been shown at the following fifteen venues within nine countries: Frankfurt (German Architecture Museum),

London (Royal Institute of British Architects), Kassel, Tel Aviv (twice in the Bauhaus Centre), Stuttgart, Cairo, Lomé, Lagos, at the XXIII UIA (Union International des Architects) World Congress of Architecture in Turin, in Bologna, Graz, Tübingen, Munich, and at the XXXV World Congress of Architecture in Durban. At most venues the exhibition was complemented by lectures, debates, and symposia.

PV: How was the exhibition received?

C&KM: The overall resonance to the exhibition by visitors and the media was very positive. Reviews were headlined *Design-Jewel in the Savanna*, *Picture Book of the Modernity*, *Unique Architectural Jewel*, *Africa's Rome in Asmara-blue*. We are particularly happy about the comments from African specialists. Gaetan Siew, from Mauritius and then president of the International Union of Architects (UIA) and Charles Majoroh from Nigeria, former President of the African Union of Architects, spoke and wrote very positively about the exhibition. However, critical comments appeared as well. They draw their criticism from the fact that the exhibition does not focus on the crimes of the Italian colonisers and on the brutal war context of the main Asmara urban development, while at the same time not disregarding these crimes. Raimund Rütten, Professor at Frankfurt University, and Aram Mattioli, for example, laid their focus on the racicm and nationalism of the Italian colonists. Most of those critics have not even seen the exhibition and did not study the accompanying material of the exhibition, in particular the book by Gebremedhin, Denison and Yu Ren. They base their information on secondary sources or quotes out of context. A sad example is Harald Bodenschatz in this volume. Criticising the exhibition, he quotes from a book that was published parallel to the exhibition but which was never the book of the exhibition. By referring to "Asmara as the *citta piu progressista del continente* – Africa's most progressive city!" Bodenschatz insinuates the exhibition would portray Asmara as a progressive role model for Africa. But this was never stated and never intended by the exhibition. The exhibition maintains that Asmara entails the most comprehensive urban ensemble of classical Modernist architecture in Africa and not only in Africa. There is no other city in the world with a similar comprehensiveness of such architecture. Bodenschatz claims: "The wide range of myths and associations implied by the exhibition demonstrated the lack of reflection regarding fascist Italian architecture and urbanism." And he asks "who was able to stay in the hotels pictured and could watch films in the Cinema Impero (one notices the name)? Who was able to fill his car at the winged service station and who could live in the many houses?" The exhibition does not omit that this was all built originally for the Italian colonisers. But after a protracted liberation struggle the buildings are now owned and used by

Eritreans. The exhibition does not deny the historical context in which Asmara was built. Naigzy Gebremedhin replies to the criticism that Eritreans have appropriated, completely and unequivocally, the colonial architecture in their capital city. This appropriation has never implied minimisation of the evils committed by fascist Italy in Eritrea. Eritreans will never forget the humiliation of the excesses of racial discrimination, but they no longer harbour any quarrel with the buildings that have survived. The exhibition simply contributes to the wise decision to put these buildings to good use. It does not extol racism, it is an exhibition about architecture that survived against all odds.

PV: How much of the past is in present-day Asmara? Does Italian colonialism still echo in the Eritrean present?

C&KM: This is an interesting question raised within postcolonial discourse. We do not deny the necessity to critically analyse influences of the past on present identities. But the mainstream postcolonial discourse wrongly overstates such influences; it determines people as objects of influences while they are mainly subjects of their destiny; it victimises Africans of colonial and neo-colonial influences while – in the long run – they were and are liberating themselves despite and against terrible odds. We prefer to acknowledge the positive rather than the negative potential of people. Asmara is a good case in point. Two examples may signify this. One of Asmara's first Modernist buildings is the former Bank of Eritrea in Harnet Avenue 175, which for some time had served as a military prison. After the independence of Eritrea in 1991, the building was due to be demolished to make way for high-rise buildings proposed by a German architectural consultancy. There was an outcry among local Eritreans about this disregard for the historic architecture in the centre of Asmara. Former inmates of the prison appealed to the President of Eritrea to shelve the project. And they succeeded. The fine example of Novecento architecture has survived. This is one of the few cases where civil society intervention has succeeded in independent Eritrea. Saray Erican cynically terms such concern of Eritreans for their heritage love with a city that represents Eritrea's darkest history of Italian fascism, Italian apartheid, Italian Nazism. The other example of public concern was the Nakfa House built in 1995 which dwarfs the Fiat Tagliero Service station. This exciting example of futurist architecture has become the icon of Asmara classical Modernist architecture. As a result of the public debate about such developments, CARP succeeded with the government to establish the historical perimeter of the city centre of Asmara in 2001 as a national monument. Christoph Rausch denounces this achievement as collusion of the Eritrean Officialdom in fostering outsider's colonial nostalgia, accepting international funding toward preservation of the colonial built heritage, all while manipulating this heritage's value for national sentiment. This is another case of wild defamation of the work of CARP.

PV: Thank you very much.

C&KM: Thank you and may Asmara architecture survive such vilifications and be celebrated as a UNESCO World Heritage site.

Note

1 See: Dossier y– Asmara. Africa's Secret Capital of Modern Architecture, in http://www.asmara-architecture.com/Dossier_engl.pdf

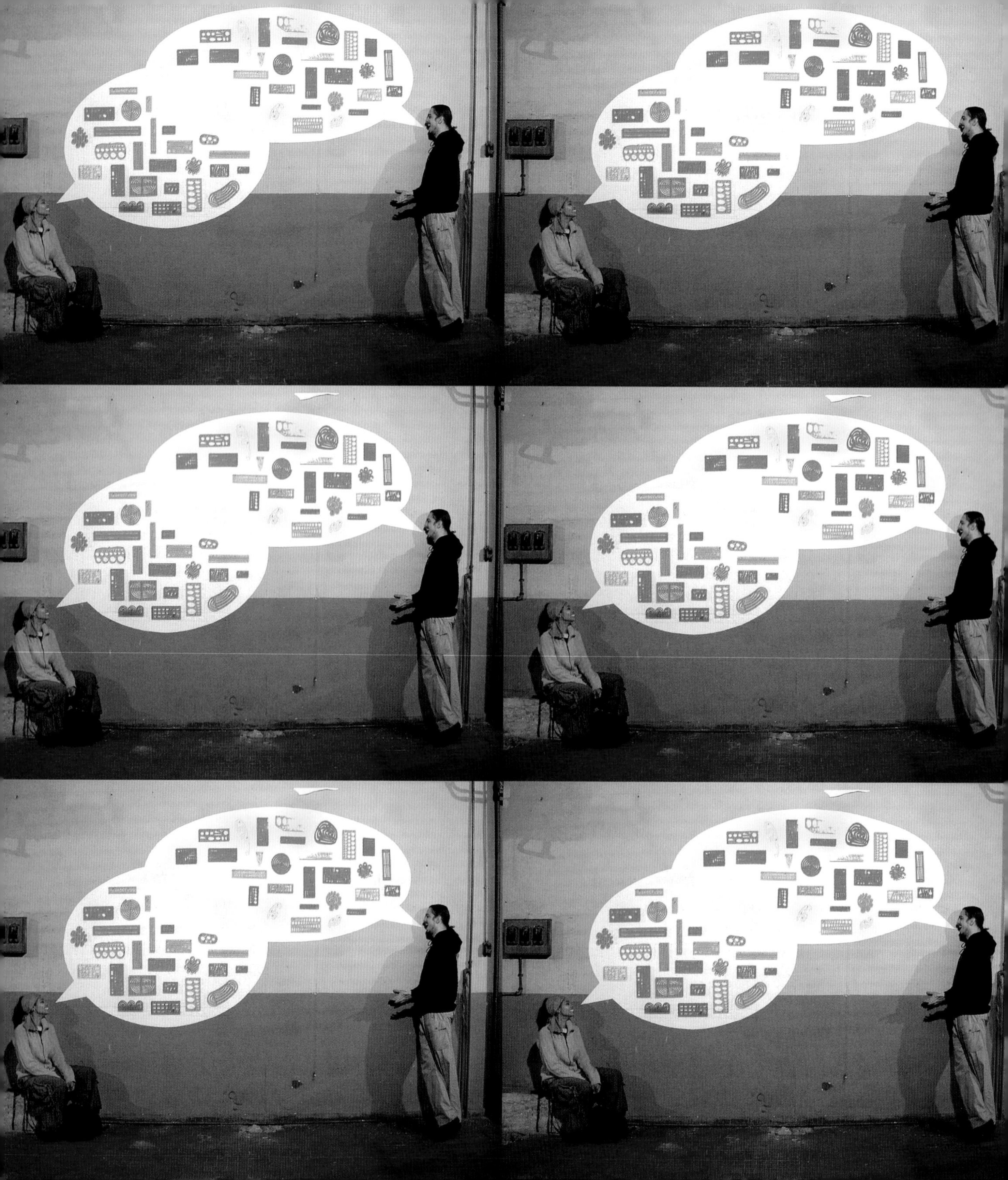

Interview
Peter Volgger Talks with Alan Maglio and Medhin Paolos

Asmarina Project (2015)

Alan Maglio is a photographer-director who has presented his works across different exhibitions and festivals in Italy and abroad. His style is a mix between portraiture, street photography and documentary and often tackles different topics related to cultural identities. *Asmarina* is his second film after *Milano Centrale – Stories from the Train Station.*

Medhin Paolos is a photographer, electronic musician and an activist. Her career path has taken her from an international experience with Fiamma Fumana to her current work within *Rete G2 – Seconde Generazioni*, a national organisation for citizenship rights. *Asmarina* is her debut film as a director.

Asmarina Project, 2015
Source: www.asmarinoproject.com, courtesy of A. Maglio and M. Paolos

Peter Volgger: For those who have not seen the Asmarina film, can you give us a sort of a short description about what the film is about?

Alan Maglio/Medhin Paolos: *Asmarina* is a film documentary about the Eritrean/Ethiopian diaspora. The Eritrean/Ethiopian community has been present in Italy for at least half a century and has been actively included in the social and cultural life of Italian society. Starting from the collective memories of the community, on the basis of photo documents, the film gathers together the legacy of personal stories, exploring the different shades of identity, migration and the aspirations of the people. Weaving together the experiences and identities of those who have lived in Italy for generations with those of newly arrived refugees, *Asmarina* traces the complex networks of colonial legacies, transnational migrations, family ties, and diasporic politics. The result of our research is a collective tale which brings to light a postcolonial heritage that has been little scrutinised up to now: the everyday life stories of those who have lived in the city for years, those who were born in Italy and the daycare of the refugees who have just arrived. The filmmakers approach this reality empathically and get involved in it, patiently trying to create a relationship with the protagonists. In addition to the documentary, the project involves the realisation of a photographic book: a collection of shots from private and institutional archives found during the making of the film. In *Asmarina*, photos are a form of collective praxis, deeply embedded in social relations and indeed formative of social relations. Photos – family photos, photojournalism, candid snapshots – are the material by which kinships and connections are traced among people, places, and time; they allow for the transmission of embodied knowledges and histories.

PV: The Asmarina Project "*brings to light a postcolonial heritage,*" *you say. Keeping alive visions of the colonial past in the present is also the task of Italy's contemporary postcolonial artists, video makers, and writers. Now, what are the challenges as a filmmaking team, to produce at this level? How do you see, more generally spoken, the engagement of Italians with their colonial past?*

AM/MP: One of our main goals was exactly this, exploring the colonial past and therefore bringing to light a postcolonial heritage that is very much present. The challenge is allowing the freedom that you have as a completely independent production team, to work in your favour. There's a certain amount of unpredictability in filming a documentary, and that could bring you off track. So it's important to allow the truth of each situation you film to come to fruition in the most genuine way, while still serving your vision for the project. *Asmarina* is not a documentary about immigration, not just a story about Ethiopians and Eritreans – it was intended to be a story about

Milan. *Asmarina* is not about the hidden Milan, it is Milan. And Bologna. And Italy ... Italy and Eritrea produced one another. This also forces a serious reconsideration of what we mean when we talk about Italy and Italians.

PV: How did the making of the film change you? Do you think it changed you?

AM/MP: Both the research and the filming of *Asmarina* lasted one year and a half in total. I think Asmarina gave me a clear idea that there's a shared need of bringing to light different parts of history past and recent, that are usually hidden.

PV: Medhin, you define yourself as a photographer, electronic musician ... and an activist. Why did you want to do this project in the first place? During the making of the film and the research, do you see yourself as an activist as well as photographer and a filmmaker?

MP: If you look closely, there's a common thread in my projects: whether it's through folk music, photography or social/political activism. I'm a story listener more than a story teller. I like connecting the dots between past and present, unveiling history through stories and understanding how people negotiate their ever changing identity.

PV: The Asmarina Project explores the visibility and invisibility of the legacy of colonial relations and the represenation of the colonial past within the habesha community in Milan. How present is the city of Asmara in this legacy?

AM/MP: Asmara is sort of the invisible character, just like in our film. It's there in memories and pictures old and new. It plays a big role whether you've been to Asmara or not. It's evocative.

PV: The film gathers together the legacy of personal stories, exploring the different shades of identity, migration and the aspirations of the people. The style is a mix between portraiture, street photography and documentary. How important is it to choose the right style?

AM/MP: In this case the right style, so to speak, was using all the media that the project naturally called for. Plus the media that is the most familiar to us, which is photography. Because we shot in very different types of situations, we tried to be flexible and always ready.

Source: M.Hudovernik 2012

Authors

Benno Albrecht
is full Professor of Architectural and Urban Design at Università Iuav di Venezia. He is the Director of the School of Doctorate Studies. Benno Albrecht is currently a member of the Scientific Committee for the Global Award for Sustainable Architecture. He is chairman of many research programmes financed by government and institutions. He devotes himself to research on sustainable urban design and has carried out projects in architectural and urban sustainable development. He has held seminars, conferences and workshops in Italy and abroad. Benno Albrecht's architectural and urban design projects are published in reviews, international magazines and books. He has received architectural prizes, won international competitions and held exhibitions in Italy and abroad.

Sean Anderson
is senior lecturer and undergraduate programme Director at the Faculty of Architecture, Design and Planning at the University of Sydney. His book *Modern Architecture and its Representation in Colonial Eritrea (1890–1941)* illustrates the evolution of public and private spaces in Asmara and speculates on the notion of a colonial interior as both a metaphor for colonialism and as a gendered site in the making of a colonial modernity. The Museum of Modern Art has appointed Sean Anderson as Associate Curator in the Department of Architecture and Design. His responsibilities will include overseeing MoMA's *Issues in Contemporary Architecture* exhibition series, assisting in curatorial supervision of the Young Architects Program (YAP) both at MoMA PS1 and with international partners, and serving as the primary liaison to architecture communities both locally in New York as well as globally.

Victoria Bernal
is Professor of Anthropology at the University of California, Irvine. Her scholarship addresses questions relating to politics, gender, migration and diaspora, war, civil society and activism, and digital media. Her most recent book is *Nation as Network: Diaspora, Cyberspace, and Citizenship* (2014). With Inderpal Grewal she co-edited the anthology *Theorizing NGOs: States, Feminisms, and Neoliberalism* (2014). Victoria Bernal has carried out ethnographic research in Sudan, Tanzania, Eritrea, Silicon Valley, USA, and cyberspace. Her current project focuses on privacy, cybersecurity, and digital surveillance.

Rino Bianchi
was born in Anagni in 1965. He started photographing for case, attracted by the image that he saw in the hole of a TLR Twin lens reflex (Rolleiflex). Rino Bianchi studied journalism at the school directed by Gino Pallotta. He deals with photojournalism, works with newspapers and magazines and, in recent years, took part in many projects related to memory. The themes that he prefers to develop are custom, fashion, and people. He retracts writers, poets, historians, essayists, philosophers and Nobel laureates and published *Piombo e Carta; La Bestia. Narrative invaders*; *Sant'Anatolia di Narco*; *Sukran Moral Apocalypse*; *Made in Mompeo haiku and photo*, with Riccardo Duranti; *Rome denied. Postcolonial Paths in the City* (*Roma negata. Percorsi postcoloniali nella città*, 2014) and *14 fotografi in cerca d'autore* (2016).

Harald Bodenschatz
is a sociologist and urban planner. From 1995 to 2011 he was full Professor for Sociology of Architecture and Urban Planning at the Technische Universität Berlin. Since 2012 he has been an Associate Fellow of the Centre for Metropolitan Studies at the Technische Universität Berlin and of the Bauhaus-Institut Geschichte und Theorie der Architektur und der Planung at the Bauhaus-Universität Weimar. From 2004 to 2009 he was speaker of the Schinkel Centre at the TU Berlin and from 2009 to 2010 a speaker of the Transatlantic Graduate Research Training Group *Berlin – New York* funded by the DFG German Research Foundation. His research projects are related to the history of urban design and post-industrial urban design. Harald Bodenschatz is author/co-author or editor/co-editor of a number of publications and research activities on urban issues and dictatorship (Soviet Union, fascist Italy, Salazar's Portugal, and Franco's Spain), among other things.

Stefan Boness
is a photojournalist based in Berlin and Manchester. His photos have received several awards, including a World Press Photo Award. His work has been published in quality magazines and newspapers throughout the world. His long-term documentary projects in the tradition of Conceptual Photography include reflections on urban landscapes as well as street photography. His book project entitled Flanders Fields is a photographic search on the battle elds of World War I in Belgium. In *Asmara – The Frozen City* he uncovers the legacy of Italian colonial avant-garde architecture in the capital of Eritrea. A new, changed and revised edition of the photo book was published by Jovis in 2016: *Asmara – Africa's Jewel of Modernity*. Other book projects include: *Japan – Fleeting Encounters* (2016), *Hoyerswerda – The Shrinking City* (2012), *Tel Aviv – The White City* (2012), *Southern Street* (2010). Stefan Boness has worked in Eritrea on a regular basis since 1997.

Annalisa Cannito
was born in 1984 in Acqui Terme (I). She is a transdisciplinary artist and political activist working on topics that deal with history politics, EU immigration policy, common goods and art in public spaces. Her artistic investigations into the past and present impact of the relations between fascism and colonialism are exposed in different forms within the long lasting project *In the Belly of Fascism and Colonialism*. She studied at the Academy of Fine Arts Vienna, Post Conceptual Art Practices (Marina Gržini, degree 2013), attended the Visual Arts Fellow (10/2014–06/2015) at Künstlerhaus Büchsenhausen Innsbruck, participated in the exhibition *A Hole in the Sea* (May 21–August 21, 2016) at the Württembergischer Kunstverein Stuttgart. She currently lives and works in Algiers (June 2016).

Federico Caprotti
is an Associate Professor in Human Geography at the University of Exeter. His main research interest is in nature and the city, and in broader debates around nature, society and technology in modernity. He has carried out both historical urban research, with a focus on fascist Italy, and more contemporary research on eco-urbanism in Europe and China. His latest book, *Eco-Cities and the Transition to Low Carbon Economies*, was published by Palgrave in 2015. A geographer by training, he has lectured at the universities of Leicester, Oxford, University College London, Plymouth and King's College London, and his research has been funded by national funding agencies including the ESRC, NERC, and by learned societies including the Royal Geographical Society, the British Academy, and the Nuffield Foundation.

Filippo De Dominicis
was born in 1982 and studied architecture in Brussels and Rome. Erasmus and Cornelius Hertling EU Fellow, he holds a Ph.D in Architectural Design and Theory. Between 2012 and 2015 he was a post-doctoral researcher at the University IUAV of Venice and Massachusetts Institute of Technology, Aga Khan Program for Islamic Architecture. His research investigates

the relationship between the sub-Saharan environment and the multi-scale planning process, with a special focus on the spatial and ecological mechanisms set up across the southern border of the Great Desert. Filippo matches his academic involvement with a solid professional training. As architect and urban designer he has been involved in several projects in Morocco, Mauritania, Mali, Saudi Arabia and Malaysia, having collaborated with NGO and international institutions.

Fassil Demissie
is a faculty member of the Department of Public Policy Studies. He received his Ph.D in Urban Planning from the University of California – Los Angeles. Before joining DePaul, he served as an urban planner for the Department of Housing and Community Development, State of California. He has published a number of books including *Colonial Architecture and Urbanism in Africa: Intertwined and Contested Histories*; *Postcolonial Cities in Africa*; *Africans on the Move: Migration, Diaspora and Development Nexus*; *African Diaspora and the Metropole*; *African Diaspora in Brazil: History, Culture and Politics*; *Land Grab in Africa: The Race for Africa's Rich Farmland*. Fassil Demissie is Founding Editor of *African and Black Diaspora: An International Journal* (Routledge) and Series Editor, *Routledge Studies on African and Black Diaspora*. Currently he is working on a book project on contemporary Addis Ababa, Ethiopia, with a particular focus on the relationship between globalisation and the changing urban landscape of the city.

Edward Denison
is an architectural historian, writer and photographer specialising in twentieth-century architecture. He has worked as a heritage consultant to numerous international organisations and is a research associate and teaching fellow at the Bartlett School of Architecture (University College London). His latest book is titled *Ultra-Modernism in Manchuria* (HKUP, 2015). Others include *Asmara: Africa's Secret Modernist City* (Merrell, 2003), *Luke Him Sau* (Wiley, 2012), *McMorran & Whitby* (RIBA, 2009), *Modernism in China – Architectural Visions and Revolutions* (Wiley, 2008), and *Building Shanghai: The Story of China's Gateway* (Wiley, 2006).

Jacopo Galli
was born in 1985 and studied architecture at Università degli Studi di Parma and at Università Iuav di Venezia where he received his Ph.D in architectural design. His research focus is on modern architecture in Africa and on cosmopolitan architecture related to the work of international organisation and transnational groups. He has curated exhibitions in international venues such as La Triennale Milan, CIVA/La Cambre Brussels and La Biennale di Venezia, as well as conducted research projects in Italy and the UK and professional work in Italy and Spain.

Domenica Ghidei Biidu
is an independent scholar and a lawyer. Among other things she is a member of the European Commission against Racism and Intolerance (ECRI) in respect of the Netherlands; Deputy Human Rights Commissioner, Netherlands Institute for Human Rights, Utrecht, Netherlands; Vice-Chair, *Geschillencommissie Passend Onderwijs* (Commission for Disputes on Inclusive Education), Utrecht. She is also a freelance trainer, consultant and keynote speaker in the areas of transcultural and inclusive leadership; transcultural communication; diversity management; equal treatment and anti-discrimination on the grounds of gender, race, LGBTI, handicap and chronic illness. She also has a special focus on diaspora and refugee issues.

Stefan Graf
is an architect and art historian. The academic field of architectural theory gave him the opportunity to satisfy his multifaceted interests in art, architecture and cultural theory. He wrote his diploma thesis about Asmara and was part of the research project *Asmara – The Sleeping Beauty*. His field of research includes history, urban planning and the relationship between the historic part of CARP and Greater Asmara.

Rebecca Hopkins
is currently associate lecturer of English at the Johns Hopkins University School of Advanced International Studies (Bologna, Italy). Previous positions include adjunct Professor of Comparative Literature and Global Culture at New York University (Florence, Italy). Her publications mainly focus on novels in English and Italian that deal with issues of Italian colonialism, migration, and gender. Since 2007 she has served on the Editorial Board of *Scritture Migranti*, a peer-reviewed journal (University of Bologna) dedicated to themes of migration, displacement, and transnationalism in world literature. She received her Ph.D. in Comparative Literature from the University of California, Los Angeles in 2007.

Kathleen James-Chakraborty
is Professor of Art History at University College Dublin and Vincent Scully Visiting Professor of Architectural History at the Yale School of Architecture. She has also taught at the University of Minnesota, the University of California Berkeley and the Ruhr Universität Bochum. She was educated at Yale and the University of Pennsylvania. Her books include *Erich Mendelsohn and the Architecture of German Modernism* (Cambridge, 1997), *German Architecture for a Mass Audience* (Routledge, 2000), *Architecture since 1400* (Minnesota, 2014), and the edited collections *Bauhaus Culture from Weimar to the Cold War* (Minnesota, 2006) India in Art in Ireland (Routledge, 2016).

Chris Keulen
born in Heerlen 1959, Nederlands. Studied Dutch language and literature at the University of Nijmegen, and Visual Arts at the Royal Academy of arts in The Hague and lives in Maastricht. For twenty-five years he has worked on long-term photo projects that resulted in exhibitions, publications and books. In this book about Asmara he shows us the cycling stages in the Eritrean capital. Keulen followed the *Giro d'Eritrea* twice for his photobook *Hete glassplinters; le tour d'Afrique*. The book follows the most important cycling races in Africa (Burkina Faso, Eritrea, Senegal, Cameroon) but is much more a social document on the power of the continent. Keulen has received two World Press Photo Awards for his work.

Eric Lafforgue
was born in 1964 and lives in Toulouse, France. Ever since he was young, he has been fascinated by far away countries and travelling, and spent some time in Africa, unknowingly retracing Monfried and Joseph Kessel's footsteps when he was ten years old in Djibouti, Ethiopia and Yemen. He started taking photographs in 2006. Quickly, magazines from all over the world began using his work for illustrations on North Korea, Papua New Guinea, the tribes of Ethiopia, etc. His work has been published in *Time Magazine*, *National Geographic*, *New York Times*, *CNN Traveller*, *Discovery Channel* magazine, *BBC*, *Sunday Times*, *Lonely Planet*, *Morning Calm Korea*, *GEO* (sixteen countries), *International Herald Tribune*, and many more.

Cristina Lombardi-Diop
is senior lecturer and Director of the Rome Studies Program at Loyola University Chicago, where she holds a joint appointment in Modern Languages and Literatures and Women's Studies and Gender

Studies. Cristina is the editor and translator of Ngugi wa Thiong'o's *Moving the Centre*, and was also the recipient of the 2001 Nonino Prize. She is a co-editor with Caterina Romeo of *Postcolonial Italy: Challenging National Homogeneity* (Palgrave 2012, published in Italian as *L'Italia postcoloniale* by Le Monnier-Mondadori in 2014) and a co-author with Gaia Giuliani of *Bianco e nero. Storia dell'identità razziale degli italiani* (Le Monnier-Mondadori 2013, winner of the 2014 Prize of the American Association for Italian Studies). Her essays on white femininity, fascism and colonialism, Mediterranean migration, and African Italian diasporic literature have appeared in a variety of edited volumes and journals. Most recently, she has published on the need for a postcolonial and race theory approach to Italian American Studies, and on the visual grammar of fascist colonial comics strips.

Linde Luijnenburg
is a Ph.D candidate and part-time teaching assistant at Warwick University in the School of Modern Languages and Cultures. Her Ph.D research examines the deconstruction of the colonial narrative in several films of the *commedia all'italiana*, and argues that critically and politically engaged film directors of the *commedia all'italiana* both ridicule and question the concept of Italianness by exaggerating it in their films, contrasting it against the concept of the *Black Other*. Ms. Luijnenburg's research interests include Italian Studies, Postcolonial Theory, Film Studies, and Comparative Literature. She is a collaborator for *Italinemo* and *InteRGRace*, and member of the board of editors for *Incontri*, the European journal for Italian Studies. Later this year, her documentary on the Somali Dutch community in Birmingham, UK, will come out.

Francesca Locatelli
is a lecturer in African History at the University of Edinburgh. Her research interests concern urbanism, crime, migration and border spaces. Her publications *Beyond the Campo Cintato: Prostitutes, Migrants and 'Criminals' in Colonial Asmara (Eritrea), 1890–1941* and *African Cities: Competing Claims on Urban Spaces* and her research deals with the social history of Asmara.

Pier Giorgio Massaretti
is an architect and researcher in History of Architecture, incardinated in the Department of Architecture (DA) of the University of Bologna. He is a specialist in the history of architecture and national cities during the fascist period and is co-author with Giuliano Gresleri of the exhibition catalogue *Architettura Italiana d'Oltremare 1870–1940* (Venice, 1993) and *Italian Architecture Overseas – Iconographic Atlas* (Bologna, 2008). Since 2002 he has been part of the body's National Inter-Scientific Committee: We Reclaim History.

Gianmarco Mancosu
is a Ph.D student in Italian Studies at the University of Warwick. His main research interests are the representations of colonialism in Italy between fascism and the Republic, and related legacies in contemporary visual products. His current doctoral research focuses on how newsreels, early TV shows, and documentaries about colonialism/decolonisation have re-defined the aesthetic borders of Italian national identity after World War II. He is currently working on a monograph about the activity of the *Reparto Foto-Cinematografico Africa Orientale Istituto Luce* which made and spread cinematographic representations of the fascist empire, topics which he explored in his first Ph.D dissertation (Cagliari, 2015). He collaborates with the *Archivio Storico dell'Istituto Luce* (Rome) and with the *Istituto Italiano di Cultura* in Addis Ababa.

Sabrina Marchetti
(Ph.D) is Associate Professor at the University of Venice Ca' Foscari. She is mainly specialised in issues of gender, racism, labour and migration, with a specific focus on the question of migrant domestic work. Amongst her publications are *Black Girls. Migrant Domestic Workers and Colonial Legacies* (Brill, 2014) and *Employers, Agencies and Immigration: Paying for Care* (Ashgate 2015, with Anna Triandafyllidou).

Christine Matzke
taught literature and theatre at the Department of New Literatures in English at Goethe-University Frankfurt am Main (2001–2003) and the African Studies Department, Humboldt-Universität zu Berlin (2003–2010), before joining the University of Bayreuth in spring 2011. She has spent well over a decade researching Eritrean theatre arts and cultural production. Her publications include the co-edited *African Theatre 14: Contemporary Women* (2015), *African Theatre 8: Diasporas* (2009) and *Postcolonial Postmortems* (2006) on transcultural crime fiction. She teaches Anglophone literature and theatre at the University of Bayreuth. Her research and teaching interests include African theatre and performing arts (with a focus on the Horn of Africa, particularly Eritrea), British drama since 1890, Shakespeare in performance, Anglophone African literature, popular literature (esp. crime fiction), women's writing, sports and literature, concepts of diaspora, and historiography.

Steven McCarthy
(MFA, Stanford University) is Professor of Graphic Design at the University of Minnesota, Twin Cities campus. His long-standing interest in theories of design authorship – as both scholar and practitioner – has led to lectures, exhibits, publications and grant-funded research in a dozen countries. His book on the topic of authorship, *The Designer As... Author, Producer, Activist, Entrepreneur, Curator and Collaborator: New Models for Communicating* was published in 2013 by BIS Publishers, Amsterdam. McCarthy has been in over 120 juried and invitational exhibitions and his artist's books are in prestigious collections. He also serves on the board of the Minnesota Centre for Book Arts.

Christoph Melchers
is an architect and worked from 1968 until his retirement in 2005 for the Federal State Baden-Württemberg in the Building Department. He was also Chief of the Building Department in Reutlingen and worked in different committees within the architectural association. Christoph Melchers is the coordinator of the project group *Asmara* and initiator of the *Asmara* exhibition.

Konrad Melchers
is an economist and journalist. He is chief editor of the journal *eins – Entwicklungspolitik* and works as an expert for the Federal Ministry for Economic Collaboration and Development (BMZ). Melchers is a member of the project group *Asmara* and initiator of the *Asmara* exhibition.

Tanja R. Müller
is senior lecturer in Development Studies at the Global Development Institute, and founding member and former Director of Research (2010–2014) at the Humanitarian and Conflict Response Institute, both at the University of Manchester, UK. She is the author of *The Making of Elite Women. Revolution and Nation Building in Eritrea* (Brill, 2005) and *Legacies of Socialist Solidarity – East Germany in Mozambique* (Lexington, 2014). She has written on the Horn of Africa, and on Eritrea specifically, for more than a decade. She also conducted a British Academy-funded research project among Eritrean refugees in Tel Aviv between 2010 and 2013, and still visits Eritrea in regular intervals. Her articles on Eritrea have appeared in leading

journals. She was recently commissioned to write a country report on Eritrea for the *World Politics Review*. On her blog, *aspiration&revolution*, she often engages with topics at the heart of Eritrean Studies themes.

Silvana Palma
(MA, Ph.D in African History) teaches African History at the University L'Orientale in Naples, where she is member of the Ph.D programme in International Studies. She is a historian who has combined fieldwork (Eritrea and Ethiopia) and archival research (Europe, Boston and Washington where she obtained a fellowship by the Smithsonian Institute) in her studies on the colonial period. In Italy she carried out extensive research on colonial photography and in particular has been responsible for curatorship and research aspects of the substantial photographic collections of the richest colonial archives, that of an ex-colonial museum in Rome (project funded by the National Council of Researches), and also that of the Neapolitan *Società Africana d'Italia*. Her main areas of research focus on the history of Eritrea and Ethiopia in the colonial period; photography as source for African history, and colonialism and its postcolonial legacies and memories.

Gian Luca Podestà
holds a degree in Modern History, Genoa University, a Ph.D in Economic and Social History, Bocconi University Milan, and obtained a Masters degree in Business Administration, Bocconi University Milan. He is a full tenured Professor of Economic History at Parma University and an adjunct Professor at Bocconi University in Milan. He has written, among other works, *Colonists and 'Demographic' Colonists. Family and Society in Italian Africa*, in *Annales de Démographie Historique*, 2, 2011, 205-231; *I luoghi della cultura nell'Impero fascista* (Culture Sites in the Fascist Empire) in S.Luzzatto and G.Pedullà (eds.), *Atlante della letteratura italiana* (Atlas of Italian Literature) 3, *Dal Romanticismo ad oggi (*From the Romantic Movement to the Present*)*, D. Scarpa (ed.), Turin 2012, 655-670; *Building the Empire. Public Works in Italian East Africa (1936–1941)*, *Entreprises et Histoire*, 70, 2013, 37-53; *Race as a Myth. The Empire, Mixed-Blood People, Apartheid, Fascist Racism*, in G.Brunet (ed.), *Mariage et métissage dans les sociétés coloniales. Amériques, Afrique et Iles de l'Océan Indien* (*XVIe-XXe siècles*), Bern:Peter Lang 2015, 321-338.

Jean Robert
has been capturing the Earth's natural diversity on film for the past twenty years as a photographer and journalist. He has stepped foot in more than 100 countries over the last ten years. Currently, he is in charge of the travel section of the French magazine *Terre Sauvage* (www.terre-sauvage.com), the biggest French magazine about nature, and is working on a freelance basis for a large panel of magazines (*Figaro, Magazine*, *Animan*, *Paris Match*...). He is travelling more than ten days each month to a different country looking for nature, eco-tourism or outdoor subjects. He has conducted several reports on the effects of Chernobyl on the environment; worked on the problems posed by Bangladesh's water being contaminated by arsenic poisoning, and climbed Mount Kilimandjaro, Mount Kenya and Mount Ruwenzori in Ouganda to shoot the last ice of Africa.

Michelangelo Sabatino
is an architect and historian whose research broadly addresses intersections between culture, technology, and design in the built environment. From his research on pre-industrial vernacular traditions and their influence on modern architectures of the Mediterranean region to his current project, which looks at the transnational forces that have shaped the architecture, infrastructure, and landscape of the Americas over the course of the nineteenth and twentieth centuries, he has shed new light on larger patterns of architectural discourse and production. Sabatino is Professor and Director of the doctoral programme at the Illinois Institute of Technology College of Architecture in Chicago.

Belula Tecle Misghina
was born in Asmara-Eritrea in 1981. Is a researcher and consultant to professional architectural practices which specialise in architectural design, urban design and restoration. She obtained a Masters degree in Architecture in the year 2006 and a Ph.D in Architectural Composition and Design Theory in the year 2010 from the Sapienza University, Rome. Belula Tecle has participated in several university research projects at the Department of Architecture and Design of Sapienza University of Rome. During the years 2007–2009 she served as an assistant lecturer at the Faculty of Architecture *L.Quaroni* in teaching architectural planning. In July 2014 her book, *Asmara: An Urban History*, was published. She also actively participated, as a facilitator and instructor, in the international workshops of the UNESCO Chair for Sustainable Urban Quality and Culture in China (2013) and South Africa (2014).

Medhanie Teklemariam
is an urban planner who obtained his postgraduate degree at the University of Erasmus within the Institute for Housing and Urban Development Studies. Currently, he is the coordinator of the Asmara World Heritage Project which is responsible for preparing Asmara's application to UNESCO for World Heritage listing. He was a director of the Urban Planning Division – Department of Public Works Development, from 1998–2010, during which time he designed many medium- and large-scale urban development projects. He has also managed various multi-sector studies and projects, including the *Asmara Infrastructure Development Study* funded by the African Development Bank and the National Heritage Programme funded by the EU, and presented his work at numerous international conferences in Africa, Europe and the USA. He has written various research papers on urban development and heritage-related subjects in Eritrea. Medhanie Teklemariam is a member of the National Committee for World Heritage Convention and chairperson of the tangible heritage subcommittee. He is also a member and Secretary of the Asmara World Heritage Committee.

Alemseged Tesfai
is a prominent historian, essayist, novelist and dramatist. Born in the town of Adi Quala, Eritrea, in 1944, he graduated from Haile Selassie I University (now Addis Ababa University) with an LLB degree in 1969, and attained a Masters degree from the University of Illinois at Urbana-Champaign in 1972. In1974, Tesfai abandoned his Ph.D studies at the University of Wisconsin, Madison, to join the fledgling Eritrean People's Liberation Front. He has written several books and plays and his novel, *Wedi Hadera*, is based on the experiences of a bandit turned freedom fighter. *Two Weeks in the Trenches* (*Kilte Qne ab Difa'at*) is a collection of childhood memories, war diaries and plays which won Eritrea's highest literary award, the Raimock Prize, in 1997. He has also published two children's novels. His three-volume work on the history of Eritrea covering the period 1941 to 1962 is a treatise on the events that led to Eritrea's thirty-year war of independence. Tesfai writes mainly in his native language of Tigrinya, with some works translated into English. He is also working on a collection of short stories in English that he hopes to publish over the next few years. His screen adaptation of *Wedi Hadera* will feature in Eritrean theatres in two parts.

Magnus Treiber
holds a Ph.D in Anthropology from Munich University (2005) and received his *venia legendi* in 2016 from Bayreuth University, where he has also been assistant professor. He taught at Munich, Bayreuth and Addis Ababa universities and is affiliated to the German Felsberg Institute (www.fibw.eu). Since April 2016 he is a Professor of Anthropology at Munich University. His main fields of interest are urban anthropology, migration, anthropological theory and methodology as well as political conflict in the Horn of Africa. He conducted fieldwork in Asmara between 2001 and 2005 and studied Eritrean emigration at different stages thereafter.

Igiaba Scego
is an Italian writer (born 1974) of Somali origin. After graduating in Foreign Literature at the First University of Rome (La Sapienza), she obtained her doctorate in pedagogy. She collaborates with many magazines that deal with migrant literature, in particular *Carta*, *El-Ghibli* and *Migra*. In 2003, she won the Eks & Tra prize for migrant writers with her story *Salsicce*, and published her debut novel *La nomade che amava Alfred Hitchcock*. She collaborates with the newspapers *La Repubblica* and *Il manifesto* and also writes for the magazine *Nigrizia* with a column of news and reflection. Bibliography: *Rhoda* (2005), *Pecore nere. Racconti* with Gabriela Kuruvilla, Ingy Mubiayi, Laila Wadia (2005), *Quando nasci è un roulete. Giovani figli di migranti si raccontano* (2007), *Amori Bicolouri* (2007), *Oltre Babilonia* (2008), *L'albero in Nessuna Pietà* (2009), *La mia casa è dove sono* (2010), *Roma negata* (2014), *Adua* (2015).

Peter Volgger
studied philosophy, history and art history at Innsbruck University. Since 2003 he has worked as a freelance architect. In 2012 he wrote his dissertation on migration and its impact on urban structures. Recently he joined the Institute for the History and Theory of Architecture and the Institut für Gestaltung at Innsbruck University (assistant professor) and the Institute for Architecture and Planning at Liechtenstein University (guest professor) as a teacher and researcher. He was invited to the renewed Archtheo-Conference in Istanbul and, more recently, to the John D. Calandra Institute in New York. From 2010 to 2013 he attended meetings of the European Network for Architectural Theory. He is a member of the *kulturhauptstadt 2024* initiative in Vienna. Since 2012 he has conducted research work in Eritrea. He is a member of the Research Centre for Migration and Globalisation in Innsbruck.

Günter Wett
was born in 1970, studied architecture and is an Innsbruck-based photographer specialising in architecture and interiors. Employing his own personal style, Günter Wett is able to craft beautiful images that evoke a sense of place and being. He enjoys the opportunity to work closely with architects to understand each project. His projects include: *Architektouren nach Japan und China* (2006); *Rovina di una villa modern* (2007); *Spuresnsuche in Brasilien* (2009); *Fotografisches Stadtportrait Prishtina* (2008/09); *Italienische Architektur in Asmara* (2011), and a number of exhibitons.

Tekle Woldemikael
(Ph.D., Northwestern University) is Professor of Sociology and International Studies at Chapman University, Orange, California. He has served as Chair of the Department of Sociology and Director of Masters in International Studies at Chapman University. He has taught at University of Redlands, where he was the Chair of Sociology and Anthropology; Hamilton College, where he was the Chair of Africana Studies; University of Hartford, and University of Gezira in the Sudan. His research interest involves studying nationalism and ethnicity, immigrants and refugees, and language and public policy. He is an author of the book *Becoming Black American: Haitians and American Institutions in Evanston, Illinois*. He co-edited a book titled *Scholars and Southern Californian Immigrants in Dialogue; New Conversations in Public Sociology*. He also edited a special issue of the *Africa Today* journal titled *Postliberation Eritrea* and a special issue of *The American Sociologist* on *Racial Diversity in Becoming a Sociologist*. He teaches courses in Social Theory, Field Work and Writing a Senior Thesis, Race and Ethnic Relations, and Cultural Diversity and Ethnic Identities in a Globalised World.

Hadas Yaron
is a social anthropologist. She currently works as a lecturer at the School of Government and Society at the Academic College Tel Aviv Yafo. In addition she is an activist, researching and operating together with Israeli NGOs and in particular the African Refugees Development Center. Hadas completed her Ph.D at the Department of Social Anthropology at the University of Cambridge in 2006. Her Ph.D focused on land lement and politics in Israel and was published by academic press in June 2010. Her current research focuses on African refugees living in Israel, examining the interaction between refugees, Israeli society, and the state. During her stay in Berlin she will investigate the life of African migrants and forced migrants in the country in comparison to their lives in Israel.

Massimo Zaccaria
is a graduate in Oriental Studies at the University of Venice, and holder of a doctorate in African Studies (1994, University of Siena) and post-doc (1998–1999, University of Pavia). In 2000 he obtained his LIS Diploma from the University of Bologna (sede di Ravenna). Since 2000 he has been a researcher in African History at the Department of Political and Social Science of the University of Pavia. Massimo's current research interests lie in the social history of the Horn of Africa during the colonial period with special emphasis on Eritrea and Sudan.

Stefano Zagnoni
was born in 1954 and is currently associate Professor of History of Architecture at the University of Udine. He has also taught and carried out research activities in other scientific institutions, including the universities of Ferrara, Bologna and Milan Polytechnic. His research work is mainly focused on Italian contemporary architecture, both in the Motherland and abroad (former Italian colonies and the Mediterranean area). He has edited some books and published several essays, articles and reviews on books, proceedings and magazines. He has extensive experience in architectural editing and has organised symposia and exhibitions.

The *Deutsche Bibliothek* lists this publication in the *Deutsche Nationalbibliografie*; detailed bibliographic data is available on the Internet at *http://dnb.d-nb.de*

ISBN 978-3-86922-487-9

Proofreading
Clarice Knowles

Design
Stefan Graf

Printing
Tiger Printing (Hong Kong) Co., Ltd.
www.tigerprinting.hk